THE COMPLETE GUIDE TO PATHWORKS

PATHWORKS for VMS and DOS

THE COMPLETE GUIDE TO PATHWORKS

PATHWORKS for VMS and DOS

KENNETH L. SPENCER

CBM
BOOKS

Copyright © 1993 CBM Books, a division of Cardinal Business Media, Inc.

The information in this book is subject to change without notice and should not be construed as a commitment by the author or the publisher. Although every precaution has been taken in the preparation of this book, the publisher assumes no responsibility for errors or omissions.

Printed in the United States of America.

Cover design by Michael Cousart.

Trademark Acknowledgments

PostScript is a trademark of Adobe Systems Inc.

Macintosh and AppleTalk are registered trademarks of Apple Computer Inc.

DECnet, DECwindows, PATHWORKS, ULTRIX, VAX, and VMS are registered trademarks and CI, DEClaser, DECmcc, DECquery, DECrepeater, DECserver, DECsystem, DSSI, LA75, LA324, LAT, PATHWORKS Links, PrintServer, Rdb, TeamLinks, VAXcluster, VAX Notes, VAXsimPLUS, and VMSmail are trademarks of Digital Equipment Corporation.

Intel, 386, and 486 are trademarks of Intel Corporation.

OS/2, MVS, MVT, Proprinter, and SNA are trademarks of International Business Machines Corporation.

MS-DOS and Power Point are registered trademarks and Windows and Windows NT are trademarks of Microsoft Corporation.

NetWare is a trademark of Novell Inc.

OSF and OSF/Motif are registered trademarks of Open Software Foundation Inc.

UNIX is a registered trademark of UNIX System Laboratories Inc.

WordPerfect is a trademark of WordPerfect Corporation.

Ethernet is a trademark of Xerox Corporation.

All other trademarks are the property of their respective owners.

Library of Congress Cataloging-in-Publication Data

Spencer, Kenneth L., 1951-
    The complete guide to PATHWORKS : Pathworks for VMS and DOS /
Kenneth L. Spencer.
      p. cm.
    Includes index.
    ISBN 1-878956-22-1
    1. PATHWORKS for VMS. 2. PATHWORKS for DOS 3. Local area
networks (Computer networks) – Computer programs. I. Title
TK5105.9.S64   1992
005.7'1369—dc20   92-25716
                                        CIP

Please address comments and questions to the publisher:

CBM Books
101 Witmer Road
Horsham, PA 19044
(215)957-4287 FAX (215)957-1050

Contents

CHAPTER 10: PRACTICAL APPROACH
TO NETWORK MANAGEMENT

Preface

During the past 12 years, I have installed, used, and managed a number of different computer systems, including a variety of networks. It became apparent throughout the years that there was a tremendous amount of technical documentation available on how these systems worked, but in most cases very little information about how to implement and use them in a business environment.

During several courses I gave on various systems in the late 1980s and 1990, numerous people suggested that I write a book on networks that would both discuss the technical aspects of the network and offer suggestions about how to make the network a functional part of an organization. After a lot of thought (I never considered myself a writer), I contacted Professional Press, and to use an old quote, "The rest is history."

THE PATHWORKS PERSPECTIVE

There are great misunderstandings about computers and networks and how they should be used. Currently, a lot of debate exists over what type of system to purchase (PC, RISC, or minicomputer) and what to do with it. The issue is clouded daily with the introduction of yet another system or network.

Despite the wide variety of options to consider when purchasing a system, there are many viable alternatives in the network arena. I consider the Digital PATHWORKS product to be one of the best and most flexible networks available because of its ability to mix different systems (PC, Apple Computer's Macintosh, Digital's VMS, and UNIX) and networks (Microsoft's LAN Manager, Novell's NetWare, and Apple's AppleTalk) on the same system. The client/server products available from Digital and other vendors further add to the tremendous potential of this network. When you add to these factors the arrival of Microsoft's Windows NT product and Digital's Alpha chip, the PATHWORKS network is the best bet for most organizations.

Networks also are one of the fastest growing segments of the systems market and are likely to experience the greatest growth in the 1990s. Networks are indispensable for linking disparate parts of an organization and serving as the glue to facilitate communications and sharing of data. A properly implemented network will bring about an unprecedented change in an organization and lower the long-term computing costs compared with a minicomputer or mainframe.

GOALS FOR THIS BOOK

The goals for this book are twofold:

1. To introduce the PATHWORKS network and to explain its most important technical aspects.

2. To provide examples of how to use and manage the network.

This book is designed to provide insight into the PATHWORKS network operating system within a local-area network (LAN) environment and how an average organization would use it. It provides typical installation procedures, tips on managing the network, practical information about how the network operates, and information about how to use the network from a user's perspective and a manager's perspective.

New system managers will gain useful insight into the day-to-day operations of the network and will learn how to plan and manage a new system.

Several chapters guide users through the use of the network and give them a better understanding of what services the network offers. Most of the PATHWORKS commands are discussed in some detail, and this information serves as a reference guide suitable for answering most questions. Where appropriate, the book also points to other documents of interest, such as PATHWORKS manuals.

Managers who are considering purchasing a LAN or switching to PATHWORKS will also benefit from this book. By browsing through each chapter and delving into the details of certain areas, they can gain an in-depth, practical insight into PATHWORKS and see how it will provide a systems foundation for their organization.

HOW THIS BOOK WAS DEVELOPED

This book not only was an exercise in the difficult and fun task of writing, but it also served as my own test bed for Microsoft Windows V3.x and its suitability for day-to-day applications. I have used Windows since version 1.0 but have never had more than one or two applications, such as Micrografx Designer, that I really used under Windows. For the PATHWORKS project, I purchased a Dell 320LT laptop and loaded it to the gills with Windows software. The laptop has a 120-MB disk and 8 MB of RAM. (It started life with 4 MB.) The processor is a 320sx. The only non-Windows applications I used were an MS-DOS-based communications package (PC Anywhere) and a DOS editor (Kedit), which was normally run from within Windows.

The primary applications used during the preparation of this book were:

◆ Microsoft Word for Windows (V1.1 and V2.0)

◆ Micrografx Designer V3.0

◆ Inbit's Fullshot

◆ The Backup program from the Norton Desktop

In addition to these products, I used or reviewed a number of other packages for specific tasks for inclusion in the book. I performed every task possible under Windows, except for tasks such as redirecting the output of a program to a file. I captured NETSETUP screens using Fullshot to capture the screen while the program ran in a DOS window. Fullshot is a remarkable product that you can use to capture any Windows screen or portion of a screen. As mentioned, this includes DOS programs that are run in a DOS window. The graphics of the DOS V5.0 shell were captured in this same manner. Microsoft Word for Windows was used exclusively to manage the many documents that make up the book.

As the book neared completion, I began to realize how beneficial the Windows environment was in producing a document of this magnitude. Portions of the book were written in airports, on airliners (I am writing this at 29,000 feet), in hotel rooms, and in my den at home. Using Windows, I could build and incorporate screen snapshots and other graphics into the document in minutes. I developed entire graphics with Designer from start to finish, including incorporating them into the document, in 3 to 5 minutes.

Styles, the button bar, the ribbon bar, and many other advanced features of Word saved many of the tedious hours that a project such as this requires. The user interface removed the headaches of producing the documents.

After 7 months on this project, the bottom line is this: It would have been impossible to complete the project on time without the Windows environment and superb products such as Word and Designer.

CONVENTIONS USED IN THIS BOOK

This book uses the following conventions: In example sessions with the computer, all commands are shown in Letter Gothic typeface. In these sessions, commands that the user inputs appear in bold, and the parts of these commands for which the user must supply the information are also italicized.

ACKNOWLEDGMENTS

There are a great many people whom I need to thank for helping with this project. The top person on the list is my wife, Patricia, for putting up with my many late nights and weekends spent with my laptop or upstairs in my office. I also appreciate the patience of my children, Ken Jr. and Jeffrey.

Joe Catalonotti from Digital provided a great deal of help. This included arranging for loans of hardware and software, providing access to internal Digital resources, and providing encouragement and feedback throughout the project

I also owe a great deal to Tracey Langenbach for her help in editing, proofing, indexing, and numerous other tasks. She has been a great friend, inspiration, and invaluable participant in this project. Dick Pankratz also helped greatly in the editing process and provided a tremendous amount of useful feedback throughout the project.

Steve Harvey is another good friend who has offered counseling and support throughout.

There were many people at numerous vendors who helped by making things happen in their organizations. Lisa Cawley, Julie Barney, and Sherry Cathey from Digital provided support and helped facilitate this project. Lisa deserves special mention for her technical support and advice and for helping with the introductions to the right people. Joe is a super person who has spent many hours on the phone with me over the past 7 months and has been a key factor in making this book possible by providing support, information, and access to the right products and people.

When I think of large corporations, I often picture organizations that must be very hard to deal with. Christy Gersich from Microsoft and Jill Houston from Raxco refuse to believe that this must be true. Christy has been extremely helpful throughout this project by cutting through the red tape and providing access to the products and information I needed. She is also a pleasure to work with. Jill has exemplified the same kind of attitude since our first discussions and has gone out of her way to provide information on Raxco and to have Raxco personnel review the book.

I would like to extend my thanks again to everyone who helped on this project. It really feels good to complete a project like this, especially when you have made many new friends in the process.

CHAPTER 1

Introduction

Digital's PATHWORKS product offers an exciting environment for connecting personal computers (PC), Apple Computer Inc.'s Macintoshes, Digital's VAX computer systems, and other computers and devices in a typical business environment. It provides the foundation and tools necessary to provide a transparent interface to the user, and it allows the user to maintain access to software located on many different systems.

PATHWORKS is a collection of software modules that comprise a network operating system and that work with a Digital local-area network (LAN) to allow PCs, Macintoshes, VAXs, and other computer systems to function together as a single, integrated system. The entire network becomes one system, providing resources to the user on the basis of his or her functional requirements. PATHWORKS also provides the management information system (MIS) staff with a flexible system foundation with which to build state-of-the-art systems. It also provides users with the technology they demand for third-party products. In addition, PATHWORKS protects end-user and corporate investments in hardware, software, applications, and training.

The PATHWORKS product family includes:

◆ PATHWORKS for VMS

◆ PATHWORKS for ULTRIX

◆ PATHWORKS for DOS

◆ PATHWORKS for Windows

◆ PATHWORKS for DOS (TCP/IP)

◆ PATHWORKS for DOS (NetWare Coexistence)

◆ PATHWORKS for OS/2

◆ PATHWORKS for OS/2 (TCP/IP)

◆ PATHWORKS for Macintosh

THE PATHWORKS APPROACH TO INTEGRATION

The PATHWORKS approach to integration is illustrated by the support for a wide variety of products and applications. Two major factors that differentiate PATHWORKS from other LAN packages are its support for standards and its ability to let you painlessly build a LAN that supports a variety of clients (e.g., PCs and Macintoshes) and server hardware platforms (e.g., Digital VMS, IBM OS/2, and Digital ULTRIX machines). PATHWORKS provides the ideal platform for sharing information among different systems and building powerful client/server applications. Networks based on PATHWORKS provide the reliability for mission-critical applications that businesses require.

The support for different servers brings a tremendous amount of flexibility to a network. A PATHWORKS server may be a PC running OS/2, a VAX running VMS or ULTRIX, or a DECsystem running ULTRIX. The future promises to open the server options to many more platforms, providing a virtual smorgasbord to the network manager. Flexibility in server selection is critical to a network's success, because networks that rely only on PC servers are often brought to their knees by multiuser applications with large numbers of concurrent users. PATHWORKS for VMS takes advantage of the power of the VAX platform in this type of environment, especially if the application uses client/server technology. Figure 1-1 illustrates Digital's approach to integration.

Future versions of PATHWORKS will support even more servers and clients, including Microsoft Windows NT, Santa Cruz Operation Inc.'s (SCO) UNIX, Digital's Alpha-based systems, and who knows what else.

Network Application Support

Digital's Network Application Support (NAS) is a comprehensive set of software products that includes DECnet, PATHWORKS, VMS, and many other products relevant to a 1990s multivendor computing environment. NAS provides software that is designed to standards such as Portable Operating System Interface (POSIX), UNIX, X/Open, CCITT X.400, American National Standards Institute (ANSI) X.12, Digital's SQL Access Services, and CODASYL FIMS. Digital has embraced standards from numerous standards bodies, as it seeks to provide users with a fully functional computing environment for systems from different vendors. There are many cases in which Digital has dropped or changed a product to use an industry standard. For example, DECwindows was changed to the industry-standard Open Software Foundation (OSF)/Motif. PATHWORKS moved from the former DECnet DOS product to a product based on Microsoft LAN Manager.

As a member of the NAS architecture, PATHWORKS inherits the ability to work with systems running under ULTRIX, UNIX, OS/2, VMS, Systems Network

Architecture (SNA), IBM's MVS, IBM's VM, Remote Job Entry (RJE), Transmission Control Protocol/Internet Protocol (TCP/IP), Network File System (NFS), Token Ring, and other popular environments. This ability provides the typical enterprise with the foundation to build systems with hardware and software that meets its business needs, without creating islands of automation (or islands of frustration) within the organization.

PATHWORKS managers may also use the tools designed for managing complex NAS and VAX networks, which further simplifies their management chores. Products such as Network Control Program (NCP), Local-Area Transport Control Program (LATCP), DECmcc, and others provide PATHWORKS managers with a mature set of tools that have evolved over many years. All other PC-based network operating systems are faced with a shortage of full-featured, mature, integrated management tools.

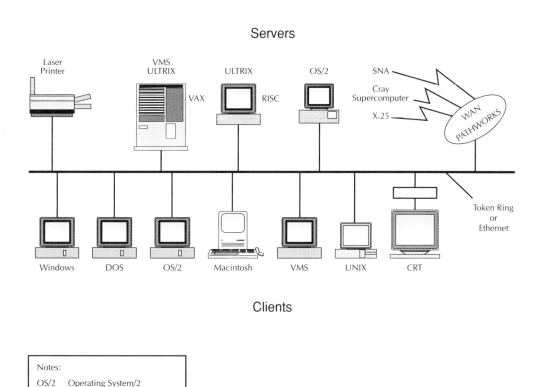

Figure 1-1. Digital's Approach to Integration

Layered products that work with PATHWORKS are an important part of this picture. Digital's TeamLinks for Windows, PATHWORKS Links for Windows, ALL-IN-1, and others are Microsoft Windows-based products that integrate cleanly into a PATHWORKS network. Other products or features such as Digital's NetWare Coexistence allow PATHWORKS to fully operate in an environment originally designed for Novell Inc.'s NetWare systems.

Standards

PATHWORKS supports a number of standards including compatibility with Microsoft's LAN Manager and NetWare. Each of these architectures has a large industry base and is considered an industry standard by most experts. PATHWORKS products based on these architectures provide a common platform for companies with existing systems.

The network architectures supported by PATHWORKS also provide a great degree of flexibility to an organization. LANs based on Token Ring or Ethernet can be smoothly integrated into a common system. Support for DECnet, TCP/IP, and Internetwork Packet Exchange (IPX) adds further flexibility for existing or new systems.

X Window System. The X Window System standard is supported by PATHWORKS via the DECwindows products included with PATHWORKS and optionally with the Digital eXcursion product for Microsoft Windows.

The eXcursion product brings the ability to access almost any X application to Windows users. The X client may be a VMS or UNIX machine anywhere on the network, as long as it is running the client software. Note that X clients and X servers are reversed from the normal client/server roles. That is, the host is actually the client.

Microsoft Windows. Windows is another de facto standard that has been embraced by PATHWORKS and is now a part of the NAS architecture. PATHWORKS is directly supported by Windows V3.1 via the network drivers in the Windows installation kit. The WIN3SETU program included with PATHWORKS will further configure Windows to support the LK series keyboards and older DEPCA mice.

In late 1991, Digital began releasing a number of Windows products. PATHWORKS Links and ALL-IN-1 for Windows are just the beginning of a wide range of products specifically designed for client/server Windows systems.

Application Control and Management System. Application Control and Management System (ACMS) is Digital's management tool for high-powered transaction-processing environments or systems that require large numbers of users to access a large database. PATHWORKS and other network clients can access a database via ACMS from a wide variety of mechanisms, including VT320 terminal emulation and client/server applications.

ACMS provides the tools to create dedicated database servers that allow the database functions to be handled by a VAX dedicated to that task. The performance of the overall system improves because the tasks are split over multiple processors sized appropriately for the task they are managing.

NetBIOS. NetBIOS is an industry-standard application programming interface (API) for developing network applications. NetBIOS is built into PATHWORKS and is used for many PATHWORKS tasks. Most applications designed for NetBIOS networks will work "out of the box" on a PATHWORKS network.

LAN Manager. PATHWORKS V4.1 supports full LAN Manager V2.0 APIs for clients connecting to OS/2 LAN Manager servers. Clients may simultaneously access OS/2, VMS, and ULTRIX servers.

Terminal Services

A variety of terminal services are provided to PATHWORKS clients. The Local-Area Transport (LAT), CTERM, and TELNET protocols are used by the SETHOST and VT320 programs shipped with PATHWORKS. These protocols allow a PATHWORKS client to access hosts residing on LANs and wide-area networks (WAN), including the Internet via TELNET.

Video terminals and printers can attach to the network via direct Ethernet connections or by their connecting to a terminal server or connecting directly to a host or client machine. This flexibility of connecting devices is a big advantage over most other PC networks.

BENEFITS OF PATHWORKS

PATHWORKS is a foundation for access to almost all the other Digital products. Instead of being afterthoughts that have access to host-based services, PATHWORKS clients are peers with the other systems on the network.

The close integration of PATHWORKS with other Digital products and third-party products provides a stable foundation for building robust and reliable business systems. PATHWORKS enables systems running on VMS or UNIX hosts to be cleanly integrated with the latest client applications. Data can be easily shared between systems, either in real-time or in a batch mode. Client users can easily move data files from one system to another, such as from a Macintosh to a PC, dramatically increasing productivity.

CHAPTER 2

PATHWORKS Installation

This chapter discusses the installation of PATHWORKS on a VMS server and a DOS client. The discussion assumes a medium level of experience with both the VMS and the DOS operating systems. If PATHWORKS is already installed on your system, you can skip this chapter.

You should install PATHWORKS in a test environment in your organization to provide a limited-access system that you can test and configure. Once you are satisfied with the configuration and have completed the necessary planning, you can add users to the network in a step-by-step fashion.

This chapter will concentrate on helping you to quickly install the server and client software and go online for the first time. Future chapters discuss performance tuning, standards, and other ways of making your system successful. Try each step of the process on your system to make sure it runs properly, and plan for this time in your implementation process so you can correctly set the expectations for the user population and management.

Before you begin the PATHWORKS installation process, it is vitally important to consider several factors. As anxious as you may be to get the system up and running, taking a few minutes to plan your installation and taking several precautions could save you hours. PATHWORKS can be installed in as little as 2 hours, including the PC configuration, if you follow the correct procedures.

INSTALLATION COMPONENTS AND OVERVIEW

The PATHWORKS software consists of three major components: PATHWORKS for VMS server software, PATHWORKS for DOS server software, and PATHWORKS for DOS client software. PATHWORKS for VMS is loaded on the VAX and provides the server functions. The first step in installing PATHWORKS requires loading PATHWORKS for VMS on the server.

One of the advantages of PATHWORKS modularity is the ability to upgrade the server while still running the former version of the server and client software. You can upgrade clients over time, instead of using the all-or-nothing upgrade process of most other systems.

The rest of this chapter focuses on how to install the server software, server client software, and client software.

PATHWORKS FOR VMS SERVER SOFTWARE

This section covers the installation of the PATHWORKS for VMS software. The media will usually be a TK-50 tape cartridge, magnetic tape, or CD-ROM for your VMS server.

Preinstallation

Before installing PATHWORKS on the server, you need to check and possibly modify a number of items;

- ◆ Take into account the status of your server. If the machine is currently used in a production environment with real users, you may have to plan around their activities. You should also check the VMS version and make sure it is correct for your version of PATHWORKS. For example, PATHWORKS V4.1 requires VMS V5.3 or higher.

- ◆ Some parameter changes will require you to run AUTOGEN and reboot the server. If the machine is in production, you may have to reboot over lunch or at night.

- ◆ Be sure to consult your installation guide for the version of PATHWORKS you are installing, and verify *all* parameters listed in the preinstallation section.

- ◆ Make sure you follow the installation steps listed in your user manual very carefully, including the sections on rebooting the server.

Disk Requirements

The amount of disk space and the configuration of the disks are areas of potential conflict. You should check your installation guide to determine the amount of space used on the system drive and application drives. Also note the amount of free space used during installation.

You also need to have the proper directory structure, even if logical names are defined to point to the exact location. One critical directory on a VMS system is the SYSHLP directory. It is normally located under the SYSCOMMON directory ([000000.sys0.syscommon.syshlp]). If this directory is not in its proper location, the VMSINSTAL procedure will fail, and you will spend many hours rectifying the situation.

To verify the structure of your system and prepare for the PATHWORKS server installation, you should perform several tasks:

1. Perform a full backup of your system.

2. Create a directory listing of your system disk and capture it to disk. Make sure you save this file.

3. Check free disk space on the system disk. You will need 6,000 blocks during installation and 4,500 blocks after installation. Also check free disk space on all disks PATHWORKS will use.

4. Capture to disk and/or print a listing of all logical, environmental, and symbol names.

5. Check system parameters.

6. Verify that the following files are in their correct location:

```
SYS$COMMON:[SYSHLP]
  Help Files
SYS$COMMON:[SYSEXE]
  SYSUAF.DAT
  NETPROXY.DAT
SYS$SYSTEM
  RIGHTSLIST.DAT
```

7. Disable disk quotas until the installation is complete.

8. Check for group code 360 in the user authorization file (UAF). If 360 is in use, find a free group code for PATHWORKS.

9. Verify that DECnet is running.

The directory listing is useful if there is an installation problem. It is also useful if you wish to find out what files the installation placed on your disks. You can use a file compare procedure to find the difference in your postinstallation and preinstallation directory structures. You should also note the time the installation begins. If other users are not creating lots of new files on the drive you will use for PATHWORKS, you can use the command DIR /SINCE=TIME SYS$SYSDEVICE:, where TIME is the time the installation began. If you execute this command, it will produce a directory listing of all new files added since the installation began. The listings of logicals and symbols are also useful to document any problems with conflicting names.

Review the *Client Installation Guide* for disk and system requirements for the server portion of the client software that will be loaded on the server. These include the client applications and DECnet interface software that reside on the PCSAV41 service.

SYSGEN Parameters

PATHWORKS has certain minimum system requirements that may necessitate changes to the SYSGEN parameters for your system. These parameters will be checked during the VMSINSTAL procedure. Table 2-1 shows some of the system parameters required for PATHWORKS V4.1. Check the system parameters for your version of PATHWORKS in the *Server Installation Manual*. Remember that the system parameters for PATHWORKS affect resources that are also used by other software running on the server.

Table 2-1. SYSGEN Parameters

Parameter	Value
SCSNODE	Same as node name (clusters only)
SCSSYSTEMID	DECnet address for a VAXcluster (Area * 1024) + node number
	Example: DECnet address 1.200 (1 * 1024) + 200 = 1224
MAXBUF	Equal to or greater than 8192
GBLSECTIONS	10 or more free
GBLPAGES	120 or more free
CHANNELCNT	(open files per client + 1) * no. of clients) + 10 (minimum of 256)
MIN_SPTREQ	Equal to 5176

If the SYSGEN parameters are not sufficient for PATHWORKS, the installation procedure will probably append a new section to your system's MODPARAMS.DAT file and request that you reboot the system. Below is a typical section of MODPARAMS.DAT that was added by the PATHWORKS installation process. The MIN_SPTREQ line was added after the initial PATHWORKS V4.0 release. These parameters may vary for the version of PATHWORKS you are installing:

```
! Added for PATHWORKS
MIN_CHANNELCNT = 500
MIN_MAXBUF = 8192
MIN_PROCSECTCNT = 60
ADD_NPAGEDYN = 300000
ADD_GBLPAGES = 10000
```

```
ADD_GBLSECTIONS = 500
MIN_PQL_MBYTLM = 16384
MIN_SPTREQ=5176
```

If the file server does not boot after installation, increase the MIN_CHANNELCNT and MIN_SPTREQ parameters. According to Digital, you can increase both of these significantly with little impact to other areas of your system. The primary influence on these two parameters seems to be the number of users specified in the PATHWORKS configuration screen. As the number of users goes up, so must these two values.

After checking and updating the SYSGEN parameters, verify that DECnet is running. The screen below illustrates the use of Network Control Protocol (NCP) on a VMS system to determine the state of DECnet. Start NCP from DCL by using the $MCR NCP command. At the NCP> prompt, use the SHOW EXECUTOR command to display the current status:

```
NCP>sho exec

Node Volatile Summary as of 1-NOV-1991 14:56:39

Executor node = 1.200 (KENS)

State                  = on
identification         = DECnet-VAX V5.4-1, VMS V5.4-2

NCP>
```

The DCL command SHOW NETWORK will display the same basic information as NCP SHOW EXECUTOR:

```
VAX/VMS Network status for local node 1.200 KENS on 21-DEC-1991 15:33:48.81

This is a nonrouting node and does not have any network information.

The designated router for KENS is node 0 KENS.
```

If DECnet is running, your display will be similar to one of the screens above, depending on which method you use. If the state is off, you can start it by issuing the command @SYS$STARTUP:STARTNET.

On a new system, the display may show a 0 for the node address. (Our example is 1.200.) If your system shows a 0, you need to run the NETCONFIG command procedure, located in SYS$MANAGER, by executing the command

$@SYS$MANAGER:NETCONFIG. Before running NETCONFIG, verify that the appropriate licenses are loaded by using the SHOW LICENSE command. Look for the license entries DVNETEND (DECnet End Node License) or DVNETRTG (DECnet Routing Node License). All new VMS systems include the DVNETEND license, but it may not be loaded. Consult with your installer or system manager to load the license, if necessary.

After verifying that the license is loaded, run the NETCONFIG procedure. This procedure will ask for node name and address, as well as ask several other questions. The defaults should suffice, except for the node name and address, which are explicit for your VAX.

When NETCONFIG completes, DECnet should be up and running on your system. Be sure to add the command @SYS$STARTUP:STARTNET to your system startup procedure, if it is not already enabled.

Installation

After performing the preinstallation steps, including any others not mentioned here that are listed in your server installation manual, you may install the PATHWORKS server software. At this point, you should refer to your installation guide and follow the installation steps explicitly.

The VMSINSTAL utility is used to install PATHWORKS on the server. The installation process is much improved for PATHWORKS V4.1. If system parameters are not sufficient for PATHWORKS, VMSINSTAL will now complete the installation successfully and allow you to change the system parameters in the PCSA$CONFIG program.

If the installation procedure reports that the installation was successful, proceed to the next step. If you did not get this message, refer to the troubleshooting section of this book (Chapter 12, "Problem Solving") and to your PATHWORKS manuals.

At this point, you are almost done with the initial installation. Before proceeding to the next step, you will need to run PCSA Manager and configure the server. You accomplish this by logging into a privileged account and executing the command $@SYS$STARTUP:PCSA$CONFIG. This will bring up the menu shown in Figure 2-1. You can also access this particular screen via the Utility/Configuration menu selections of PCSA Manager. Figure 2-1 shows the default values.

For your initial system installation, the default values will probably suffice. You can select the default values for the configuration or modify them with your best guess according to your network specifications. As you begin to understand how the network will perform in your environment, you can update the configurations later.

Figures 2-2, 2-3, and 2-4 summarize the actual installation steps for the server. These figures should serve as a guide, not as all-inclusive installation procedures, because

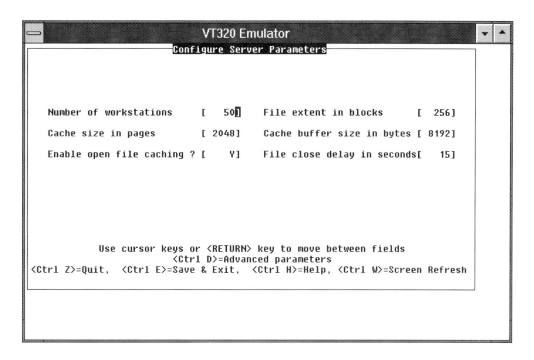

Figure 2-1. PCSA Configuration Screen

the steps may change with new versions of PATHWORKS. Use the documentation provided with your PATHWORKS software to guide you during installation.

Here is a list of the basic steps for installing PATHWORKS:

1. Log into a privileged account.

2. Determine available disk space.

3. Back up the system disk.

4. Verify device and logical names.

5. Disable disk quotas.

6. Configure DECnet:

   ◆ Start DECnet if it is not running.

   ◆ Increase/verify parameters, such as logical links and pipeline quota, and then enable remote boot services.

   ◆ Set up DECnet TCP/IP if required.

13

7a. First-time installation only:

   ◆ Verify free space on the system disk and data disks via $SHOW DEVICE D.

   ◆ Plan disk usage for system files, user files, and applications.

7b. Upgrades only:

   ◆ Save copies of ESS$LAD_STARTUP.DAT and ESS$LAST_STARTUP.DAT.

   ◆ Disconnect all PATHWORKS nodes.

   ◆ Stop file and disk servers via PCSA STOP FILE_SERVER CONNECTIONS-ALL_SERVICES and PCSA STOP DISK_SERVER CONNECTIONS.

If you reinstall VMS versions earlier than version 5.4-3 after PATHWORKS is loaded, you will need to reinstall PATHWORKS V4.1 or later to reload the correct version of the LAT symbiont. Versions 5.4-3 of VMS and later have the correct symbiont.

You should save these data files because VMSINSTAL may overwrite these files during the upgrade. If you have made changes to these files, you must restore the files from your backup copy before restarting the server.

Figure 2-2 illustrates the steps required to install the PATHWORKS for VMS software. This includes installing the file server, disk server, and other services. The critical parts of this procedure are running VMSINSTAL and making sure the installation verification procedure (IVP) is successful. Use your *PATHWORKS for VMS Server Installation Manual* as a guide for installation of your version.

Figure 2-2. Installation Tasks for PATHWORKS for VMS

Log into a privileged account, and run VMSINSTAL:
```
$SET DEF SYS$UPDATE:
$@VMSINSTAL PCSA041 DEVICE options N
DEVICE = Tape Drive (EX: MKA500)
```

Verify the installation was successful.
You will see the following message:
```
IVP completed successfully at 25-Oct-1991
```

If the installation failed:
Modify system parameters and reboot. Then rerun the VMSINSTAL procedure.

Log out.

After the server is installed, you must run PCSA Manager to configure the server and load PATHWORKS. This also includes returning the system to its normal configuration (e.g., re-enabling disk quotas) and updating the system startup files (e.g., SYSTARTUP_V5.COM), if necessary. Figure 2-3 provides a general outline of the steps required.

Figure 2-3. Postinstallation Tasks for PATHWORKS for VMS

Configure the file server:

```
$RUN SYS$STARTUP:PCSA$CONFIG
```

Re-enable disk quotas (if used):

```
$RUN SYS$SYSTEM:DISKQUOTA
DISKQUOTA> ENABLE
DISKQUOTA> EXIT
```

Update system startup files:

```
SYS$STARTUP:SYSTARTUP_V5.COM
```

Add:

```
$@SYS$STARTUP:LAD_STARTUP  if disk services will be used.

$@SYS$STARTUP:PCFS_STARTUP if file services will be used.
```

To start the server, you must execute the server startup command files, shown by the last two lines in Figure 2-3. This is accomplished by executing PCFS_STARTUP.COM and LAD_STARTUP.COM, found in the SYS$STARTUP directory. These commands will start the appropriate PATHWORKS server modules for your system. The command $@SYS$STARTUP:LAD_STARTUP should be placed in your SYSTARUP_V5.COM file only if you are going to use disk services. If you are using only file and print services, this command is not required and will waste valuable system resources.

You must execute the PCFS_STARTUP.COM command file before loading the DOS software on the server. The commands for manually starting the various PATHWORKS servers are shown in Figure 2-4.

Figure 2-4. Manual Start of the Server(s)

Start the server(s):

Reboot the server machine or enter the following commands:

$@SYS$STARTUP:LAD_STARTUP if disk services will be used.

$@SYS$STARTUP:PCFS_STARTUP if file services will be used.

CLIENT INSTALLATION ON THE SERVER

You are now ready to install the portion of the client software that will be loaded on the server. This portion of the installation loads DOS applications and other DOS files that are included with PATHWORKS. These files are moved to the PCSAV41 service.

The PATHWORKS file server must also be running before you begin this portion of the installation procedure. To verify this, execute the SHOW VERSION command:

```
$ PCSA SHOW VERSION
LAD$KERNEL          Version : LAD$KERNEL V1.2
LADDRIVER           Version : LADDRIVER V1.2
PGFS_SERVER         Version : PATHWORKS for VMS S4.0E
PCSA_MANAGER        Version : PCSA_MANAGER S4.0E
```

This PCSA SHOW VERSION command reports the status and version of each PATHWORKS component. For the installation of the client software, PCFS_SERVER must be running. If it is not running, this command will show Not Available, and you must start the server using the PCFS_STARTUP command discussed in the server installation section.

Check the installation guide for any parameters or special disk requirements for this portion of the installation. After the installation procedure completes, check for error and completion messages. If the procedure reports that the installation was successful, proceed to the next step. Otherwise, consult the troubleshooting information. The steps for installing the client software on the server are listed in Figures 2-5 and 2-6.

The first step in installing the client software is to perform the preinstallation tasks listed in the Figure 2-5 and include any preinstallation requirements found in your *DOS Software Installation Manual*. This process verifies that the system is in the proper configuration for installing the software and prepares your system for the upgrade if an earlier version of PATHWORKS was installed.

Figure 2-5. Preinstallation Tasks for PATHWORKS for DOS

Log into a privileged account.
Verify that DECnet is running:

```
$MCR NCP SHOW EXECUTOR
```

or

```
$ SHOW NETWORK
```

Verify that PATHWORKS is running:

```
$PCSA SHOW VERSION
```

Plan disk usage and verify free space.

Check the system disk and data disk(s):

```
$SHOW DEVICE D
```

After the preinstallation tasks are complete, you are ready to install the client software on the server. Figure 2-6 shows the required steps. This process is similar to loading the server software and uses the same VMSINSTAL routine.

Figure 2-6. Installation Tasks for PATHWORKS for DOS

Log into a privileged account, and run VMSINSTAL:

```
$SET DEF SYS$UPDATE:
$@VMSINSTAL PCSACLIENT041 device options N
   device=system tape drive (EX: MKA500)
```

Verify the installation was successful.
You will see the following message:

```
VMSINSTAL procedure done at 25-Oct-1991 19:05
```

If the installation failed:
Check for adequate free space on all disks.
Rerun the VMSINSTAL procedure.

Log out.

Once the installation is complete, verify that it was successful by using the PCSA SHOW FILE SERVICE command:

```
$PCSA SHOW FILE SERVICE -
  /REGISTERED/SERVICE=PCSAV41
PCSAV41 service should be listed.
```

```
$PCSA SHOW FILE SERVICE -
  /AUTHORIZED/SERVICE=PCSAV41
PCSAV41 should be listed with groups that have
  access — normally system (RWC) and public (R).
```

This command verifies that the new PATHWORKS system service, PCSAV41, is both registered and authorized.

If your results show that PCSAV41 is registered and authorized, your system is ready to use. The only thing left is to configure the client software on the workstations.

CLIENT CONFIGURATION

Once the server is installed, you may begin configuring the PC client software. This process is very simple and should be completed in 10 to 15 minutes. As with the server installation, there are a few simple preconfiguration checks that can save you a lot of time.

Preconfiguration

The first area of concern is the PC you will configure as the first workstation. This machine should be a plain PC, with no special memory-resident programs, video cards, or other internal equipment. Most standard clones with a hard disk and with or without a VGA monitor will work fine.

After choosing the PC, print a listing of the root directory and save it for future reference. Then check to make certain there is not a DECnet directory located off the root directory of the boot drive (e.g., c:\DECNET). If this directory exists, move the files into another directory and delete the directory. The configuration procedure will recreate it.

Next, print the AUTOEXEC.BAT and CONFIG.SYS files from your boot drive. You may want to compare these to the files after the configuration is complete. You should also run a memory utility such as CHKDSK, MEM, or MEMMAN and print the output both before and after the configuration to document the amount of RAM left after PATHWORKS is loaded. These are the preconfiguration commands for the PC:

```
C:\>DIR c:\*.* > LPT1:

C:\>MEM > LPT1:

C:\>PRINT C:\AUTOEXEC.BAT

C:\>PRINT C:\CONFIG.SYS
```

Make sure the CONFIG.SYS file has a shell statement that includes the /E: entry with a minimum value of 1,024. The following is an example of a CONFIG.SYS shell statement:

```
SHELL C:\COMMAND.COM /E:1024 /P
.
.
```

Next, shut down the PC and install a Digital ThinWire Ethernet card. Use the default settings on the card for this initial installation. After installing the card, you may restart the PC.

The network card for at least one client on your network should use a ThinWire Ethernet card and cable from Digital. This may cost slightly more than a clone card, and you may be planning on twisted-pair, but you will find it invaluable to have at least one ThinWire workstation. The main reason to have a ThinWire node is to assure yourself of a simple network connection. ThinWire connects straight to the VAX and client, with no bridges, routers, or repeaters. It is clean, simple, and easy to test, especially on a new network.

Buying the card from Digital will assure you of starting out with a card that is supported by Digital and will work with your release of PATHWORKS. You will not have to deal with other vendors and go through the trial-and-error process on the first machine. This card will also serve as your standard when troubleshooting PC and network problems.

Configuration

After completing the preconfiguration procedures, run the client installation procedure. For PATHWORKS V4.1, the configuration process uses a program called NETSETUP.EXE and is found on the client disk set and the PCSAV41 service. In this section, all references to NETSETUP refer to NETSETUP.EXE.

NETSETUP will create a network-key disk by copying files from the server or client disk set to a PC disk. The disk may be a bootable hard disk, floppy, or network disk service. The STARTNET.BAT file and EXECINFO.BAT files are created by NETSETUP and placed in the DECNET directory on the boot disk. The other files placed in this directory are copied from the system service PCSAV41 or the client disk set.

If you have access to a DOS client on an existing PATHWORKS network running the same version of PATHWORKS, you can run NETSETUP on this machine to create the initial key disk for your new network. If you do not have access to an existing PATHWORKS client node or key disk, you should run NETSETUP from the client disk set supplied with your media and documentation kit.

NETSETUP will ask for the drive letter of your boot disk. This can be either a floppy or the local hard disk. I like to build all configurations onto a floppy and copy the files onto the hard disk, if necessary. This prevents NETSETUP from overwriting any files that should not be overwritten, such as AUTOEXEC.BAT and CONFIG.SYS. When using this approach, you may need to reset the BOOT environment variable to point to the hard disk instead of the floppy, and possibly edit the drive letters in the CONFIG.SYS and AUTOEXEC.BAT files.

Your system administrator should provide the DECnet address and node name for your client machines. The address is a standard DECnet address, in the form area.node. The area parameter is a number from 1 to 63 and designates the logical area of the network to which this node belongs. This parameter provides a method of segmenting traffic on a network. The node parameter is also an integer, from 1 to 1,024, and it uniquely identifies a particular node on the network. The network shown in most of our examples uses a server named KENS with an address of 1.200. NETSETUP also requires the address and name of the primary PATHWORKS server.

After entering the node address and name, select the parameters shown in Figure 2-7 and choose the write disk option. This will write the configuration files to the boot disk you specified. The figure shows a NETSETUP screen in the advanced operator mode. See Chapter 4, "Client Configurations," for a detailed explanation about how to customize NETSETUP's operation.

You should also make sure that LANSESS is flagged to load in NETSETUP. When LANSESS is loaded, the Local-Area Systems Transport (LAST) will automatically be used for file services, providing much faster performance than DECnet. DECnet still must be loaded if you will be using PATHWORKS Mail.

The memory configuration parameters for loading PATHWORKS components are on a separate screen that is accessed by selecting the MEMORY CONFIGURATION MENU prompt. NETSETUP will also allow you to select Ethernet or Token Ring support for the node. NETSETUP provides access to different versions of the LAN Manager Redirector: basic and enhanced. Additional features include numerous NDIS drivers and support for CD-ROM drives on Digital's InfoServer 100.

NETSETUP will write the setup parameters and files to the disk specified as the boot disk. If this disk is a floppy, copy the files from the floppy \DECNET directory to the \DECNET directory on the target client machine. You must also edit AUTOEXEC.BAT to insert the call to STARTNET.BAT, to execute the PATHWORKS startup procedure. You should check the CONFIG.SYS file on the floppy to determine if you should modify the client's CONFIG.SYS. I will discuss the CONFIG.SYS file in more detail in Chapter 4, "Client Configurations."

After this step is complete, reboot the PC, and you should be connected to the network. To check your connection, enter the USE command:

```
C:\>USE
USE Version V4.1 Digital Network Connection Manager

Status Dev  Type  Connection name                      Mode    Size
------ ---  ----  --------------- ----                 ----    ----
       D:   FILE  \\SERVER\PCSAV41
C:\>
```

The output of the USE command verifies that the client has connected to the VMS server and shows that drive D: is connected to the file service PCSAV41 on the server named SERVER. The drive letter for PCSAV41 will vary, depending on the

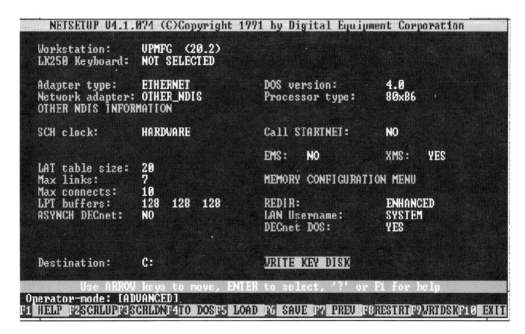

Figure 2-7. NETSETUP Screen in Advanced Operator Mode

number of local drives on your workstation. For example, if you have a hard disk and RAM disk, the PCSAV41 may be connected via drive E:. If you receive an error message, the client is not connected to the server, and you should consult the troubleshooting section of this book (Chapter 12) and your network documentation.

DOS V5.0 Clients

If you are upgrading a DOS V5.0 client to PATHWORKS V4.1, you should remove the SETVER references to any PATHWORKS components, as PATHWORKS V4.1 directly supports DOS V5.0. This includes REDIR.EXE, USE.EXE, MEMMAN.EXE, LAD.EXE, SHOW.EXE, NETSETUP.EXE, and any other PATHWORKS files. The format of the command is:

```
C:\>SETVER file.ext /delete
```

Replace file.ext with the name of each file to reset. If your network has a large number of clients, you may want to include the SETVER reset commands in a batch file, to use for quickly upgrading other clients.

TESTING THE INSTALLATION

If the USE command is successful, you are ready to access the network. To access the PCSAV41 service, simply refer to the D: drive as you would any other drive. Executing the command C:\>DIR D: will list files installed by the installation process on the server. If you try to create a file on this service, you will receive an error message. The default access to this service is read only for the group Public (all users).

At this point you will have only one file service on the server. You can access any server directory by executing the following command:

```
C:\>USE ?: \\Server\DKA300:[000000]%Username * /log.
```

DKA300:[000000] should be the directory specification required for your particular server. This example uses the VMS format. This command will set the next available drive letter to the root directory on the drive DKA300:, provided your username and password allow you to access this directory. Any directory on the server can be accessed in the same manner. The following example illustrates a sample USE command, which accesses a normal VMS user directory:

```
C:\>USE ?:\\VAX\DKB300:[000000.USERS.JOHN]%%JOHN *
```

This command sets the next available drive letter to point to the user directory named JOHN on the DKB300: drive on the VMS server named VAX. If this command is successful, you may now access any files in the directory tree that meet the DOS file conventions, such as file name restrictions of an 8 character name + 3 character extension. You can also connect to your personal login directory on the server by using USE in the following statement:

```
C:\>USE ?:\\VAX\JOHN%JOHN *
```

You can also try using a network printer. If existing printers are connected to your network, you can execute the following commands to access any printer to which you would have access. Substitute your server and printer names for SERVER and LA324 respectively:

```
C:\>USE LPT3: \\SERVER\LA324
C:\>COPY C:\CONFIG.SYS LPT3:.
```

The USE command in this example redirects the LPT3: local printer name to the LA324 print queue on the server named SERVER. Printing from within an application or DOS and referencing this printer will direct the output to the network print queue LA324. If these two commands are successful, your CONFIG.SYS file will print on the printer specified in the first command.

CHAPTER 3

Network Configurations

A network is made up of discrete components. The very word *network* implies a number of things that are connected together and work as a whole. A particular PATHWORKS implementation will have file servers, bridges, routers, and any number of other devices (including the client PCs) attached to the network. Each component plays a role in making the network function, and each can be a critical element in the reliability of the system.

This chapter will focus on the configuration of the file server, give an overview of network architectures available with PATHWORKS, and discuss cabling. The discussions presented are not intended to be the last word in any particular area but should serve as a guide to how the system is put together and how it functions. The details of each area (PATHWORKS, DECnet, network architectures, and so on) are changing at a rapid pace and are outside the scope of this book.

SERVERS

A server on a PATHWORKS network provides a number of services to clients. File, print, time, disk, and numerous other services may be provided to all or some users on the network. The standard features of the VMS operating system enable VMS servers to provide many of these services. For example, VMS print queues are accessible to PATHWORKS users with no special configuration or modifications. Queue management features apply to all files using a queue, whether they originate from VMS or PATHWORKS. Print queues created with PCSA Manager are actually VMS print queues. PCSA Manager simply automates the configuration process for creating and configuring the queue by creating DCL command procedures to create the queue. Time and file services operate in the same fashion, using standard VMS system features.

Figure 3-1 illustrates how VMS file services are used to store both VMS files and client user files, using PATHWORKS file services. VMS sees no difference between DOS or VMS, and it makes all files available to either interactive users or PATHWORKS DOS users. All PATHWORKS services are handled transparently as far as the user is concerned.

The PATHWORKS server software is a collection of different programs and files. Some programs and files are standard VMS programs such as AUTHORIZE and NCP, while others are specific to PATHWORKS, such as PCFS_SERVER and LAD$KERNEL. The PATHWORKS-specific software is usually broken down by categories for the file server, disk server, and management.

The server software is installed and functions like any other VMS-layered product. VMSINSTAL is used to install the various pieces of software on the file server, including the server software and parts of the client software. Once installed and configured, the server software is started and runs as a background process. You can start only the file server or only the disk server if you are using one or the other and not both. This can save on the overhead of the PATHWORKS software and improve overall performance of the server for both VMS and PATHWORKS users. The block diagram in Figure 3-2 illustrates how the various pieces of software work with the standard VMS utilities.

In general, PATHWORKS is an I/O-intensive system and does not place a great deal of demand on memory. Keep this in mind when designing your server and choosing

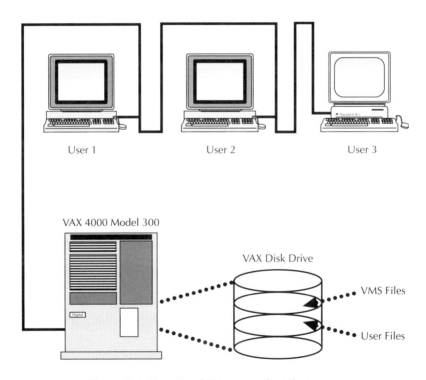

Figure 3-1. Functional Diagram of a File Server

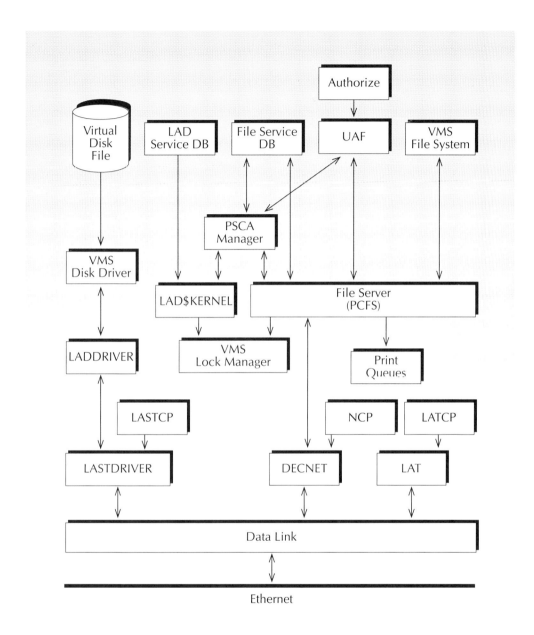

Figure 3-2. Relationship of Server Software to VMS Utilities

the I/O devices. Chapter 11 covers managing disks and how to spread the PATHWORKS services across several disks.

Figure 3-3 shows an example of a typical network with a file/print server. Notice that the print file moves from the PC to the server and then to the printer. The command executed by the user is the standard DOS COPY command. In most networks, the application need not be network specific or even written to run on a network. The network software handles all disk requests and reroutes any access requests for network services to the server. This is normally handled by a shell program on the PC that intercepts requests for disks and passes data transparently to the server when required.

PATHWORKS works in the same fashion as the typical LAN by using driver programs on the PC to provide the interface to the PATHWORKS server software on the VAX to provide access to VAX services. As PC users store files on network drives, the data is stored on the PATHWORKS server as record management services (RMS) files. These files may be accessed by any PC user or VAX user with the proper application software and security authorization.

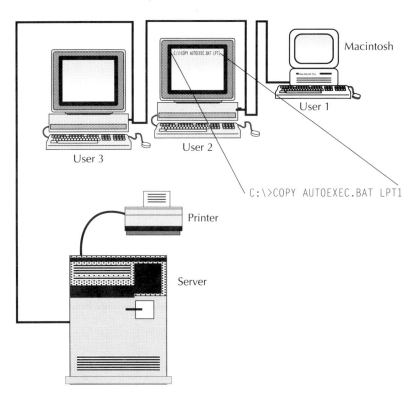

Figure 3-3. Network File/Print Service

Figure 3-3 illustrates PATHWORKS programs and VMS utilities used by the various services. Notice how the PATHWORKS software interfaces with standard VMS programs and databases. The interface to all services is provided through DECnet, LAT, and LAST in the same manner as to other VMS nodes. By using the standard VMS services, PATHWORKS utilizes VMS features instead of re-creating them. It also inherits the richness of many VMS features such as the C2 security rating. VMS benefits from this interface because it sees every access to the server as it arrives at the server.

I will now briefly discuss the components of the file server and disk server. Refer to Figure 3-3 for the various processes and files that make up the server.

File Server

The PATHWORKS file server is controlled by the PCFS_SERVER process. PCFS_SERVER works with a number of standard VMS services to provide access to VMS services from client workstations. Standard services such as DECnet, the VMS security system, VMS print services, VMS Lock Manager, the VMS file system, and others are used by PCFS_SERVER.

DECnet and LAST provide the network architecture over which PATHWORKS communicates between the file server and client. Because DECnet is the standard Digital network software, PATHWORKS can integrate with the many other systems that have access to a DECnet network. When a request is sent or received by the file server, it is handed over to or from DECnet. PATHWORKS can also use LAST for file services, providing increased performance over the LAN. DECnet is a protocol that may be used in any network (LAN or WAN), but LAST may be used only locally — that is, not over bridges and routers.

PATHWORKS coordinates with RMS to perform read/write operations to VMS files. PCFS_SERVER does not actually use RMS but directly accesses the VMS file system, which provides for faster access to files. There is a lot of overhead in file services, as VMS files must be converted to and from DOS files when a client accesses a file. Even though PATHWORKS does not use RMS to access the files, it uses all of the RMS security features.

PCFS_SERVER uses the UAF to maintain some of the security information for access to the server. This file is the same file as VMS uses, and information for VMS users is interchangeable with that for PATHWORKS users. Any users listed in the UAF can access the server on the basis of the permissions allowed through the UAF and RMS. If you can access a file from VMS, you can access the same file from PATHWORKS via the username and password, if the file is accessible by DOS.

PATHWORKS uses the VMS Lock Manager to provide concurrent access control over files located on the file server. When two or more users try to access the same file, the Lock Manager decides who can access the file and when. This is critical when PATHWORKS is used in a cluster environment.

Another interesting feature of PATHWORKS is the print system. Most networks must create a print system from scratch, whereas PATHWORKS uses the powerful VMS printing features. When a print request is received by PCFS_SERVER, it is handed over to a standard VMS print queue. PATHWORKS queues are managed by managing VMS queues.

The PATHWORKS file server uses information in the PCFS$SERVICE_DATABASE.DAT database. This file is maintained by PCSA Manager. The information contained in this database includes directory locations for file services, file service connection limitations, file service security (using access control lists, or ACLs), and print services.

Disk Server

The disk server is also controlled by several processes that are part of PATHWORKS. PATHWORKS disk services are referred to as local-area-disk (LAD) services and are known as virtual disks, which indicates that there is no physical disk drive.

A LAD disk is actually a file located on the server disk, which is called a container file. The size of this disk may range from 360 KB to 32 MB. A virtual disk can be accessed by one user at a time in read/write mode or by many users in read-only mode. The disk can be accessed over LANs and extended LANs, but not over a WAN. Although this file is a VMS file, it cannot be accessed directly from VMS without using the PCDISK utility described in Chapter 10, "Practical Approach to Network Management."

A container file is a standard VMS file that has a contiguous fixed-record-length (512-byte) sequential structure. One RMS record of the file equals a DOS sector. A container file will appear as a standard VMS file with the .DSK suffix.

Disk services are provided by two VMS processes, LAD$KERNEL and LADDRIVER. The LAD$KERNEL process interfaces with both PCSA Manager and the VMS Lock Manager to control the LADDRIVER process. LADDRIVER is implemented as a device driver and interfaces with the VMS disk driver. This process does not interface with RMS, but accesses the disk directly through the VMS disk driver.

The LADCDRIVER process is used to enable the PCDISK utility to access a disk service. This process does not require loading if you are not using PCDISK.

The disk server uses LAST not DECnet. LAST is faster than DECnet for accessing files, but it is a local protocol and cannot be routed over a WAN. LAD services are not available over Token Ring or asynchronous DECnet.

PCSA Manager creates the LAD$SERVICE_DATABASE.DAT for maintaining information relative to LAD services. This database is similar to the databases used by PCFS_SERVER but contains information used by the LAD$KERNEL process.

Disk Services Versus File Services

Disk services and file services offer different levels of performance and functions to the PATHWORKS client. Table 3-1 summarizes the key features of each.

Table 3-1. Key Features of Disk Services and File Services

Feature	Disk Service	File Service
Maximum Size	512 MB	Unlimited
Read Access	Multiple Users	Multiple Users
Read/Write Access	One User	Multiple Users
VMS Access to Files	PCDISK Only	Yes
Available in a WAN	Using NDU	Yes
Access Speed	Fastest	Fast
Remote Boot	Yes	No

File services are by far the most flexible of the two services. New releases of PATHWORKS also support using LAST instead of DECnet as the protocol for file services, which increases performance. All security features of VMS may be used for an application file service, greatly extending the power to secure your network. File services also allow any VMS directory or print queue to be used by client workstations. Even though a VMS service is not defined as a PATHWORKS service, all VMS directories are available to PATHWORKS.

Disk services offer faster access times than file services. If you have remote boot clients, they must use disk services because remote boot is not yet supported under file services. Drawbacks to disk services include the use of more RAM on the client — a device driver must be loaded — and the addition of another layer of complexity to network management, including system backup.

Print Services

Print services are provided to PATHWORKS by the standard VMS printing system. This allows PATHWORKS users to use all the functions available to a VMS user, including queue management, LAT printers, and device control libraries. PATHWORKS also inherits the VMS tool sets, including third-party tools to manage and enhance your printing capabilities.

Figure 3-4 is a high-level block diagram that depicts how PCFS_Server receives a print request from a client and passes it to the standard VMS print queue system for processing. Notice that all printing is handled by PCFS_Server, even if you are not using file services.

A client user prints the file with the DOS PRINT command. The output of this command is captured by the PATHWORKS client routines and routed over DECnet to the server, where it is handed over by PCFS_Server to the VMS queue subsystem.

Other Services

In addition to file, disk, and print services, a PATHWORKS server provides other services to clients, including mail, time, and client/server functions.

Mail services are provided using VMSmail, which is included with VMS. The client can use PATHWORKS Mail, which is included with PATHWORKS, PATHWORKS Links, or ALL-IN-1 Mail for Windows for accessing mail on a client. DECnet must be loaded on the client to send or receive mail.

Time services provide client workstations with a simple means of setting the date and time on the client from the server. This is usually accomplished when the client

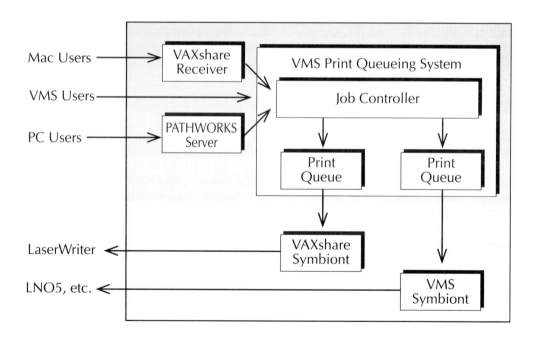

Figure 3-4. Print Server Diagram

boots and possibly when a user logs into the network. A client can obtain the time from a particular server or from any server providing time services.

PATHWORKS provides the optimal client/server environment for building truly powerful application environments in a distributed manner. You can design and build these applications by using Digital's ACMS transaction processing software, DECquery, and third-party tools, and by using powerful client software packages such as Microsoft's Visual Basic, C compilers, and Borland International Inc.'s Rdb Link. Building a client/server application does not require writing operating system-level code, as with some PC networks.

Another major benefit of the PATHWORKS client/server environment is that you can use whatever hardware is required for a particular task. Environments such as large multiuser systems can burn a traditional PC LAN to the ground. Upgrading to more expensive 80386 or 80486 servers may not improve the situation, because the constraint is often the network operating system and the server architecture. Most 80386 and 80486 machines share the same architecture. Building complex systems with PATHWORKS allows part of the application to run on the client, such as the user interface and maybe some of the graphics, and lets the heavy database applications run on the server or a separate database server. The server can be a dedicated VAX of whatever size you need for the task.

Miscellaneous Server Files

Miscellaneous files used to start the file and disk servers include:

- ◆ PCFS_STARTUP.COM — Starts the file server.
- ◆ LAD$STARTUP.COM — Starts the disk server.
- ◆ PCFS_LOGICALS.COM — Defines PATHWORKS logicals.

Both PCFS_STARTUP.COM and LAD$STARTUP.COM are normally executed in the startup procedures for the server. PCFS_LOGICALS.COM is automatically called during this process, and it establishes the logical names used by PATHWORKS.

Server Clustering

In addition to offering the file, print, and security features of VMS, PATHWORKS also inherits VMS' ability to add load-balancing and fault-tolerance features by grouping servers in a cluster. These features are enabled by creating a VAXcluster, which consists of multiple VAXs. The many possible combinations of servers is truly mind boggling. You can cluster small MicroVAX machines up to the mainframe-level VAX 9000. These machines can be grouped in many different configurations, and you can combine machines of different models. Many other network vendors have been trying to build redundant server functions into their products for several years, although at the time of this writing none has produced a successful product that provides a fully redundant server. VAXclusters, introduced in 1983, provide this capability to any VMS installation. As with any product that has been improved for almost 10 years, the current state of clustering is very reliable and robust. Figures 3-5 through 3-8 illustrate a few possible clustering configurations.

Figure 3-5 shows two MicroVAX 3100s connected in a Local-Area VAXcluster (LAVc), using Ethernet as the connection between the two machines. This is a simple and cost-effective method of building a cluster. Using an LAVc provides the ability to cluster multiple servers, but it suffers from the speed limitation of Ethernet, which is 10 Mbps. This type of cluster should be used in areas where you require server redundancy and some sharing of files from the different servers. If users will be extensively sharing files from one server while logged into the other, you should consider one of the more powerful Digital Storage Systems Interconnect (DSSI) or Computer Interconnect (CI) clusters.

VAXs with a DSSI bus provide an interesting capability to network servers or interactive implementations. You can connect a DSSI cable between the two machines, linking the bus of each VAX. Once this connection is made, every device attached to the bus of either machine appears as if it were locally attached to both machines. That is, if you connect two machines, each with two disks, both machines will have access to all four disks. At the time of this writing, three VAXs with DSSI buses can be clustered in this manner. (See Figures 3-6 and 3-7.)

The expansibility of the DSSI bus provides a very cost-effective method of building a cluster. If you add a secondary equipment cabinet and another DSSI cable, the disk drives can be moved out of the CPU boxes, providing an almost fault-tolerant VAXcluster. Digital provides a special configuration of several models that is truly fault tolerant.

The CI cluster (see Figure 3-8) provides a high-performance system by using Digital's CI to connect the various VAXs to disk and tape devices. This type of cluster is available on systems using the VAX 6000 and higher models. At the time of this writing, up to 16 VAXs can be clustered using the CI.

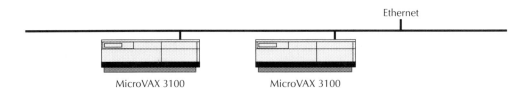

MicroVAX 3100   MicroVAX 3100

Figure 3-5. LAVc with Two MicroVAX 3100s

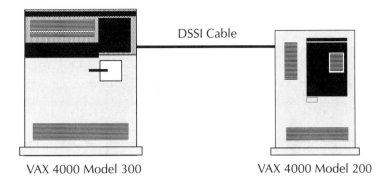

VAX 4000 Model 300   VAX 4000 Model 200

Figure 3-6. DSSI VAXcluster

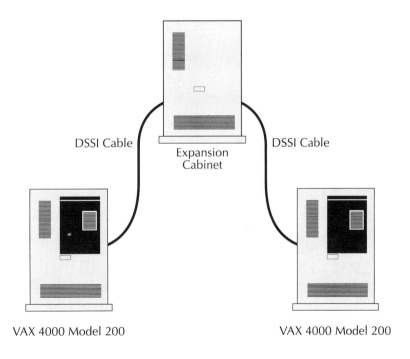

DSSI Cable   Expansion   DSSI Cable
                     Cabinet

VAX 4000 Model 200   VAX 4000 Model 200

Figure 3-7. DSSI VAXcluster with External Disks

When you install PATHWORKS on a cluster, the file and disk server programs run on each node in the cluster. Users may connect to the services through any node. The PATHWORKS programs and databases can be stored on the boot devices or other devices available to the cluster.

Because the cluster capabilities of PATHWORKS will change with new releases, you should consult your documentation in detail and use DSN Link and Digital Customer Service to check for any known problems with any particular version.

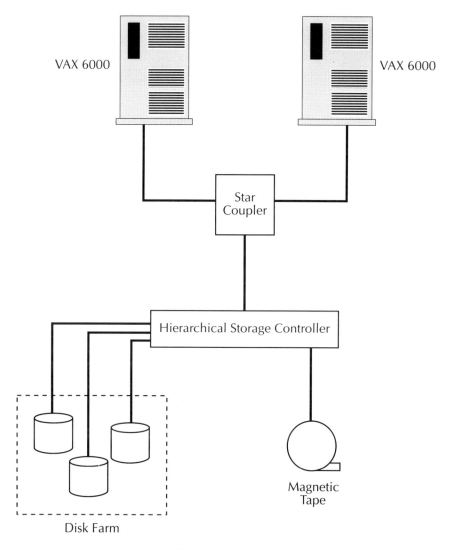

Figure 3-8. CI Cluster

NETWORK ARCHITECTURES

This discussion so far has centered on the file server, and I have touched on components of the network itself, such as DECnet, LAT, and LAST. In this section, a brief overview of the available network options for PATHWORKS is provided. This is a relatively high-level discussion and does not delve into a tremendous amount of detail. For further discussions on networks, refer to "Suggested Readings and Online Services" at the end of this book.

The network options for PATHWORKS let you integrate almost any other system into your environment. The two most popular LAN types today are Ethernet and Token Ring, both of which are supported by PATHWORKS. These two network architectures account for more than 70 percent of all network implementations.

Ethernet

Digital's implementation of Ethernet meets the IEEE 802.3 standard. It operates at 10 Mbps over coaxial or twisted-pair cable. Configurations are available to support LAN and WAN systems, including those using fiber-optic, leased-line, and microwave technologies. High-performance networks can be built using both Digital and third-party, off-the-shelf products.

Ethernet is one of the oldest network standards and as such has proved itself in business environments for many years. Attempts to supplant Ethernet with other standards have led to products having only incremental performance gains over Ethernet, which will be greatly outdistanced by the speeds of Fiber Distributed Data Interface (FDDI).

While newer technologies may bring short-lived improvements in one or two areas, Ethernet continues to provide a leading role in network implementations. It is still the most popular network standard for current implementations. The configuration options available for Ethernet from Digital and third-party vendors provide almost limitless options for configuring and managing your network. Tools are readily available for small, medium, and large networks in a number of configurations.

FDDI is a newcomer to the networking arena and is boosting the speed in some applications to 100 Mbps over fiber-optic cable and some types of copper cable. FDDI also provides advantages in security and in freedom from electrical interference. Digital and other vendors provide standard products for integrating FDDI into your Ethernet network. FDDI provides a high-performance medium for use as a network backbone or in areas requiring extremely high speeds, such as graphic-intensive applications and demanding database environments.

Token Ring

Token Ring is fast becoming the network of choice for many people. By adding support for Token Ring, Digital has removed the issue of Token Ring vs. Ethernet from the network software selection process. Digital's implementation of Token Ring operates at either 4 or 16 Mbps and conforms to the IEEE 802.5 standard. For now, I would suggest staying with Ethernet, unless you have a compelling reason to use Token Ring, such as your having a large Token Ring installation currently. Ethernet has many advantages, especially for WANs, and its network hardware is widely available.

Protocol Support

PATHWORKS supports DECnet, TCP/IP, LAST, LAT, CTERM, Maintenance Operations Protocol (MOP), Appletalk, NetBIOS, and NetBUIE. NetBUIE is supported on Token Ring and Ethernet, and Appletalk is supported only on Ethernet. The other protocols are supported on both Token Ring and Ethernet.

PATHWORKS can operate over any of these protocols, and it supports multiple simultaneous protocols. In other words, DECnet and TCP/IP can be used at the same time for a server that has both DECnet and TCP/IP clients. There are some limitations on how the networks are physically configured, but there do not appear to be any limitations on which protocols can run simultaneously.

DECnet is a Digital standard that has been used for many years. It is robust and is supported by almost everything Digital makes. VMS and PATHWORKS support for DECnet includes management tools on both the client and the server.

TCP/IP is popular for UNIX networks. Almost every UNIX system on the market supports TCP/IP. While TCP/IP is supported by PATHWORKS, it lacks some of the functions available with DECnet. However, TCP/IP provides the ability to connect to the Internet and many other systems.

LAST is used by the PATHWORKS disk server and possibly the file server. It is highly optimized and works only on a LAN.

LAT or CTERM may also be used on your network. LAT manages terminal servers and client terminal services with a terminal emulator. Like LAST, LAT is highly optimized for a LAN and does not function over a WAN. CTERM is an alternative to LAT for networks requiring WAN terminal access. CTERM uses DECnet as the transport. Both LAT and CTERM are supported by SETHOST and VT320. Make sure that users on the LAN are using LAT to improve the efficiency of the network, not CTERM, which should be used only when required for access to services over a WAN.

VMS uses MOP for any device that boots over the network. This includes PATHWORKS clients that boot remotely from the server. MOP is also a local transport and is designed specifically for boot services. VMS nodes that boot from other nodes and some terminal servers also use MOP.

NETWORK CABLING AND CONNECTIONS

One of the most overlooked LAN components is the cabling system, called the cable plant. It is one of the most important components for determining the long-term maintenance requirements and cost of your network. Penny-pinching or lack of planning in this area will cause you untold grief for many years to come.

Network designers most frequently review the technical aspects of a LAN, leaving the cable scheme and components until the last minute. Many installations turn the cable system design and installation over to a local contractor, often one that specializes in telephone or electrical wiring. In the process of designing your LAN, you must consider several factors to ensure the success of your investment.

It is critical to the success of your LAN to analyze why the LAN is being installed or expanded, and where the system will grow in the future. You must consider user needs and requirements in order to ensure that the system will accommodate their future plans.

This section reviews cable systems for a typical PATHWORKS LAN. I will review cabling schemes, connectors, and other functional components and discuss their growth aspects and cost implications. Most of the discussion on cabling is from a manager's point of view and is not particularly detailed. Digital and other vendors provide books on their various cabling systems. Refer to "Suggested Readings and Online Services," and note the documents available from Digital and Anixter on cabling.

Almost every VAX system has a built-in Ethernet port. The modern-day VAX was originally designed as a networking machine, with support for DECnet incorporated into the VMS operating system. Each VAX is usually shipped with a ThinWire and/or ThickWire connection, providing immediate access to the network. Adding a VAX to a network can be as simple as unpacking the machine, plugging in the network connection, booting the machine, and starting and configuring DECnet. Within a minute or two, the entire network will be aware of the new machine.

Planning the Cable Scheme

The cable scheme used in your LAN will determine the growth potential, cost of growth, flexibility, and reliability of your system. Ethernet is a forgiving system, allowing you to mix different types of cable in one system. For instance, you can add twisted-pair cable to a ThinWire system by adding a 10Base-T repeater. The hard part of changing cabling plants comes when you totally change from one scheme to another and try to justify to your management why you are spending money without adding functions.

Structured Versus Unstructured Cabling

Installing network cable is like working on any other project. Cable can be installed willy-nilly on an install-as-you-go basis, or it can be logically thought out and planned. A structured cable plant is one that is well designed and has a standard plan for its implementation and growth. Structured cabling also means that the cable and components used lend themselves to the planning and growth of the network.

Unstructured cable systems normally use wiring components that are easily moved from one place or station to another. ThinWire is usually used in this environment, with workstations simply connected in a daisy chain. Twisted-pair or ThickWire cable can also be used in this type of environment but are not normally installed in wiring closets or otherwise structured.

Structured cable plants are often broken down into areas such as campuswide, vertical, and horizontal. In a structured cable system, wiring plans are organized for each area of the system, and structured wiring components, such as concentrators, patch panels, and face plates, are used to connect all wiring and devices. Any type of wiring can be used in a structured system, but its use must be carefully planned and documented.

Neither of these approaches is inherently bad or good, but each serves as a point of reference for planning a reliable and flexible cable system. Because the cable system is the root of 95 percent of network problems, it pays to make it reliable, using whichever system is best for a given network.

The goal of any cable system should be to provide a reliable and flexible foundation for your network. Just as the foundation of a house is vital to its reliability and flexibility, the cable system will be the foundation of your network. When you need to add a node or section to the network a year from now, you should be confident that the network will not go down when you make the change. By establishing a clear plan for your cable system and using modular components, you can achieve this fairly easily.

Digital's DECconnect wiring system provides standard components for wiring almost anything. In addition, most of these components are available from other vendors such as Anixter. With a little ingenuity, you can configure a cost-effective system using a few of these tools. In a small office, I have used DECconnect faceplates wired directly to a DECrepeater 90T (10Base-T repeater) that was connected to the server via a short ThinWire segment. This was fairly inexpensive and very effective. You can also use standard RJ45 jacks at the faceplate to connect to the network. It does not matter what or whose components you use, as long as you plan for now and the future, and properly install the components.

If you have a very complex environment, that is, one with lots of potential interference or a large network (over 50 nodes), you should consult your network designer and do further research in this field.

ETHERNET

To configure a typical Ethernet LAN, you must consider several factors, including the cable type (coaxial, twisted-pair, fiber-optic), number of nodes (servers, clients, terminal servers), and overall layout of the network. This section covers the basics of the network cabling system, including several types of network components and the basic structure of the network.

Segments

Ethernet networks are organized into segments. Each segment is a logically separate section of the network, usually consisting of a length of cable. The cable may be a single piece (from one node or device to another) or may be multiple sections of cable that connect numerous devices. All nodes on a segment are isolated from nodes on other segments by a repeater, bridge, or router. A node can communicate with other nodes on the entire network, but each is protected from problems that occur on other segments, unless the segment is downstream from the problem segment (i.e., the problem segment is between the server and your segment).

An Ethernet cable segment consists of all cable sections up to a repeater, router, or bridge, with each cable attaching to the device belonging to another segment. Each type of cable has a unique set of rules governing the number of nodes that can attach to the cable, overall length of the cable segment, number of bridges between nodes, and so on. These rules were established because of the characteristics of the different cables and devices available for a particular cable type.

When planning your network, you should logically separate different areas by breaking them into segments. It is also beneficial to establish redundancy in your network by adding redundant devices where uptime is critical or by possibly laying alternate cable runs to other devices. In the event of a failure, you can quickly bypass the faulty equipment by moving a connection or two. New devices such as Digital's DEChub products (DECrepeater 90T, DECrepeater 90C, and DECbridge 90) make this affordable and easy to manage.

ThinWire

Digital's ThinWire specification conforms to the IEEE 10Base-2 standard. ThinWire uses traditional coaxial cable, meeting the RG-59 specification. ThinWire is very flexible and easy to install. In workgroup environments, you can build your network easily by installing short pieces of cable to connect each node. ThinWire also works well in the computer room or office environment to connect servers and other devices to the network. Connections to ThinWire cable segments are made by using a T connector to attach to the device, with the ThinWire cable attaching to either side of the T. Other devices such as a ThinWire repeater may attach directly to the cable.

ThinWire also provides some EMI and RFI protection for areas with other equipment that may cause interference, such as in manufacturing plants and engineering environments. Machines in these environments typically generate electronic frequencies that may interfere with the network wiring scheme. In any type of environment, adhere to the rules for the type of cable being used. Day-to-day devices such as a simple fluorescent light may also wreak havoc with the typical network if cables are placed too close to the light.

ThinWire is suitable for workgroups and small, stable systems. Pay special attention to the words *small* and *stable*. Interference from moving the network cable, certain types of lights (e.g., fluorescent), antennae, machines, and so on, have a major effect on a ThinWire segment. This interference will drive you crazy if it hits your network. The best cure is prevention, so use ThinWire selectively and cautiously.

ThickWire

The original Ethernet specification was designed and implemented using baseband cable. Digital's implementation of baseband meets the IEEE 10Base-5 specification and is usually referred to as ThickWire. This is a heavily shielded coaxial cable that is very tough and provides a high level of interference protection. ThickWire is very hard to manipulate and requires a special device and transceiver cable for connections from the ThickWire cable to a node or other Ethernet device. The bending radius of ThickWire is also very large, making it unsuitable for tight spaces.

ThickWire is frequently used for backbones or long runs between segments, such as from one building to another. It is also well suited for areas that have a high degree of noise or interference, such as factories.

Twisted-Pair Wire

Twisted-pair wire is relatively new to the Ethernet scene and is based on the IEEE 10Base-T standard. It is flexible, inexpensive, and easy to install, and it is the same wire that is used for telephones. The 10Base-T specification uses unshielded twisted-pair cable in runs up to 100 meters. Twisted-pair wire connects devices in a point-to-point fashion, with a maximum of one device on each end of a cable segment.

In contrast to ThinWire and ThickWire, twisted-pair is easy to manipulate and is usually extremely forgiving. It is the medium of choice for most office environments where several workstations are located in a relatively close area. The DEChub product family supports 10Base-T with the DECrepeater 90T, which provides eight twisted-pair ports. Twisted-pair cable can also be used to connect terminals and printers to a server or terminal server.

Fiber-Optic Cable

One of the newer cabling technologies, fiber optics, offers a number of advantages to computer networks over traditional cabling. Fiber is simple in principle. It uses a light source and a cable that is similar to a monofilament fishing line. Electrical energy is converted into light pulses that are transmitted over the cable, resulting in a very high-speed connection that is virtually immune to interference.

Digital and other vendors have offered fiber-optic cable options for several years, providing a high-performance growth path but at a steep price. Affordable fiber options are becoming available that allow fiber to be used as a high-speed backbone and to connect high-performance desktop systems.

The FDDI ANSI standard specifies fiber in a ring configuration to provide network services at 100 Mbps. Digital and others are developing an addition to FDDI to allow twisted-pair cable to be used as the desktop interface and still provide speeds of 100 Mbps.

Topologies Used with Ethernet

Ethernet has traditionally used a bus (daisy-chain) topology to connect devices along the network but can also use a star or ring topology.

Bus. Bus networks are broken into segments, each consisting of a section of cable that may connect numerous devices. The network cable connects one node to another in a series. A section of cable runs from each node to the next, where it is connected to a T connector (ThinWire only) or transceiver (ThickWire only) that attaches to the network interface on the node. The T connector is simply inserted between two segments of cable or has a terminator installed on one side if there are no additional nodes downline from the current node. ThickWire uses a transceiver that connects to the ThickWire cable and uses a transceiver cable to connect to the AUI port on the device.

A bus network is easy to install and is usually the first component of a new network. ThinWire is usually installed to connect the server with terminal servers or other equipment located near the server, and ThinWire is initially low in cost. Invest in a network card and cable section, and you are in business. This cost will grow substantially as you add new nodes in far-flung sections of your organization.

One major disadvantage to a bus network is the effect of a network problem on other nodes. If a problem occurs on a segment of a bus network, all nodes on that segment will go down. If the segment includes repeaters or terminal servers, all devices connected to these components may also go down.

The bus network is an important component of any Ethernet system, but you must carefully plan for its use. It must be installed in the proper environment and carefully maintained. Figure 3-9 illustrates several PCs connected to a ThinWire segment with T connectors.

Star. The relatively new 10Base-T standard supports the star topology for unshielded twisted-pair (UTP) wiring. In a star configuration, each node is connected to the network by a single cable that runs from the node to a concentrator, or repeater, that is attached to the network cable. (See Figure 3-10.)

Star configurations are normally easy to install, upgrade, and maintain. Each user is physically isolated from other nodes on the network. If a problem occurs in the cable that connects to a particular node, the problem will not affect other nodes.

While the star configuration has many benefits over the bus configuration, it is usually more costly to install. However, it provides a lower long-term cost. The cost

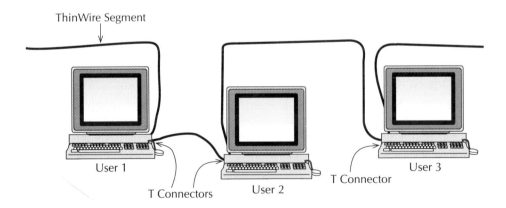

Figure 3-9. Bus Configuration

picture is continually changing, as newer and lower-cost network components are introduced. The DECrepeater 90T, a good example of this star technology, costs about $1,600. It provides a ThinWire connection to the network and a connection for eight twisted-pair connections to client workstations, such as DOS, Macintosh, ULTRIX, or VMS nodes. Twisted-pair wire is also much cheaper than ThinWire and can be installed in new buildings at the same time as the telephone system, using the same outlet boxes. See the section "Structured Versus Unstructured Cabling" earlier in this chapter. If you are installing a system in an existing building, unused twisted-pair cabling may already be installed. Unused wiring is often a great benefit. The only problem is trying to identify it and trace the ends of the cable.

Ring. In a ring topology, each computer is connected to the next by a cable that eventually returns to the first computer, forming the ring. FDDI is based on the ring topology. FDDI uses two rings made of fiber-optic cable that run in parallel. It

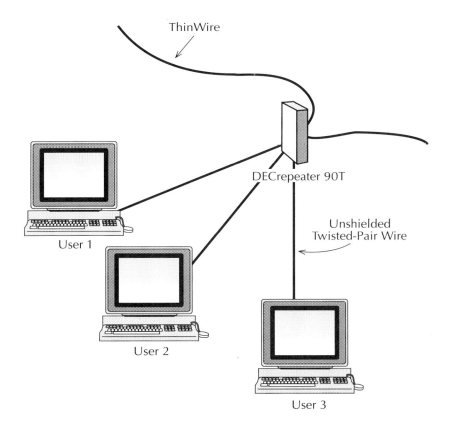

Figure 3-10. Star Configuration

45

provides a degree of fault tolerance by automatically switching to the backup ring if a failure occurs in the primary ring. Connections to an FDDI ring are made through a device such as a concentrator or bridge.

Active Devices

Ethernet uses a number of components called active devices to enhance and manage the network. Devices such as repeaters, routers, bridges, gateways, and terminal servers provide the network with different types of capabilities.

Repeaters. A repeater takes the network signal and passes it on to other devices. The signal is not checked for route information or integrity. Repeaters are most often used in ThinWire and twisted-pair environments to connect two segments or to extend the length of the LAN. Examples of commonly used repeaters are the DECrepeater 90T and DECrepeater 90C from Digital. Figure 3-11 shows the DEChub 90 with several DECrepeater 90Ts, and one DECrepeater 90C installed.

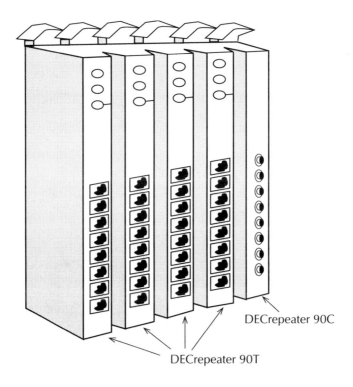

DECrepeater 90C

DECrepeater 90T

Figure 3-11. DEChub 90

Repeaters may be used within a LAN to segment the network or to allow the addition of more stations. They may also be used to connect remote networks. They are available for twisted-pair, ThinWire, ThickWire, and fiber-optic cable.

Bridges. A bridge is one step above a repeater. It provides some store-and-forward services in addition to extending the LAN and allowing the addition of more workstations. Bridges also handle LAT and DECnet, allowing you to extend your network. Most products permit the use of a repeater on one side of the connection and a bridge on the other. In addition to extending the LAN, bridges provide traffic isolation and tools for managing the network. Bridges normally do not perform any protocol emulation or translation services, although some hybrid units may offer these services.

Bridges can improve the performance of a LAN by isolating traffic on the LAN. If you install redundant paths for all nodes, bridges can also provide high availability of the network. They are usually protocol independent.

Digital provides local, remote, and fiber-optic bridge products. The Vitalink bridge products sold by Digital also support remote printers and terminals via a DECserver. DECbridge 90 is member of the DEChub family and adds remote management capabilities when installed in a DEChub with or without other products.

Some products incorporate both bridge and router services into one unit, creating what is usually called a bridge-router, or brouter. These devices selectively route or bridge protocols simultaneously, depending on which method is best for a particular protocol.

Routers. Routers are normally cheaper than bridges and provide additional intelligence to selectively route LAN traffic. They employ learning techniques to determine automatically which addresses should be routed over the WAN and which addresses should be kept on the LAN. Because routers are implemented at a higher level on the Open Systems Interconnect (OSI) model than bridges, they are protocol specific. LAT and LAST will not work across a router because they are LAN protocols. Multiprotocol routers that route numerous protocols simultaneously are also available.

Routers are effective in a WAN where there are a low number of users on the remote side of the network. Low-speed routers will also support asynchronous DECnet over a phone line. Figure 3-12 illustrates a network with bridges, routers, and repeaters. The Vitalink bridges are used to extend a LAN over phone lines.

Gateways. A gateway is a step up from a router and serves as a link between two networks, each of which uses a different network architecture. The gateway performs the conversion and emulation tasks to translate from one protocol to the other and vice versa. A DECnet system that is connected to a X.25 network is an example of this type of network. The gateway will translate DECnet to X.25 and back.

Terminal and Printer Connection Devices

Terminal servers from Digital and other vendors provide support for attaching video terminals, printers, modems, foreign hosts, and other permanent, dedicated connections to the network, such as PLCs attached to the terminal server. Any device connected to a terminal server has access to and from any host attached to the network. In a cluster environment, devices attached to a terminal server do not depend on any particular host being up for access to the cluster. Connections to a terminal server are normally made using RS-232 or EIA 423 cables and connections.

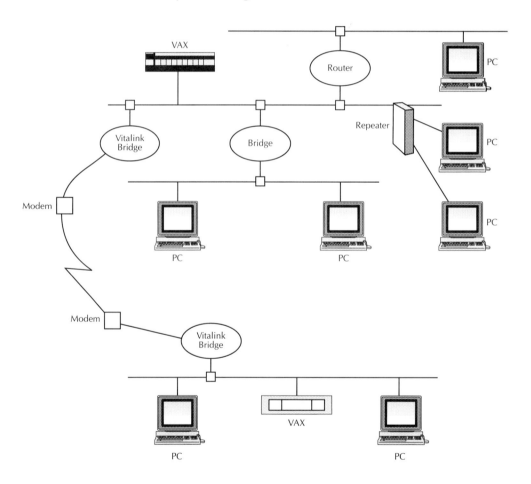

Figure 3-12. Bridges, Routers, and Repeaters

Features of most terminal servers include status lights, security levels, centralized management, remote testing, and numerous other services. Terminal servers may also provide sophisticated management tools that are accessible over the network. The DECserver 90L is an eight-port terminal server that is a member of the DEChub product family.

Ethernet Rules

Every network has certain requirements for the cabling system. These usually involve lengths of cable runs, maximum number of devices, types of cable, and so on. Here are several general guidelines for Ethernet networks:

◆ Use backbones in all but the smallest systems.

◆ Separate segments by using repeaters, bridges, or routers.

◆ Use structured cable plans and modular components.

◆ Use twisted-pair wiring whenever possible.

◆ Use care in running *all* cables. Do not run cables within 2 to 3 feet of fluorescent light fixtures, and do not run them *anywhere* near a radio transmitter.

◆ Install connections carefully on in-house cables.

Remember that the more care used in planning, documenting, installing, and testing your cable system, the more reliable and flexible your network will be.

There are also fixed rules for Ethernet components and segments that you must follow to have a successful LAN. The Ethernet restrictions are listed in Appendix A.

TOKEN RING

Digital's Token Ring support for PATHWORKS is designed to allow integration of Token Ring systems into open, enterprise networks as part of the NAS strategy. This provides access to services and applications on Digital and non-Digital systems for PC users connected to Token Ring systems. Users that were restricted to Digital or non-Digital systems will be able to share applications and data across systems. Others who were restricted to a particular type of network topology by the Ethernet versus Token Ring battles can now choose either topology. Users with mixed systems can integrate them in a clean, straightforward way.

Digital's foray into the Token Ring market is based on the Proteon Inc. product line. Digital has selected and certified certain Proteon products to perform within Digital's NAS to provide access to VAX and PATHWORKS systems from Token Ring networks. Proteon's products are field proven and provide state-of-the-art functions not available from other vendors. Some products have been enhanced to Digital specifications to ensure compatibility with standards and NAS applications.

The initial product offerings and service agreement targets several product areas. This includes the 4- and 16-Mbps PC adapters for connecting PC workstations to the network. Support for Series 70 Intelligent Wiring Centers provides a product set to serve as a foundation for a structured wiring system. WAN and extended LAN capabilities (including integration with Ethernet networks) are provided by the series of local and remote bridging routers. The DEQRA adapters install in a VAX and allow it to actually sit on the Token Ring network. Up to two adapters can be installed in a VAX and can coexist with an Ethernet adapter. Finally, network management support is handled by the TokenView Plus and SNMP product set.

Ring Topology

The Token Ring topology is implemented by using a logical ring design with a physical star-wired cabling scheme. The token actually travels in a ring around the network, even though the physical diagram depicts a star network. The multistation access unit (MAU) is internally structured to physically implement the ring inside the box.

A Token Ring network operates by transmitting a token from one node to the next. A node is allowed to transmit over the network only when it has captured the token, and only one token can be on the ring at one time. Every station on the ring will see all transmissions. There must always be a token on the ring, even if there are no transmissions.

Figures 3-13 and 3-14 show logical and physical views of the ring. Notice the directional arrow in Figure 3-13, which indicates the direction the token travels. In the physical view of the same network (Figure 3-14), each PC has a cable that runs to a concentrator, the small box at the top of the figure.

Active Devices

Repeaters, bridges, and routers are used to extend and interconnect rings in a fashion similar to their counterparts on an Ethernet LAN.

Multistation Access Units. The concentrator is the main component of the ring configuration. All wiring in a single ring terminates at the concentrator. The concentrator is referred to as a MAU.

A MAU can support up to eight stations. Two other ports are used to attach the MAU to the ring. One port is used for the ring in (RI) connector, and the second is used for the ring out (RO) connector. Multiple MAUs can be serially connected to expand the ring.

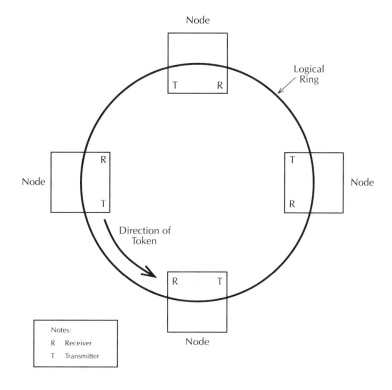

Figure 3-13. Logical Token Ring Representation

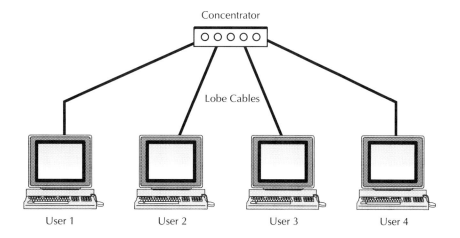

Figure 3-14. Physical Token Ring Representation

51

MAUs can be connected by linking the RO connector of one unit to the RI connector on the next unit. This will expand the number of connections to the ring. The last MAU on the ring must connect its RO connector to the RI connector of the first unit (see Figure 3-15).

Notice how the cable from the RO port on the right MAU connects to the RI port of the left MAU. The ring actually loops through each MAU, out to each PC and back, and then out of the RO port to the next RI port. The long cable between the RO and RI points completes the ring's main path.

The connectors in the MAU automatically short together when a lobe cable is removed, providing a complete path for the ring as nodes are added and removed.

Bridges and Routers

A Token Ring network uses bridges and routers to perform the same tasks as they do in an Ethernet network. The main difference is the method of routing the traffic on the network.

Bridges are used to connect multiple Token Ring networks. Token Ring networks use a concept called *source routing*. Source routing is implemented by the sending device, which places routing information within the data it places on the ring. The routing information specifies the path the data must travel to its destination.

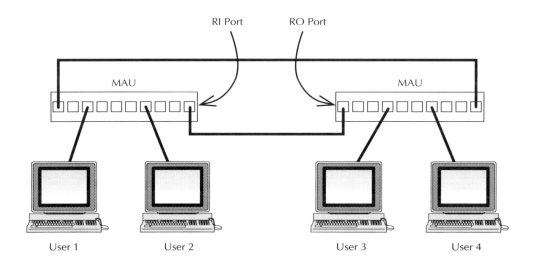

Figure 3-15. Sample Ring Using Multiple MAUs

A router can connect a Token Ring network to an Ethernet network. The router will attach to the network and listen for frames destined for the other network. It will copy any frames that have destinations on the other network. A VAX can be used as a router between a Token Ring network and an Ethernet network or between two Token Ring networks. Using a VAX for a router is best suited to casual usage, where sustained high-volume traffic would not be routed through the VAX.

Brouters can also be used in Token Ring networks. A brouter can serve as both a bridge and a router simultaneously or operate as either a bridge or a router.

The Proteon router offered by Digital is a combination bridge/router. It can be used to connect an Ethernet network to a Token Ring network or to connect two Token Ring networks. A PC-based bridge can also connect two Token Ring networks, provided the traffic is relatively low (1 to 2 Mbps).

Network Connections. Nodes connect to a Token Ring network via a Token Ring-compliant adapter. PCs typically use an 8- or 16-bit card. Other interfaces are available for attaching printers, minicomputers, and mainframes to the network. (Digital provides adapters for connecting PCs and VAXs to a Token Ring network.) Current adapters run at either 4 Mbps or 16 Mbps. The 802.5 specification covers only the 4-Mbps transmission speed. All devices attached to a ring must operate at the same speed.

The connection between a workstation network adapter and the ring typically uses a shielded twisted-pair (STP) or UTP cable. This cable is also referred to as a *lobe cable*.

CHAPTER 4

Client Configurations

As we begin a detailed review of PATHWORKS, let's consider one of the key elements in this puzzle, the PC. Most companies consider PCs to be commodity items, with very little to differentiate them from one another. PCs can be purchased for $600 to $12,000 from many different sources. Many networks use 80286 machines as workstations. People usually purchase these machines using price as the determining factor.

While PCs adhere to the standards of the open PC architecture, there is a drastic difference in quality from one brand to another. Some inexpensive machines available through mail-order channels are assembled in "assemble-only" operations, where components are purchased from low-cost bidders, with little thought for quality.

PC CONFIGURATION FILES

When planning your PATHWORKS network, consider the CONFIG.SYS and AUTOEXEC.BAT files on each PC. These files determine what happens each time the PC reboots, and they can mean the difference between an easy-to-maintain, efficient network and a nonstandard, slow network. PATHWORKS requires that one or more programs be loaded in one or both of these files.

CONFIG.SYS

The CONFIG.SYS file is loaded each time your PC is turned on or rebooted. After the internal tests are completed, CONFIG.SYS is loaded from the boot drive of the PC before any other commands are executed. Commands in this file set various DOS parameters such as the number of buffers DOS will use (BUFFERS=) and the maximum number of files the PC may have open simultaneously (FILES=). Other commands may control the number of drive letters allowed (LASTDRIVE=) and modify the configuration of the PC's memory. Programs may also be loaded into memory via entries in the CONFIG.SYS to control various aspects of the PC's operation.

A device driver is a special type of program that controls the operation of a particular device, such as extended memory, a disk cache, or a RAM disk. Some peripherals such as scanners and mice also require device drivers for their operation. A device driver works with DOS to manage the interface to its particular device. Most device drivers are loaded in CONFIG.SYS, and some drivers may be loaded in AUTOEXEC.BAT as well.

A common device driver used by PATHWORKS is the HIMEM.SYS program that is shipped with Windows, DOS, PATHWORKS, and a number of other packages. This program controls the operation of extended memory and allows programs to exceed the memory limitations of DOS. Be very careful which version of this program your CONFIG.SYS references. A PC may have a copy of this file in its DOS, Windows, and DECnet directories, to name a few. If your CONFIG.SYS file uses the wrong version, programs that use extended memory may not function.

The following CONFIG.SYS is typical of a PATHWORKS client machine with extended memory:

```
DEVICE=C:\DOS\HIMEM.SYS
DOS=HIGH
FILES=30
BUFFERS=2
SHELL=C:\COMMAND.COM/P/E:1024
DEVICE=C:\DOS\SMARTDRV.SYS
DEVICE=C:\windows\ramdrive.sys 1024/e
```

This system is set up to run Windows using DOS V5.0. There is no PATHWORKS-specific information in CONFIG.SYS, but there is plenty of information relative to DOS and Windows. Even though the HIMEM.SYS statement is not specific to PATHWORKS,

Figure 4-1. Analysis of CONFIG.SYS for Windows Using DOS V5.0.

shell=command.com/P/E:2048	Loads command.com and sets the environment to 2,048 KB.
DEVICE=C:\DOS\HIMEM.SYS	Loads the HIMEM driver for extended memory.
DOS=HIGH	Loads DOS into extended memory.
FILES=30	Allows 30 files to be open at once.
BUFFERS=2	Sets up 2 cache buffers.
SHELL=C:\COMMAND.COM/P/E:1024	Uses COMMAND.COM as the DOS shell and sets the environment for 1,024 bytes.
DEVICE=C:\DOS\SMARTDRV.SYS	Loads the SMARTDRV disk cache.
DEVICE=C:\windows\ramdrive.sys 1024/e	Sets up a RAM disk for 1 million bytes, using extended memory.

it is useful for allowing certain PATHWORKS drivers to load into extended memory via the STARTNET.BAT file. Figure 4-1 examines this file line-by-line.

A typical CONFIG.SYS for a DOS V4.01 or lower is illustrated below:

```
DEVICE=C:\DOS\HIMEM.SYS
FILES=30
BUFFERS=2
SHELL=C:\COMMAND.COM/P/E:1024
DEVICE=C:\DOS\SMARTDRV.SYS
DEVICE=C:\windows\ramdrive.sys 1024/e
```

The only difference in these two examples is the DOS=HIGH statement in the DOS V5.0 example. This line loads a large part of DOS into memory above 640 KB, freeing up conventional memory. Earlier versions of DOS do not support loading DOS into extended memory.

The shell statement in both examples is very important to the operation of DOS, because it controls which command interpreter is loaded and it may modify how the interpreter works. For our purposes, I will limit this discussion to COMMAND.COM and the parameters that are useful to PATHWORKS. A typical shell command is shown below:

```
SHELL=C:\COMMAND.COM/P/E:2048
```

The two parameters /P and /E used in the examples control the start-up functions of COMMAND.COM and the amount of memory used for environment variables. The /P parameter causes COMMAND.COM to load itself as the permanent command interpreter and execute the AUTOEXEC.BAT file located in the root directory of the boot drive as the system boots. The /E:2048 parameter specifies that DOS will allocate 2,048 bytes for environment variables. This includes the PATH statement, PROMPT statement, and any variables created with the SET command. Environment variables are set within batch files or from the DOS prompt by using a statement similar to SET THIS_VAR=TEXT. The statement in this example sets a variable called THIS_VAR in memory and initializes its contents to TEXT. The PATH and PROMPT commands establish environment variables named PATH and PROMPT. Entering SET without parameters will display all current variables.

PATHWORKS uses the SET command in batch files such as STARTNET.BAT as it loads the network components at system start-up. The LOGON.BAT program may set additional variables as a user logs into the server. Be careful to allocate more space than you expect to use for the environment, because a program will most likely fail when it runs out of environment space. In most systems, 1,024 bytes will be more than sufficient. The values for the /E parameter may range from 160 to 32,768 bytes. The following code shows a typical DOS V5.0 environment with PATHWORKS loaded. This example was produced by using the command C:\>SET:

```
MOUSE=C:\BALLPT
TEMP=d:
PROMPT=$p$g
REFLECT2=C:\REFLECT
BOOT=C:
PCSA=C:\DECNET
_SYSD=E:
PATH=C:\UTIL;C:\NDW;C:\WIN30;C:\WINWORD;C:\DSR;C:\EXCEL;C:\D
                    ECNET;C:\DOS;C:\WINSPT;E:\P
                    CAPP;E:\DECNET;E:\437USA
HELP=E:\HELP
USER=system
SERVER=vax1
```

If the /E: value is set too low, programs may not have enough memory to create the variables they require. Some programs such as Windows V3.x may also place additional demands on the environment.

I will reference CONFIG.SYS again later in this chapter when discussing how to optimize the memory utilization of the PC.

AUTOEXEC.BAT

The AUTOEXEC.BAT file is also executed as the PC starts or when it is rebooted. Note that AUTOEXEC.BAT is executed after CONFIG.SYS. This file normally contains commands that are required for a specific PC, such as the PATH and PROMPT commands, mouse drivers, and other start-up parameters.

In a network, it is important to set standards for AUTOEXEC.BAT, even though it may vary from machine to machine. By establishing a standard configuration, you can manage the differences among various PCs with minimal effort. In a typical network, the AUTOEXEC.BAT and CONFIG.SYS files will be the same on the vast majority of machines, with only the few special machines such as CAD and desktop publishing requiring customization. Figure 4-2 examines a typical AUTOEXEC.BAT file for a DOS V5.0 PC.

This AUTOEXEC.BAT is typical for a DOS V5.x system. The only DOS V.5x specific statement is the \DOS\DOSKEY line that loads the DOSKEY.EXE program. This program stores statements executed at the DOS command line, allowing you to

Figure 4-2. Analysis of AUTOEXEC.BAT for DOS V5.0

Command	Function
@ECHO OFF	Sets the echo off.
SET TEMP=d:	Sets the TEMP variable to d:. This is used by Windows.
SET GMKW=C:\GMKW\	Sets the GMKW variable to c:\GMKW\.
\DOS\SHARE	Loads the DOS SHARE.EXE program.
\DOS\DOSKEY	Loads the DOS DOSKEY.EXE program.
PROMPT pg	Sets the PROMPT.
CALL SETPATH	Calls the SETPATH.BAT program to set the PATH variable.
CALL C:\DECNET\STARTNET	Executes the STARTNET.BAT file to start DECnet.

recall, modify, and select previous commands for reuse. It also provides some macro capabilities at the command level.

The CALL C:\DECNET\STARTNET command at the end of the file executes the STARTNET.BAT file, usually located in the \DECNET directory on the user's boot drive for local-boot PCs. This batch file is created by NETSETUP, and it loads the network drivers and establishes the network connection for the PC.

Notice the CALL SETPATH statement located before the CALL C:\DECNET\STARTNET statement. This calls a batch file named SETPATH.BAT, which is located in the root directory of the PC. A sample SETPATH.BAT file is shown below:

```
REM SETPATH.BAT
REM
PATH=c:\DOS;\util;c:\decnet;\c:\mswin30
```

SETPATH.BAT is created by moving the PATH statement from AUTOEXEC.BAT to the SETPATH.BAT file. Moving PATH from AUTOEXEC.BAT prevents newly installed programs from haphazardly modifying your PATH statement.

The only drawback to placing your PATH in a separate file is the manual updating required when new applications are added to the local drive. However, this simplifies your maintenance procedures, because there will be only one SETPATH file for all PCs. This file can also be renamed to provide for many different SETPATH files

(SETCAD.BAT, SETNORM.BAT, SETMFG.BAT, and so on) to provide specific changes required by different groups of users.

PATHWORKS CONFIGURATION FILES

NETSETUP

NETSETUP is an executable DOS program that builds or modifies STARTNET.BAT, CONFIG.SYS, AUTOEXEC.BAT, EXECINFO.BAT, and CFGWS.DAT and copies certain PATHWORKS files to the local boot disk. This program is included with PATHWORKS and is located on the PCSAV41 service, usually in the PCAPP directory.

The operation of NETSETUP is controlled by the DNETWIK.V41 file from the PCSAV41\DECNET directory. DNETWIK.V41 is a template file that determines which files are copied to the client boot disk and how the configuration files STARTNET.BAT, CONFIG.SYS, and AUTOEXEC.BAT are built. The DNETWIK.V41 file shipped with PATHWORKS will work out of the box for most networks. Learning to understand this file and tailor it to your network can make managing your network a lot easier. Once you have decided how your network start-up files AUTOEXEC.BAT, CONFIG.SYS, STARTNET.BAT, and EXECINFO.BAT will look, placing the changes in DNETWIK.V41 will cause NETSETUP to make every boot disk you make the same. This is a real time saver. The basic operations of DNETWIK.V41 and NETSETUP are explained later in this chapter.

The configuration information you enter in NETSETUP, such as node name and address, is stored in CFGWS.DAT on the client boot disk. If CFGWS.DAT exists when NETSETUP is started, it will use the current configuration for modifications. One aggravation about the standard NETSETUP is that it always copies files to the boot disk, even when you want to make a simple modification. Even if you change only EXECINFO.BAT, it rewrites and recopies everything.

NETSETUP is fairly simple to operate since it uses prompts and has simple fill-in-the blank screens for entering information. In most cases, it will show you the options from which to select or try to give you an explanation of what to enter. You can toggle between basic, intermediate, and advanced modes of operation by pressing CTRL-F10. All function key assignments for operating NETSETUP are displayed at the bottom of the screen.

STARTNET.BAT

STARTNET.BAT is the network start-up file created by NETSETUP. It loads the client PATHWORKS components and typically sets the date/time and initial connections to network services. STARTNET may require some fine-tuning for your network. Having easy access to STARTNET.BAT is helpful for making these changes quickly, but it is also dangerous, because if you change STARTNET manually, your changes will be overridden the next time you run NETSETUP. As you can imagine, this can cause havoc with your client configurations.

A sample STARTNET.BAT is shown in Figure 4-3. Comment lines have been added to block off various sections of the file.

Figure 4-3. STARTNET.BAT

```
*************** Header Information *****************************
@echo off
break on
rem -------------------------------------------------------------
rem STARTNET.BAT
rem -------------------------------------------------------------
rem This batch file will start the network components for the workstation.
rem When this batch file is run, the current drive must be the drive from
rem which the workstation was booted. It is NOT recommended that
rem this file be included in the workstation's AUTOEXEC.BAT file.
rem Instead this file should be called from the AUTOEXEC.BAT file, and
rem any postnetwork start-up commands should be placed after
rem the ":end" label (for DOS V3.3 and above) in the
rem AUTOEXEC.BAT in a file called \STARTUP.BAT file or for DOS V3.2,
rem which will be chained to by this file.
rem -------------------------------------------------------------
*************** Set NCP Params ********************************
Call \DECNET\EXECINFO.BAT
cls
*************** Display Startup Info **************************
echo  -------------------------------------------------------------
echo       PATHWORKS for DOS V4.1 Network Operating Environment
echo       Created by NETSETUP.EXE V4.1.074 Configuration Utility
echo             DNETOMO.V41 V4.1.060
echo             DNETWIK.V41 V4.1.047
echo       (C)Copyright 1986-1991 by Digital Equipment Corporation
echo -*************** Chk for _SYD var ************************
rem -------------------------------------------------------------
rem If the _SYSD environment variable is already set, then either the
rem network was never unloaded or it was unloaded improperly. In this
rem case, warn the user of this and terminate this batch process.
```

Figure 4-3. STARTNET.BAT (continued)

```
rem -----------------------------------------------------------------
if "%_SYSD%"=="" goto oktoload
echo-------------------------------------------------------------------
echo     Network already loaded. You must use
echo
                                    %BOOT%\DECNET\STOPNET.B
                                    AT
echo     to unload the network.
echo -----------------------------------------------------------------
goto exit
:oktoload
*************** Begin Loading Network *************************
%BOOT%\DECNET\NETENVI 145 48
if ERRORLEVEL 1 goto exit
rem-----------------------------------------------------------------
rem Now set the PCSA environment variable that will tell programs
rem (such as mail) where there is a writable disk area. If you
rem boot from a floppy, it is a good idea to reset this variable (PCSA)
rem later in your AUTOEXEC.BAT (or STARTUP.BAT file for DOS
rem V3.2 users). For example: set PCSA=C:\
rem-----------------------------------------------------------------
*************** Start Decnet ********************************
set PCSA=%BOOT%\DECNET
if not exist %BOOT%\decnet\decnet.ini goto no_ini
%BOOT%
cd \decnet
%BOOT%\decnet\ncpdefp define exec name %_WSNODE% address
                                    %_WSADDR% state on database
                                    \decnet
%BOOT%\decnet\ncp <%BOOT%\decnet\decnet.ini
cd\
if ERRORLEVEL 1 goto error
del %BOOT%\decnet\decnet.ini
:no_ini
rem -----------------------------------------------------------------
rem Now see if STARTNET.BAT has already executed by looking at the
rem S_RUN environment variable. If it is set to "YES," then STARTNET
rem has been run before.
```

Figure 4-3. STARTNET.BAT (continued)

```
rem --------------------------------------------------------------
if "%S_RUN%"=="YES" goto already_run
set S_RUN=YES
:already_run
%BOOT%\decnet\save
*************** Load Network Components ************************
rem --------------------------------------------------------------
rem Start the network scheduler.
rem To use the hardware clock, use /H. To use the system clock, use /S.
rem --------------------------------------------------------------
%BOOT%\DECNET\SCH /H
if not ERRORLEVEL 1 goto schdone
echo ** ERROR ** Unable to start the Network Scheduler
goto error
:schdone
rem --------------------------------------------------------------
rem Start the DEPCA's datalink.
rem --------------------------------------------------------------
%BOOT%\DECNET\DLLDEPCA.EXE
if not ERRORLEVEL 1 goto dlldone
echo ** ERROR ** Unable to start the Data Link
goto error
:dlldone
rem --------------------------------------------------------------
rem Load DECnet Network Program
rem --------------------------------------------------------------
%BOOT%\DECNET\DNNETHAT.EXE /rem:2 /nam:n /fc:0
if ERRORLEVEL 1 %BOOT%\DECNET\DNNETHAT.EXE /rem:2 /nam:n /fc:0
if ERRORLEVEL 1 goto decneterror
rem --------------------------------------------------------------
rem Start the redirector.
rem --------------------------------------------------------------
%BOOT%\DECNET\REDIR.EXE /L:10 /P1:128 /P2:128 /P3:128 /himem:yes
if NOT ERRORLEVEL 1 goto rdrdone
:rdrerror
echo ** ERROR ** Unable to start the Redirector
goto error
:rdrdone
```

Figure 4-3. STARTNET.BAT (continued)

```
******** Begin Setting Workstation Specific Parameters ***********
rem ----------------------------------------------------------------
rem Set the workstation name.
rem ----------------------------------------------------------------
%BOOT%\DECNET\SETNAME %_WSNODE%
rem
rem Uncomment the next line if you will be connecting to
rem an OS/2 server that is running with user-level security.
rem This will enable you to connect to the server.
rem %BOOT%\decnet\setlogon
*************** Connect to Server ********************************
rem ----------------------------------------------------------------
echo Now attempting connection to the system file service:
rem ----------------------------------------------------------------
echo \\MFG\PCSAV41
set _SYSD=?:
%BOOT%\DECNET\USE ?: \\MFG\PCSAV41%% /ENV=_SYSD
if not ERRORLEVEL 1 goto c_sysdone
echo ** WARNING ** Unable to connect to \\MFG\PCSAV41
echo         Retrying...
%BOOT%\DECNET\USE ?: \\MFG\PCSAV41%% /ENV=_SYSD
if not ERRORLEVEL 1 goto c_sysdone
echo ** ERROR ** Unable to connect to \\MFG\PCSAV41
set _SYSD=
goto error
:c_sysdone
rem ----------------------------------------------------------------
echo Setting Path and Environment Variables
rem ----------------------------------------------------------------
set HELP=%_SYSD%\HELP
if "%path%"=="" goto nopath
path %path%;%_SYSD%\PCAPP;%_SYSD%\DECNET
goto pathdone
:nopath
path %_SYSD%\PCAPP;%_SYSD%\DECNET
:pathdone
path %path%;%_SYSD%\437USA
*************** Check/Set Decnet Params ********************
```

Figure 4-3. STARTNET.BAT (continued)

```
rem ---------------------------------------------------------------
if exist %BOOT%\DECNET\DECNODE.DAT goto decnetdone
if not exist %BOOT%\DECNET\DECNODE.txt goto decneterror
%_SYSD%
cd \decnet
ncp <%BOOT%\DECNET\DECNODE.TXT
cd\
%BOOT%
if ERRORLEVEL 1 goto decneterror
goto decnetdone
:decneterror
echo ** ERROR ** Unable to start DECnet
goto error
:decnetdone
******* Load Remaining Network Components *********************
rem ---------------------------------------------------------------
rem If you want to load RCV, then uncomment the next line:
rem ---------------------------------------------------------------
rem %_SYSD%\DECNET\RCV /r:2
rem ---------------------------------------------------------------
%_SYSD%\DECNET\LATCP define service table 20
if exist %BOOT%\DECNET\DECLAT.DAT goto latcpdone
%_SYSD%\DECNET\LATCP add 3.100 NODE1 MFG
%_SYSD%\DECNET\LATCP define multicast on
:latcpdone
rem ---------------------------------------------------------------
%_SYSD%\DECNET\LAT
if not ERRORLEVEL 1 goto latdone
echo ** WARNING ** Unable to start LAT
goto error
:latdone
rem ---------------------------------------------------------------
rem If you want to run CTERM, uncomment the next line:
rem %_SYSD%\DECNET\cterm
rem ---------------------------------------------------------------
rem If you want to run NML, uncomment the next line:
rem %_SYSD%\DECNET\nml
echo ---------------------------------------------------------------
```

65

Figure 4-3. STARTNET.BAT (continued)

```
************** Set Date and Time ****************************
echo Setting the date and time...
%_SYSD%\PCAPP\NETTIME MFG
if not ERRORLEVEL 1 goto timedone
echo ** WARNING ** Unable to set date and time from network
echo ---------------------------------------------------------
:no_2boot
echo Enter the date and time:
date
time
:timedone
************** Wrapup Messages ******************************
echo ---------------------------------------------------------
echo                                      To complete workstation
                                          initialization, enter the
                                                        command:
echo         LOGON server-name user-name [password or *]
echo ---------------------------------------------------------
echo         To unload the network use: %BOOT%\DECNET\STOPNET.BAT
echo ---------------------------------------------------------
goto exit
:error
rem Reach here if any errors
echo ---------------------------------------------------------
echo                   There were start-up errors.
echo ---------------------------------------------------------
rem Restore old path and exit
path %_path%
set _SYSD=
:exit
set _WSNODE=
```

This is a very imposing file to most new PATHWORKS users and managers. The very length of the file and all the error-checking code makes for a confusing start-up file. As confusing as it may appear, it is vitally important for a network manager to understand the workings of this file and how to tune it for a particular system. Knowing how STARTNET functions greatly simplifies the task of managing your network and preventing problems.

In the balance of this section, I will discuss what STARTNET does from a high-level perspective. For specifics on each component of this procedure, you should consult your PATHWORKS documentation, especially the Client Commands Reference and Memory Solutions for Client Administrators manuals. For you to understand any principle fully, nothing is a substitute for a little experience. The best way to understand STARTNET or any other procedure is to use a single workstation and play with the many different options. Spending 2 to 3 hours with STARTNET is cheap education that will pay off many times over.

Pay special attention to the bold italic lines in the STARTNET.BAT example in Figure 4-3. These lines have been modified from the standard STARTNET.BAT configuration. Here are the reasons for these changes:

◆ CALL \DECNET\EXECINFO

The \DECNET\EXECINFO line should be changed to CALL \DECNET\EXECINFO only if your clients will be running DOS V3.3 or above. If you are not running version 3.3 or above, I strongly suggest that you upgrade to DOS V5.0 or higher. The reason for the awkward method of calling EXECINFO in the original STARTNET.BAT file is because versions of DOS prior to version 3.3 did not provide a procedure to call other batch files. The CALL statement was introduced in DOS V3.3.

For this change to work, you should also modify EXECINFO.BAT by deleting or "commenting out" the last line:

```
set _WSNODE=KEN
set _WSADDR=20.1
REM \DECNET\STARTNET.BAT RUN               Comment out this line
```

◆ %_SYSD%\PCAPP\NETTIME *IT.1*

The second change is the line that calls NETTIME.EXE. This command sets the date and time of the client machine from the server. This minor change adds the server name as a parameter to NETTIME, so that when NETTIME executes in STARTNET.BAT, the date and time will be obtained from the specified server, MFG in this example. If the server name is not added, NETTIME will obtain the time from the first MS-NET sever it finds listed in the NCP database.

STARTNET.BAT is functionally divided into several sections. Each section executes a series of tasks for starting and configuring the network. Let's examine each section.

Initialization. When STARTNET.BAT begins executing, it calls a batch procedure named EXECINFO.BAT. EXECINFO sets environment variables for the node name and address of the workstation (_WSNODE and _WSADDR). These variables are used by STARTNET.BAT. After the SET PCSA= statement, the next section creates the DECnet database only if the DECNET.INI file exists. At the completion of this section, the DECNET.INI file is deleted.

Load Network Components. The Load Network Components section is the heart of STARTNET and loads several drivers used by PATHWORKS, such as the datalink driver, DECnet, LAST, LAT, the redirector, and the network scheduler. The actual programs loaded will depend on the options set when you ran NETSETUP and the configuration of your DNETWIK.V41 file if it has been modified. This is the section that will require the most tuning, since it affects the amount of memory the network uses on the client and affects the functions the client may perform on the network. For example, LAT or CTERM must be loaded for terminal emulators to work.

This section loads the scheduler (SCH), the datalink driver (DLLxxx), and if you are using a NDIS driver, runs NETBIND. Further down in the file, it loads the redirector (REDIR). These steps are mandatory on any PATHWORKS client, since the network will not function if they are not loaded. In fact, when STARTNET executes, the failure of one of these programs will trigger numerous error messages as other components try to load.

DECnet, LAST, and LANSESS are loaded between the scheduler and redirector commands. This section of STARTNET.BAT will vary from network to network, depending on which components are loaded on each client. For example, if you are not using DECnet, then the DECnet section will not be written by NETSETUP. After the main network components are loaded — REDIR is the last — the workstation name is set with the SETNAME command.

Connect to Server. The next section, Connect to Server, connects to the default services and resets the PATH for this workstation. This always includes the PCSAV41 service, which is the system service for PATHWORKS. It contains all the PATHWORKS client programs not found on the boot device. Other services may also be connected in this procedure if you have modified STARTNET directly or changed the DNETWIK.V41 file.

Load Remaining Network Components. This section, Load Remaining Network Components, begins by checking for the file DECNODE.DAT. If this file exists, the next section of code is skipped to the :decnetdone label. If the file does not exist, it is created.

The next step involves loading any network components that were not previously loaded. This usually includes the receiver (RCV), LAT, CTERM, and NML.

Set the Date and Time. Typically, the last thing done by STARTNET is to set the date and time on the client from the server. This ensures that the client time is the same on all machines or at least that it is the same as of the time they last booted. This can be very important, because the clock contained in most PCs is notorious for its inaccuracy. If time stamping is critical in your business, I would suggest adding the same line to every user login procedure, via the STD_STDS procedure discussed in chapter 5, "Network Access." This will ensure that the time is reset for each user every time he or she logs in.

Once the date and time have been set, the procedure exits by skipping to the :exit label and deleting the variables set by EXECINFO.BAT (_WSNODE and _WSADDR).

The :error label several lines before the :exit label is used if an error occurs in the DECnet load process in STARTNET.BAT.

Startup Files

The client network software is made up of several executable and driver files that are normally loaded by STARTNET.BAT and CONFIG.SYS. Each of these routines provides a particular function for the network. Table 4-1 provides a brief description of the most common components.

Table 4-1. Common Client Network Software Components

Driver Name	Description
SCH	This is the real-time scheduler that is used by the network software and must be loaded on the client. PATHWORKS V4.1 introduces a new version, SCHK, that has additional features and reduced memory requirements on 80286 or higher clients. The PATHWORKS V4.1 versions of SCHK require less memory than the SCH version shipped with version 4.0.
DLLxx	DLLxx.EXE is the data link driver for a network adapter. The actual file name will be DLLDEPCA, DLLNDIS, DLLNDIST, or DLL802, depending on which network card is used.
DNNETH	DNNETH.EXE is the DECnet driver for the client. It is used for both DECnet and NetBIOS. DNNETH provides full-function DECnet services for client workstations, allowing the client to participate in any DECnet network. DNNDCPLD and DNNDCPPC load the asynchronous version of DECnet and NetBIOS for use over serial communications lines. DNNDCPLD loads into expanded memory, while DNNDCPPC loads into conventional memory. DNPDCPPC loads asynchronous DECnet without NetBIOS into conventional memory.

Table 4-1. Common Client Network Software Components (continued)

Driver Name	Description
EMSLOAD	This program is used to load DNNETH, LAD, LAST, LANSESS, LAT, and RCV into expanded memory.
REDIR	This is the LAN Manager Redirector program for network transport services. It manages redirection of devices such as printers and disk/file services.
	REDIRx.EXE is included with PATHWORKS and loads the basic LAN Manager Redirector. When NETSETUP copies the files to the boot disk, the redirector is renamed to REDIR3.EXE, REDIR4.EXE, or REDIR5.EXE, depending on which DOS version is used. This file is not used for enhanced redirector services.
LANSESS	This is the LAN session manager. It must be loaded if you wish to access file services via LAST instead of DECnet. Using LAST and LANSESS for file and print services provides a significant speed increase over using DECnet only. When LANSESS is loaded, LAST will automatically be used as the transport layer, and LANSESS will provide the session layer, overriding DECnet.
LAST	LAST.EXE is the driver for the virtual disk transport. It must be loaded on the client to use disk services or to enable LAST for file and print services.
LAD	LAD.EXE is the LAD driver. It uses LAST to communicate with the disk server. If you are using disk services, this driver must be loaded on the client.
LAT	This is the LAT driver used by terminal emulators over the LAN.
LADDRV.SYS	This is the DOS device driver for disk services. It is loaded in CONFIG.SYS via a DEVICE= statement. It must be loaded on the client if disk services will be used.
PSC	This is a terminate and stay resident (TSR) utility that provides support for printing screens to a network printer and timed closing of redirected printers.

Table 4-1. Common Client Network Software Components (continued)

Driver Name	Description
RCV	RCV is a TSR program that is required to receive broad-cast messages from other nodes and notification of new mail.
PROTMAN	PROTMAN.SYS is the protocol driver for NDIS network adapters. This file is loaded in the CONFIG.SYS file.
NETBIND	The NETBIND program is used to bind the protocol-layer and MAC-layer NDIS drivers.
xxxxxx.xxx	This file is the NDIS driver for a particular network card and is supplied by the network card vendor. For example, the file for the Xircom Inc. Pocket Adapter is PE_NDIS.DOS, whereas a DEPCA card uses DEPCA.DOS. This file is loaded in the CONFIG.SYS file.

Although file and print services can now use LAST, DECnet provides a number of benefits, including WAN support and access to VMSmail. DECnet is slower than LAST/LANSESS because it has many more layers and offers higher-level functions. If you are using NetBIOS applications, they may require DECnet, because DECnet fully supports NetBIOS, whereas LAST provides only minimal support. You must load DECnet or TCP/IP if you are using mail. If LAST and DECnet are both loaded, PATHWORKS will automatically use LAST for file services to improve the performance.

Miscellaneous Client Start-Up and Management Files

In addition to the numerous executable programs, there are several other files used on the client in the start-up process and possibly afterwards. These include DECNODE.DAT, NODEDEF.TXT, and DECNODE.TXT.

DECNODE.DAT is the DECnet executor database for the workstation. It contains binary data and is stored in the DECNET directory on the client. The DECNET.INI file is used to create DECNODE.DAT if it does not exist.

NODEDEF.TXT stores the DECnet node names and addresses of servers on your network. NETSETUP uses this file to create the node definition files (DECNODE.TXT and DECNODE.DAT). This file should be kept in the DECNET directory on the PC used to run NETSETUP for other workstations in order to keep all workstations configured correctly.

71

DECNODE.TXT contains the same information as NODEDEF.TXT, which NETSETUP uses to create this file. If NODEDEF.TXT does not exist, NETSETUP prompts for the node name and address. This is a very important file, because a server must be defined in this file before a DOS client can connect to it without specifying the server name in the USE statement. When the client boots to the network with STARTNET.BAT, this file is used to define the servers to NCP. If you review the STARTNET.BAT file, you will notice how the NCP command uses this file to obtain its input. DECNETNODE.DAT is the command sequence to load MS-NET server nodes:

```
C:\>NCP
NCP> define node 1.200 name KENS ms-net
NCP> define node 1.300 name JOE ms-net
```

In addition to these files, there are several other files that may appear on a client. They include the LAT database, DECLAT.DAT, and other DECnet files, such as DECPARM.DAT, DECACC.DAT, DECALIAS.DAT, DECOBJ.DAT, and DECREM.DAT.

NDIS Network Cards

Network Device Interface Specification (NDIS) is a specification for network drivers created by Microsoft and 3Com Corp. It was designed to simplify the hassles of having a different network driver for every different network card and vendor. Most vendors are starting to adhere to the NDIS standard, although some may do a better or more thorough job than others because of their interpretation of the specification. This variety may cause some boards to function on specific networks but not on others.

The network adapter (Ethernet or Token Ring) vendor supplies the network driver. This driver is known as the media access control (MAC) driver. Drivers from different vendors will normally be named NAME.DOS (e.g., DEPCA.DOS, ELNKII.DOS, or PE_NDIS.DOS), or they may not have DOS in the name.

The protocol driver is specific to the LAN and is supplied by the LAN vendor. NETSETUP will use the DLLNDIS.EXE file from the system service directory \LMDOS\DRIVERS\PCSA.

The protocol manager is named PROTMAN.SYS and is used to supply configuration information to the protocol and MAC drivers. Once these drivers are bound together by NETBIND, PROTMAN.SYS is unloaded.

PROTOCOL.INI is the configuration file used by the protocol manager. Information on the hardware and software is stored in this file and is used by PROTMAN.SYS to provide information about the MAC and protocol drivers. The bulk of information in this file is supplied from Digital and is specific to PATHWORKS. The network card vendor supplies the sections on the network interface.

NETSETUP places references to these files in the CONFIG.SYS and STARTNET.BAT files. To access an NDIS driver from NETSETUP, select the driver Other for the Ethernet controller type. NETSETUP will ask for the location and file name of the NDIS driver. It will also ask for the location of the PROTOCOL.INI file.

Here is an example of a PROTOCOL.INI file for a Xircom Ethernet Adapter:

```
; PROTOCOL.INI file

[protocol manager]
DRIVERNAME = PROTMAN$

[XIRCOMNET]
 DRIVERNAME = XIRCOM$
 INTERRUPT = 7
 PRINTERPORT = LPT1


[DATALINK]
DRIVERNAME = DLL$MAC
LG_BUFFERS = 16
SM_BUFFERS = 6
OUTSTANDING = 32
HEURISTICS = 0
BINDINGS    = XIRCOMNET
```

In this example, the [XIRCOMNET] and [DATALINK] sections are supplied by the card vendor.

These are the related NDIS lines from a CONFIG.SYS:

```
DEVICE=C:\DECNET\PROTMAN.SYS
DEVICE=C:\DECNET\PE_NDIS.DOS
```

These are the NDIS-related drivers in STARTNET.BAT:

```
DLLNDIS.EXE                 DLL (Datalink Layer)
NETBIND.EXE                 Bind Protman with MAC Driver
```

CONFIGURATION MANAGEMENT

To simplify the maintenance of your network, I suggest moving parts of the start-up process to the network. This may seem like a time-consuming and fruitless exercise at first, but it will save you many headaches down the road.

If each PC has unique start-up files located on its hard disk or floppy, someone will have to visit each PC when it is time to update the files. Putting the process on the network prevents someone from deleting a critical start-up file and not having a backup. I will discuss this topic at length in Chapter 8, "Application Installation and Use."

The things that should reside on a local boot disk (or remote boot key disk) are programs or files that are specific to the hardware for a specific machine and programs or files that are required to connect the machine to the network. Examples of these files are CONFIG.SYS, STARTNET.BAT, and (to some extent) AUTOEXEC.BAT. The entire CONFIG.SYS file must reside on the boot disk for a PC to boot. AUTOEXEC.BAT must start on the boot disk but may call other procedures or programs on the network once the network connection is available.

Likewise, STARTNET.BAT must be on the boot disk, remote boot key disk, or other local disk, but it can call other programs from the network once a network connection is made.

The goal for these three files should be to contain the minimum amount of information necessary to boot the PC and connect to the common network services. Once the connection is made, any further commands should be executed by common command procedures located on the network. Resetting the path, connecting to printers, and setting the workstation time are examples of functions that can be performed cleanly from the network.

Notice that the printers started in AUTONET.BAT will be the ones located close to the PC. This is a good example of what can be accomplished by using environment variables. Since PCs usually do not wander around very often, you can create a variable called LOC, short for location, which will allow you to connect to the printer closest to the PC. Let's define this variable in the AUTOEXEC.BAT file as ACT1. ACT1 stands for accounting department, first floor. In this example, the accounting department has a laser printer named LASERACTG and a dot-matrix printer named LA324ACTG. Here are the last three lines of the AUTOEXEC.BAT file used for this example:

```
CALL SETPATH
Call \DECNET\STARTNET
USE ?:\\SRVR\SITESYS /ENV=_H
%_H%:\NET\AUTONET ACTG
```

The AUTOEXEC.BAT procedure executes the STARTNET procedure after all of the PC-specific code is executed. Once STARTNET.BAT completes, it returns to the AUTOEXEC.BAT procedure, which then connects the SITESYS service and executes AUTONET.BAT, located in the \NET directory. Note how the USE command connects to the first available service and places the drive letter in the _H variable. This variable will be used again later.

The AUTONET.BAT example below is a simple procedure that checks for one parameter. If this parameter is set to ACTG or ENG, the USE command is executed to connect the PCs to the appropriate printers or plotters. AUTONET.BAT also sets the current drive to the NET service and changes the directory to \LOGIN:

```
REM AUTONET.BAT
if not %1# == ACTG# goto NOACTG
CALL SET_PRT 2 KENS LASERACTG
CALL SET_PRT 3 KENS LA324ACTG
:NOACTG
if not %1# == ENG# goto NOENG
CALL SET_PRT 2 KENS LASERENG
CALL SET_PRT 3 KENS HP7551EG
:NOENG
%_H%:
CD \LOGIN
```

This procedure has a couple advantages over the plain start-up files. First, when a new printer is added to any department, updating one procedure activates this printer for all users. Second, by placing commands in this file to change to the F:\LOGIN directory, all users see the same thing when they boot a PC, no matter where it is located.

AUTONET.BAT calls a standard command procedure for connecting the logical printer devices to the print queues. This procedure sets an environment variable indicating that the printer was connected and performs a few other housekeeping chores. Chapter 6 shows an example of the SET.PRT procedure.

REMOTE-BOOT CLIENTS

PATHWORKS provides the ability to use remote-boot PCs, which boot from a server located on the network. Some of the advantages of remote booting over locally booting each PC are:

◆ Central management from the server.

◆ Local disks are not required on a client PC.

◆ Start-up files can be protected.

As with anything else, there are also disadvantages:

◆ Each PC must use a separate boot disk.

◆ LAD must be enabled.

◆ Troubleshooting PCs without a disk is a pain.

◆ It is more difficult to set up the network initially.

Each PC that boots remotely from a server must have its address and node name entered in the server's NCP database before the client can boot remotely. The NCP database tracks the Ethernet address, DECnet name and address, type of load file, and other information for the PC. This database is used when a remote-boot request is received to determine the address of the PC and the type of load file to send. NETSETUP automatically stores this information when the boot disk is created.

You can enable remote booting for PCs with any Digital network card and some third-party cards by changing a jumper or a switch on the card. Once this is complete, the card will request remote-boot services from the network when the client boots. If a particular network card is not supported for remote boot, PATHWORKS also supports a Floppy Remote Boot (FRB) diskette that will generate the remote-boot services request to the network.

When a PC boots using the PATHWORKS remote-boot services, it transmits a MOP request to the server. The boot server will respond by sending a load file to the requesting PC. Once this load file is received, the boot server will start a mininetwork between the PC and the server and request a remote-boot disk service connection. This disk service will contain the CONFIG.SYS, AUTOEXEC.BAT, and STARTNET.BAT files for the PC. Once the disk service is connected, the PC will continue booting with the start-up files located on this service.

NETSETUP will automatically create and mount the remote-boot disk service and enter the client in the NCP database. NETSETUP will not display the local or remote boot prompt unless LAD is loaded and active on the PC. This minor detail is not explicitly covered in the manual. The basic steps for creating a remote-boot disk are outlined below:

1. Start NETSETUP. Select Remote Boot.

2. Configure the PC by responding to the NETSETUP prompts. Select Load DOS from Server.

3. Set the jumpers or switches on your network card.

4. Reboot the PC.

If the PC is using DOS V5.0 or Windows 3.x, load the Redirector into conventional memory. After you have responded to all prompts, select the WRITE KEY DISK option. This will cause NETSETUP to read the PC's Ethernet address, create and mount a 1.2-MB network key disk, and register the PC as a remote-boot node.

Remote-boot services is an area that will probably see changes with future releases of PATHWORKS and new network cards. Be sure to consult the documentation for your system before implementing remote-boot services. Chapter 7 in the *Client Installation and Configuration Guide for the VMS Server* covers setting up remote-boot clients.

PATHWORKS FOR DOS (NETWARE COEXISTENCE)

PATHWORKS for DOS (NetWare Coexistence) lets PATHWORKS clients coexist with a NetWare network, using the same Ethernet adapter. NetWare Coexistence allows a DOS client to simultaneously use DECnet or TCP/IP to connect to a PATHWORKS server and IPX to connect to NetWare servers on the same network. Clients running this product can access file and print services on VMS, ULTRIX, OS/2, and NetWare servers. The clients can also access WAN services over DECnet.

Using NetWare Coexistence, NetWare clients can seamlessly integrate into VMS, ULTRIX, or OS/2 networks, gaining access to the value-added features available on these systems.

Overview

NetWare uses an IPX driver (IPX.COM) and a NetWare shell (NETx.COM) for communicating with the network. NetWare's IPX normally communicates directly with the Ethernet adapter in the PC. NetWare Coexistence provides a driver for generating a new IPX with WSGEN, which will communicate with the NDIS driver supplied with PATHWORKS. NetWare Coexistence allows simultaneous loading of the standard PATHWORKS drivers and the NetWare drivers. As connections are made to services over either network, the appropriate network components handle accessing the particular service. The user will see no difference in the operation of either system.

NETSETUP is used to generate a boot disk with both sets of drivers and will copy both IPX.COM and NETx.COM to the PATHWORKS boot disk. IPX will be loaded in STARTNET.BAT immediately after DLLNDIS. To load NETx.COM, modify STARTNET, update the WIK file to call NETx, or add the command to the AUTOEXEC.BAT program.

NetWare uses all drives after LASTDRIVE, and PATHWORKS will use all drives up to and including LASTDRIVE. If LASTDRIVE is set to R in the CONFIG.SYS file, PATHWORKS can use drive letters up to and including R, while NetWare can use any drive letters from S to Z. If LASTDRIVE is set to Z, NetWare will not be able to access any services.

Memory Issues. Loading the NetWare drivers in addition to the PATHWORKS drivers will add approximately 50 KB to memory requirements for the network. IPX requires approximately 35 KB and NETx requires 15 KB.

You can use Quarterdeck Office Systems' QEMM or some other memory manager program to load the network components in the upper memory block (UMB), expanded memory specification (EMS), or extended memory specification (XMS). The safest approach to loading components is to use EMSLOAD for PATHWORKS components and to load the NetWare components in UMB with LOADHI. Only one transport can be loaded in EMS or XMS at a time.

Installation

NetWare Coexistence is very straightforward to install. The installation involves building a NetWare IPX driver with WSGEN, loading NetWare Coexistence on the PCSAV41 service, and then using NETSETUP to configure the clients.

Generate IPX.COM. The first step is to use WSGEN to create a new IPX driver that supports NDIS. A separate IPX.COM must be created for each different configuration of Ethernet controller. If only the configuration parameters change (base address, memory address, IRQ), the changes may be made with the Jumpers utility after the boot disk is created.

Run WSGEN from either a floppy or a hard disk, and select the NDIS driver NDIS\MAC V1.02EC (901022) on the NetWare Coexistence disk. After WSGEN finishes, you should probably change to the Ethernet II frame format to prevent any possible conflicts with other Ethernet services on the network. The following command will accomplish this:

```
C:\NETWARE> ECONFIG IPX.COM shell:e 8137
```

If you change the frame format of the IPX.COM file, the NetWare server must also be updated to use the Ethernet II format. This will not create a problem for existing clients, because multiple copies of the Ethernet driver can be running simultaneously on the server. See your NetWare system administrator for more information on updating the server.

After the new IPX.COM file has been generated, save it to a floppy for use in updating the PCSAV41 service.

Update PCSAV41 Service. Before creating a boot disk with NETSETUP, you must copy the new NETSETUP and several other files to the PATHWORKS system service, PCSAV41. Follow these steps:

1. Connect to PCSAV41 service as SYSTEM (or some other username with RW access):

```
C:\>USE E: \\server\PCSAV41%SYSTEM *
```

2. Place the LAN_DRV_DEC disk in the floppy:

   ```
   C:\>UPDATE A: E:
   ```

3. Copy the new IPX.COM and the NetWare shells to the system service:

   ```
   C:\>MD E:\NETWARE

   C:\>COPY A:IPX.COM E:\NETWARE

   C:\>COPY A:NET*.* E:\NETWARE
   ```

Build Client KEY Disks. The process of building the boot disks involves running NETSETUP from the PATHWORKS system service. The boot disk should contain all the DOS files needed for booting a PC. NETSETUP will copy the PATHWORKS startup files, NetWare components, and NDIS drivers to the boot disk. The client must be a local boot client.

The following steps are required for building the boot disk:

1. Connect to PCSAV41 service (if not connected):

   ```
   C:\>USE E: \\VAX\PCSAV41
   ```

2. Run NETSETUP. Choose DECnet or TCP/IP for your transport. Select Yes to the prompt:

   ```
   Should the workstation be set up to run NetWare (R)?
   ```

   After completing screens, select WRITE KEY DISK. Enter the PROTOCOL.INI settings for the network adapter.

3. Reboot the client PC.

Accessing Services. After the client is rebooted with both correct drivers, you should be able to connect to services on both a NetWare and a PATHWORKS server. Execute the USE command for connecting to PATHWORKS file and print services and NetWare file services. You can also use the MAP command for connecting to NetWare file services. To connect to NetWare print services, use the CAP-TURE command.

The USE command without parameters will display all connections on all servers. The MAP and CAPTURE /SHOW commands will display only NetWare file and print services, respectively. Figure 4-4 shows current connections on a PATHWORKS server (\\VAX) and a NetWare server (\\SERVER1). Notice how the NetWare drives start at R:.

Figure 4-4. Current Service Connections (Displayed by USE)

```
USE Version V4.1.23 Digital Network Connection Manager

Status    Dev    Type    Connection name              Access    Size

          H:     FILE    \\VAX\PCSAV41

          R:     FILE    \\SERVER1\SYS \

          Y:     FILE    \\SERVER1\SYS \

          Z:     FILE    \\SERVER1\SYS\PUBLIC
```

The MAP command produces a listing similar to the USE command but is restricted to NetWare connections. The following lines show the output of MAP. Notice how drives A through Q are listed as local drives. The PATHWORKS connections that are entered in PATH show up only as search drives:

```
Drive A: maps to a local disk.
Drive B: maps to a local disk.
Drive C: maps to a local disk.
Drive D: maps to a local disk.
Drive E: maps to a local disk.
Drive F: maps to a local disk.
Drive G: maps to a local disk.
Drive H: maps to a local disk.
Drive I: maps to a local disk.
Drive J: maps to a local disk.
Drive K: maps to a local disk.
Drive L: maps to a local disk.
Drive M: maps to a local disk.
Drive N: maps to a local disk.
Drive O: maps to a local disk.
Drive P: maps to a local disk.
Drive Q: maps to a local disk.
Drive R:=SERVER1\SYS: \
    - - - - -
SEARCH1 :=Z:.[SERVER1\SYS: \PUBLIC]
SEARCH2 :=Y:.[SERVER1\SYS: \]
SEARCH3 :=C:\U
SEARCH4 :=C:\WIN31
SEARCH5 :=C:\WW
SEARCH6 :=C:\DSR
```

```
SEARCH7  :=C:\DECNET
SEARCH8  :=C:\DOS
SEARCH9  :=C:\WINSPT
SEARCH10 :=NU
SEARCH11 :=H:\PCAPP
SEARCH12 :=H:\DECNET
SEARCH13 :=H:\437USA
```

When the USE command connects to a NetWare file service, the command format is basically the same as for PATHWORKS services, except that a username and a password are not required. The following command will connect the T: drive to the SYS volume on the NetWare server SERVER:

```
USE T:\\SERVER\SYS
```

Notice that the SYS volume reference in the USE command does not include the colon (:).

Windows V3.x can see all services on both NetWare and PATHWORKS servers that were connected before starting Windows. Only services on the network specified in the SYSTEM.INI file can be connected to after Windows is loaded, unless both sets of network drivers are loaded.

LOADING DOS ON THE NETWORK

One of the best ways to manage network clients is to load DOS on the network server. This places the DOS files for each version used in your network in a separate directory on the server. When clients boot to the network, you can easily reset their PATH and possibly the COMSPEC environment variable to point to the appropriate network directory. This will force the client to use the DOS programs and utilities located on the server, which should be up-to-date, complete, protected from user destruction, and virus-free.

PATHWORKS provides the DOSLOAD utility to automate this process. This program is very easy to use and operates in a manner similar to NETSETUP. The information that must be supplied includes the server name, directory name to store the files, DOS version, source drive, number of disks, and the VMS account name to use. The account name must have privileges sufficient to write to the PCSAVxx service (xx=version). You can also use DOSLOAD to display the current DOS versions stored on the server and to remove a DOS directory. The DOSLOAD screen should look similar to Figure 4-5.

Once DOSLOAD has completed, STARTNET.BAT will automatically enter the new DOS directory in the PC's PATH statement at boot time, if the Load DOS from Server: prompt was set to yes when you ran NETSETUP.

With PATHWORKS V4.1, DOSLOAD supports DOS V5.0 and loading DOS from a network service or hard disk. This new version of NETSETUP makes it very easy to load DOS directly from a client hard disk to the PCSAV41 service. If you will be using any of the DEC DOS enhancements, you can copy them into the new directory. I usually leave these files in their normal directory (\DOSENH on the PCSAV41 service) or copy the ones required on a particular system into the public UTIL directory, which is located above DOS in the PATH statement. The DOS COPY command can be used to copy any of the files to the new directory. It is a good idea to keep the DOS directory pure, that is, containing only DOS files. This makes it much easier to manage and upgrade the DOS files, because you know that DOS and only DOS is in this directory.

When locating DOS on the server, update the PATH statement to point to the server directory. If the PC has only a floppy disk, it would be a good idea to change the COMSPEC variable to point to the server. You can accomplish this in a number of ways. One of the simplest is to create a batch procedure that executes when a PC boots. This can be triggered at the end of the STARTNET procedure or from the AUTOEXEC.BAT procedure.

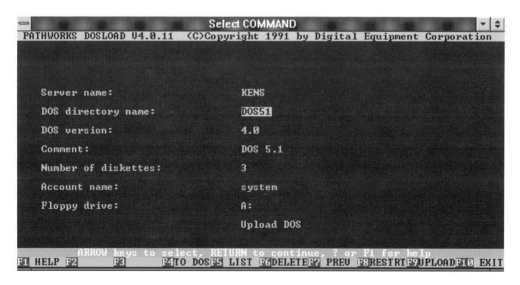

Figure 4-5. DOSLOAD Screen

The following lines of code should be placed in the SETNPATH.BAT program, which resets the PATH statement and sets the COMSPEC variable to the network directory. This file should be called from AUTOEXEC.BAT, STARTNET.BAT, or preferably AUTONET.BAT. If you use DOSLOAD to load DOS, NETSETUP may reset PATH for you automatically. Be sure to check your configuration before using the following file:

```
REM SETNPATH.BAT
REM
SET DOSDIR = %SITE%\DOS50
if not %1# == #  set DOSDIR = %SITE%\%1
PATH=%SITE%\util;%DOSDIR%;%_SYSD%\decnet;
   %_boot%\decnet;%_sysd%\pcapp;%_sysd%\mswin30


SET COMSPEC=%DOSDIR%
SET DOSDIR=
```

This procedure sets an environment variable (DOSDIR) to the directory containing the DOS programs. The SITE variable referenced here should be set in STARTNET.BAT or AUTONET.BAT to point to the drive letter containing your site-specific files. You can override the default directory (DOS50) by including a new directory on the command line with the program CALL SETNPATH DOS41. The PATH statement resets the path by placing the UTIL directory at the head of the path, followed by the new DOS directory. Error checking is not performed in this example, because this procedure will not be used interactively, except during testing. It would be fairly simple to add error checking and maybe even the intelligence to check the environment for the version of DOS being used, and reset the path on the basis of this information.

The SET COMSPEC statement resets this variable to point to the DOS directory on the server. Each time DOS must reload COMMAND.COM, it reloads from the file pointed to by COMSPEC. This file should be located on a fast device. If the PC has a hard disk, you may not want to reset this variable unless the hard disk is slow, because it will force the PC to reload COMMAND.COM over the network. If your network has many machines with hard disks and some without, you should add an environment variable to indicate the type of disk on the PC. This should be set in the AUTOEXEC.BAT program on each PC.

Once the SETPATHN procedure executes during the startup process, the PC will load all DOS utilities from the network directory.

CONFIGURING NETSETUP WITH DNETWIK.V41

NETSETUP may modify either or both of the CONFIG.SYS and AUTOEXEC.BAT files during the PATHWORKS installation on a client PC. You should review the PATHWORKS documentation on NETSETUP to determine how these files will be modified. By using a configuration file (DNETWIK.V4.1), NETSETUP also can allow customization of how the modifications take place. Modifying the DNETWIK.V41 file can tailor how the following files are created or edited: AUTOEXEC.BAT, CONFIG.SYS, PROTOCOL.INI, STARTNET.BAT, STOPNET.BAT, and DECNODE.TXT. By using the features of DNETWIK.V41, you can tailor NETSETUP to automatically check for the DOS version and add the appropriate statements into CONFIG.SYS and AUTOEXEC.BAT. You should review the documentation for your version of PATHWORKS carefully to determine the features available in customizing the DNETWIK.V41 file. The syntax for PATHWORKS V4.1 is shown in Appendix E.

The example in Figure 4-6 is intended not to be an all-inclusive explanation of the DNETWIK.V41 file, but to offer some insight into its operation and how to make some simple changes to the CONFIG.SYS and AUTOEXEC.BAT sections. If you will be making complex changes to DNETWIK.V41, refer to the PATHWORKS manuals and test your changes carefully.

Figure 4-6 shows a CONFIG.SYS and AUTOEXEC.BAT section of a typical configuration file for NETSETUP. Several lines in the figure have been added from earlier examples. Compare this section to the DNETWIK.V41 file in your DECNET directory on the PCSAV41 service.

Notice that the syntax is similar to most programming languages, with BEGIN and END statements separating procedural sections and IF statements triggering different actions. Most of the information entered in NETSETUP can be accessed in DNETWIK.V41 via the IF command and keywords. You can cause files to be deleted, copied, created, or not created, and cause a host of other things to happen when NETSETUP runs. This in turn will trigger the reaction when the PC boots and runs STARTNET.

You should tune DNETWIK.V41 (save a backup of the original) to perform exactly as you want it to for your network. If you don't use DOS V3.2 or earlier, delete the lines controlling things for version 3.2 and tune it for your version of DOS. You should at least update the sections for CONFIG.SYS, AUTOEXEC.BAT, and STARTNET.BAT to look exactly how you want them to look.

The sections of DNETWIK.V41 that refer to the use and creation of DECNET.INI, DECNODE.TXT, and any other files with these extensions are also good candidates for modification. Once you have decided what your network will look like and have configured these files, you may want to place them on the server and have them automatically copied to the PC's boot drive when they change.

Figure 4-6. Modified DNETWIK.V41 Section

```
$BEGIN CONFIG.SYS
        DEVICE=C:\DOS\HIMEM.SYS
$if strequ(DOSVERSION, "5.0")
        DOS=HIGH,UMB
$end_if
        FILES=30
        BUFFERS=2
        SHELL=C:\COMMAND.COM /P /E:1024
        DEVICE=C:\DOS\SMARTDRV.SYS
        DEVICE=C:\windows\ramdrive.sys 1024 /e
$END CONFIG.SYS

$BEGIN AUTOEXEC.BAT
        @ECHO OFF
        SET TEMP=d:
        $if strequ(DOSVERSION, "5.0")
        LH \dos\doskey
        $end_if
        \dos\share
        PROMPT $p$g
        PATH = c:\DOS;\util;c:\decnet
        STARTNET
$END AUTOEXEC.BAT
```

PC MEMORY ORGANIZATION

PC memory is stored on the motherboard or on add-in boards that attach to the PC bus. Most systems shipping today that use 80286, 80386, or 80486 processors support up to 16 MB on the motherboard. PCs are shipping with more and more memory, and it is not unusual to find an 80386 PC for sale at mail-order prices with 2 to 4 MB as standard equipment. As more sophisticated programs and environments increase in popularity, this trend will continue.

PC memory is organized into five basic types when you are using the DOS operating system:

◆ Conventional memory

◆ UMB

◆ High memory

- ◆ Expanded memory (EMS)

- ◆ Extended memory (XMS)

PC memory is physically organized into three basic areas: conventional (0 - 640 KB), other (640 KB - 1 MB), and extended (above 1 MB). Software memory managers must be used to access all memory above 640 KB.

Conventional memory, located between 0 and 640 KB, is also known as low memory. Practically every program that runs under DOS uses some low memory. It is also the most critical memory on your PC because it is limited to 640 KB and cannot be expanded. Figure 4-7 shows the memory map of a PC.

Expanded memory is defined by the Lotus/Intel/Microsoft (LIM) specification and is located above 1 MB. EMS is used for storing programs or data and works much like a paging operating system. When a program or data segment is required by the system, the EMS manager will swap the segment from EMS into a block of upper memory, called a window. When the next segment is requested, EMS repeats the process. EMS was one of the first methods to access memory above 640 KB. EMS386.EXE or a third-party memory manager is used to create EMS memory.

The major difference between EMS and XMS memory is that XMS memory is a contiguous block of memory that does not require swapping of program segments. Programs such as Windows use XMS to provide a large memory area (more than 640 KB) to programs.

Extended memory can be directly accessed by many programs via the extended memory specification.

You may be wondering what happened to the area between 640 KB and 1 MB. This memory is the UMB, and it is used by DOS for special DOS functions, such as video RAM and BIOS code. There are unused areas, or holes, in this memory that vary in size from one PC to another, depending on the type of video adapter used and other parameters. A section of this memory is also used by most network cards to map their memory into DOS. Some systems can use special drivers that can reclaim some or all of this memory for use within DOS, sometimes providing up to 768 KB of conventional memory. DOS V5.0 can also use some of this memory for itself and allow other programs to use it via HIMEM.SYS and EMM386.EXE.

Which Is Best — EMS or XMS?

Most DOS programs are beginning to focus on XMS instead of EMS. EMS was used extensively several years ago when DOS was unable to use extended memory. XMS is contiguous memory and requires less overhead than EMS, because it does not require swapping parts of programs in and out of the EMS window.

I would suggest standardizing on XMS and not using EMS at all, unless your application will not use XMS or if you are not running an 80386 or 80486 machine. The EMM386 driver works only with 80386 or 80486 PCs because of the memory management limitations of the 80286 processor. If you will be running XMS, you may still use the EMM386 driver with DOS V5.x to allow the use of the UMB for programs and drivers by using the NOEMS qualifier.

Where Does Memory Go?

In the previous section, I mentioned running out of conventional memory. It is important to understand what happens to this memory and what you can do to reclaim as much as possible for your application programs.

The biggest user of conventional memory is typically DOS itself. It is normal to have only 550 KB or 540 KB left after just loading DOS V4.x or lower, while DOS V5.x

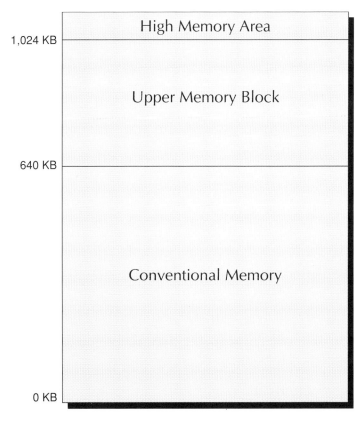

Figure 4-7. PC Memory Map

may leave 595 KB free. As the system boots, the command interpreter, COMMAND.COM, is loaded by the system and remains resident in conventional memory. With DOS versions through 4.x, each new version used more memory. You will see how that changes with DOS V5.x's ability to move part of itself into XMS.

Other big users of conventional memory are the small utility programs that often find their way into CONFIG.SYS and AUTOEXEC.BAT. ANSI.SYS, MOUSE.SYS/ COM, DOSKEY.EXE, SHARE.EXE, and RAMDISK.SYS are examples of programs that occupy some portion of low memory. They may be very small (10 to 12 KB) such as MOUSE.COM or relatively large (40 to 50 KB) such as some third-party programs.

The last major user of low memory is PATHWORKS. The network uses various PC programs to control different aspects of its operation. When these programs load via STARTNET.BAT, most of them load into conventional memory, with the exception of a few programs or drivers that may load into extended memory. Most PATHWORKS files can also be loaded into expanded memory.

On a DOS V4.x system or earlier, it is not uncommon to find PCs with only 470 KB free after the network loads. This sounds like a lot of RAM, but some programs require more than 500 KB to run. For example, Symantec Corp.'s Time Line requires 540 KB. Future applications are going to be very memory hungry as well, making it imperative to provide as much available memory as possible.

As we explore how to resolve some common memory problems, keep in mind the earlier discussions on standard configurations. By planning to relieve the memory problems from the outset, you can spare yourself and others many frustrating problems in the future, as users begin to explore different applications that will require more and more memory.

Before installing PATHWORKS on multiple client machines, you should install it on one or two clients and test the modifications to CONFIG.SYS and AUTOEXEC.BAT. This testing should include booting the machines and checking memory utilization with a memory display tool, such as MEM with DOS V5.x or MEMMAN, which is included with PATHWORKS. Be sure to notice how the available extended, conventional, and expanded memories change. You typically should strive for more conventional memory by moving programs and drivers to extended memory. One important part of the testing is to check the performance of each client between changes to the start-up files. You may notice a degradation in performance after moving some drivers to extended or expanded memory.

Displaying Memory Information

MEMMAN. This command is used to display information about memory on a client machine and optionally to unload network components from memory. It is very useful for assessing the impact of the memory requirements of different programs. When you initially configure a network, MEMMAN is invaluable for evaluating the requirements of the various network components, including drivers that may be loaded via the CONFIG.SYS file. You should always redirect the output of this command to a printer or file when testing memory configurations. This will allow you to evaluate the impact of changes to your system in a step-by-step fashion.

MEMMAN's DOS counterpart is the MEM command. MEMMAN provides more information than the MEM command and provides additional unique features.

The MEMMAN /X parameter is useful when using extended memory. Using /X and redirecting the output to a file is a handy trick when testing your system. To display a memory map, including extended memory, use:

```
C:\>MEMMAN /X
```

Use /E to display detailed information on expanded memory usage. You must have an expanded memory driver loaded via the CONFIG.SYS file for this command to work:

```
C:\>MEMMAN /E
```

/M is the default parameter and displays the memory map for DOS.

Use /S to display summary information for all types of memory in the client machine:

```
C:\>MEMMAN /S
```

/U unloads all network components from conventional memory. All components up to and including the PCSA memory mark are unloaded.

MEM. The MEM utility is included with DOS and has been enhanced in DOS V5.x. To display a summary of memory using MEM, enter the following command:

```
C:\>MEM
```

Here is the output of this command:

```
655360 bytes total conventional memory
655360 bytes available to MS-DOS
478336 largest executable program size
7340032 bytes total contiguous extended memory
      0 bytes available contiguous extended memory
4992000 bytes available XMS memory
    MS-DOS resident in High Memory Area
```

89

To display a memory map of the PC's memory, including the upper memory area and programs, use this command:

```
C:\>MEM /C
```

The output from MEM /C will show which programs are loaded into memory (including upper memory) and how much memory is free.

Processor Configuration

What does the processor type have to do with memory problems? The Intel 80386 and 80486 processors have improved memory management facilities over the 80286 chip. There are several products available today that take advantage of the 80386 and 80486 processors' ability to manage memory. Most of these products will run only on an 80386 or 80486 processor.

Operating systems are also becoming more power hungry every year and are using features found only in the newer processors. Application software is becoming more powerful as well, requiring more powerful processors. Some programs that are very useful on a LAN (such as QEMM) will work to full function only on an 80386 or 80486 machine. By investing in new technology, your users can run virtually any software required and your organization protects its investment for the future.

In today's markets, the 80386 is only marginally more expensive than an 80286 machine. 80386 and 80486 processors have narrowed the gap to where it makes no sense to buy an 80286 machine, unless you know exactly what the machine will do and know for certain that it will never be used for anything else and that you will never upgrade the software running on it. Although it may seem expensive to pay $300 or more per PC for 80386 and 80586 machines, it is far more expensive to scrap numerous 80286 machines 1 or 2 years from now or, worse, to prevent employees of your company from using applications that could drastically improve their efficiency and, in many cases, directly impact the bottom line of your organization.

Memory Managers

Memory managers such as QEMM and Qualitas Inc.'s 386Max are designed to work around the 640-KB memory limitations of DOS. They can move programs into upper memory (between 640 KB and 1 MB) and into expanded or extended memory. They typically feature additional functions, such as providing statistics on memory usage and workarounds for machines with particular memory architectures, such as clones that have particular memory quirks.

DOS V5.x

You may wonder what DOS V5.x is doing in this section on memory managers. DOS seems to be moving in the direction of solving some of the nagging problems we have lived with for many years, although at a very slow pace. DOS V5.0 broke new ground by allowing part of the operating system to be loaded into high memory if it is available. The laptop I have used to write this book has 625 KB of free conventional memory, with no memory managers or PATHWORKS loaded.

DOS V5.x also supports loading parts of itself, other programs, and drivers into the UMB. You can insert the statement DOS=HIGH,UMB into the CONFIG.SYS file to trigger loading DOS into the HMA. Device drivers can be loaded into the UMB by using DEVICEHIGH instead of DEVICE in CONFIG.SYS. You can also load other TSR programs into UMB by placing LOADHIGH or LH in front of the program name when it is loaded. This sounds very simple: Just edit two or three files (CONFIG.SYS, AUTOEXEC.BAT, and STARTNET.BAT), and save tons of memory. But, alas, this is not a perfect world, and this solution helps only to a degree.

The size of the UMB is finite and will vary from PC to PC, depending on the model and vendor. The rule "a VAX is a VAX is a VAX" does not necessarily translate to "a PC is a PC is a PC." The type of monitor, type of BIOS, whether your PC shadows ROM to RAM, and other factors affect how much of this memory you can use for DOS and driver-type programs.

The most important memory-related item in CONFIG.SYS is loading the memory manager's EMM386.EXE and HIMEM.SYS. When you load EMM386, the NOEMS qualifier is used to load EMM386 without using EMS. The example below is for a laptop with 8 MB of RAM, a VGA monitor, and PATHWORKS V4.1. It should work with most 80386 and 80486 PCs:

```
SHELL=C:\COMMAND.COM /P /E:2048
DEVICE=C:\DOS\HIMEM.SYS
DEVICE=C:\DOS\EMM386.exe NOEMS
DOS=HIGH,UMB
FILES=60
BUFFERS=5
devicehigh=c:\decnet\protman.sys /i:c:\decnet
devicehigh=c:\decnet\pe_ndis.dos
lastdrive=z
```

Other factors that affect how UMB memory is used include the order in which programs are loaded and the type of programs that are loaded. If you load a large program first and try to load other large programs, you may be able to load only one program. If, on the other hand, several small programs are loaded, they may all fit. Some programs also take more memory when they are loaded and then shrink afterward. This creates a problem for DOS V5.x, because it will make sure the program has enough RAM available when it starts. This amount will not be reduced after the program is loaded, unless the SIZE= qualifier is used on the DEVICEHIGH line in CONFIG.SYS.

To determine the order of loading, review all of the drivers and programs that you plan to load, and record the file sizes. The file size usually indicates the memory requirements of the file. Next, determine the amount of high memory available on your PC. The MEM /X command will report the total high memory used and the total memory that can be used for high memory. By spending a few hours figuring out how much high memory you have available and trying different combinations of programs, you can determine a standard configuration for all 80386 clients. Standardizing PCs by type and vendor makes configuring and managing the clients much easier.

QEMM

QEMM will allow you to move parts of PATHWORKS and other programs into high, expanded, and extended memory.

When using QEMM, make sure you have the right version. Windows is especially picky about memory managers such as QEMM. If you will be running Windows, make sure the QEMM version you are using is the latest release. The following lines show a typical CONFIG.SYS file using QEMM instead of HIMEM.SYS. The functions of HIMEM.SYS are included in QEMM:

```
shell=c:\dos\COMMAND.COM /e:1024 /p
device=c:\qemm\qemm386.sys frame=E000 maps=16 ram
files=8
buffers=2
break=on
device=c:\qemm\loadhi.sys c:\windows\smartdrv.sys 4096 2048
device=c:\qemm\loadhi.sys c:\decnet\laddrv.sys /D:4
device=c:\qemm\loadhi.sys c:\mouse\mouse.sys
device=c:\qemm\loadhi.sys c:\decnet\ladddrv.sys /N:4
lastdrive=z
```

The DOS V5.0 DEVICEHIGH statement is replaced by QEMM's version, which uses the DEVICE statement to load the LOADHI.SYS driver, which in turn loads the device driver. The CONFIG.SYS file also sets the statements and buffers to very low values. The values are reset in AUTOEXEC.BAT with the files and buffers options of the LOADHI command to reduce the amount of memory used by these commands.

The following AUTOEXEC.BAT file uses the QEMM features of LOADHI and files and buffers:

```
c:\qemm\loadhi /r:1 share /f:4096/1:60
c:\qemm\loadhi: files=30
c:\qemm\loadhi: buffers=20
prompt $p$g
REM Insert any keyboard internationalization and character set information
        here.
REM Executing network startup procedure
if not exist \DECNET\STARTNET.BAT goto nostartup
call \DECNET\STARTNET
goto end
:nostartup
echo ** WARNING ** STARTNET.BAT file not found. Network functions not
        performed
:end
```

Instead of using the LH command included with DOS V5.x, QEMM uses its own LOADHI program, which is found in the C:\QEMM directory. The LOADHI command has numerous options, which you should explore if your system requires every inch of RAM possible.

One word of caution when using QEMM with an NDIS driver: Do not use LOADHI.SYS to load PROTMAN.SYS into upper memory. If PROTMAN.SYS is loaded into upper memory with QEMM, the PC will lock up when PROTMAN.SYS loads.

QEMM offers numerous advantages over DOS V5.x for squeezing every ounce of conventional memory out of a PC. However, it has two disadvantages: It costs extra, and it will probably lag behind new versions of DOS, PATHWORKS, and Windows. This delay can be a severe disadvantage if you need to run the latest versions of these programs and can't afford to wait for a new version of QEMM. Most of the advantages and disadvantages of QEMM also apply to other third-party memory managers.

Using High Memory with PATHWORKS

Several PATHWORKS components can be safely moved into the UMB. You should test your version to verify what works and what does not. With version 4.1, DLL*, SCH, DNP, REDIR, LAD, LADDRV, LANSESS, CTERM, and LAST safely load into the UMB. I expect future versions of PATHWORKS to require less conventional memory, just as the memory restrictions of DOS are lessened with changes to DOS, changes to new utilities, and programming language improvements.

If you are using a memory manager such as QEMM, you should test everything thoroughly with it. Components that cannot be relocated with DOS V5.x may work with QEMM, because some memory managers provide improved capabilities over DOS.

You can also use the EMSLOAD program shipped with PATHWORKS to load DNP, LAST, LAD, and LAT into EMS memory. This is useful on PCs that do not support XMS memory or when there is no room in XMS for all of the network components.

CHAPTER 5

Accessing the Network

This chapter explains the network directory structure, the most important client functions for accessing the network, and the commands to accomplish them on a DOS PATHWORKS client. These commands are grouped with other commands that perform similar or related functions. The detailed explanations illustrate how and why the commands are used in a networking environment. A more complete listing of PATHWORKS standard client commands with qualifiers and parameters is included in Appendix E.

Client commands are used to perform a number of tasks on the network, including managing memory utilization, accessing your personal account on the server, and connecting to various services on the server. Most commands are used from the DOS command line, with a few exceptions such as mail and setup programs. Program information files (PIF) are also available for several programs, to facilitate the use of these programs under Windows. A few client commands, such as FAL, NFT, and VT320, are full-featured Windows programs, providing the full functionality of Windows, such as cut-and-paste functions and multitasking.

This chapter does not try to duplicate information found in the command reference for your system; nor does it define all options for each command. It details the most important commands for the majority of installations. The appendixes in this book list the major PATHWORKS commands and their entire command sets.

THE USER'S PERSPECTIVE

A typical business must focus on its business objectives and use all of its resources to accomplish them. With the increase in competition in today's markets, especially from overseas, a company must apply every resource in the most effective manner and assure that it is focused on the objectives of the organization.

One example of a critical resource is the companywide computer system prevalent in most organizations. This system must serve as the backbone of the company, providing critical information and communications across the organization. A computer network extends this system into many different areas of the company, where people having various degrees of exposure to a computer system are now *users* of the network.

It is vitally important to understand that the most important person involved with any network is the user. Users are actually the employees within functional departments of the organization who enable the company to achieve its goals. Their usage of any computer system is a means to an end, not the end itself. By classifying people as end users, we often view their use of the system as the end result.

Function-Driven Users

A user's view of the system is almost always function driven. An example is the controller who uses Borland International's Quatro Pro or Microsoft Excel to manipulate data pulled from the accounting database. The controller is not concerned about the neat software being used in the engineering department or the fancy methods established by MIS for pulling the data into the PC. The controller's focus is on how quickly he or she can obtain the analysis at hand and use the results to reduce costs.

Application-Oriented Users

To adequately perform the required functions in today's dynamic business world, users are normally application oriented. During the course of a typical day, various tasks will require them to manipulate documents, manage lists, access a PC database, type a letter, review or send electronic mail, and access a corporate database. Each of these tasks requires interacting with a particular application at various times of the day and possibly using a particular application only once a year. This can be very frustrating to users as they try to accomplish their jobs efficiently with a bewildering array of different computer tools, each with its own set of rules, interfaces, and behaviors. In many cases, the LAN adds another layer of complexity to users' tasks and increases the frustration factor. Instead, the LAN should serve as a medium of communication and provide ready access to the tools they require.

USER REQUIREMENTS

In the following sections, I will look at functions such as accessing a VAX application from the PC, retrieving files from the server into the PC, printing on network printers, and performing various other typical user tasks. I will present several software packages and technologies to demonstrate how these applications fit into a typical 1990s business.

File Sharing

The first and most visible user requirement for a PC network is the ability to access common files and output devices such as printers, modems, and plotters. PATHWORKS provides for services ranging from simple file and printer sharing to complex integration of file sharing, including client/server applications.

PATHWORKS stores client files on the server disks, in the format of the application creating the file, by using the standard file system of the server. This provides one of the major advantages of PATHWORKS: The same file may be accessed by a PC, a Macintosh, and a server with no changes to the file. This means that a file produced by a VMS program's print facilities may be read by a PC program without using a translator or other piece of intermediate software. A person using a Macintosh can also read a file produced by a compatible application running on a PC (such as Aldus Corp.'s PageMaker).

A network server provides the interface between itself and the client workstations and other systems on the network. In a typical system, a PC user uses Microsoft Word to edit a file that is stored on the VMS server disk drive. A Macintosh user later uses Microsoft Word for Macintosh to edit the same file. This also relieves the different users from using the tried-and-true (and aggravating) "sneakernet" to move files from one machine to another. Because only one copy of the file exists, it also precludes the problems that arise when many people have a copy of the same file (invariably with different revisions) on different disks or in multiple directories on a file server.

Properly performed backups are also critical to any organization using a computer system. Most users of standalone PCs or Macintoshes do not perform routine backups of their files. When (not if) a failure occurs, users will scream and complain about the loss of data. In most organizations, not only is this an inconvenience, but it may also involve the loss of critical data that may be costly or impossible to replace. One big benefit of almost every LAN is that a backup of the server also provides a backup of the client files on the server. PATHWORKS carries this one step further by allowing the server to collect files located on client machines and include them in the backup.

Access to printers, plotters, and other devices attached to the network can be transparent to PC, Macintosh, and server users. PC and Macintosh print requests are simply rerouted by PATHWORKS to a printer on the network. This printer may be physically attached to the server, PC, Macintosh, or another network device such as a terminal server. Once the proper definitions and access methods are established, the user need not care where or how the printer is attached. When a user wants to print a file on the laser printer connected to the server, he or she uses the familiar DOS printing methods normally used with a DOS printer. In this case, the user needs to know only where to pick up the output from the printer.

Printing via PATHWORKS also allows the administrator to minimize the number of similar devices on the network while providing a smaller number of more sophisticated devices for use by network users. Adobe Systems Inc.'s PostScript-capable printers, large plotters, and color printers are devices that are in great demand but are typically too expensive to attach to each user's PC or Macintosh.

Sharing printers provides a hidden advantage to the users because PATHWORKS will use the server print queue system for managing devices. This provides management control and print spooling, which increase the productivity of client users. LOGON.BAT can automatically redirect the LPT printer names to a network printer as the user logs in, allowing standard print procedures to print on a network printer as if it were locally attached. The complexity of how this happens and how the USE command operates to redirect the printer is hidden from the user. For a more in-depth view of how PATHWORKS manages printers, see Chapter 7, "Network Printers."

Access to Corporate Applications

The next reasonable expectation of a network is to provide client users with access to corporate applications running on the network. The network makes this easy by providing users with direct connections to all systems on the network, without extra cables, terminal servers, and other hardware.

Accessing VMS- or UNIX-based applications over the network normally requires the use of a software package commonly referred to as a terminal emulator. As its name implies, this type of software emulates the functions of a typical terminal, including screen and keyboard functions. This allows a client to appear to the server as a normal terminal.

Most programs available today also provide functions such as local print functions, screen capturing to a Macintosh or DOS file, and keyboard mapping features that allow your keyboard to send key sequences from user-selected keys. Some programs also provide the ability to record sequences of keystrokes into macros. You can replay a macro at any time, sending many keystrokes with the press of a key.

An increasingly popular method for accessing VMS and UNIX applications is through the use of front-end programs such as Digital's DECquery product. This program allows users running Windows to build interactive queries to a VAX database such as Rdb. This uses the power of the client workstation to process the results of the query, without adding a lot of overhead to the server. DECquery also provides a simple and easy-to-use interface that gives a quick and intuitive method of building complex graphical reports. Other programs are starting to appear that will allow people to develop complete front-end programs for VMS and UNIX.

At this point, you may be thinking, "This sounds great, but how do I pull it together?" Volumes upon volumes exist that explain how to set up the file server and workstation, how to use PATHWORKS commands, how to configure printers, and so on. The missing link in most of these books is how to successfully implement all these tools in a common network, one that is easy to use and manage. The balance of this chapter will focus on how you set up PATHWORKS for easy access, while providing users with the proper tools, without creating a management nightmare.

Most PC networks are confusing to the typical user. Tasks as simple as accessing a directory on the server require detailed knowledge of strange commands and many different parameters. A PC network typically uses a wide variety of commands for connecting to file services and print services and other functions. PATHWORKS improves on this by offering help on most commands users will encounter. Even with the information provided by the help facilities, there is a tremendous number of commands to master with PATHWORKS. When a user is confronted with a great number of network commands, the user invariably grabs a note pad and creates a cheat sheet that becomes the bible for using the network.

To prevent the short-term and long-term chaos that occurs when this happens, let's look at the network from a high level and see how to make life easier for everyone who uses the network — end users and network administrators.

NETWORK ACCESS

As with any computer system, the user and the computer must have some method to recognize each other, and at the same time, the system must provide appropriate levels of security for different users. Most computers, including those running VMS and UNIX, and networks use the familiar login procedure. By properly configuring several batch files (including AUTOEXEC.BAT, LOGON.BAT, AUTOUSER.BAT, and STARTNET.BAT) for each client PC or user on the network, the network administrator may configure custom login and start-up procedures that establish the proper access privileges, set up the appropriate printers, and start the user's menu or windowing interface.

This login procedure should require the user to enter the minimal amount of information possible, such as C:\>Logon MyName (cr). The more difficult the network login process is, the less effective your network will be for the users.

AUTOEXEC.BAT, CONFIG.SYS, and STARTNET.BAT are normally tailored for a specific PC. LOGON.BAT is an exception to this rule; it may be tailored to a specific PC or a particular group of users.

Let's review the login procedure that users execute to access their personal directories on the server. When a user executes the login procedure, the logical drive letter M: is connected to his or her personal account on the server.

Standard LOGON.BAT

The first thing you notice about the standard LOGON.BAT file is its length. If we included the entire file here, it would take several pages. Batch programs are executed by interpreting each line of code at run time and then executing the command. The longer the program, the longer the run time. When most users log into the system with LOGON.BAT, they begin to wonder if the PC has locked up. LOGON.BAT is a general-purpose login procedure with a lot of complexity built into it to handle different situations. Let's review a replacement for LOGON.BAT that will simplify and speed the user login process.

The first step in simplifying the login procedure is to streamline LOGON.BAT. Figure 5-1 shows a high-level flowchart for a modified version of this program. It illustrates the chain of batch programs that execute when a user logs into the server. The normal PATHWORKS procedure is to use LOGON.BAT, which is illustrated by the second box in the figure. LOGON.BAT connects the M: drive letter to the user's home directory on the server and eventually calls the AUTOUSER.BAT program that should be found in the user's M: drive root directory. Both LOGON.BAT and AUTOUSER.BAT perform error checking, and they display messages to the user if problems occur.

New LOGON.BAT

The procedure in Figure 5-2 is a new version of LOGON.BAT that takes a very different approach to the process of logging in. The user may or may not enter information when executing the LOGON.BAT command. If no information is supplied, the procedure uses a default server and then prompts the user for his or her username and password. If the server or username is already set, the procedure will display it to the user and allow it to be changed. The new LOGON.BAT also calls a new procedure called AUTOSYS.BAT, which sets standard directory, application, and printer access.

This logon procedure calls several routines that set parameters for general classes of network users. Standard applications such as mail would typically be set via a standard procedure for all users. Calling one standard procedure from the logon procedure simplifies the management of your network by placing common connection commands in one procedure. When this procedure is updated, it affects all users on the network.

This streamlined version of LOGON.BAT removes many lines of code from the standard logon procedure while adding functionality. All comment lines from the beginning of the procedure have been eliminated. Since DOS batch programs are interpreted at run time, comments drastically slow the execution of a command procedure. One or two comment lines do not have a big effect, but 15 or 20 are a totally different story.

The PASSWORD program following the :noserv and :novars labels is a Pascal program that prompts the user for the server name, username, and password, eliminating the need for lots of parameter checking at the beginning of the program. The /n parameter on the first PASSWORD line invokes the program without asking for the server and user names. In either case, PASSWORD creates environment variables for the username, server name, and user's password. PASSWORD is an executable file (.EXE) written in Turbo Pascal V6.0, using the Turbo Object Professional toolkit. The source for this program is shown in Appendix F. This program was written by

Figure 5-1. Procedures Executed at Login

Figure 5-2. New LOGON.BAT

```
@ECHO off
REM: LOGON.BAT
break on

if %1@ == /s@ goto novars
set server=KENS
if %1@ == @ goto novars
if %2@ == @ goto noserv
 set server=%2
:noserv
 set user=%1
 password /n
goto cont

:novars
 password

:cont
echo ...
REM: Making username%username
set_user=%USER%
set_user=%_USER%%%
set_user=%_USER%%USER%

:cM
rem: Drive M: is not connected
set_USR=M:
use m:\\%SERVER%\%_USER% %pass%/network/R
if not errorlevel 1 goto setenv

:oM
rem: Drive M: is not connected
echo Attempting reconnection
use m:\\%SERVER%\%_USER% %pass%/network/R
if not errorlevel 1 goto setenv
echo ? Error connecting to personal drive
goto error
```

Figure 5-2. New LOGON.BAT (continued)

```
:setenv
set_user=
%_USR%
Call AUTOSYS
if exist%_USR%\autouser.bat call autouser

:error
rem: Clean up environment space
set_VP=
set_sw=
set_user=
set_USR=
set password=
```

Alan Sharkey and is in the public domain. You may obtain PASSWORD from the Digital Customer Support Center and from the disk accompanying this book.

After the password, USE statements similar to those in LOGON.BAT connect the M: drive to the user's personal directory.

Most sites will use file services for user directories, which makes the deletion of the lines for virtual drives fairly safe and easy. If only selected users are using virtual drives, you may want to copy LOGON.BAT to LOGONV.BAT or move it to a directory higher in the users' PATH statement. Separating the LOGON.BAT programs between users who connect to virtual drives and those who use file services will allow you to strip the unnecessary code from LOGON.BAT, thus making the procedure much faster.

You can easily customize the login procedures for groups of users on the basis of where the PCs are located and what servers they normally connect to. You can accomplish this by placing different versions of the LOGON.BAT file in separate directories on the server and placing the appropriate directory in the PATH statement of different PCs. Chapter 6 discusses directory structures and use of the PATH statement.

We have also removed the error messages for a missing AUTOUSER.BAT. The user will realize that AUTOUSER.BAT is missing when he or she cannot print or access applications. This simple modification removes several more lines of code.

Using simple DOS batch programs to call the various PATHWORKS commands is useful with PATHWORKS. This type of program is simple to write and completely hides the mystery of the PATHWORKS command structure. DOS batch programs are also useful for calling many of your own batch programs, especially those that require several parameters that change only occasionally, such as the server name. Most of the commands that I will examine follow the same format of simplifying the user interface or providing a front end to standard PATHWORKS commands.

The environment variables SERVER, USER, and PASS are set by PASSWORD at the beginning of the login process and remain until LOGON.BAT terminates. Immediately before termination, LOGON.BAT will delete the PASS variable. Any batch files called during the login process may use the variables. Batch files may also access the SERVER and USER variables after the user is logged in.

AUTOSYS.BAT

AUTOSYS is a standard batch file executed by all users when they log in. This file may be very short, as shown in the example below, or may become very complex as the usage of your system grows.

The purpose of the AUTOSYS procedure is to establish the environment for all users on your system. Items to place in this file are things that every user requires. The following example has only one command, the LIST command. This command is used to display the file NEWS.TXT, which contains important news for the network's users:

```
@ECHO off
REM AUTOSYS.BAT
LIST F:\NEWS\NEWS.TXT
```

AUTOUSER.BAT

What happens to the user after he or she executes LOGON.BAT? The last thing the login procedure does is call the AUTOUSER.BAT procedure for this particular user. By creating a file named AUTOUSER.BAT in the user's home directory, you can very easily customize each user's login procedure, including setting up printers and establishing links to various disk drives each time the user logs in. AUTOUSER.BAT is called by LOGIN.BAT each time the user logs in. AUTOUSER.BAT should include the items listed in Table 5-1.

AUTOUSER.BAT is an absolutely key program in a successful installation. Here is a sample AUTOUSER.BAT:

```
@ECHO off
REM AUTOUSER.BAT
CALL set_drv L MfgDB
CALL Set_stds Mfg
CALL StrtMenu Win
```

Table 5-1. Functions to Include in AUTOSYS.BAT

Function	Description
Printers	Connect the user to the normal printers and devices.
Directories	Set up access to the user's normal directories, including those needed by application programs specific to this user or the user's department. See Chapter 6, which discusses directory structure, for more information.
Path	Modify the PATH statement to include standard network directories and specific requirements for this user.
Variables	Set up any standard environment variables required by programs, batch files, or specific network functions.
Interface	Set the user's interface to either a menu or a graphical user interface.
Logout	If the user is a restricted user (i.e., limited to menu or graphical user interface access), log the user out when the user exits from his or her interface.

Figure 5-3 examines the AUTOUSER.BAT file line by line.

The sample AUTOUSER.BAT in Figure 5-3 calls numerous batch programs to make service connections for printers and file services. The SET_STDS command also sets standard connections and parameters for the group MFG. By customizing the SET_STDS program and building other modules called by SET_STDS, you can very easily build standard login procedures for various groups and departments in your organization.

SET_STDS.BAT

Most networks will have certain services that will be used by all users on the network. This is especially true on small networks where there are only two or three network printers and one or two shared services. Connections to these services can be placed directly in AUTOUSER.BAT, LOGON.BAT, or STARTNET.BAT. Depending on how many services fit this category, how often they change, or how they are used, one method may be required over another.

The AUTOUSER.BAT file in Figure 5-3 uses the file SET_STDS.BAT to connect to these services. This file can be called from AUTOUSER.BAT, LOGON.BAT, or STARTNET.BAT. I suggest calling SET_STDS.BAT from either AUTOUSER.BAT or LOGON.BAT.

Figure 5-3. AUTOUSER.BAT with Explanations

@ECHO off	
CALL SET_PRT Laser_Office 1	Call the SET_PRT.BAT file to set up LPT1 as the office laser printer (using the VAX queue Laser_Office).
CALL SET_PRT LA324_System 2	Call the SET_PRT.BAT file to set up LPT2 as the LA324 printer in the computer room (using the VAX queue LA324_System).
CALL SET_PRT HP7550_Eng 3	Call the SET_PRT.BAT file to set up LPT3 as the HP7550 plotter in the computer room (using the VAX queue HP7550_Eng).
CALL SET_DRV L MfgDB	Call the SET_DRV.BAT file to set up access to the MfgDB directory via the L: drive letter.
CALL SET_STDS MFG	Call the SET_STDS.BAT file to set up network standard for the MFG group. This could include setting the search path, drive mappings, variables, and printers.
CALL STRTMENU	Call the STRTMENU.BAT file to start the user's interface program.

SET_STDS.BAT is very useful because it places all the standard service commands in one place. When you must make a change because a service has changed or a new service is added, you can quickly place this change in SET_STDS.BAT. If SET_STDS.BAT is called from either LOGON.BAT or AUTOUSER.BAT, the changes will be picked up when the next user logs in.

If the connection commands had been placed in each user's AUTOUSER.BAT file, it would take a long time to update every file. Every command used by more than one person is a candidate for placement in a common batch program. The following example shows a common SET_STDS.BAT file:

```
USE Z:\\KENS\SHARE1 /R
USE H:\\KENS\WORD20 /R
USE LPT2: \\MFG\LASER /R
```

Menu Interface

The last step in this AUTOUSER.BAT procedure should also set up the interface through which the user will access the various applications he or she requires. The standard interface for DOS computers is some type of menu system. Menus can be tailored to set up printers and other disk drives and to perform many other functions users require. Users should select applications from a menu and return to the menu after finishing with an application.

Most users should also be logged out of the system when they exit the menu. This provides a level of control for the system manager and comfort to the user, who does not need a lot of shorthand notes and ready access to a help desk for DOS or network command questions. A very simple menu example is shown below:

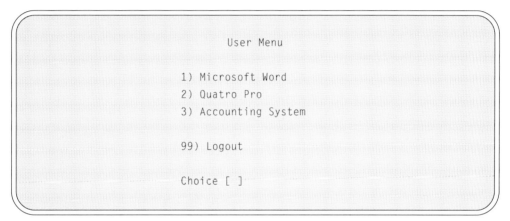

```
                         User Menu


                     1) Microsoft Word
                     2) Quatro Pro
                     3) Accounting System


                     99) Logout


                     Choice [ ]
```

STRTMENU is used to execute the menu for a particular user. This is usually a very short file called by the AUTOUSER.BAT program and used by users who work in DOS and use a menu. The menu can either be a traditional menu or a graphical interface such as Windows.

The program shown below loads a menu program called QuickMenu from Crescent Software. The login username is supplied to the menu program with the %USERS% variable. This command could be changed to LOAD AUTOMENU or any other menu or interface program. It may also be necessary to connect to a particular drive or service with the USE command to access the necessary files. All commands necessary to start the menu should be included in this program:

```
@ECHO OFF
REM STRTMENU.BAT
Q%USER%
```

DOS Shell

DOS Versions 4.x and above are shipped with a user interface called the DOS shell. The shell provides a simple interface that allows the user to use the arrow keys or mouse to execute applications. The interface is intuitive and easy for a user to understand.

The shell first appeared with DOS V4.0 and has undergone vast improvements with DOS V5.0. Features pioneered in Windows are slowly moving to the DOS shell, providing the user with a simpler interface and with features such as task switching and a graphical directory structure. Figure 5-4 shows the DOS shell main screen.

Figure 5-4 illustrates the flexibility of the DOS shell. All disk drive letters are displayed across the fourth line of the screen. Notice that there is no difference in the appearance of local drives A through D and network drives E, F, M, N, and S. Clicking on a drive letter will change the file and directory display to that drive.

The bottom of the screen is used for application menus. Submenus (groups) are shown in brackets. To execute an application or menu, simply click on the item with the mouse, or use the arrow keys to highlight the item and press enter. In Figure 5-5, the drive has changed to the M: drive, which is a personal drive on the network. Notice how the directory and file windows have been changed to the new drive. The menu screen has also changed to the Application menu, showing the options for Word and the Main menu.

This type of interface provides a simple system for the user and a level of control for the system manager. The shell will allow a user to exit to DOS and perform numerous DOS functions. (Note that this may cause security concerns in some organizations.)

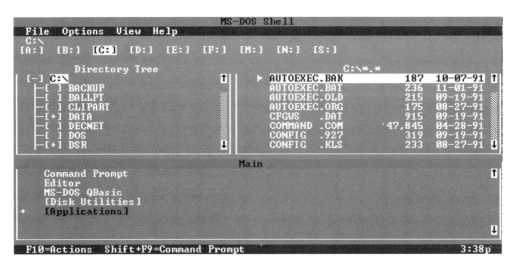

Figure 5-4. DOS Shell Main Screen

Windows Interface

When we discuss the user interface, it is impossible to ignore the graphical user interface that is quickly becoming a best seller. If I were asked to pick two topics that were the most discussed, pro and con, today, they would be LANs and Windows. As part of this discussion on user interfaces, let's take a brief look at Windows, specifically at the importance of Windows for LANs.

Windows can be a very complex environment to set up on a LAN. Any advanced user interface for a computer in today's world is complex and requires planning before implementation. Even the simple menu system will turn into a mess without proper planning and design. What troubles many people about Windows is the fact that Windows might not run if the proper configurations have not been set up. Windows applications are typically very memory hungry and are picky about settings in various .INI files. Temporary directories and network memory configurations further compound the successful implementation of Windows in any network environment.

With the number of potential problems, you may begin to wonder why you should bother with Windows when it would be easy to get started with a simple little menu program. Let's consider several important factors. One of the foremost involves planning for the future. A look at DOS V5.0 indicates that the graphical user interface is moving into the DOS world as a standard feature. Given this fact and considering that Microsoft produces Windows, you will find it makes sense that Windows and DOS will be moving closer together over time. A review of the latest and greatest applications also indicates the newest software is moving to Windows at a startling pace.

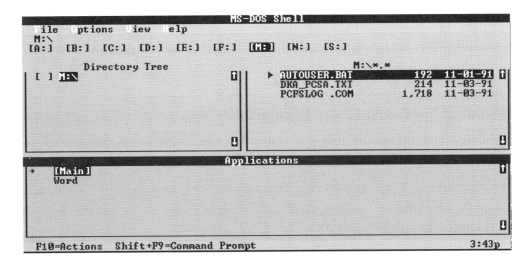

Figure 5-5. DOS Shell Menu Features

Current versions of Windows provide a number of built-in network features. Future Windows versions (Windows 3.x and Windows New Technology [NT]) will also provide built-in network features. Windows NT will support PATHWORKS as both a client and server platform, bringing the power of the NT architecture to PATHWORKS. As LAN Manager also moves to the world of Windows, PATHWORKS will become more closely tied to the Windows environment.

Also consider that it is important to provide a common user interface with which users need learn a minimal amount of new commands to run a new program. Training and standards are easier to maintain because of this interface. Data sharing alone is a great reason to consider Windows. Cutting and pasting graphics and text is so easy that it makes generating a document a pleasure, not a chore. For demonstrations of an integrated manufacturing product, my company's standard demo uses the VT320 terminal emulator shipped with PATHWORKS and NOTEPAD.EXE. We cut and paste data from a VMS application straight to NOTEPAD, without closing either application. Many manufacturing personnel I know go crazy for lack of this capability.

When you add up all these benefits, it equals a lessened workload for the support staff in areas such as training, data access, problem solving, and day-to-day questions. It is also important to remember that some applications are available only under Windows. Applications such as Micrografx Inc.'s Designer and Aldus PageMaker do not have full-featured DOS counterparts. By embracing Windows, administrators not only will reduce their workload, but will be positioned for the future and will provide a logical growth path for users.

One of the biggest concerns for anyone purchasing software or hardware is the possibility of buying something that is out of date by the time it is installed. Windows is at the center of most debates concerning what platform to bet on for the future. Microsoft has invested a great deal in Windows, with support for non-Intel processors such as MIPS Technologies Inc.'s RISC processors and with the development of the Windows NT operating system.

Improving the PATHWORKS/Windows Interface

WinBatch. Some of the first tools to add to your PATHWORKS Windows arsenal are the WinBatch products from Wilson WindowWare. WinBatch is a batch language for Windows that includes numerous tools for accessing PATHWORKS services. WinBatch also provides functions for displaying dialog boxes, requesting user input, manipulating files, and executing DDE. WinBatch is a shareware program included on the disk accompanying this book.

The WinBatch compiler will compile WinBatch (and Norton) batch programs into EXE files. The resulting EXE files are ideal for a network because of their cost (there are no run-time fees), speed (they execute faster than a DOS batch file), and security (it's hard to edit EXE files).

AUTOEXEC.BAT. The first step in the boot process for PATHWORKS is the AUTOEXEC.BAT program. As previously mentioned, the STARTNET.BAT program is usually called from AUTOEXEC.BAT to load the PATHWORKS network software and possibly establish some network connections. Immediately after STARTNET.BAT completes, AUTOEXEC.BAT loads Windows. When Windows loads, the PC is connected to the default printer and to default services. Before the user takes control of his or her system, Windows is loaded and all network connections are established except for the user's personal service and other file or disk services the user may require.

Connecting to Network Services

The network functions of WinBatch work very well in a PATHWORKS environment, especially for connecting to file and print services. I created the following examples using the WinBatch compiler. The total amount of time to get these programs working on a network was less than 1 week (in spare time).

NETLOGON.WBT. NETLOGON.WBT is very similar to the LOGON.BAT program and is used by all Windows users on the network to connect to their specific network services. These services include personal drives, shared drives, and special applications. NETLOGON.WBT will also execute a file called AUTOUSER.WBT, if AUTOUSER.WBT is located in the user's personal directory. One interesting note: On a typical 80486 machine, NETLOGON.WBT executes quicker than LOGON.BAT!

When NETLOGON.WBT executes, it looks in the WIN.INI file for a field called username. If the field exists, it is used as the default account name for the user. If it does not exist, the default account is MyInitials (to prompt the user for his or her initials). The username field is displayed to the user via a simple dialog box. After the user completes the dialog box, he or she is presented with another dialog box requesting a password. The password is the last item the user will input before connecting to the network.

The core of the NETLOGON.WBT program uses the NET functions from WinBatch to handle the network interface. NETCANCEL is used to cancel a connection, while NETADCON adds a new network connection. These two commands are similar to the PATHWORKS USE command. The code for NETLOGON.WBT is shown in Figure 5.6.

Figure 5-6. NETLOGON.WBT Program

```
prevmode = ErrorMode(@off)                              ; Set error checking
                                                         ; Load Winbox.exe
Run("e:\u\winbox.exe","Network Logon|Please Wait - Network Connections are in progress")

hwnd=IntControl(21,"Network Logon",0,0,0)                ; Determine the WinBox window handle
                                                         ; and tuck it away for later.
defchg = "false"                                         ; Set change flag to false

defuser = IniRead("NetworkInfo","username","NoUser")     ; Get default user name from INI file

if defuser <> "NoUser" then goto defok                   ; Error check for a vaild user name

defuser = "MyInitials"                                   ; Set def user
:defok
                                                         ; Get user name
user = askline("Network Login New","Enter your UserName",defuser)

if defuser == User then goto skn                         ; If user = default, skip change flag
defchg = "true"
:skn
                                                         ; Get password
pwd = askpassword("Enter password","Network Account %user%")

path = "\\Srvr01\%user%%%user%"                          ; Set path = network path
drv = "M:"                                               ; Set drive to M:

avail = diskscan(0)                                      ; Find available drives
drvlen = strlen(avail)                                   ; Get the length of AVAIL
if drvlen == 0 then goto none                            ; If no available drives, exit

found = strindex(avail,drv,1,@FWDSCAN)                   ; See if M: is connected

if found == 0 then netcancelcon(drv,1)                   ; Cancel M:

rslt = netaddcon(path,pwd,drv)                           ; Connect M: to personal service

if rslt == @TRUE then goto con                           ; Error check for a good connection
message("Network Error","Error connecting to Personal Drive %drv% %path%")
if WinExist("Network Logon") then WinClose("Network Logon")
exit
:con

mydir = "%drv%\"                                         ; set MYDIR to M:

if defchg <> "true" then goto skipadd                    ; Check for change flag
rslt = IniWrite("NetworkInfo","username",user)           ; Update INI with new username
:skipadd

rslt = DirChange(mydir)                                  ; Change to personal drive

fex = FileExist("e:\u\std_use.wbt")                      ; Look for Std_Use.wbt on SiteSys
                                                         ; Execute Std_Use.wbt
if found if fex == @TRUE then call("e:\u\std_use.wbt","%user% %pwd% %avail%")

fex = FileExist("m:\autouse.wbt")                        ; Look for AutoUse.wbt on M:
                                                         ; Execute AutoUse.wbt
if found if fex == @TRUE then call("m:\autouser.wbt","%user% %pwd%")

playwaveform("c:\windows\chimes.wav",1)                  ; Play chimes if successful
                                                         ; If Network Logon window exists,kill it
if WinExist("Network Logon") then WinClose("Network Logon")
```

STD_USER.WBT. The STD_USER.WBT program is called from NETLOGON.WBT for every user. (See Figure 5-7.) STD_USER establishes connections that are common to all users (such as to shared drives). STD_USER may also display systemwide messages via Notepad or Browser.

Figure 5-7. STD_USR.WBT Program

```
user = param1
pwd = param2
avail = diskscan(0)
path = "\\Srvr01\share"
drv = "N:"
;message("Std user",avail)
found = strindex(avail,drv,1,@FWDSCAN)
if found == 0 then netcancelcon(drv,1)
rslt = netaddcon(path,"",drv)
drv = "Z:"
path = "\\Srvr01\app"
found = strindex(avail,drv,1,@FWDSCAN)
if found == 0 then goto ok
rslt = netaddcon(path,"",drv)
:ok
fex = FileExist("m:\setup\setup.nam")
;message("Call next","autouse")
if fex == @TRUE then goto skipbld
rslt = dirmake("m:\setup")
if rslt == @TRUE then FileCopy("e:\u\setup.nam","m:\setup",@FALSE)
:skipbld
```

AUTOUSER.WBT. The AUTOUSER.WBT program may optionally be executed as the user logs in. NETLOGON.WBT will execute this file automatically if it exists and will do nothing if it does not exist. AUTOUSER is a good place to handle user-specific tasks such as connecting to special shared or personal services and accessing special output devices. I also use AUTOUSER to call the FILMNGR.WBT program for users that use File Manager, shown below:

```
call("e:\u\set_drvs.wbt","\\Srvr01\newserv %param1% %param2%")
call("e:\u\filmngr.wbt","")
```

FILMNGR.WBT. FILMNGR is a simple little program that starts the File Manager if it is not running and activates it if it is running. The only other task it performs is to update the File Manager windows to the new connections made during the login process:

```
if WinExist("File Manager") == @FALSE then run ("WinFile.exe","")
res = winactivate("File Manager")
```

NETLOGO.WBT. NETLOGO is similar to LOGOUT.BAT and is used to close the nonstandard network connections for a user. The PC is returned to the same state it was in after it booted. (See Figure 5-8.)

Figure 5-8. NETLOGO.WBT Program

```
; Logout.wbt
prevmode = ErrorMode(@off)              ;Turn error mode off
; ------Remove Standard Drives Section---------
NetDrvs = diskscan(4)                   ;Obtain a list of current network drive
                                        ;assignments.
DrvNo = Itemcount(NetDrvs," ")          ;Get a count of current network drives
if drvno == 4 then exit                 ;If only standard drives, then exit
Loc = ItemLocate("D:",NetDrvs," ")      ;Remove Standard drives (D:,E:,F:,Z:)
NetDrvs = ItemRemove(Loc,NetDrvs," ")
Loc = ItemLocate("E:",NetDrvs," ")
NetDrvs = ItemRemove(Loc,NetDrvs," ")
Loc = ItemLocate("F:",NetDrvs," ")
NetDrvs = ItemRemove(Loc,NetDrvs," ")
Loc = ItemLocate("Z:",NetDrvs," ")
NetDrvs = ItemRemove(Loc,NetDrvs," ")
DrvNo = Itemcount(NetDrvs," ")          ;Reset DrvNo to the number of remaining

                                        ;Network connections.
                                        ;------Killdrvs Section---------
:killdrvs
if DrvNo < 1 then goto OK               ;Exit if DrvNo < 1
drv = itemextract(DrvNo,NetDrvs," ")    ;Obtain a drive letter to remove
rslt = netcancelcon(drv,0)             ;Remove the connection
if rslt == @FALSE then goto error       ;Goto error section on an error
DrvNo = DrvNo - 1                       ;Decrement DrvNo
goto killdrvs                           ;Return to remove the next connection
:error
;------Error Section---------
drv = itemextract(DrvNo,NetDrvs," ")
playwaveform("c:\windows\not.wav",0)
```

Figure 5-8. NETLOGO.WBT Program (continued)

```
Message("Error Disconnecting","Files are Still Open on Drive %drv%")
;------Finish Section---------
:OK
playwaveform("c:\windows\chimes.wav",1)
```

Using the WinBatch Programs. To use the WinBatch programs included in the examples and on the disk, you will need to change the lines in the ALL.WBT file all that point to a specific drive and directory. On our test system, this is the e:\u directory, which is on the SITESYS service. The AUTOUSER.WBT file is usually located on the M: drive after the user logs in.

Logging Off the Network

Almost all systems require some method for disconnecting, or logging off, the network or system. The easiest way to accomplish this with PATHWORKS is to create a small batch procedure called LOGOUT.BAT. Here is a sample logout file:

```
@echo off
if %1. == ?. goto help
C:

USE* :/DISCONNECT/EXCEPT=%_SYSD%S:

goto end
:help
echo-------------------------
echo.
echo Command Format: logout
echo.
echo-------------------------
:end
```

CHAPTER 6

Network Directories and Client Commands

One of the biggest problems facing a network manager is configuring the directory structure for ease of use and effective management. The large number of options for storing application and data files further complicates the problem. This chapter will cover how to access PATHWORKS file and print services and describe common techniques for using PATHWORKS client commands.

FILE SYSTEMS

LAN file systems are often paradoxical. Users find they have the space to store everything they ever wanted without having to be concerned with the upkeep or backup of anything. At first, this seems to be a dream come true. Over time, however, the dream begins to fade, as users are frequently fussed at via electronic mail to clean up their files. They also run into problems as they try to find files from others in their organization that are stored somewhere on the vast server disks.

This problem is compounded by the network's ease of use and promises of endless access to everything. The poor network administrators begin to pull their hair out fighting fires and justifying the purchase of more disk space. The solution to file management problems on a LAN begins with the same process as many other solutions: planning and design. Planning the structure of the directories on the server offers a method of arranging directories to provide access and controls for both end users and administrators. Our discussion on directories begins with an overview of server and PC directory and file structures.

VMS Directory Structure

The VMS operating system stores files in groups by establishing directories (common locations) for certain types of files. Each directory can store any type of file, including application programs, data files, or other legal VMS files. It can also store other directories, creating a tree structure that is very good for organizing groups of files. An example of a VMS directory is shown in Figure 6-1.

Each directory name is subject to the same naming conventions as normal VMS files. The name may consist of alphabetic and numeric characters, including some special characters (e.g., _, $, .). Names must also be from 1 to 39 characters long, and must not begin with a hyphen or dollar sign. VMS directory trees are limited to a maximum depth of eight levels. Keep this in mind during the discussion of client directory structures, which are not limited to the same depth as VMS. If users create DOS directories that are deeper than eight levels, operations such as backup procedures can fail unless special precautions are taken.

If you execute the VMS DIR command in a directory containing files and other directories, you will see information similar to this:

```
$ DIR
      LOGIN.COM;8, MYFILE.TXT_OLD;3,
      WP_FILES.DIR
$
```

The file specifications with the .DIR suffix are VMS directories. The directory file specification appears in this listing as a normal file, with all the attributes of any other file. You may search for directories by using the VMS command DIR *.DIR, which will list all directories *in* the current directory. The command DIR [...]*.DIR will perform the same search but will search for all directories in and under the current directory.

A VMS file name has the same characteristics as a directory name, except for the extension. A file may use an extension that is separated from the file by a period and is from 1 to 39 characters long. VMS files are also maintained by version, providing a convenient backup of new files. The version must be separated from the file type by a semicolon or period. In directory listings, the semicolon is used.

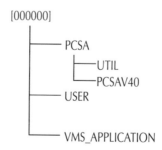

Figure 6-1. VMS Directory Structure

The VMS root directory serves as the common point for the origination of all directories on a particular drive, similar to the root of a tree. The name for the root directory on any drive is always [000000].

Every VMS disk has its own name (e.g., DUA1:, DKB300:, DKB0:) and directory structure. Issuing a DIRECTORY or other DCL command with a disk specification prefixing the directory will cause the command to access the directory on the specified disk. Command procedures and programs can also access directories and files on other disks by using this technique. The following command displays a directory from the device DKA300: and its root directory:

```
$ DIR DKA300:[000000]
```

DOS Directory Structure

DOS directories are structured along the same lines as VMS directories, using a separate directory structure for each disk. (See Figure 6-1.) The root directory is denoted by a \ instead of the [000000] used on VMS. All directories on a disk, except the root, are subdirectories and originate from the root directory. A PC file or directory name must be eight characters in length or less, with a suffix (file type) of three or fewer characters. The \ character is also used as the separator in a directory name. Figure 6-2 shows an example of a DOS directory structure.

You can access a DOS file by prefixing its name with the full path name (directory specification) or by placing the directory name in the PATH variable (for executable files). DOS directory names and file names are limited by a length of 64 or fewer characters in the total path name. DOS programs and commands access directories

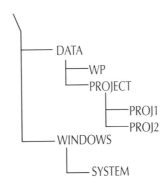

Figure 6-2. DOS Directory Structure

119

and files in the same manner as their VMS counterparts. The following command displays the directory for drive D::

```
C:\>DIR D:\
```

One area of potential conflict between VMS and DOS users sharing files is the difference in file names. DOS or a DOS application can see any file on a VMS server (if the user has the right permission) that meets the DOS file name rules. The area that causes the most problems for DOS users is trying to access a VMS file that is longer than eight characters or has an extension longer than three characters. If a directory has 10 files that meet the DOS name rules and two that are 12 characters long, a DOS DIR command on the directory will display the 10 files. DOS will not provide a clue that the other files exist. Make sure your users are aware of this rule and understand that all files targeted for DOS users must meet the DOS file name specifications.

DOS provides several shortcuts to accessing directories. I have already mentioned how the back slash (\) is used to indicate the root directory. The period and double period are used as shortcuts to access the current directory and the parent directory, respectively. Anytime either of these two characters is used, it has the same effect as specifying the entire directory path. For instance, if the current directory is C:\DATA\FILE\LTR, using .. will point to the directory C:\DATA\FILE. The period can be used in place of *.* to indicate all the files in a directory.

Network Directories

The design of your file server and client workstations directory structures is a key element to the success of your network. This design will determine whether your server and client workstations are easy to maintain, provide a usable method for users to share data, and provide for easy enhancements, or are the source of continual pain for you and your users. It also plays a large part in the ease or difficulty of installing new PC applications and backing up the system.

As you begin to consider the structure for your server, many different factors will come into play. Things as unrelated as user departments and functions, applications required by users, types of applications planned for the network, and the size of your tape drive should be considered in your design. A server directory structure is much like a child's balloon, with many forces pulling on it and pins headed for it from every direction.

Home or User Directory. The home directory for a user is normally the current server directory when the user logs into the server. This is usually the directory where the user's personal files are stored, such as word processing memos, letters, and documents; spreadsheet files; and other miscellaneous files that are for the user's use only. If the user is a VMS user, this will probably be his or her home directory for

VMS as well. A home directory and its subdirectories are usually accessible by only one user. Files stored in these directories are considered private.

Figure 6-3 shows a sample user structure for a network drive. Note how each user directory is located under a common directory (USER). The USER directory is key to making the maintenance of user directories an easy task. By placing all user directories under this one directory, functions that must be performed on more than one user directory at a time are easy to perform. I will discuss this in more detail as this chapter progresses.

Users should create subdirectories under their home directory to organize their files. The exact organization of these directories is up to the discretion of the user, but it should be logical and relate to the way the user works. Files stored in a user's personal directory are normally personal and do not require frequent sharing with other users. When someone needs access to a file stored in a personal directory, the file can be copied to a shared service or mailed to the user. Personal directories should be personal, with limited access for other users.

This is an area in which proper education and training is essential to maximizing the utilization of the network and reducing the support load. The user may not need to understand DOS but should have a good understanding of directories — how directories are used, how to access them through the system's interface, and how to manage files. Users also need an understanding of standard files, such as MAIL.MAI, LOGIN.COM, AUTOUSER.BAT, and any other standard files that may show up in a user's directory.

Data Files. Most computer systems today have some type of business applications resident, such as database programs and off-the-shelf software packages. Many of these programs access files that are shared by more than one user. Often some of these files are shared by many users.

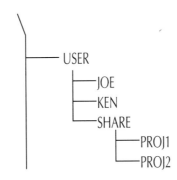

Figure 6-3. Home Directory Structure

121

Users in any organization need to share certain files with other users. This becomes complicated, because certain files must be shared with some users and other files shared with a different group of users. This requires a well-thought-out directory structure that builds in the ability to share files and imposes the appropriate restrictions to prevent unauthorized access.

Data directories for shared database files normally involve read/write access by several users at once. It is usually handy to establish subdirectories under a common shared directory for these different types of application projects. You should create the top-level directory for each major group as a service. You should create groups with the appropriate access and users assigned to them. This is a handy way to control access to the shared service.

Shared data directories can be broken up by application (such as a structure for a database application), department (Engineering, Manufacturing), project (Sales\ThisSale, Sales\ThatSale), product (Sales\Widget1, Sales\Widget2), and so on. It is normally better to establish directories by project than application. With this type of structure, users have only one place to look for a file relating to a particular item, instead of having to look through each application directory for a

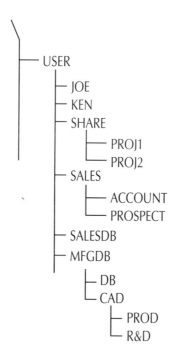

Figure 6-4. Data Directory Structure

particular file. Figure 6-4 shows a common format for shared directories. Notice how everything is located under one common directory called USER. New applications also make it easy to integrate file types into one application.

Education and training are also key elements for users sharing data files with applications such as word processors and spreadsheets. Even though the files are stored in a project directory (such as \USERS\SALES\HOUSE), it is important to establish conventions for file names. DOS does not help much in this regard with its eight-character restriction on file name length.

The file extension can be useful for indicating the purpose of the file. The only problem with this is that most applications tag their own extension to files to indicate the application that created the file. Most packages allow you to use your own extensions, but default to their original extension when displaying file lists.

Using a one- or two-digit prefix in the file name to indicate the purpose of the file will usually work. The prefix SL could indicate Sales Letters, SQ could be Sales Quotes, ES is Engineering Specifications, and so on. With a well-thought-out directory structure, a one-digit prefix may suffice. Documents stored in the \USERS\SALES\HOUSE\LTR directory may not require an indicator in the name, since they are identified by the directory. In this case, the file name could be used to indicate the actual name of the file. Most applications only display files sorted by name, making the first few digits the key to looking at a directory of files.

Many applications will augment the DOS file name by storing a short description of the file in the file itself. They will usually provide some way of viewing files and the short titles. Microsoft Word for Windows V2.x allows the user to store the title, subject, author, several keywords, and comments with the file itself. Understanding how DOS and your applications treat files and display them in directory-access procedures simplifies the process of designing the structure of your network. The method a program uses to access its files is also an important point to consider when you choose new applications for your network.

Application Directory Structure

Structuring directories for applications is slightly more difficult than designing the user directory structure, depending on how you choose to use your system. If you are using PCs with DOS, the structure may be different from a system using DOS and Windows.

Applications themselves further complicate the problem by requiring particular directory configurations. Have you ever noticed that every application wants to have its directory in the DOS PATH? On a typical network, you will notice a problem after installing the 10th or 12th application. This is because PCs will no longer access the network because their PATH is too long. PATHWORKS requires that the DOS PATH be less than 78 characters for STARTNET to load properly. Chapter 8, "Application Installation and Use," goes into further detail about how to avoid this problem.

The best way to manage application directories on PATHWORKS is to use application services. Application file services should be created on the basis of the types of applications on your network, how they will be used, and the number of users.

If your system is running only DOS applications, a separate application file service should be created for each application. Using simple DOS command files, you can connect to the application service when the application is accessed. Figure 6-5 shows the application services WW and QPRO. Note that these services are located below the APPS directory. File services should always be created beneath one subdirectory and never directly off the root. PCSA Manager may delete the entire disk if you delete a file service that is located directly on the root.

Applications can also be placed on disk services, providing concurrent read-only access to many users. If applications will use disk services, several applications should be placed on the same service. Creating a separate disk service for each application will cause additional overhead on the server, because each disk service must be mounted before it can be accessed.

Use short directory names for applications that will be placed in the PATH statement because of the limitations on the PATH statement length. Most users will not need to understand the directories their applications are stored in, so using short names is not a problem. Instead of using the name UTIL, change it to U. WINDOWS becomes W3 or W31, with WINWORD becoming WW. The example in Figure 6-5 illustrates a typical subdirectory structure for Word for Windows and Quatro Pro.

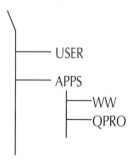

Figure 6-5. Typical Application Directory Structure

NATIVE DOS COMMANDS AND THE NETWORK

The DOS operating system provides a number of commands for manipulating files and directories. Some of these commands, such as DIR, COPY, and MKDIR are internal to the DOS command processor (COMMAND.COM), while many others are external programs (e.g., XCOPY, ATTRIB, DISKCOPY). DOS utilities are included with DOS and are usually stored in a directory named DOS or DOS50 (DOS50 stands for DOS V5.0) on the PC's hard disk. If the PC has only a floppy disk, some of the external files are on the boot floppy.

Most DOS utilities will function properly when used with a PATHWORKS service. A user will normally not know the difference between a command executed on a standalone PC directory or a network service. Exceptions to this are native DOS commands that modify or directly access the disk, such as CHKDSK, and third-party programs that perform similar functions, such as disk optimizers and tuning utilities. Most third-party DOS utilities will work correctly on a PATHWORKS service.

DOS commands and utilities are an important part of the network operating environment. Although this chapter is not a DOS reference, I will cover several commands and utilities that are useful for network operations.

DOS COMMAND PROCEDURES (BATCH FILES)

DOS provides a simple batch language for automating various tasks. It includes facilities for calling other batch procedures and programs, performing IF/THEN logic, setting and using environment variables, and performing several other tasks. The DOS manual shipped with a PC will normally have a description of the entire batch language for that particular version of DOS. You should also reference any of the DOS books on the market.

In this book, my goal is not to teach the DOS batch language. However, several important features of the DOS batch language are described, specifically as they relate to PATHWORKS commands or batch procedures included in this book. Each of these commands is outlined below:

CALL	Executes another batch procedure and returns control to the original procedure.
ECHO	Displays a message or messages on the screen, or turns the display of commands on or off.
FOR	Repeats a command for a group of files or directories.
GOTO	Skips from the current procedure line to the line specified by the label.

IF	Checks a condition specified by the test parameters, and executes the command following the condition if it is met.
PAUSE	Stops execution of the current program until the Enter key is pressed.
REM	Signifies a remark (nonexecutable) line in your program.
SHIFT	Changes the position of parameters in the replaceable parameters list.

Percent Sign Parameters

DOS provides command line parameters %1 through %9 for passing information to a batch program. These parameters are always entered following the batch program name and separated from the name and each other by at least one space. To specify three parameters with the values 1, 2, and 3 to the TEST.BAT program, enter:

```
C:\>TEST ONE TWO THREE
```

The program test can reference these values by using %1, %2, or %3 within the program:

```
ECHO "PRINT :" %2
PRINT: TWO
```

These parameters can be used with environment variables to provide many different types of information to a batch procedure. Environment variables are frequently used to provide a default condition set within a particular batch procedure. If the command line parameter is blank, the default is used; otherwise, the specified parameter is used.

An interesting quirk of DOS that can make you lose your hair (I know from experience) is the requirement that all percent signs in a batch program be prefaced by a percent sign, unless they signify either a command line or an environment variable (e.g., %1 and %DRV%). This can be troublesome for files using the PATHWORKS USE command, because it also uses the percent sign as a separator for usernames. The following command will work in a batch program:

```
USE ?:\\KENS\DKB300:[000000]%%SYSTEM *
```

When the command executes in the batch program, the %% is translated to a single %.

Redirecting Input and Output

One of the most useful features of the DOS batch language is the ability to redirect information from or to another file. This feature is useful for many programs that request one or more parameters when they execute, although it loses its usefulness for interactive programs that require many responses or for programs that do not have predeterminable responses. To direct the output of a program to a file, use the greater than symbol (>). If the information should be appended to an existing file, use two symbols (>>). If only one symbol is used, the new file will overwrite any existing file by the same name. Redirecting input from a file uses the less than symbol (<). The following examples use the redirection feature to capture the output of the directory command to a file:

```
C:\> DIR *.BAT > DIRBAT.TXT
```

You could append another directory listing to this same file with this command:

```
C:\> DIR C:\U\*.BAT >> DIRBAT.TXT
```

The following command executes the delete command for all the files in a directory and automatically fills in the yes response from a file called YES:

```
C:\> DEL C:\TMP < C:\U\YES
```

Control Commands

The IF statement is often used for testing a particular condition and executing a command based on the result. The format of this command is very straightforward:

```
IF CONDITION ACTION
```

The condition must always evaluate to either true or false (if the NOT prefix is used). If the test is successful, the action will be executed. When two items are tested, such as in checking a variable against a string, the two parts must be separated by two equal signs (==). The following command checks the match between %1 and TEST and turns echo on if it is true:

```
IF %1 == TEST @ECHO ON
```

A quirk of this command is its inability to handle a blank match, as in the case of a command line variable that may or may not be specified. The easiest way to handle this problem is to develop a standard method of entering IF commands, using some type of character on both sides of the equation. Let's use our last statement to see how this works:

```
IF (%1) == (TEST) @ECHO ON
```

Notice how parentheses have been added around both %1 and TEST. If %1 happens to be blank, the left side of the IF statement will still equate to (), which will not

127

match (TEST). This works because DOS simply concatenates the strings (, TEST, and) together before making the test. The following methods are also acceptable:

```
IF %1# == TEST# @ECHO ON
IF %1@ == TEST@ @ECHO ON
IF "%1" == "TEST" @ECHO ON
```

It doesn't matter which method is used, as long as you are consistent.

The EXIST option is very useful for checking for the existence of a file. For instance:

```
IF EXIST C:\DECNET\STARTNET.BAT GOTO OK
    Statement one
    Statement two
:OK
```

If the file STARTNET.BAT exists, the GOTO OK command will be executed, causing DOS to skip all lines down to the :OK label.

Another major control command is the GOTO statement mentioned in the last example. GOTO simply transfers control to the label following the command. For example:

```
:REPEAT
ECHO Test - CTRL-C to Stop
COPY c:\config.sys e:\test.txt
GOTO REPEAT
```

This command simply repeats ECHO and COPY by returning to the :REPEAT label until someone hits CTRL-C (or turns off the machine). The label is indicated by the colon (:) preceding the label name. GOTO will use only the first eight characters of the label. If a label is not found, the following message will be displayed:

```
Label not found.
```

The CALL command was introduced in DOS V3.3 to allow one batch program to call another and return control to the calling program. You can pass parameters to the called program by entering them after the program name, separated by spaces. CALL executes just as if the same command were executed from DOS, as illustrated in the next example:

```
IF "%1" == "TEST" @ECHO ON
ECHO This is a test
    .
    .
    .
CALL PROG2
ECHO This statement is never executed
```

This fictitious program will load the batch program PROG2 and pass control to that program. When PROG2 completes, control will return to the original program and execute the line after the CALL command. One quirk to watch out for is the ability of a batch program to execute another program by using just the program's name. The next example seems to be equivalent to our last example, except for the missing CALL command before PROG2. When this batch program executes, it will call PROG2 as in our last example, but control will never return to the original program:

```
IF "%1" == "TEST" @ECHO ON
ECHO This is a test
   .
   .
   .
PROG2
ECHO This statement is executed after PROG2 returns
```

This feature of DOS usually causes problems when a second or third program is called and the called program contains a reference to another batch program without using the CALL statement. Before calling batch programs from another program, check them for references to other programs and test them thoroughly.

SERVICE CONNECTIONS

In normal operations of a DOS client, the most commonly used commands are the various NET commands and the USE command. These commands control most of the operations of the client, such as managing files, managing and using printers, changing passwords, changing file attributes, and managing disk services.

Connecting to a Service

The USE command is one of the most powerful commands on the network. It provides access to network-file, virtual-disk, and print services. USE also provides information about network services by using numerous status and usage displays.

USE is most frequently used to connect to file or disk services. When connecting to file or disk services, USE will map a DOS drive letter to point to a drive or directory on the server. The new drive letter will appear to the user and application programs as just another drive. This command is also used with file and disk services to change the way a service is connected and to remove the connection to a service.

Another common USE operation is to connect to and manage print services. When accessing printers, the USE command works in the same manner as for accessing file or disk services. USE maps a DOS print device name to a print queue on the server. USE can also display usage and status information about print services.

Because of its power, USE is often a confusing command. Many users are confused when confronted with a command that controls both printers and file or disk services. Further confusion occurs because USE also provides information about the status and availability of print services. One frequent solution to this problem is the creation of a series of batch files to call the USE command for specific tasks.

Network Directory Access

After the USE command has redirected a drive letter to a directory or service on the VAX, that directory will appear as a normal DOS directory to DOS application programs, including DOS utilities. This is transparent to the program and user. Most programs are not even aware that they are accessing a network drive.

The logical drive letters used for accessing network services should be standardized for each network. If random drive letters are used for different users, supporting the network becomes a nightmare, and developing standard command procedures and menus becomes an almost impossible task. Table 6-1 lists standards for drive letters on a typical system. Except for drives A: through C:, this is not set in concrete. Drives A: through C: are established by DOS and cannot be changed, unless you have no local drives or have a floppy-only system, in which case only A: and B: will be defined.

Table 6-1. Drive Naming Conventions

Drive Letter	Typical Use
A-B	Local Floppy Drive
C	Local Hard Disk or RAM Disk
D-E	Local RAM Disk or System Service (PCSAV41)
E-F	Site-Specific Service (PCSASITE)
G	Network Default Drive
H	Spare
K-L	Shared Group Data
M	Personal Directory
N-R	Spare
S-T	Shared Data
U-Z	Applications

The G: drive is used as the default network drive when a PC connects to the network. The purpose of the G: drive is to make sure that all PCs connect to the same service at boot time and provide exactly the same interface to all users. It also ensures that users have access to the required files that may be located in the DEFAULT service. This is usually accomplished in the boot process via STARTNET.BAT. The last thing this procedure does is connect the G: drive to the DEFAULT service.

To connect to a file service, a command similar to the following will work. This command connects the next available drive letter to the service STD_APPS on the server MFG. Notice that this command connects to the service with the default account and does not explicitly specify a username and password:

```
C:\>USE ?: \\MFG\STD_APPS
```

The two back slashes (\\) before the server name (MFG) are used as separators and designate that a server name follows. The back slash after the server name is just a separator between the server name and the service. This format is standard for the USE command for all services.

If the client has used drive letters from A: to D:, the service will connect to drive E:. In many instances, it is useful not only to connect to a service with an available drive letter, as in our example, but also to know which drive letter is used. The /ENVIRON qualifier accomplishes this by causing USE to place the drive letter used for the connection in the DOS environment variable placed after the qualifier. The following command connects to the same service and places the drive letter in the variable DRV:

```
C:\>USE ?: \\MFG\STD_APPS /ENVIRON=DRV
```

This is very useful for batch files that establish a service connection and then refer to the drive explicitly. The next example shows a section of a batch file that uses our example command and then executes a program located on this drive. The last command in this example disconnects the service:

```
C:\>USE ?: \\MFG\STD_APPS /ENVIRON=DRV
%DRV%:\WP\WP %1 %2 %3 %4
C:\>USE %DRV%: /D
```

A file service does not need to be defined before a client can connect to the service, as long as it exists as a VMS directory that is located on a PATHWORKS server. The following command connects to the DKB0:[000000.USERS] directory on the server KENS. Once this connection is made, the service is available for use just as if it were a defined service:

131

```
C:\>USE I: \\KENS\DKB0:[000000.USERS]
```

If a file, disk, or print service is protected in any way, you must supply a username and password with USE to connect to the service. The username must be separated from the service by a percent sign (%). When a USE command with a username occurs in a batch program, the username must be separated by two percent signs:

```
C:\>USE ?:\\KENS\DKB300:[000000]%%SYSTEM *
```

Defining services with PCSA Manager actually requires some overhead on the server, because each service is stored in the file service database and must be referenced each time a user connects to the server, in addition to the user's checking of the normal protections (RMS and ACLs). Connecting directly to a VMS directory uses less overhead, as VMS checks only the normal protections.

Sometimes you must reuse a drive letter that is currently connected to a service. This occurs with a standard service in which general applications are stored or with any other service that may be connected to a frequently used drive letter. The following example replaces the I: connection with a new service:

```
C:\>USE I: \\KENS\DKB0:[000000.USERS.KEN] /REPLACE
```

Another handy option of the USE command is the ability to change the current directory to the new service automatically when the connection is made. The /SETDIR qualifier accomplishes this just as if you had connected to the service and then issued the commands to change to the new drive and service. This is illustrated in the following command:

```
C:\>USE I: \\KENS\DKB0:[000000.USERS] /LOG
```

The command to connect to a disk service is almost identical to the one used for a file service. One difference between the two connection methods is that if you are connecting to a disk service, you do not have to specify the server name, unless the same service is offered on multiple servers and you want to connect to a particular server. If the server name is specified, the /VIRTUAL qualifier must be included to identify the service as a disk service. If no server name is specified, /VIRTUAL can be left off the command because PATHWORKS will assume that the service is a disk service. For example, to connect to the service MYDISK without specifying a server, use:

```
C:\>USE I: MYDISK
```

To connect to the same service specifically on the server KENS, use:

```
C:\>USE I: \\KENS\MYDISK /VIRTUAL
```

If you forget the parameter format for the USE command, the /CONNECT qualifier will cause USE to prompt for each piece of information:

```
C:\>USE ?: /CONNECT /NETWORK

Server name: KENS
Service: STD_APPS
Username: KEN
Password:              (The password will not show.)
```

The /NETWORK or /VIRTUAL qualifier should be used with /CONNECT to specify whether the service is a file (/NETWORK) or a disk (/VIRTUAL) service. The password will not be displayed when entered with the /CONNECT command.

When a connection is made to a service, PATHWORKS normally does not display any information to the user. This is very useful in batch files or other cases in which you want to connect to a service and do not want to clutter the screen with information. If for some reason (such as to inform a user what has happened within a batch file) you wish to display the status of the connection, use the /LOG qualifier. This forces USE to display the result of the command:

```
C:\>USE I: \\KENS\DKB0:[000000.USERS] /SETDIR/LOG
```

Disconnecting from a Service

The /DISCONNECT qualifier is used to disconnect a drive or printer identifier from one or multiple services. The LOGOUT command uses /DISCONNECT in conjunction with the /EXCEPT qualifier to drop all connections except for the standard connections. To disconnect drive I:, use:

```
C:\>USE I:/DISCONNECT
```

To disconnect from all services except H, use:

```
C:\>USE *: /DISCONNECT /EXEC=H:
```

Displaying Service Information

In addition to making connections, one of the most frequent tasks for the USE command is displaying information about connections or available services. Simply typing USE will display a brief listing of your current services, including any connections with errors. This is the same as entering:

```
C:\>USE /LIST /BRIEF
```

To obtain a list of available services, use the /SHOW qualifier. Figure 6-6 shows the command to list file and print services on the server KENS, followed by the output.

Figure 6-6. Command to Show Available File and Print Services

```
C:\>USE \\KENS /SHOW

USE Version V4.1 Digital Network Connection Manager
Service information for \\KENS
File Server Authorized Services:

User name      Alias name    Service name    Access    RMS protection
---------      ----------    ------------    ------    --------------

<PUBLIC>       BACKUP        BACKUP          RWC       S:RWED,O:RWED,G:,W:
<PUBLIC>       BOOKS         BOOKS           RWC       S:RWED,O:RWED,G:,W:
TRISH          BOOKS         BOOKS           RWC       S:RWED,O:RWED,G:,W:
KEN            BOOKS         BOOKS           RWC       S:RWED,O:RWED,G:,W:
<PUBLIC>       DOC           DOC             R         S:RWED,O:RWED,G:,W:
SYSTEM         DOC           DOC             RWC       S:RWED,O:RWED,G:,W:
<PUBLIC>       HP_LAND       HP_LAND         RWC       S:RWED,O:RWED,G:,W:
<PUBLIC>       HP_PORT       HP_PORT         RWC       S:RWED,O:RWED,G:,W:
<PUBLIC>       JUNK          JUNK            RWC       S:RWED,O:RWED,G:,W:
<PUBLIC>       PCSAV41       PCSAV41         R         S:RWED,O:RWED,G:,W:
```

The NET FILE SERVICES command will display exactly the same information as the command in Figure 6-6. A server name is required with the NET FILE SERVICES command.

If you specify the /VIRTUAL qualifier, the command will list only disk services. When /SHOW is used to display virtual disk services, it displays the service name, server name, type of service (BOOT, USER, SYSTEM, or APPLICATION), rating (priority), access mode (RO or RW), maximum connections, current connections, and status of the service (MNT, PERM, PEND, and DSMNT). NET DISK SERVICES will display the same information as the /VIRTUAL qualifier.

Specifying a service with /SHOW will list all servers that have that service. This is handy in a multiple server environment when several servers may offer the same service but others do not. To list all servers with the disk service SPREADSHEET, type:

```
C:\>USE SPREADSHEET /SHOW
```

The information displayed for the servers will include the server name, rating (priority), whether a password is required, access mode (RO or RW), maximum connections, current connections, and network address and node address of the server.

The /X qualifier is useful if you need to determine the remote boot servers from which your node may boot. To display remote boot services, type:

```
C:\>USE /X /SHOW
```

The /STATUS qualifier displays current connection information, including information about which network components are loaded, the station and hardware address, the type of Ethernet adapter, and the number of drives (both physical and logical). Figure 6-7 shows the command and a sample of its output.

Figure 6-7. USE /STATUS Command

```
C:\>USE /STATUS

USE Version V4.1 Digital Network Connection Manager
Copyright (C) 1988-1991 by Digital Equipment Corporation

Component Information

    Scheduler is installed
    Datalink is installed and is running
    DECnet is not installed
    Session is installed
    Redirector is installed
    LAT is not installed
    LAST is installed
    LAD is not installed
    CTERM is not installed

Client Information

    Station address: AA-00-04-00-0A-50
    Hardware address:      08-00-2B-1E-13-08
    Ethernet hardware:     DEPCA
    Physical drives: 4 (A:-D:)
    Logical drives:  26 (A:-Z:)
```

Figure 6-7 shows something interesting about this particular workstation. Notice that DECnet is not running as indicated by the "DECnet is not installed" message. Some of the PATHWORKS commands use DECnet to access the server. DECnet must be running and properly configured for this command to execute properly. If the

"Service not Available" or "Not Listening" message ever occurs, USE/STATUS is a good place to start looking to check on DECnet.

One other interesting tidbit is the Ethernet address. Our example shows two addresses. How is this possible, and what is going on? The hardware address is actually the Ethernet address for the network card and hence the PC. The station address is used only for DECnet internals and should never be used for any other purpose.

Error Checking and the USE Command

When USE executes, it always sets the DOS ERRORLEVEL variable to 0, unless an error occurred, in which case it is set to a nonzero value. This is useful for monitoring the success of the command when it is executed from a batch program:

```
USE I:\\KENS\STD_APPS
IF ERRORLEVEL == 0 GOTO OK
ECHO An Error occurred in connecting to drive I:
:OK
```

The /CHECK qualifier performs error checking on active network service connections and is normally used only in batch procedures. It is used to check an active device and replace it if there are any network errors on the device. This command is usually followed by a check of the error level and USE/REPLACE if an error occurs. The following example illustrates this:

```
USE I:/CHECK
IF ERRORLEVEL == 0 GOTO OK
USE I: /REPLACE
ECHO An Error occurred in connecting to drive I:
:OK
```

Connecting to a Print Service

The USE command manages print service connections in the same manner as file services. Instead of redirecting a DOS drive letter to point to the network service, you use the logical printer names (LPT1:, 2:, and 3:). Once the connection is made, any application printing to this device will print to the network printer automatically. To connect to the printer service LA424, using LPT1, type:

```
C:\>USE LPT1: \\KENS\LA424
```

This command redirects printing designated for port LPT1: to the queue LA424 on the server KENS. Executing any print command or printing from an application to LPT1: will cause the document to print on the printer attached to the LA424 print queue. A network printer does not have to be defined as a print service to be used by a DOS client.

The USE command will also accept wildcards for connecting to the next available printer. Using a wildcard, you can attempt to connect to an open device, test for the success of the connection by checking the ERRORLEVEL, and reset the device if necessary. The /ENVIRON qualifier can also be used to trap the printer device in an environment variable. The following command connects to the first available printer and sets the variable PRTR with the device name:

```
C:\>USE LPT?: \\KENS\LA324 /ENV=PRTR
```

SET_PRT.BAT

SET_PRT.BAT is a handy tool for removing the toil and tedium from redirecting printers. The format of the command procedure requires the LPT number (without the letters LPT), the node, and the print queue name.

The PRTDEV environment variable is set in the batch program indicating the number of the redirected printer. The actual name of the variable is PRTDEV1, PRTDEV2, or PRTDEV3, depending on the local printer number. These variables are used by PRT.BAT to determine the default printer for print requests. (See Figure 6-8.)

Figure 6-8. SET_PRT.BAT

```
@echo off
if %1. == .goto error
if %2. == .goto error
if %3. == .goto error
set prtdev%1=%1

use lpt%1: \\%SERVER%\%3 /log/replace

goto end
:error
if %1. == .set err1=No Printer Number
if %2. == .set err2=No Server Name
if %3. == .set err3=No Queue Specified
echo ----------------------------------------
echo    Command Format: SET_PRT n1 Node Queue
echo
echo      n1 = Printer No (1,2, or 3)
echo      Node = Server Name (MFG)
```

Figure 6-8. SET_PRT.BAT (continued)

```
echo        Queue = Queue Name
echo
if %1. == .echo    %err1%
if %2. == .echo    %err2%
if %3. == .echo    %err3%
echo
:end
set err1=
set err2=
set err3=
```

Windows

Windows V3.x provides direct access to the network and its printers. Windows uses printer drivers for controlling different types of printers. Other drivers are used to establish access to the network and provide network services for Windows. Access to printer drivers and connections is controlled through the Windows Control Panel (CONTROL.EXE). Figure 6-9 shows a control-panel screen for a typical Windows client. In this example, the PC is not connected to the network, and the network button is grayed out.

To access a PATHWORKS network printer from within Windows, you must redirect the LPT port number to a specific network print queue, just as with any other DOS

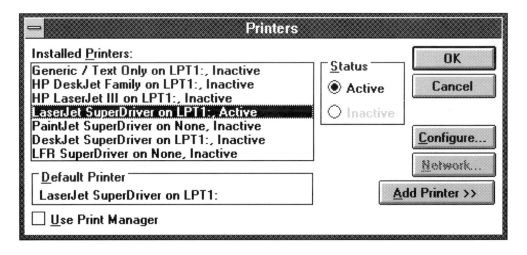

Figure 6-9. Windows V3.0 Printer Control Panel

application. Establishing a connection with the USE command before starting Windows provides your applications with the ability to print within Windows. The Control Panel Printer Network function may be used for this connection, but it is more time-consuming and error prone.

Figure 6-10 illustrates the Windows V3.1 Control Panel, which has improved support for network printers. Notice how the Connect window shows that LPT3: is connected to the network printer \\KENS\PCFS$HP_LASERJET. The network capabilities of each new version of Windows continues to improve.

Once the print queue connection is established, any Windows application can print to the printer. The connection will remain in force until the network connection is lost through a client reboot, by executing STOPNET.BAT, through a cable problem, or some other action. I normally redirect printer LPT3: to an HP LaserJet queue in the client start-up procedures (either STARTNET.BAT or AUTOEXEC.BAT). Since Windows uses the printer connections for the logical print device as the active printer, all of my Windows applications print correctly on the LaserJet, with no intervention. If you have multiple network printers that are regularly used by Windows, you can redirect up to three of them at once (LPT1:, LPT2:, and LPT3:). The Windows printer definition for each printer should point to the standard printer name, such as LPT2:. This makes accessing network printers through Windows as easy as connecting to DOS printers.

The NetPrint program on the accompanying disk provides a clear way of accessing print services. NETPRINT.WRI is the documentation file for the program.

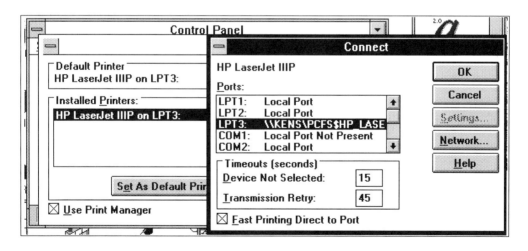

Figure 6-10. Windows V3.1 Printer Control Panel

USING NETWORK SERVICES

After you make a connection to a network service, it can be accessed by the client. This normally involves using a DOS command or application in the same manner as the application is used on a standalone workstation. Most users will not be aware that they are using a network service, unless they are directly using extended network features such as ACLs or extended print services, or they run into a security problem when trying to access a file.

File and Disk Services

The standard DOS methods of accessing a file or directory involve the same functions on a PATHWORKS service. This includes using most DOS commands, the shortcut names for directories (. and ..), and the wildcard characters (* and ?). For example, to change the current drive to a network service, either file or disk, type the drive letter and a colon (:), and press enter. To change to drive M:, type:

```
C:\>M:
```

The command for changing to a directory on a network service is also exactly like the command for a standalone PC and is accomplished with the DOS change directory (CD) command. This command has several interesting properties. If CD is executed with no parameters, it will display the current directory on the current drive:

```
M:\>CD
```

To change to another directory (\FILES) on the current drive, type:

```
M:\>CD \FILES
```

A feature of DOS that most users are unaware of is the ability to have a different current directory on multiple drives. This is very useful in a network environment where directory structures are normally several levels deep. The following example uses a service named DOC (P:) with subdirectories called BOOK\ONE and BOOK\TWO. A second service is also used, which is the personal service for the test user (M:) and has the subdirectories FILES and LETTERS:

```
M:\>CD LETTERS
M:\LETTERS>CD P:\BOOK\ONE
M:\LETTERS>COPY P:CH1.TXT CHP1.TXT
M:\LETTERS>COPY P:CH2.TXT CHP2.TXT
M:\LETTERS>CD P:\BOOK\TWO
M:\LETTERS>COPY P:CH3.TXT CHP3.TXT
```

The copy commands in this example use the P: prefix to the source file to indicate that the file is located on that drive. Because the CD command on the second line changed the directory on drive P: to BOOK\ONE, the files are pulled from this directory. This saves several keystrokes by shortening the parameters on the copy commands. It also makes it easy to verify where the files will come from by using the command:

```
M:\LETTERS>DIR P:CH*.TXT
```

This command will perform a directory list of drive P: and display any files that begin with CH and have a TXT extension. Using different default directories is also very useful when referring to multiple drives in batch procedures.

If you are using Windows, accessing a network drive is very simple. Note in Figure 6-11 that the network drives all have a network symbol in the icon.

Accessing files using Windows, via File Manager or another utility, functions the same as using DOS. This provides an excellent interface for users, because all file access is point and shoot.

Printing Files

There are a number of ways to print files over network printers. Once a printer service connection has been made, any method of printing to the device will work,

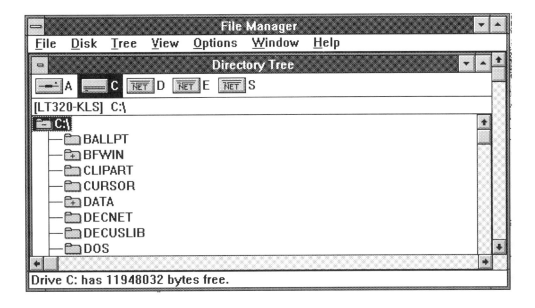

Figure 6-11. File Manager Network Drives

141

from either DOS or an application. Three of the handiest methods of printing are available to PATHWORKS clients at no additional cost, via the NET PRINT command included with PATHWORKS and the COPY command included with DOS. These are DOS COPY, NET PRINT, and PRINTQ. In addition to these programs, third-party tools and in-house programs are useful.

DOS COPY. The DOS COPY command is a handy utility for printing files. Any valid file-oriented device can be the target for this command. Specifying the printer device as the target causes the file to print on the appropriate printer. If the network printer is connected to device LPT3:, the following command prints MYFILE.TXT on the printer:

```
M:\>COPY MYFILE.TXT LPT3:
```

COPY is useful to quickly print a file or to test a printer without going through a print command. It can also be used in a batch file to print directly to the printer.

NET PRINT. This command is useful for printing files and managing printers from a client workstation. It allows you to print files on network printers and display information about print requests that are waiting to print.

NET PRINT is a useful addition to the DOS command set because of the flexibility it adds to the print process. The DOS PRINT command is very limited compared with NET PRINT and uses valuable client memory that is not released when printing is completed. DOS PRINT also has problems with the PATHWORKS drivers. NET PRINT executes from DOS in the same manner that the DOS PRINT command does but offers many more printing options. With NET PRINT, you can specify which device to print on, whether to print a header page, how many copies to print, whether to delete a previously entered print request, which form to use, and many other options.

As you can, NET PRINT offers many options for managing printers and print requests. It also works with PATHWORKS in a transparent manner to provide the client with a full-function printing environment. NET PRINT is also a useful tool for batch procedures.

Printing with NET PRINT is almost as simple as using PRINT. The only mandatory extra requirement is the addition of the print device name. NET PRINT also requires that the print device be a valid connection to a network printer. To print a file on LPT3, type:

```
C:\>NET PRINT MYFILE.TXT LPT3:
```

When NET PRINT is used to print a file, the file is immediately queued to the network printer and NET PRINT is released from memory. NET PRINT also understands network printer queues and other features of VMS. For instance, if your printer is located some distance from your office and you wish to be notified immediately when the file prints, you can have a message automatically sent to the system operator requesting that you be notified by phone:

```
C:\>NET PRINT MYFILE.TXT LPT3: /OPERATOR=(CALL_ME_@_X234)
```

There are also qualifiers to specify when the file prints, which form to use, and the number of copies to print. Other qualifiers trigger the printing of header or trailer pages, print specific notes on the header or trailer, and set the parameters as the default for future print requests.

To print a file with a burst page and cause the file to print after midnight, type:

```
C:\>NET PRINT MYFILE.TXT LPT3: /BURST /AFTER=TOMORROW
```

To print the same file and make the qualifiers the default, use the /SET qualifier:

```
C:\>NET PRINT MYFILE.TXT LPT3: /BURST /AFTER=TOMORROW /SET
```

After this command executes, any files printed on LPT3: will have a burst page printed before the file and will not print until midnight. The defaults are set only for LPT3:, not any other printer connections. If you normally use one printer with different parameters, you can connect the print queue to multiple devices, such as LPT1 and LPT3, each with a different set of defaults. The defaults can be returned to their normal state with:

```
C:\>NET PRINT LPT3: /SET
```

If you need to reset only one or two parameters, /* retains all parameters but the ones you change:

```
C:\>NET PRINT LPT3: /NAME=KEN /* /SET
```

The /COPIES qualifier will print multiple copies of your request:

```
C:\>NET PRINT MYFILE.TXT LPT3: /COPIES=2
```

Network printing often requires using different forms on a printer at different times of the day. This creates problems when there are several print requests in a queue that require more than one type of paper. The /FORM qualifier handles this by allowing a form request to be entered on the print request. Once a print job is entered requesting a particular form, VMS will not print the file until that form has been mounted. The form may be entered with the form number or name. If the system has a form named WIDE11x17, with a form number of 10, you can use:

```
C:\>NET PRINT MYFILE.TXT LPT3: /FORM=WIDE11X17
                 or
C:\>NET PRINT MYFILE.TXT LPT3: /FORM=10
```

NET PRINT will also allow you to override the default Device Control Library module used for a particular print request. The /SETUP parameter will notify the VMS print system to use the specified module. This is a slightly dangerous qualifier, because the library module is not verified until the job actually begins to print.

Another useful feature is the ability to print a range of pages. This is especially handy after your printer has jammed or when for some reason a certain page or pages are damaged. To reprint only pages 5 and 6, type:

```
C:\>NET PRINT MYFILE.TXT LPT3: /PAGES=(5,6)
```

Occasionally a problem will occur with a system, especially during off hours. If this happens and your print request is in the process of printing, the request may not complete. To prevent this from happening, especially if the request will print over-night or over a weekend, use:

```
C:\>NET PRINT MYFILE.TXT LPT3: /RESTART
```

An interesting feature of the NET PRINT command is the use of PRINTQ.EXE as the actual print module. Accessing PRINTQ directly is faster than executing NET PRINT because the NET module is not loaded first. For instance, the following command is equivalent to using NET PRINT:

```
C:\>PRINTQ MYFILE.TXT LPT3:
```

The batch programs in the following sections can help simplify printing operations for users and managers. These programs should serve as examples for the customization of your particular environment.

PRT.BAT. The PRT.BAT program serves as a front end to the PATHWORKS NET PRINT function. The example in Figure 6-12 uses the PRTDEV variable set in SET_PRT.BAT to specify the print device. If the print device is not specified on the command line, the default printer is the lowest printer currently redirected. If a client is connected to LPT2 and LPT3, the default printer will be LPT2. The file to be printed is specified on the command line as the second parameter.

Notice that the /header qualifier is included in Figure 6-12. Other qualifiers can be included to automatically change the operation of the print command. This can include adding headers, numbers, and any other qualifiers supported by NET PRINT.

Figure 6-12. PRT.BAT Program

```
@echo on
rem PRT.BAT
if %1. == .goto error
if not exist %1 goto nofile
set device=lpt%2
if not %2. == . goto devok
if not .%prtdev3% == .set device=lpt3
if not .%prtdev2% == .set device=lpt2
if not .%prtdev1% == .set device=lpt1
:devok

NET PRINT %1 %device%: /header %3 %4 %5 %6 %7 %8

goto end
:nofile
echo File %1 not found
goto end
:error
if %1. == . set nofile=No File
if %2. == . set err1=No Printer Number
echo --------------------       ---------
echo
echo   Command Format: PRT File Prtr
echo
echo     File = File Name
echo     Prtr = Printer No ((1,2,or 3)
echo -------------------------------------
echo
if %1. == .echo          %err1%
if %2. == .echo          %err2%
echo
echo -------------------------------------
:end
set err2=
set err1=
set device=
:end
```

LA324.BAT. Remember the batch file SET_PRT.BAT for redirecting printers? SET_PRT.BAT requires the input of the server and printer names, forcing the user always to enter the information, even if the user uses the same printer on the same server every day. The LA324.BAT program serves as a front end to SET_PRT.BAT, supplying both the server and printer names. The user simply enters LA324 to redirect printing LPT3: to the SYSTEM$LA324 printer. Creating a copy of this file for each printer on your network can greatly simplify the interface to printers for your users. (See Figure 6-13.)

Figure 6-13. LA324.BAT Program

```
@echo off
rem LA324.BAT
if %1. == ?.goto help
if %1. == .set _PRT=3

call SET_PRT%_PRT%mfg system$la324

goto end

:help
if %1. == .set err1=No Printer Number
echo ------------------------------------
echo
echo Command Format: La324 n1
echo
echo    n1 = Printer No (1,2,or 3)
echo ------------------------------------
echo
if %1. == .echo      %err1%
echo
echo ------------------------------------
:end
set err1=
set nonode=
set noq=
echo ------------------------------------
echo
echo Command Format:La324 n1
echo
echo    n1 = Printer No (1,2,or 3)
echo ------------------------------------
:end
set _prt=
```

Managing Print Queue Entries

NET PRINT also provides several options to control and display the status of entries in a print queue. It will display all the entries in all the print queues on a server, display only the entries in one queue, display only the entries for a user, display the status of one entry, and delete entries in a print queue.

To display all entries in all print queues on a server, type:

```
C:\>NET PRINT \\KENS
```

To display all entries in the print queue LASER, type:

```
C:\>NET PRINT \\KENS\LASER
```

You can display the entries for a queue by using the DOS print device:

```
C:\>NET PRINT LPT3:
```

Frequently, a user will be concerned with only his or her print requests and may not want to look at other users' entries in a queue, particularly if the queue has many entries. This is accomplished by specifying:

```
C:\>NET PRINT LPT3: /USER=KEN
```

This command shows all the entries in the queue connected to LPT3: for the user KEN. If KEN only wanted to find out the status of entry 10, he would type:

```
C:\>NET PRINT LPT3: /10
```

MANIPULATING FILES

Transferring files between a client and a server is a straightforward and simple task. A user on a client workstation issues a command from the operating system or program, requesting information from a drive that is redirected to a server drive. As far as the client programs are concerned, the server drive is simply another drive on the client.

The standard DOS COPY and XCOPY commands can be used to copy files on the server and to or from a client. As with the CD command, these standard DOS commands perform the same functions on network drives as on a local PC.

COPY is the traditional command for moving files from one place to another or creating a second copy of a file with a different name. It is an internal DOS command and has been around since the earliest versions of DOS, with a few enhancements along the way. COPY is most efficient when only one or a small number of small files must be copied. To copy C:\TEST.TXT to the network drive M:\, type:

```
M:\> COPY C:\TEST.TXT M:\
```

This could also be abbreviated, because M:\ is the current directory and drive:

```
M:\> COPY C:\TEST.TXT .
```

DOS V3.3 introduced the XCOPY utility. This program is an external utility (.EXE file) and is located with the other DOS commands, usually in the DOS directory. XCOPY is much more powerful than COPY and offers many unique options, such as the ability to copy an entire directory structure and to copy only files that have been modified. XCOPY is usually more efficient than COPY because it uses the PC's memory as a buffer during the copy process. When numerous files must be copied or COPY does not provide the necessary features, use the XCOPY command.

One of the most frequently used XCOPY options is the /S parameter for coping an entire directory and its subdirectories. This is handy when you want to copy numerous directories and files from a client or server directory to another drive and create the same directory structure. For example:

```
M:\> XCOPY C:\DATA M:\ /S
```

This command copies the DATA directory and all of its subdirectories to drive M:. XCOPY also provides a quick way to copy a subset of a directory to a new drive or directory.

The /M parameter is also very useful for networks. I used a simple batch command called COPYBOOK.BAT to backup the files for this book from my laptop to a network drive. Without the /M parameter, the command takes about 30 minutes to execute as it copies every file. When /M is added, the command takes only 3 to 5 minutes and copies only the modified or new files. The new version of this command is:

```
XCOPY C:\DATA\BOOKS\PW E:\BOOKS\PW /V /m
```

The /V parameter causes XCOPY to verify the files after the copy command has completed.

Other Methods of Copying Files

Sometimes it is necessary to transfer files between two clients, from a server to a client, or from a client to or from a node that is not a PATHWORKS client. One of PATHWORKS' often hidden and very powerful features is the ability to work with other systems. Users on any DECnet node that is capable of running a FAL program can copy files from or to the node, delete files on the remote node, and print files on a printer at the remote node.

The next two sections cover the DOS client versions of NFT and FAL. NFT and FAL are fully documented in Digital's *PATHWORKS for DOS — DECnet User's Guide* and *DECnet Network Management Guide*.

NFT. NFT is the Network File Transfer program for DOS clients that allows them to remotely access files and printers on a DECnet node that is not a PATHWORKS server. NFT is a powerful program with a rich command set that provides facilities for combining files, copying files, deleting files, listing files, displaying files, running remote command files, printing files, and defining and displaying access control information.

The NFT program, NFT.EXE, is a Windows program and a DOS program. NFTNOWIN.EXE is a smaller DOS-only version of the same program. NFT is a full-featured Windows program that offers traditional Windows features such as cut and paste and multitasking. When executed from DOS, NFT commands can also be entered interactively or from the DOS command line. This provides a rather unique ability for a DOS program to run interactively from DOS, from a DOS batch file, or in a Windows environment. When NFT runs from the DOS command level, the DOS error variable, ERRORLEVEL, is set to 0 if the command is successful or 1 if the command fails. The ERRORLEVEL is usually checked when NFT is executed from a batch file. NFT can also take advantage of the redirection feature of DOS and execute a number of commands from an input file. The example below shows all three methods of executing NFT from DOS:

```
Single Command from DOS
        C:\> NFT SHOW KENS::

Interactively
        C:\> NFT
                NFT> SHOW KENS::
                NFT>
Redirected Command Input
        C:\> NFT <SHOW.TXT


SHOW.TXT Contents
        SHOW KENS::
```

Figure 6-14 shows an NFT Windows screen. The Windows screen is easy to use and is recommended for interactive access to other nodes if you are running in a Windows environment. The DOS level of NFT is also very useful when a series of commands must be executed repeatedly, when NFT commands must be executed from within a batch procedure that also does other tasks, or when you are working in DOS and must execute an NFT task quickly. The Windows interface for NFT that is shipped with PATHWORKS V4.1 is vastly improved over the 4.0 version. The interface is much nicer and supports the drag-and-drop method of copying files. In Figure 6-14, a file can be moved from one client to another by simply pointing at the file with the mouse, holding down the left button, and dragging the pointer to the destination directory.

NFT commands for the DOS version are straightforward and, in many cases, are similar to DOS and VMS commands. All NFT commands can be abbreviated to the first three characters. Remote file specifications must include the node specification, consisting of the node name and the username and password, if required. The node name may be either the actual node name or the node address (e.g., 1.200). The username and password should be included in quotation marks, and the entire specification must be followed by a double colon. If you omit the password, the command will prompt for a password. The next example shows a file specification for the directory USER on node KENS:

```
KENS"JOE password"::[USER]
```

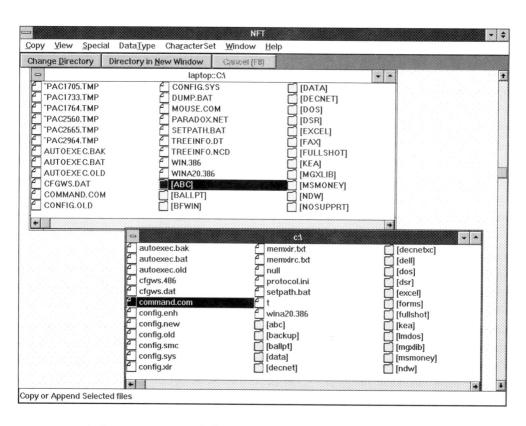

Figure 6-14. NFT Windows V3.0 (NFT for PATHWORKS V4.1)

NFT offers an alternative to entering the full node and file specification by using the SET command to temporarily record the information in memory. Once the SET command has been used, simply use the node name to access the remote node. You can also enter node specifications through NCP to permanently record the information in the NCP database. The following example shows the use of the NFT SET command and how the data stored with SET is used with the standard NFT command:

```
NFT> SET KENS"JOE password"::[USER]

NFT> DIRECTORY KENS::
Directory of: KENS"JOE password"::[USER]

LOGIN.COM;1 2              11-25-91       14:05:00
TEST.COM;1  3             11-12-91       11:02:00
```

When a file specification is entered without the full node and account information, NFT checks the NFT session and then the NCP database. If the information is not found within the current session or the NCP database, NFT assumes the remote node does not require secure access and attempts the connection.

You can change access information for a node by reissuing the SET command with the new information or entering any other NFT command for the same node with different access information. This will automatically change the temporary access information held by NFT.

If the file specification references a DOS file or directory, you must use the standard DOS file specification (Drive:Path\Name.Extension). The following command illustrates the file specifications for both local and remote files, including a DOS and a VMS file:

```
NFT> COPY C:\DOS\INFO.TXT KENS"JOE"::[USERS]INFO.TXT
```

When NFT encounters a file name of more than eight characters, and the destination node is a DOS client, NFT truncates the name to eight characters to conform to the DOS file name restrictions. File names must be in the format of the node on which they reside. In other words, if the file is copied to a VMS node, it must meet the VMS file specification requirements.

Some commands allow the specification of more than one input file. These files include the Append, Copy, and Type commands. Each of these commands allows up to 10 input files in a file list. Each file in the list must be separated by a comma and may not contain wildcards. If a node, device, directory, or file type is included with a file in a list, the information becomes the default for any subsequent files.

To copy a file from a DOS client to a VAX node named KENS, type:

```
C:\> NFT COPY CONFIG.SYS KENS"JOE"DKB300:[JOE]
```

To print a remote file on a remote printer, use the command:

```
C:\> NFT PRINT KENS"JOE"DKB300:[JOE]CONFIG.SYS KENS::
```

To print a remote file on a local printer, the COPY/PRINT command cannot be used. The COPY command will work if the DOS print device is used as the target file, as in a normal DOS COPY command. If the local printer is LPT3:, the following command copies the file CONFIG.SYS to the printer:

```
C:\> NFT COPY KENS"JOE"DKB300:[JOE]CONFIG.SYS LPT3:
```

FAL. FAL is the File Access Listener program shipped with PATHWORKS. FAL is used on a DOS client to listen to and execute remote requests for file access. It can run as a single task under DOS or with other programs in the Windows environment. DOS and Windows versions are contained in the FAL.EXE program. FALNOWIN.EXE is included for users who are not using Windows. It is smaller than FAL.EXE and takes less disk space.

FAL can be executed from the Job Spawner or from DOS by using the C:\FAL command. It can also be executed directly from the Program Manager or File Manager within Windows.

Before running FAL from the Job Spawner, install it in the DECnet Object database (DECOBJ.DAT). This should have been done as part of the installation procedure if you ran the PATHWORKS for DOS configuration procedure. Use the C:\NCP LIST KNOWN OBJECTS command to determine whether FAL is correctly entered in the database. If it is there, the LIST command will show the task name of FAL and an object number of 17. If FAL is not entered correctly, use the following command to add the entry:

```
C:\> NCP DEFINE OBJECT FAL NUMBER 17 FILE FAL.EXE (OPTIONS).
```

OPTIONS represents the parameters for the FAL command.

The following command loads FAL with error checking for overwriting files and specifies that all requests be recorded in the file FALL.LOG:

```
C:\> FAL /ERROR /LOG:FALL.LOG
```

Running FAL under Windows provides the ability to execute it as a background task and allow the user to continue with normal work. When FAL is running in this manner, it is usually minimized but still collects information on connections. Figure 6-15 shows the FAL log window.

PERMIT. Occasionally you must move a file from one PC to another, and neither user has access to a common server drive, or you do not wish to move the file to the server first. This requires a connection from one PC to the other to directly copy the file. PERMIT provides a means to make this happen, by allowing another client workstation to connect to your local client disk as a file server. Only one client can connect at a time.

When PERMIT is executed, it waits for a client to connect to the service. After the connection is removed, PERMIT returns to DOS. To allow the node JOHN to copy a file from the C:\DATA\WP directory on node KLS, use these commands:

```
From node KLS:
C:\>PERMIT COPYKLS=C:\DATA\WP /R JOHN

From node JOHN:
C:\>USE L: \\KLS\COPYKLS
```

This example allows node JOHN to connect to node KLS and read files in the C:\DATA\WP directory structure, including any subdirectories. If * is used in place of a username, any user can access the service. Once the connection is disconnected, PERMIT will terminate and return control to the operating system.

When a client connects to another node with PERMIT, the drive on the client is accessible like any other network drive. DOS and Windows programs and commands can access and create files in the normal manner. The access restrictions established with PERMIT will limit other users' abilities to read, write, and create files on the disk or directory. The drive and directory offered as a service by PERMIT can also limit access to certain disks or portions of a directory. The example offers the C:\DATA\WP directory as a service, allowing the user JOHN to read any files in this directory or its subdirectories. Files located on parent directories (C:\DATA\) are not accessible or visible to JOHN. Figures 6-16 and 6-17 illustrate accessing a remote node from DOS and from Windows, respectively.

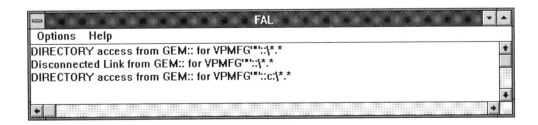

Figure 6-15. FAL Log Window

Figure 6-16. Using PERMIT and DIR

```
C:\> DIR L:
Volume in drive L is SCSI-KLS
Directory of L:\

ANYWHERE         <DIR>              10-08-91 8:33a
CLIPART          <DIR>              10-08-91 8:34a
CSERVE           <DIR>              10-08-91 8:36a
DOS              <DIR>              10-08-91 9:17a
DECNET           <DIR>              10-08-91 9:01a
DATA             <DIR>              10-08-91 9:19a
DESIGNER         <DIR>              10-08-91 9:21a
DIET             <DIR>              10-08-91 9:21a
EXCEL            <DIR>              10-08-91 9:23a
FAX              <DIR>              10-08-91 9:25a
WW               <DIR>              11-11-91 5:38p
INSTALL          <DIR>              10-08-91 9:26a
MATH             <DIR>              10-08-91 9:26a
NDW              <DIR>              10-08-91 9:27a
FULLSHOT         <DIR>              01-02-92 1:53p
PCLFONTS         <DIR>              10-08-91 9:29a
PRODPACK         <DIR>              10-08-91 9:29a
TEST              915               09-19-91 12:07p
CW               <DIR>              11-08-91 8:07p
UTIL             <DIR>              10-08-91 9:34a
WINDOWS          <DIR>              10-08-91 9:34a
TMP              <DIR>              10-18-91 3:54p
WINUTIL          <DIR>              10-26-91 10:52a
WINSPT           <DIR>              11-01-91 3:13p
MLSA             <DIR>              01-04-92 7:01p
MAIL             <DIR>              01-11-92 5:33p
    26 file(s) 915 bytes
    6825984 bytes free
```

Figure 6-17 shows the Windows File Manager displaying a drive from another PC using PERMIT. Notice that the drive name is SCSI-KLS, which is the disk label for the 80-MB SCSI drive on that PC.

The drive accessed via PERMIT acts exactly like a standard file service. These two examples show how easy it is to work with a file on another system. The only problem I have found to date is that Windows File Manager will not copy a file to the PERMIT drive, even though the access is CRW (create, read, write). The DOS copy commands work fine. Windows will allow you to copy a file from that service to a local drive or to the server.

SAVING AND RELOADING NETWORK CONNECTIONS

NET SAVE stores current network connections that may be restored later with NET LOAD. The user can temporarily change network connections after a NET SAVE command and then restore the connections by a simple NET LOAD command.

The following example saves the connection configuration in the file CONFIG, and then resets the connection to drive E: via the USE command. After ANYPROGRAM runs, the connections are reset by running NET LOAD:

```
C:\>NET SAVE CONFIG
C:\>USE E:\\KENS\MYDRIVE%JOHN *
C:\>ANYPROGRAM
C:\>NET LOAD CONFIG
```

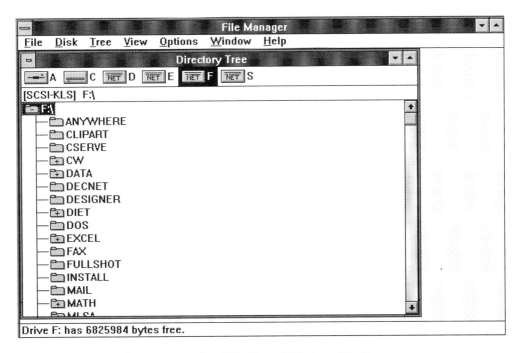

Figure 6-17. Using PERMIT and Windows File Manager

NET PAUSE and NET CONTINUE perform functions similar to the NET SAVE and NET LOAD commands. NET PAUSE will suspend the network connections to all file or print services. You cannot disconnect only a particular service with NET PAUSE.

NET PAUSE and NET CONTINUE use the parameters DRDR for file services and PRPR for print services. To halt all print connections, type:

```
C:\>NET PAUSE PRDR
```

Once this command executes, all print devices can be used for local printers or redirected to other network printers. To re-establish the same print services, type:

```
C:\>NET CONTINUE PRDR
```

One major difference between NET PAUSE/NET CONTINUE and NET SAVE/NET LOAD is how NET PAUSE controls client connections. When NET PAUSE is executed, it actually suspends client connections for the specified services. This means that the services will be unavailable to the client until NET CONTINUE is executed. NET SAVE will store all connection information but will not suspend the connections. One advantage that NET PAUSE has is the ability to suspend only file services or only print services. For most uses, NET SAVE/NET LOAD will be the best alternative, unless you need to temporarily halt and then restore print services.

PATHWORKS V4.1 includes an updated USE command with support for saving and reloading network connections. The /SAVE and /LOAD options perform the same function as NET SAVE and NET LOAD. The following examples illustrate how these two commands are used:

```
C:\>USE MYCONNN.SAV /SAVE /LOG
C:\> Other Commands
C:\> USE MYCONNN.SAV /LOAD /LOG
```

The USE /SAVE and USE /LOAD commands will work even if the network is stopped after the USE /SAVE command is executed.

SETTING CLIENT DATE AND TIME FROM A SERVER

The NETTIME command will set the date and time for the client from the file server specified on the command line or the first available file server. This command is useful for synchronizing the date and time for all clients on the network. It is usually called from the STARTNET.BAT program on the client PC. It is also frequently called from the AUTOUSER.BAT program to ensure that the time is set each time the user logs in. This is important for sites that leave their machines on and do not reboot frequently.

The time is also displayed as the command executes. You can suppress this by redirecting the output to the NULL file:

```
C:\>NETTIME KENS > NULL
```

To set the time from the first available server, type:

```
C:\>NETTIME
```

When the time is set in this manner, at least one server must be listed in the DECnet database on the client and must have the MS-NET bit set with NCP. If you have multiple servers, each server must be listed in this database for the client to be able to set the time from the servers.

SETTIME.BAT is a simple procedure to set the time for a workstation from the server. SETTIME.BAT obtains the time from the server named MFG. SETTIME.BAT should be called from LOGON.BAT or AUTOUSER.BAT to synchronize the workstation time with the server each time a user logs in:

```
@ECHO off
REM SETTIME.BAT
NETTIME KENS
```

SENDING AND RECEIVING MESSAGES

The BCAST command sends a broadcast message to a client or list of clients over the network. The message will interrupt other screen activity on the client machine and will appear in its place, prompting the user to clear the message.

BCAST is useful for notifying users of an important event. You can send messages such as "Let's go to lunch at 11:45," or "The system is going down at 4:00 p.m." It may also be used in programs and batch files to notify users when a program's status changes.

To send the message "Let's go to lunch at 11:45" to the client user John, type:

```
C:\>BCAST JSMITH LETS GO TO LUNCH AT 11:45
```

The next command sends the same message to the nodes listed in the ENGDPT.DIS file:

```
C:\>BCAST ENGDPT LETS GO TO LUNCH AT 11:45
```

Note that the .DIS extension, which indicates a distribution file, is not specified on the command line. An example of a distribution file is illustrated below. The maximum number of entries in a distribution file is 200:

```
ENGDPT.DIS
  john
  joeS
  .
  .
  .
  sams
```

The RCV and TRCV commands are TSR programs that are used to receive and read messages. RCV is used on systems using DECnet, and TRCV is used for systems using TCP/IP. RCV and/or TRCV must be loaded for a client to receive BCAST messages. These commands can be used to add group names and change the way messages are stored and displayed on the client. To load RCV, type:

```
C:\>RCV
```

You can restrict message receipts to only the server:

```
C:\>RCV /R:0
```

To only receive messages from other clients, type:

```
C:\>RCV /R:1
```

To only receive messages from other clients and servers, type:

```
C:\>RCV /R:2
```

The /T: qualifier can restrict messages by their destination. To restrict messages to only those sent to you, type:

```
C:\>RCV /T:0
```

To only receive messages sent to all users, type:

```
C:\>RCV /T:3
```

You can also restrict messages sent to you and to a group by using the /A qualifier to specify the group name. The group name cannot be a node name used on the network. The name can be up to 16 characters. For example:

```
C:\>RCV /A:ENGINEERING
```

After RCV has been loaded, any messages sent to your node and available for reception will be displayed on your screen. The exception to this rule is when you are in graphics mode, such as Windows or a CAD or Paint program. When this happens, RCV will beep and store the messages, up to a default total of 10 messages. To display stored messages, type:

```
C:\>RCV /D
```

The screen will display the message and a broadcast header. Press Alt-N to view the next message or Alt-Q to quit.

CHANGING FILE ATTRIBUTES

The NET ATTRIB command is used to set, display, and change ACL and RMS protections. NET ATTRIB is useful when you need to set or access information about file protections in DOS. This is particularly necessary when you have just created or copied a file and other users cannot access the file. It is also handy when a file must be protected after creation or copying.

Be very careful with the parameters for NET ATTRIB. This command is picky about the parameter format. The command C:\>NET ATTRIB *.bat will not work, whereas the command C:\>NET ATTRIB M:*.bat will work correctly. The entire path must be specified.

NET ATTRIB is useful for managing file and directory security from a client without your having to log into the server as an interactive user. For simple security, it is a vast improvement over the DOS ATTRIB command. The following command establishes the RMS security for MYFILE, located on the M: drive. The second command displays RMS protection information for the same file:

```
C:\>NET ATTRIB M:\MYFILE /PROT=(S:RWED,O:RWED,G:R,W:)
C:\>NET ATTRIB M:\MYFILE
```

Protection attributes are determined for four categories of users:

System (S)	Users with system access.
Owner (O)	Users with the same user identification code (UIC) as the owner of the file or directory.
Group (G)	All users who belong to the same group as the owner.
World (W)	All users.

159

Privileges are established for each file or directory by using the characteristics listed below:

Read (R)	Allows users to read the file and display directory information about it.
Write (W)	Provides write access to the file or directory.
Execute (E)	Allows the user to execute the file. If used on a directory, it allows the user to execute all files in the directory. It will not allow directory or wildcard searches for files in the directory.
Delete (D)	Allows delete access.

Setting ACLs on files and directories can be a time-consuming task if you must log into the server each time. NET ATTRIB provides an easy way to accomplish this from the client. The command below sets an access control entry (ACE) for a directory named DOC on the M: drive. This allows members of the group TECHWRTR to access files and subdirectories of the M:\DOC directory:

```
C:\>NET ATTRIB M:\DOC TECHWRTR /ACCESS=WRITE
```

For more information on ACLs and how they apply to files, services, and directories, see Chapter 13, "Network Security."

CHANGING PASSWORDS FROM THE CLIENT

Network passwords must be changed occasionally, either when the change is forced by the server or requested by the user. The most effective way to manage this is to have the user change the password with the NET PASSWORD command. To change the password for KLS on KENS:

```
M:\>NET PASSWORD \\KENS\KLS
Old password:
New password:
Verification:
```

The user enters the existing password, the new password, and then the new password again to verify its correctness.

The SET_PWD.BAT program uses the PASSWORD program to request the server name and username before feeding this information to the NET PASSWORD command. If the user has logged into the server, and the server name and username are currently loaded into environment variables, PASSWORD is skipped and the existing variables are used:

```
@ECHO off
if not %server%# == # goto pw
if not %user%# == # goto pw
goto ok
:pw
 password

:ok
net password \\%server%%%user%
```

This simple program insulates the user from the complexity and syntax of the NET PASSWORD command.

NET HELP displays information on function and syntax for the most commonly used client commands.

CHAPTER 7

Network Printers

Printers are a part of the network puzzle often placed on the back burner. They do not receive the planning and care the rest of the network does. This lack of planning is compounded by the fact that the printer is one of the most used devices on the network.

Managing and installing printers on any LAN can be one of the most trying experiences imaginable. To successfully install a printer involves many of the same issues as installing the network itself: cabling, software, and nonstandard items from mail-order dealers. If the printer is the first or second printer installed on your system, it can be doubly frustrating, because you may not have a standard printer configuration to test.

Printers and print queues seem to grow by magic on a computer system. Every user wants or needs access to one or more types of printers. To further compound the system manager's problems, everyone needs access to printers *now*. Periods of deadlock can occur during various times of the month or when critical projects are due.

User demand for printers and the normal day-to-day problems of managing a computer system can lead to the fire-fighting method of managing printers. Printers and queues are added to the new system on demand, with each new printer or queue adding some new capability. Soon there are several printers on the network, with many different configurations of queues and cabling.

To overcome this problem, you should plan and manage your printer resources in the same manner as other system resources. By carefully defining printer requirements, designing and testing command procedures, and using the proper management tools, you will find that managing printers becomes a simple task and not a multiheaded monster.

This chapter will focus on the physical (hardware) and interface (software) issues having to do with printers, cabling, print queues, LAT, and print servers.

PHYSICAL CONNECTIONS

Unfortunately, every printer used on a computer system requires a physical connection to the system via some type of cable. This can be both the simplest connection of any device possible and one of the most difficult tasks of installing the entire network.

Most minicomputers, including Digital's, use serial or parallel connections for printers. Serial printers are by far the most difficult, because different printers may use different cable configurations depending on the manufacturer. Documentation for most printers and many software packages contain sketches for building printer cables for various printers. Building printer cables can be a very time-consuming process, especially for printers that are not popular or do not use standard cables.

Digital printers use industry-standard cables for connecting printers. Desktop printers use either serial or parallel cables, while print servers connect directly to the Ethernet network. Because of these standard connections, connecting any Digital printer to the network is a simple task.

One major advantage PATHWORKS has over other PC networks is the support from the DECdirect technical support staff for users trying to match non-Digital serial printers and the physical printer connections for their network. Connecting a printer can be as simple as determining the connection on your printer (serial with a DB25 connector, or serial with a DB9 connector), determining to which device you wish to connect (VAX, PC, or DECserver), and calling the DECdirect hot line. The support staff will most likely provide you with a part number for ordering from the sales staff at DECdirect. I am not trying to sell Digital hardware and cabling. However, you will miss a very valuable resource if you overlook the hot line service.

Digital cables are trouble-free and use modular connectors, similar to the jack used on a telephone. Some third-party suppliers will also provide standard Digital cables if you know the Digital part number.

When planning the installation of printers for your system, use the following guidelines and plan ahead. List the types of printers you will install, the quantity, and where they will connect to the system (both the physical location and network location). Then consult with your system supplier or DECdirect to determine the cable and adapter requirements. If your printers are from a vendor other than Digital and have not been installed on your system, you should obtain the suggested adapters and cable and *test* them on your system. If the system will be installed at the same time as the printers, consider ordering connectors for all your printers from one vendor, with an agreement that you may return the unused adapters.

Because a variety of network applications may use the printers on your network, make sure that all printers are popular devices, such as HP or Epson America Inc. printers, and that they are supported by mainstream PC and VMS applications. The list of applications should include those you are planning to run on the network now and ones that may be added in the future. Be sure to budget ample time in your project schedule for installing and fine-tuning all printers. Do not underestimate the amount of time required to configure your network software to properly work with your printers.

Server Attachment

You typically install printers directly to the file server, unless you purchase additional hardware or software to allow PCs to service your printers. (In this case, the PC becomes a printer server.) Because of the design of the systems most frequently used in a PATHWORKS network, this may be possible on some servers, but it is not the most desirable method.

Because of the design of the VAX in particular and Digital networks in general, you can connect devices such as printers, terminals, and modems to the network in a variety of ways. Attaching printers to a terminal server or client machine provides several advantages. Printers are typically character-oriented devices that accept data one character at a time. This causes the device controlling the printer to monitor the printer and continually feed additional characters to it, often in a start/stop manner. If this connection is to a server, the overhead of managing one or two heavily used printers can slow down the server. A major benefit of PATHWORKS is the performance improvements derived from offloading the printing from the server. The server queue will quickly offload the job to the terminal server or client machine, which will actual manage the print device.

Distributed printing capability is built into VMS via the use of LAT and/or DECnet. Because it is built into the operating system, Digital's distributed printing is very efficient, reliable, and robust. If your installation is running minicomputer software on the server, the printers used by this software are also managed by the same facilities as the network printers, because they are all network printers. By managing the network printers, you have managed printing for all applications using the network.

VAX Attachment

Printers may be attached directly to a VAX server if the VAX has open serial ports. The VAX will typically not directly support a parallel printer without the installation of a special card or the use of a serial-to-parallel converter. (Some of these are very unpredictable.) The MicroVAX series (3100, 3300, etc.) has several built-in ports, which are normally used for the console device, modem, and possibly a printer. Other machines (e.g., VAX 4000 Model 200 and VAX 4000 Model 300) have only one serial port for the console and will not support a printer without installation of an additional card.

Use care in attaching any device other than the console directly to a server. As mentioned in the preceding section, any directly attached character-oriented device that is heavily used will degrade the performance of the server.

To attach a printer to the VAX, you will need a cable with either a DB25 or modified modular jack (MMJ) connector on the end for the VAX. The MMJ is the standard port on Digital devices, including the VAX. There is some discussion from Digital about moving to standard RJ45 jacks, but this has not happened as of mid-1992. I expect this change to happen in the near future.

If you are connecting a Digital printer, you should consult your system vendor or the Digital Electronic Store Technical Support department. Generally speaking, any serial printer can be connected to a server or terminal server via a direct connection or using an adapter. The H8571-E adapter is a 25-pin serial connector that will work with the HP LaserJet series and other printers such as the Okidata Corp. line. This adapter is a convenient tool that connects to the printer via the 25-pin connection and to standard Digital office cable via a modular jack. The H8571-E has internal crossovers to match the printer with the standard office cable. Other similar adapters have different internal configurations to match other printers.

Client Attachment

Installing printers on client workstations is a fairly simple task, depending on how the printer is configured. A client printer may support only the client or be offered as a network printer. The client may also be used as a print server only, supporting multiple network printers.

Most PCs will support three parallel printers and from one to four serial printers. DOS supports external devices such as printers through device names. A device name is usually three characters long and may contain an additional digit to indicate a particular numbered device. All device names end with a colon (:). Examples of printer devices are LPT1:, which indicates the first logical printer; LPT3:, for the third logical printer; and COM1:, for the first serial device. Table 7-1 lists the common print device names.

Table 7-1. DOS Print Device Names

Device Name	Description
PRN:	Default Parallel Printer
LPT1:	Logical Printer Number 1
LPT2:	Logical Printer Number 2
LPT3:	Logical Printer Number 3
COM1:	Serial Port Number 1
COM2:	Serial Port Number 2
COM3:	Serial Port Number 3
COM4:	Serial Port Number 4

PRN: always references the first parallel printer attached to the PC. Any time you print to PRN:, the file will print on this printer, even if you have redirected printers to a network device. COM1: and COM2: are also physical device names, pointing to the first and second serial ports. Printing to either COM1: or COM2: will send output to these devices.

The LPT port names are slightly different from the other device names. LPTn: always points to a logical, or virtual, print device. LPT1: may point to a parallel printer, serial printer, or network printer.

DOS and PATHWORKS provide programs for connecting printers to the LPT printer devices. The DOS MODE command is used to establish the connection between the LPT name and a serial printer attached to a COM port on the PC. If you have multiple parallel printer ports on your PC, they will also use the LPT1:, LPT2:, or LPT3: name. The LPT ports are also used by PATHWORKS to connect to network print queues. The PATHWORKS command:

```
C:\>USE LPT1: \\MYVAX\LASER$QUEUE
```

will connect port LPT1: to the print queue LASER$QUEUE. Any program that prints to LPT1: will have its output sent to this queue.

The DOS MODE command is useful when dealing with local client printers. MODE is a neat little program that sets parameters for printers, serial ports, and the PC display. It is useful in this situation to map a logical printer name to a serial port. The command:

```
C:\>MODE LPT1:=COM1:
```

maps the LPT1: device to the serial port COM1:. Printing to either the LPT1: or COM1: ports will print to the serial printer attached to COM1:.

Cabling

DOS printers use either parallel or serial communications. A parallel printer is the simplest connection, attaching to either the built-in parallel connector or the parallel connector on the display adapter of the PC. Most parallel printers used on PCs adhere to the Centronics standard, which specifies a standard cable to connect from the PC to the printer. A few printers may still adhere to the Dataproducts Corp. standard, but this is very infrequent. A parallel cable for one Centronics-type printer will work on any other Centronics-type parallel printer.

Serial printers are a little more difficult to get up and running. Any two serial printers from different vendors may or may not use the same cable. When connecting a serial printer to a DOS client, you should check with the printer vendor to determine the proper cable. If this is not possible, try a local computer store or arm yourself with several different printer adapters from Digital. A little trial and error should prove successful.

Once the printer is connected to the PC, you should test the printer before proceeding. Use the DOS COPY command to print a small file to the LPT1: port (or LPT2: or LPT3: port, if used). The command:

```
C:\>COPY AUTOEXEC.BAT LPT1:
```

will print the AUTOEXEC.BAT file on the parallel printer attached to the first parallel port. The command:

```
C:\>COPY AUTOEXEC.BAT COM1:
```

will print the same file on a serial printer attached to the first serial port.

If the printer does not print, first make sure the printer is plugged in and turned on, and then check the cable. Ninety percent of printer problems are caused by cable/adapter configurations. Make sure connections on both the printer and computer are tight. If the printer still does not print, verify that the cable is correct or try a different cable if the printer is a serial printer.

Software Support

The most important part of choosing and installing a PC printer is determining the printers supported by the software you plan to use. Most PC packages will support the popular printers but may have problems with some lesser-known brands that may or may not correctly emulate a popular printer.

The process of selecting an appropriate printer is much simpler today than it was three or four years ago. Most printers will support one of several standards, including the HP PCL command sets, IBM Proprinters, and Adobe Systems Inc.'s PostScript language. These are the most popular printer languages for today's software. Almost every reliable software package supports these printers as routine installation choices.

Table 7-2 lists several Digital printers and the industry-standard drivers that support them. One or more of these drivers are standard with most software packages. Packages designed to run on VMS or ULTRIX systems will also tend to support the Digital printers and/or the industry standard. Table 7-2 can be viewed from two perspectives. If you have an IBM Proprinter and your application supports only Digital printers, choose the driver for the LA70 or LA75. Conversely, if your PC application supports only the Proprinter and you have an LA70 or LA75, use the Proprinter driver.

Table 7-2. Digital Printer Emulations

Industry Standard	Digital Printer
IBM Proprinter	LA70, LA75, and LA75 PLUS
IBM Graphics Printer	LA210
IBM Proprinter 24	LA424
HP PaintJet	LJ250, LJ252
Adobe PostScript	DEClaser 2100 with PostScript cartridge, DEClaser 2150, DEClaser 2250, DEClaser 3250, DECjet 1000 and 2000, turbo PrintServer (Standard emulation is HP LaserJet.)

Terminal Server Connection

In the VAX world, printers are normally connected to a device called a terminal server. A terminal server manages and controls terminals, printers, and modems, as well as other serial devices. The server is connected to the network cable either directly or through a transceiver, and it can be located anywhere along the network. Devices are attached to the server by either a DB25 connector or an MMJ.

Servers are available with full modem control (with DB25 connectors) or with only the XON/XOFF protocol for software control. If only printers, PCs, or terminals will be connected to a server, modem control is probably not required.

The server functions as a physical attachment point for devices and a front-end processor that offloads control of the attached devices from the server. It also allows a device to easily access multiple servers and other computers, and in the case of printers, provides a simple means of connecting a printer to the network for use by all computers on the network. Figure 7-1 shows a typical network using a DECserver to attach several printers to a network of PC, VAX, and ULTRIX machines.

Figure 7-1 illustrates a typical system with both a VMS and an ULTRIX server. Users on the network can access the printers attached to the DECserver 90L via PATHWORKS from a PC or from applications running on either the ULTRIX or the VMS server. In short, any device on the network can access any printers attached to terminal servers any place on the network. Terminal servers can also be located in user areas or other areas where the printers are used. They connect directly to the network cable like any other network node.

Printer Servers

If the printer is available to other users on the network, LAT or DECnet will be used to communicate between the printer and server. The printer will interact with the network in the same manner as a terminal server printer, offloading print management functions to the client machine.

Use care in making client printers available to network users, unless the client is used exclusively as a printer server. By offloading the print management chores from the server, the client then assumes the role of managing the printers. If the machine is also used as workstation, either the client user or the printers will suffer performance degradation.

Using a client workstation as a printer server offers a cost-effective method for managing printers, by using a low-cost PC to handle printers and offload more expensive terminal servers or VMS servers. Printer servers are also very useful for locating two or three printers in a department or work area. No cable runs are required, except for connecting the client workstation to the network, and connecting the printers to the client.

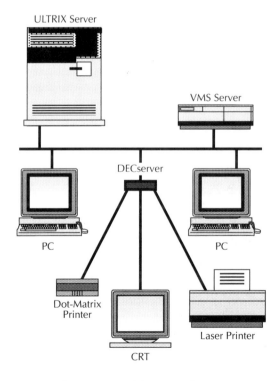

Figure 7-1. Multiserver Printers

The printer server concept also provides a simple method for connecting low-cost client printers. Printers such as the various Digital, Epson, and HP LaserJet devices provide powerful industry-standard options for your network's printing needs. Figure 7-2 illustrates a network using a printer server to manage two printers.

Managing a client as a printer server is a mixed blessing. On the plus side, you can easily test the printer by using simple DOS commands to each local device such as PRN: and COM1:. The major drawback is that this must be done locally, whereas a DECserver provides the ability for remote management over the network.

Digital Print Servers

As evidenced by its support for many different types of printers on a network, Digital long ago recognized the problems related to managing network printers. The Digital PrintServer family of products deserves mention in this chapter because of its support for the network environment and its ease of management. The turbo PrintServer 20 and PrintServer 40 are members of this family. They provide direct attachments to Ethernet and use the standard PostScript language.

Because the PrintServer attaches directly to the Ethernet, terminal servers or PCs to manage the printer are not needed. The PrintServer also has its own internal software (which is downline-loaded from a host) and management software. Users at any PC or terminal attached to the network can monitor the status of their print jobs and the status of the printer.

Attaching to the Ethernet also allows the PrintServer to communicate at Ethernet speeds, removing the bottleneck of the cable common to other printers. PrintServers

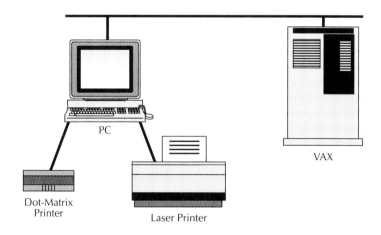

Figure 7-2. PC Printer Server

can print up to 40 pages per minute. The Ethernet connection provides the PrintServer with the ability to be located in areas where the printed documents are used, not in a computer room where additional handling of all documents is required.

PRINT QUEUES

Physical Print Queues

A physical print queue is used to control output to the physical printer port, which is either on the server or connected to a LAT device. This type of queue controls the device control library for the queue and default output parameters.

Using physical queues is a critical aspect of managing your network printers. Defining a physical queue for each printer and using multiple generic queues is very useful for dividing up the maintenance and for servicing the print queues.

Generic Print Queues

A generic print queue is a queue that accepts print requests and reroutes them to a physical print queue. Any number of generic queues can point to one physical print queue. A generic queue can also serve more than one physical print queue, feeding the print jobs out across all the physical print queues.

Different generic queues serve as the user interface to the printers. If a problem occurs, you can easily halt all generic queues and troubleshoot the physical queue. Each generic queue may also have different parameters to provide unique operation of each queue.

LAT Devices

LAT devices are useful in managing and expanding a network. Instead of connecting devices directly to the mainframe or to controllers that directly attach to the mainframe, LAT allows a terminal server or other LAT device to connect to any point on the network. Client workstations can also use LAT to connect to the server as a terminal. Figure 7-3 shows a high-level flowchart of a single server and a LAT terminal server.

In Figure 7-3, the LAT port LTA1013: is linked to port LASE1 on the terminal server. This link is established by creating a link between the terminal server name (or Ethernet address), the terminal server port name, and the LAT port name on the server. The LAT port name is used with the INITIALIZE command to link the print queue to the terminal server port.

Most LAT terminal servers offer remote management from any point on the network. Port names, addresses, speed, protocols, and access control are a sampling of the control parameters available on most terminal servers. By using NCP on the server, you can connect to any server and manage these attributes. This is useful in a large LAN, where servers may be located a fair distance from each other, possibly in far-flung corners of your organization or in the ceiling.

LATCP is another management tool for controlling LAT devices from the server perspective. LATCP is used to build and maintain the LAT database on the server.

There are also versions of NCP and LATCP for client machines. These programs are used to build and maintain their respective databases on the client machine.

Creating a Print Queue from DCL

Before configuring a physical print queue, you must configure the port for the proper communications parameters (e.g., speed), page parameters (e.g., width, length), and

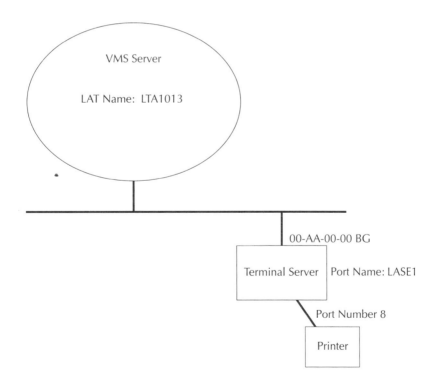

Figure 7-3. LAT Printer Overview

miscellaneous items (e.g., broadcast status). The device parameters must also be set to spool the device. The DCL commands for setting the terminal and device parameters are:

```
$SET TERMINAL/SPFFD=9600/WIDTH=80/PAGE=66 -
    /PERMANENT/NOBROADCAST TTA1

$SET DEVICE/SPOOLED TTA1:
```

After the printer port is configured with the SET command, you can define the physical queue with the INITIALIZE/QUEUE command. This command defines the queue, specifies the port to which the printer will attach, defines the device control library to use, and establishes certain default parameters. The command may also include the /START qualifier to start the queue. The INITIALIZE command creates the print queue and links the queue to the physical printer, whether the printer is attached to a terminal server, client, or server. Below is a typical INITIALIZE command:

```
$ INITIALIZE/QUEUE -
    /ON=KENS::LTA1009: -
    /PROC=LATSYM
    /LIBRARY=PCFS_DEC_LASER_DEVCTL -
    /SEPARATE=(NOFLAG,RESET=(RESET)) -
    /DEFAULT=NOFEED -
    KENS$LJ
```

The following example illustrates the INITIALIZE command for a LAT printer. A LAT print queue INITIALIZE command is very similar to the command illustrated above. The only additional parameter is the /PROC=LATSYM qualifier, which instructs VMS to use the LAT symbiont to control the printer. The ON= qualifier links the physical queue to the LAT port:

```
$ INITIALIZE/QUEUE -
    /ON=KENS::LTA1009: -
    /PROC=LATSYM
    /LIBRARY=PCFS_DEC_LASER_DEVCTL -
    /SEPARATE=(NOFLAG,RESET=(RESET)) -
    /DEFAULT=NOFEED -
    KENS$LJ
```

Once either of these commands is executed, users can access the printer from VMS and client machines and print to the physical queue.

A generic queue is created with the same INITIALIZE command, with slightly different qualifiers. The main difference is the /GENERIC= qualifier, which defines the physical queue to use and tells VMS that the queue is generic. Additional physical queues can be fed by the queue by adding their names to the /GENERIC qualifier, separated by commas. For example, you would use KENS$TTA1, KENS$TTA2. Note that the KENS$TTA1 and KENS$TTA2 parameters are queue names and not port names. The INITIALIZE command for a physical queue uses port names, whereas the generic queue INITIALIZE command accepts only physical queue names. Below is the INITIALIZE command for generic queues:

```
$ INITIALIZE/QUEUE -
      /START -
      /GENERIC=(KENS$LJ) -
      PCFS$DEC_LASER
```

Here are the steps for creating a queue:

1. Set port characteristics (non-LAT printers).

2. Initialize the physical queue.

3. Initialize the generic queue.

Creating a Print Queue with PCSA Manager

PCSA Manager can be used to create a print queue and numerous other related services. This procedure is automatic when the Add Services/Printer option is selected. PCSA Manager prompts for the physical connection name, the name of the queue, and the type of printer. Once these parameters are entered, PCSA Manager automatically generates the required functions for the printer, displaying the results of the process as it progresses. As soon as one printer is defined, you can define another by answering the questions again.

When PCSA Manager is used to add a printer, a number of functions are also performed, including building a printer start-up file and defining the print queue for PATHWORKS. All commands to define queues, define forms, and start the queue are placed in a printer start-up file, SYS$MANAGER:PCFS_PRINT.COM. This file is a DCL command procedure that contains commands to configure the printer and start the queue. A sample procedure is shown in Figure 7-4. When you add printers with PCSA Manager, the commands are added to the end of PCFS_PRINT.COM. The file shown has been edited to add some structure for readability and maintenance purposes.

Figure 7-4. PCFS_PRINT.COM

```
$ SET NOON
$!
$! DEFINE PRINTER FORMS USED BY PCFS
$!
$DEFINE/FORM -
      /SETUP=DEC_LASER_PORT -
      /NOWRAP -
      /NOTRUNCATE -
      /STOCK=DEFAULT -
      /WIDTH=80 -
      DEC_LASER_PORT 117 -
      /DESCRIPTION="HP LASERJET PORTRAIT"
$!
$DEFINE/FORM -
      /SETUP=DEC_LASER_LAND -
      /NOWRAP/NOTRUNCATE -
      /STOCK=DEFAULT/WIDTH=132 -
      DEC_LASER_LAND 118 -
      /DESCRIPTION="HP LASERJET LANDSCAPE"
$!
$! INITIALIZE/START PCFS PRINTER QUEUES
$!
$ PCFS$NODE = F$GETSYI("NODENAME") + "::"
$!
$! START DEC_LASER PRINTER QUEUE KENS$TTA1
$!     FOR KENS::TTA1:
$!
$ START_KENS = "NOSTART"
$ IF PCFS$NODE .NES. "KENS::" THEN -
      GOTO NOSTART1
$ START_KENS = "START"
$ SET TERMINAL/PERMANENT -
      /WIDTH=132 -
      /NOWRAP -
      /PASTHRU/TTSYNC -
      /SPEED=9600 -
      /DEVICE_TYPE=UNKNOWN TTA1:
$ SET DEVICE/SPOOLED=KENS$TTA1 TTA1:
```

Figure 7-4. PCFS_PRINT.COM (continued)

```
$NOSTART1:
$ INITIALIZE/QUEUE -
      /'START_KENS' -
      /ON=KENS::TTA1: -
      /LIBRARY=PCFS_DEC_LASER_DEVCTL -
      /SEPARATE=(NOFLAG,RESET=(RESET)) -
      /DEFAULT=NOFEED -
      KENS$TTA1
$!
$! START DEC_LASER GENERIC PRINTER QUEUE
$!    PCFS$DEC_LASER FOR KENS$TTA1
$!
$ INITIALIZE/QUEUE -
      /START -
      /GENERIC=(KENS$TTA1) -
       PCFS$DEC_LASER
```

PCFS_PRINT.COM sets the speed of the terminal line, defines default forms, and creates physical and generic queues. You can place a call in the SYSTARTUP_V5 command procedure to automatically start all of your PATHWORKS procedures.

After PCSA Manager has created PCFS_PRINT.COM, you should edit the file to add a structure similar to the one illustrated in Figure 7-4. This structure is similar to standard structured programming concepts and is designed to make the program easier to read and maintain.

Be careful when using PCSA Manager to define printers that use LAT. When a LAT port definition such as LTA1009: is entered as a printer port, PCSA Manager treats it as a directly attached printer. The resulting commands created for this printer *will not work*. The parameters for LAT will not be added to the INITIALIZE command, and the SET TERMINAL commands will not be necessary for a LAT device. Before defining a printer that uses LAT, review the file shown in Figure 7-5. I have modified PCFS_PRINT.COM to work with a LAT printer on LTA1009:.

This procedure has been modified to remove the unnecessary code and to modify the INITIALIZE statement for the physical print queue, KENS$LTA1009. The SET TER-MINAL command and IF statement before it were removed because the port charac-teristics for a LAT device are defined on the server to which the printer is attached.

Figure 7-5. PCFS_PRINT.COM Modified for a LAT Queue

```
$ SET NOON
$! DEFINE PRINTER FORMS USED BY PCFS
$!
$DEFINE/FORM -
      /SETUP=DEC_LASER_PORT -
      /NOWRAP -
      /NOTRUNCATE -
      /STOCK=DEFAULT -
      /WIDTH=80 -
      DEC_LASER_PORT 117 -
      /DESCRIPTION="HP LASERJET PORTRAIT"
$DEFINE/FORM -
      /SETUP=DEC_LASER_LAND -
      /NOWRAP/NOTRUNCATE -
      /STOCK=DEFAULT/WIDTH=132 -
      DEC_LASER_LAND 118 -
      /DESCRIPTION="HP LASERJET LANDSCAPE"
$!
$! INITIALIZE/START PCFS PRINTER QUEUES
$ PCFS$NODE = F$GETSYI("NODENAME") + "::"
$!START DEC_LASER PRINTER QUEUE KENS$LTA1009
$!    FOR KENS::LTA1009:
$!
$ START_KENS = "START"
$!
$ INITIALIZE/QUEUE -
      /'START_KENS' -
      /ON=KENS::LTA1009: -
      /PROC=LATSYM
      /LIBRARY=PCFS_DEC_LASER_DEVCTL -
      /SEPARATE=(NOFLAG,RESET=(RESET)) -
      /DEFAULT=NOFEED -
      KENS$LTA1009
$! START DEC_LASER GENERIC PRINTER QUEUE
$!    PCFS$DEC_LASER FOR KENS$TTA1
$ INITIALIZE/QUEUE -
      /START -
      /GENERIC=(KENS$LTA1009) -
      PCFS$DEC_LASER
```

The other main change was the addition of the /PROC=LATSYM qualifier to the INITIALIZE command. The first INITIALIZE command defines and starts the physical print queue. This is the queue that actually controls the port to which the printer is attached. The /PROC= statement tells VMS to use the LAT Print Symbiont (an executable process) to control the printer defined on LAT port LTA1009. LTA1009 is mapped to a particular port on a node somewhere on the network. If this change is not made, the LAT printer will not be recognized.

LAT Port Configuration

Just as printers directly attached to a server require that you use the SET command to configure a port, LAT devices require several additional steps. These include defining the characteristics of the port on the LAT server and defining the printer to LAT.

You must configure the server to support the printer by defining the characteristics for the port. Input and output speed, flow-control methods, and numerous other characteristics must be established to allow the server to communicate with the printer.

LAT nodes must also have a name, just as any other network node. If the server is a PC, the name will be the node name for the client, such as PSRVR1 for printer server 1. For a terminal server, the name will uniquely define the terminal server, such as DS2001 for DECserver 200, number 1.

Figure 7-6 illustrates the setup screen for a port on a DECserver 200 named DS2001, using an LA424 printer on port 8.

To access a remote terminal server over the network, you can use NCP on the VMS server. NCP will connect to the terminal server and allow you to view and change port characteristics. You can also access port characteristics by using a terminal or PC connected directly to the terminal server. Below are the commands to access a DECserver named DS200 over the network using NCP. The commands to be entered by the user are in bold:

```
$ NCP

NCP> CONNECT NODE DS200
# Access
Enter Username> *******

Local> SHOW PORTS ALL CHAR

Local> logout
# CNTRL-D

$
```

Figure 7-6. Terminal Server Printer Configuration Parameters

```
Port 8:                                             Server: DS2001

Character Size:          8                    Input Speed: 9600
Flow Control:            XON                  Output Speed: 9600
Parity:                  None
Modem Control:           Disabled
Access:                  Remote Local Switch:      None
Backwards Switch:        None     Name:            LA424
Break:                   Disabled Session Limit:   4
Forwards Switch:         None     Type:            Hard
Preferred Service:       None
Authorized Groups:       0
(Current) Groups:        0


Enabled Characteristics:
Input Flow Control, Output Flow Control


Local>
```

In addition to establishing control parameters for a port, the terminal server can test the connection to a device. The test command on the terminal server will print a test pattern on the specified port. To execute the test command, enter TEST PORT 8 at the Local> prompt. This command will execute the test command on the device connected to port number 8. If this device is a printer or CRT, a test pattern will print or be displayed on the device.

After the printer is physically connected and the port is configured, you must tell the network server about the device. LATCP is used on the network server to add the terminal server node name and address to the network server LAT database. LATCP also defines a LAT name for the device, such as LTA1000:. This step must be completed before the physical queue serving this port is initialized.

Printers attached to LAT devices also have setup requirements. LATCP must be used to create a LAT port name for the printer port. LATCP defines a LAT port name for the device that links to the device port name. The following commands are required to create a LAT port on the server:

```
$MCR LATCP

LATCP> CREATE PORT LTA321/APP

LATCP> SET PORT LTA321/NODE=AA01BBCC1233 -
     /SERVICE=MYPRTR/APP)

LATCP> EXIT
```

This sequence of commands creates a LAT port named LTA321. LTA321 is linked to the DECserver node AA01BBCC1233 and the port associated with the service MYPRTR. Once the LAT port definition has been created and linked to a terminal server port, it may be linked to an actual VMS print queue by the INITIALIZE/QUEUE command.

PC Clients as Printer Servers

The PC client offers a simple platform for managing printers and can provide other users on the network with access to its printers. In fact, printers attached to a PC can be accessed by other PATHWORKS users and users on the server machines. The most efficient way to use this feature is to use a PC as a dedicated printer server controlling several printers. The printer server will offload control of the printers from the server in a manner similar to the terminal server. This is a cheap and simple alternative to terminal servers for managing network printers. It also provides a simple way to attach inexpensive and reliable parallel printers to your network. There are no physical or license limits to the number of printer servers that can be attached to a network.

PC printers serving as network printers are controlled by LAT in a fashion similar to terminal server printers. The print queues for client printers are also the same type of queues used by other LAT printers. If the printers attached to a printer server are slow dot-matrix devices, a 12- or 16-MHz 80286 PC will probably do a good job. If laser printers or other high-performance devices are attached to the PC, you should plan to use an 80386 or 80486 machines.

Here are the steps required to set up a PC printer server:

```
C:\>LATCP
LATCP>ADD LPT1 PUR_LA424
LATCP>SHOW CHARACTERISTICS
LATCP>ADD 3.100 KENS KENS
```

These steps use LATCP on the PC to create the printer definition, display the client address, and add the server address to the client LAT database. The ADD LPT1 command creates a definition for LPT1 and names it PUR_LA434. The SHOW CHAR-ACTERISTICS command is used to display the Ethernet address of the client, which should be recorded. (USE/STATUS will also work.) The address will be needed when the port definition is created on the server. The last command creates a definition for the server KENS in the LAT database.

The commands below use LATCP on the server to create a port definition for the new printer. Notice that this definition is similar to the definition for the terminal server printer:

```
$ MCR LATCP

LATCP> CREATE PORT LTA322/APP

LATCP> SET PORT PUR_LA424 -
        LTA321/NODE=AA0023221133
        /SERVICE=PUR_LA424/APP
```

The INITIALIZE command for the client printer is also like the command used for the terminal server printer:

```
$ INITIALIZE/QUEUE/START/ON=(LTA322:)/PROC=LATSYM
        PURCH_LA424
```

Before offering the printer to the user community, you should test it. This includes testing the printer from DOS by printing a test file and testing the printer over the network. When you test the printer, be sure to use a sufficiently large file to fill its buffer. In most cases, a multipage file will work, especially on a dot-matrix printer.

To connect to the client printer as a network device, the same procedure applies as for any other network printer. The USE command will redirect printing to the server and out to the printer. Because the printer is defined using LAT, no other actions are necessary to use the printer.

CONTROLLING PRINTERS

Device Control Libraries

VMS uses device control libraries to supply printer-control commands to a printer. Each physical print queue is associated with a particular device control library when it is created with the INITIALIZE command. This feature is useful for applications that do not supply printer-control information, such as fonts or landscape printing. Most popular PC applications do not require device control libraries because they set and reset the printer each time they print. Device control libraries are very useful where numerous files are printed from applications that do not properly control printers or from DOS with simple print utilities. They are also useful for resetting the printer to a known state after each print job.

A device control library is a VMS text library that consists of various modules, each of which contains the printer-control commands to cause the printer to take a certain action. The LIBRARY command is used to create the library file and add or delete modules from the file. It also performs other maintenance chores such as listing the modules in the library. Device control libraries are stored in the SYS$LIBRARY directory and have the suffix .TLB.

PATHWORKS comes with libraries for supported printers. These include Digital printers, HP LaserJet, and IBM Proprinter. When a queue for a supported printer is created with PCSA Manager, the appropriate library is automatically assigned to the queue. If you need to modify a library module or add a device control library for an unsupported printer, refer to the *PATHWORKS Server Administrators Guide*.

Form Definitions

VMS printers also support form definitions, which allow device control library setup modules and physical page layout parameters. Each time a file prints and a particular form is active, the setup module specified by the form will be downloaded to the printer, and VMS will not print the file until the proper form is mounted.

If a printer uses more than one type of paper and does not have multiple paper-input sources, such as paper drawers on a laser printer, forms are useful for holding print requests until the proper form is mounted.

Form definitions are created with the DEFINE/FORM command. Once the form definition is created, the SET/QUEUE/FORM_MOUNTED= command is used to specify that a particular form is mounted on the printer. Any print jobs received for the print queue will be placed in a pending state if the physical characteristics of the mounted form do not exactly match the form for the print job.

VMS PRINT QUEUE MANAGEMENT

VMS provides a number of utilities for managing print queues. These include commands for displaying the status of a queue and its entries, deleting and manipulating queue jobs, resetting queue jobs, and many other functions. These utilities are part of the rich DCL command set and can be used interactively or from within a DCL procedure or VMS program.

Each of these utilities restricts user actions to the user's own files. To change or view information about other users' print jobs, the user executing the command must have Group and/or Oper privileges.

The following command descriptions provide an overview of the most frequently used VMS print queue manipulation commands. For more detailed information, consult your system manuals and the VMS HELP system.

Starting a Queue

Before a print queue can be used, it must be started. You can do this with the /START qualifier for the INITIALIZE command or by using the START/QUEUE command. START/QUEUE is also useful for restarting a print queue after it has been stopped for one reason or another. It may also be used to change the characteristics of a queue. Table 7-3 lists qualifiers for START/QUEUE. The format for this command is:

```
$START/QUEUE qualifier queue_name
```

where *queue_name* selects information for this queue only.

Table 7-3. Qualifiers for START/QUEUE

Qualifier	Function
/BACKWARD=	Causes the queue to restart at a page prior to the current page. If the page number is omitted, printing resumes at the top of the current page.
/DEFAULT	Establishes defaults for blank pages before or after a print job and forms for a particular print queue. Once a default is set, it will be in effect for all print jobs. The allowable defaults are BURST=ONE or ALL, FEED, FLAG=ONE or ALL, FORM=form, and TRAILER=ONE or ALL. The ONE or ALL keywords determine whether the specified page is printed before or after each print job or for each file in a print job. FORM establishes a default form for all jobs sent to the queue without a specific form. Default attributes can be overridden by the PRINT command.
/DESCRIPTION	Allows the creation of a queue description of up to 255 characters.
/FORM=	Sets the current form for the queue to the one specified after the = sign.
/FORWARD=	Causes the queue to restart at a page after the current page. If the page number is omitted, printing resumes at the top of the next page.
/LIBRARY=	Establishes a device control library for the queue.
/NEXT	Causes the current job to abort and resumes printing with the next pending job.

Table 7-3. Qualifiers for START/QUEUE (continued)

Qualifier	Function
/ON=	Links the queue to a specific output device, such as a serial port or terminal server queue.
/PROTECTION	Changes the RMS protection for the print queue.
/RETAIN=	Causes print jobs to remain in the queue after they are printed. The allowable options are ALL and ERROR.
/SCHEDULE	Prioritizes jobs by size, forcing small jobs to print first. This command should not be executed when there are jobs in a queue.
/SEARCH=	Begins printing with the next page containing the search string. The string can be 1 to 63 characters long and must be enclosed in quotes.
/SEPARATE	Establishes mandatory separation options for a queue. The allowable options are BURST, FLAG, TRAILER, and RESET[=module]. These options may not be overridden by a print request. The RESET option specifies one or more device control library modules that should be called before and after a print job or file.
/TOP_OF_FILE	Causes printing to resume at the top of the current file.

Stopping a Queue

To halt a network print queue or a job printing on a queue, use the STOP/QUEUE command. Several qualifiers directly affect the operation of this command, including whether it works on the queue or only for an entry in the queue.

STOP/QUEUE followed by a queue name is handy when a queue must be stopped for maintenance or for some other reason. All jobs currently in the queue will be suspended until the job is restarted. Adding the /ABORT qualifier is also very useful for a job that is currently printing and should be deleted. STOP/QUEUE /ABORT will cause the current job to stop and be deleted from the queue. Printing will begin with the next available job. Table 7-4 lists qualifies for STOP/QUEUE. With no qualifiers, this command will halt the specified queue and suspend all jobs. The format for this command is:

```
$STOP/QUEUE qualifier queue_name
```

Table 7-4. Qualifiers for STOP/QUEUE

Qualifier	Function
/ABORT	Aborts the current job and begins printing the next available job.
/ENTRY=	Aborts one or more print jobs and deletes them from the queue.
/NEXT	Stops the specified queue after all jobs currently printing have completed. No new jobs may be queued after this command is executed.
/REQUEUE	Stops the currently printing job and requeues it for later processing on the same or another queue. The /ENTRY = qualifier may be used to select only a particular entry. /HOLD will cause the job to be put on hold. /PRIORITY= will allow you to change the job's priority.
/RESET	Halts the print queue immediately, aborting any currently printing jobs.

Displaying Queue and Print Job Information

The SHOW QUEUE command is very useful for managing printers. It can be used to quickly display the status of the print queue, display detailed information about how the queue is defined, and provide information on the print jobs currently in the queue. Numerous parameters for the command tailor its operation, providing different display options.

When SHOW QUEUE is used with no qualifiers, it will display a minimum amount of information about all queues. This includes the queue status, the number of entries in the queue, and the queue name. The /FULL qualifier will display complete information, including the parameters used to define the queue and additional information about the entries in the queue. Table 7-5 lists qualifiers for SHOW QUEUE. The format for this command is:

```
$ SHOW QUEUE qualifier queue_name
```

Table 7-5. Qualifiers for SHOW QUEUE

Qualifier	Function
/ALL_JOBS	Displays information for all jobs in the queues specified. If no queue is specified, it will display information for all jobs in all queues.
/BY_JOB=	Selects information by job status. If this qualifier is used without a keyword, only queues with valid print jobs will be displayed. Valid keywords are Executing, Holding, Pending, Retained, and Timed_Release.
/DEVICE=	If /DEVICE=PRINTER is used, it selects information for all print queues.
/FILES	Displays the list of files for each print job.
/FULL	Displays all information available for the selected queues.
/GENERIC	Selects information only for generic queues.
/OUTPUT=	Allows the output to be captured in a file or printed. If only /OUTPUT is specified, or if it is used with only a directory specification, the output will be placed in a file called SHOW.LIS.
/SUMMARY	Displays summary information for each queue.

The SHOW ENTRY command is used to display information about current jobs in a print or batch queue. Only the user's jobs are normally displayed, unless the /USER qualifier is used.

This command is used to review the status of jobs in a queue, often supplying information for use by the SET command. It is helpful for determining where a particular job is in the printing sequence or for monitoring the overall status of all of your print requests for different printers. Table 7-6 lists qualifiers for SHOW ENTRY. The format for this command is:

```
$ SHOW ENTRY qualifier entry_number
```

where *entry_number* selects information for only the specified print job.

Table 7-6. Qualifiers for SHOW ENTRY

Qualifier	Function
/FILES	Displays the full file specification of entries in the queue.
/FULL	Displays all of the information available for each entry.
/GENERIC	Selects only information for entries in generic queues.
/OUTPUT=	Allows the output to be captured in a file or printed. If only /OUTPUT is specified, or it is used with only a directory specification, the output will be placed in a file called SHOW.LIS.
/USER=	Selects information only for the current user.

Deleting Entries in a Queue

To delete an entry in a print queue, use the DELETE/ENTRY command. This command will delete one or more jobs in the same or different queues:

```
$DELETE/ENTRY=entry_number
```

For currently printing jobs, use the STOP/QUEUE/ABORT command.

Modifying Queue Characteristics

The DCL SET command is used to modify the characteristics of many VMS features, including print queues and print jobs. SET QUEUE provides a tool to modify many of the parameters established when a print queue was created. It is frequently used to change the form mounted on a queue. Table 7-7 lists qualifiers for SET QUEUE. The format for this command is:

```
$SET QUEUE qualifier queue_name
```

Printing from VMS

The PRINT command is used to print a file from a VMS interactive account. If the /QUEUE= qualifier is not specified, output will be printed on the SYS$PRINT queue. Since the topic of this book is PATHWORKS, the qualifier list presented in Table 7-8 for the PRINT command is very brief. The format for this command is:

```
$PRINT file_list
```

If you are frequently using this command, consult VMS HELP or your VMS documentation.

Table 7-7. Qualifiers for SET QUEUE

Qualifier	Function
/DEFAULT	Establishes defaults for blank pages before or after a print job and for forms for a particular print queue. Once a default is set, it will be in effect for all print jobs. The allowable defaults are BURST=ONE or ALL, FEED, FLAG=ONE or ALL, FORM=form, and TRAILER=ONE or ALL. The ONE or ALL keywords determine whether the specified page is printed before or after each print job or for each file in a print job. FORM establishes a default form for all jobs sent to the queue without a specific form. Default attributes can be overridden by the PRINT command.
/DESCRIPTION	Allows the creation of a queue description of up to 255 characters.
/FORM=	Sets the current form for the queue to the one specified after the = sign.
/PROTECTION	Changes the RMS protection for the print queue.
/RETAIN=	Causes print jobs to remain in the queue after they are printed. The allowable options are ALL and ERROR.
/SCHEDULE	Prioritizes jobs by size, forcing small jobs to print first. This command should not be executed when there are jobs in a queue.
/SEPARATE	Establishes mandatory separation options for a queue. The allowable options are BURST, FLAG, TRAILER, and RESET[=module]. These options may not be overridden by a print request. The RESET option specifies one or more device control library modules that should be called before and after a print job or file.

Table 7-8. Qualifiers for PRINT

Qualifier	Function
file_list	Names the file to print, separated by commas or the plus sign. File names may include wildcard characters. If no file type is specified for a file, either the previous file type or .LIS is used.
/QUEUE=	Specifies the print queue to use.

CHAPTER 8

Application Installation and Use

A major piece of the network puzzle involves applications and how they are installed and accessed. Installing applications on a network is often a difficult task, because almost every application takes a different approach to using the network. Even if the installation is not difficult at the time, it can lead to problems down the road if you do not take care and plan well during the installation process.

Looking at the root directory of a PC that has been in use for a year or two will usually give you a good idea of how haphazard things get when applications are installed without the proper planning or preparation. It is not unusual to find a multitude of different directories, with unique names and structures. Each application may also place configuration files in its own directory or in another directory. (Let's hope it is not in the root directory!) With the problems that occur on a single PC with a 40-MB disk, just imagine what can happen to your network drives over time. Most DOS application vendors have designed their own methods for storing and accessing parameter files and for executing their applications. Applications from the same vendor may even use different methods. Many vendors have added limited support for network environments to their applications, but this has done very little to standardize a way to configure and manage their applications.

Windows V3.0 introduced some standardization to the process by the use of the various configuration files for Windows and its applications. At the time of this writing, this has still not evolved to an ideal situation. Let's hope we are in store for a positive change in the future.

The applications piece of the puzzle also has a second part: How do users access the applications loaded on the network? Accessing applications over PATHWORKS can be a simple process for some users and a very perplexing process for others on the same network because of the complexities of the network and the various differences in how applications are executed and configured. Some network implementations have users entering different commands for the same or similar applications.

This chapter offers suggestions on how to install applications on a network and how to use them. It also covers several useful applications that offer special functions for a typical network. Check the procedures and options for each application before installing it on your network, since applications change over time, as do the installation procedures.

CHOOSING THE RIGHT TOOLS

Downsizing is one of the most discussed topics in many business and computer publications. Firms are moving from large systems to smaller and more cost-effective LANs or minicomputers. A lot of confusion exists about how and what technology to use in properly downsizing.

The key to downsizing is a technique used by golfers and mechanics. Like computers, they use the proper tool for the job at hand. The golfer uses different clubs for each hole and situation. The mechanic uses different screwdrivers and wrenches for different situations and different types of screws or bolts. The mechanic's toolbox contains many different shapes and sizes of tools for different tasks.

For downsizing, the key is to use the right tool for the job. Use whatever system provides the required resources for the users and organization. This may mean using a VAX for some tasks, UNIX or VMS workstations for other tasks, and client PCs and Macintoshes for most users. New reduced instruction set computers (RISC) and VAXstations provide powerful platforms that are below the cost of similarly equipped PCs. An organization that uses a large VMS-based system may move development to several VAXstations, offloading the development processing from the main system.

PREPARING FOR APPLICATION USE

Properly installing applications on a network requires careful planning. You should develop a specification for your network that describes how the applications will function and where they will be located. The following list outlines several criteria to include in this specification:

- What type of service will be used for network applications?
- How will the service directories be structured?
- Where will the configuration files be stored?
- Which batch procedures will be used, if any?
- How will users access each application?
- Which problem applications will you need to avoid in the future?

In the planning process, you should consider the growth potential for your network. I have never seen a system installed that did not grow dramatically once the initial implementation was over and people began to see what the network could do for their organization. Growth usually involves adding workstations and new applications. If you have not planned for adequate disk space or have structured your directories in an awkward manner, making your system grow and managing it effectively will be a problem.

Upgrading application packages is another area of growth to consider. Most modern applications use numerous configuration files for storing information relative to the application and its environment. They may also store configuration files in a user's personal directory to track the user's preferences and personal information. If you have not taken into account the structure of the application directories and where these various files are stored, you may run into problems.

Have you ever purchased something at a store and then discovered that it did not work as promised by the advertising on the package, or you started using it and then found it was incompatible with another one of your favorite toys? Welcome to the world of application software and networks! I use a general rule for applications and networks: The more complex the application and the greater the number of applications, the more problems you can expect. The keep it simple, stupid (KISS), principle certainly applies to network application management. Some software packages arrive on a single floppy disk and have only one or two files. Managing these applications is fairly easy and straightforward. Some of the more complex and powerful applications such as Word for Windows and computer-aided design (CAD) software are at the other end of the spectrum. They often use compressed files and arrive on five to 10 high-density disks.

One way to minimize the problems of new applications is to thoroughly test every application. Test the application in a single-user mode and with multiple concurrent users. Keep in mind that most problems never show up until the environment is pushed to its limits. A word processor may work fine with a 10-page document but may fail miserably with a 34-page document with graphics.

An important preparation issue deals with the locations available for users to store data files. The ability to store data files on network drives is one of the biggest advantages of a network. Files can be easily shared with other users and can become part of the nightly backup of the server. Many applications support configuration parameters that can be used to establish a default data drive. For example, Word for Windows V2.0 can establish the data storage directory and several other directories in the WIN.INI file. Although this does not force users to store their data on the network, it can make it convenient to do so and inconvenient to store them on the local drive. Word for Windows V2.0 can also manage both local and network versions of template files.

Network Versus Hard Disk Storage

Network applications are easy to manage if they are stored on a network service or directory. When an upgrade is necessary, the new application can be loaded once on the network directory, and the process is almost complete. After the application is loaded and tested, making the directory public will complete the task. You may also need to update a batch file or Windows program group as part of the upgrade process.

Managing applications located on client hard disks is difficult because each hard disk must be upgraded individually. Upgrading each hard disk can be managed automatically by using custom update programs such as DOS batch files that can move application code or files directly to the local hard disk from a network drive.

Some applications will not run from a network disk, no matter what you do to them. If you must use an application that experiences problems when run from the network, you have no choice but to move it to a client disk.

Another reason to move applications to a client disk is to increase efficiency on heavily used networks already experiencing bottlenecks at the I/O or network level. Each time an application or segment of an application (i.e., overlay file) is loaded from a network directory, there is a lot of network overhead. When many users access an application concurrently, this places a tremendous load on the network. If the same application is moved to a client disk, there is no network traffic unless the application accesses data on the network. Traffic for network data files is usually very small and sporadic.

Placing applications on a client's hard disk can be used to create a sort-of fault-tolerant system, because these applications can still run when the server is down. The only problem occurs if all the user's files are on the network drive. If you plan to use hard disks for applications, you should create a reverse backup routine that the user can execute frequently (or when the user leaves at night) that copies current project files onto the user's local drive, providing access to the files should the server die.

INSTALLATION AND ACCESS

Installing Applications Directly on the Network

Installing an application directly on a network directory is becoming harder with the introduction of more sophisticated installation routines. In times past, the application files could simply be copied to a directory and they were ready to run. As applications have become more sophisticated, the installation process has grown more difficult. The larger size of applications has contributed to this problem, causing most vendors to ship their programs in a compressed format to save space.

Many applications will install correctly on a PATHWORKS network with little or no intervention. Most also determine on what type of network they are being installed and configure themselves appropriately. Some applications such as Windows V3.0 will not install on a network until they have first been installed on a hard disk and configured. Even after you install some applications on a client disk, the normal installation process may not work on the network. The only way to tell if an application will install directly on the network is by trying the normal installation process and specifying a network directory.

Before installing an application on a network directory, you should consult the software manual's section on network installations. If the manual does not have any information on networks or if the information is skimpy, you may want to call technical support before trying to install the package. Be sure to look for any information on special options to set for networks, and try to determine what configuration files are used, how they are used, and where they should be located on the server (in the application directory, user directory, or other directory).

The following steps can be used to install most applications on a network directory:

1. Connect to the network directory with sufficient privileges:

   ```
   C:\>USE X: \\KENS\WORD20%SYSTEM *
   ```

2. Run the program's installation procedure.

3. Use the network drive (X:\) for the directory name.

Installing Applications on a Client and Moving to the Network

Installing applications on a client hard disk and moving them to the network directory is a useful way of installing applications on the server and avoiding many problems associated with network installations. This usually works for applications that will not install directly on a server. Installing the application first on a hard disk has another important benefit: You can verify that the application works correctly before trying to run it from the network.

Once the application is installed on a client, moving it to the server is easy. You can use the XCOPY command to copy the entire directory structure over to the target server directory. Then run the application and test several different options after the application files have been moved to the server. After verifying that the application works correctly from the server, with no changes from the client, you can begin to change the configuration and move the setup files.

The procedure for installing applications on a hard disk and moving them to a server directory is fairly straightforward:

1. Run the program's installation procedure.

2. Test the application.

3. Connect to the network directory with sufficient privileges:

```
C:\>USE X: \\KENS\WORD20%SYSTEM *
```

4. Copy the files to the network:

```
C:\>XCOPY \winword X:\ /S /V
```

5. Test the application.

6. Change the configuration.

7. Test the application again.

Installing Applications on a Client Hard Disk

Applications located on a client disk can also access network services and data. Installing applications on the client is a useful way to cut down on network traffic, as well as to provide some backup capabilities. After installing the application on the client, configure the application for the network, if network options are supported. This may include changing the data path to the file server directories, loading a network driver, and installing the appropriate printer drivers. The installation is as follows:

1. Run the program's installation procedure.

2. Test the application.

3. Configure the application for the network.

Application Licensing and Access Issues

Standard applications present an interesting problem because of licensing arrangements. Most packages available today are licensed by the concurrent user. This means that five licenses of your favorite package will allow up to five concurrent users to access the application. If you need to give access to the sixth user, you must buy another license.

User licensing is difficult to monitor on many networks because the normal system may have five licenses for a spreadsheet and 15 for a word processing program. This problem is further compounded because you may have 25 people who need one or both of these programs at one time or another. If you have 25 PCs, you must have a license for each one. The LAN simplifies this by allowing you to share the programs over the network. Your problem now becomes how to manage the use of these programs and remain within the license agreements.

Some vendors provide site licenses for their products. These licensees usually include a base license and an incremental license for each additional user (at a drastically reduced cost). This is usually a fair method of purchasing applications, for both users and vendors.

Network-Aware Packages. Some products are becoming network aware and are taking advantage of the services of the network. Network awareness is kind of like the term *user friendly*, in that its meaning is determined by each vendor for that vendor's package. The most common feature of network awareness is to provide management facilities for allowing different users to access the package and for controlling the number of concurrent users running the software.

DOS Applications. If you are running DOS only, the licensing problem is fairly easy to manage with PATHWORKS. By creating a file service for each application (word processor 1, word processor 2, spreadsheet 1, etc.) and assigning a maximum concurrent user count for each service, you can manage DOS. The maximum number of concurrent users for a service is set using the PCSA SET FILE_SERVER SERVICE APPNAME /CONN=n command. Substitute the service name for APPNAME and the number of connections for n. To make this work, you simply create a batch file for each application that sets up access to the service via the USE command. (See Figure 8-1.)

Figure 8-1. WP.BAT, an Example Batch File

Command	Description
@echo off	
rem WP.BAT	
rem	
USE *S:* *MFG**WP*/R	Connect to the WP service
WP *%1 %2 %3 %4*	Execute the WP program
USE *S:* *MFG**STD_APPS*/R	Reset the S: drive

This simple file works because the PATH variable contains the S:. specification. The period (.) causes DOS to search the current directory on the S: drive each time an application is executed. In each batch file, the S: drive is reset to the proper directory for the application to be executed. The PATH variable should be set in the login sequence (either by AUTOUSER.BAT or LOGON.BAT) to include S:.. Before setting PATH, use the USE command to connect to the STD_APPS directory. When DOS looks for a program by checking the PATH directories, STD_APPS will be checked, but it usually does not contain any files. The WP.BAT program resets the S: directory, causing DOS to find the WP.EXE program in the MFG\WP directory.

By limiting the number of concurrent users on the WP service, you can easily find out when you need to increase the number of users covered by the license agreements. This is one of the most reliable notification systems available, and it is called UserNet. As soon as someone tries to access an application and is denied access, your phone will ring. If this happens very often, bump the user count by one or two and order the new copies.

Windows Applications. It seems that as soon as we have an easy way to manage technology, something happens to change things again. Windows complicates the security issue by changing the way applications are executed. Applications running under GUI products are executed from within the GUI itself. They normally require an icon to be set up that points directly to the application's start-up directory. Programs such as Symantec's Norton Desktop for Windows simplify this process to some extent by also allowing you to specify a start-up directory that becomes the current directory after the application is loaded. Norton Desktop for Windows does not provide any tools for license management, since it is a single-user tool like Windows.

To use Windows effectively, you must redirect drive mappings for your search drives before loading Windows. Performing the redirection before loading Windows requires that all applications reside in a limited number of file services, because the drives cannot be mapped via a batch file at execution time. Users can map drives themselves within Windows, but this is unacceptable for most users.

The WinBatch products from Wilson WindowWare can overcome this problem by creating a batch shell for Windows programs. The purpose of this shell is to connect to the service containing the application, run the application program, and disconnect from the service when the application completes. The WinExist function can also be used to determine whether the application is currently running. For more information on WinBatch, refer to "Connecting to Network Services" in Chapter 5.

Although most Windows applications request that their directory be placed in the DOS PATH, it is not a steadfast requirement. Most Windows applications store information in their subordinate files in the various INI files used by Windows. They may also create their own INI files, either in the applications directory or in the Windows directory. Because of the many variances in how these applications work, you should test your applications on the network, both with and without the application directory in the PATH.

Figure 8-2 shows the application service STD_APPS, located under the APPS directory. In this case, STD_APPS has subdirectories for Word for Windows (WW),

Windows V3.1 (W31), Windows Utilities (WU), and Designer (DSR). Mapping the STD_APPS service as the users log in or as the client boots will let all users have access to the applications on the service. The WU directory is used to store numerous utilities for Windows to keep them out of the W31 directory. This makes troubleshooting and upgrading much easier.

Applications that have a limited number of users may be installed on their own file service and mapped before the user starts Windows. Placing these applications on their own service and restricting access will control how many people have access to the application, but it will control all users who access this service, not just concurrent users.

The problem of license management is easily resolved only for packages that are network aware and manage concurrent users on their own. One or two applications are available that claim to manage the licensing of Windows applications on a network, but I have not had the opportunity to test them. By the end of 1993, this problem should be resolved for most applications as PATHWORKS and Windows become more flexible and provide more control over managing applications.

THE DOS OPERATING ENVIRONMENT

The DOS operating system provides a nice facility for managing the execution of DOS-based applications. The DOS batch language can execute most DOS applications

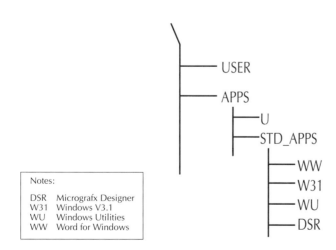

Figure 8-2. Typical Windows Application Directory Structure

199

cleanly. By using a few simple template-type batch files, you can easily install and manage applications on your network.

The key to this approach is to create a standard batch program and directory structure that works for your system. Standard applications should be placed on one or more services. Let's see how this works for a typical system.

In our example system, Word is installed on the STD_APPS service in a directory named WORD. A user named JOE is logged into the network account JOE. The server is named KENS. To access Word from DOS, JOE would enter the following commands:

```
M:\>USE T:\\KENS\STD_APPS
M:\>T:
T:\>CD \WORD
T:\WORD>Word
```

Notice that the user must know the names for the server, service, and directory where Word is stored. The user must also understand the DOS and USE commands to properly access the WORD directory. Once these steps are accomplished, he can finally enter the command to start Word.

The first instinct to resolving this problem is usually to place the directory that contains Word in the user's PATH statement. Many applications support the use of the DOS PATH for accessing their executable and data files. To use the PATH statement in our example requires placing the USE command in the AUTOUSER.BAT for this user and resetting the user's PATH statement to include the Word directory. This is illustrated in the following commands:

```
@echo off
rem AUTOUSER.BAT

USE T:\\KENS\STD_APPS

set _PATH=%PATH%

PATH=T:\WORD;%_PATH%
```

The USE statement in the code above redirects the T: drive letter to point to the PATHWORKS service containing the application programs. The next two lines change the PATH statement by adding the Word directory to the beginning of it. To execute Word, the user must simply enter c:\>WORD. Simple, right? Wrong!

Limitations of DOS include the restrictions on the PATH statement. PATHWORKS adds several directories to the PATH statement via the STARTNET.BAT procedure and will not start unless the PATH statement is equal to or less than 78 characters. As you add applications to the PATH statement, you will reach this length very quickly.

Most applications compound this problem by building their own subdirectory structures and requesting that these directories be entered into the PATH statement. Many install programs actually modify the PATH statement in the AUTOEXEC.BAT file when the application is installed. Application directory names add up in a hurry. If you add each application directory to the PATH statement via AUTOUSER.BAT, PATH grows with each new application. You must also add each new application directory to each user's PATH statement. All this requires a lot of work.

One simple answer to this dilemma is to create custom batch files for each DOS application. This process is easy to manage, because most DOS applications can use the same procedure, with minor modifications.

The secret to creating custom batch files is to combine a minor change to the PATH statement with the DOS CD command. The following two programs illustrate this procedure. In these examples, the T: drive is pointing to the STD_APPS service and the PATH statement is C:\DOS;T:.;C:\NORTON;. The first procedure executes an application called ANYAPP:

```
@echo off
rem Std Batch Procedure for Apps.
CD T:\ANYAPP
ANYAPP %1 %2 %3 %4 %5
CD T:\
```

The next procedure executes Word:

```
@echo off
rem Std Batch Procedure for Apps.
CD T:\WORD
WORD %1 %2 %3 %4 %5
CD T:\
```

PATHWORKS can also manage the number of users concurrently running an application via the file or disk services features. By creating a service named WORD and assigning a maximum number of users=5 (with PCSA Manager), you could limit the number of WORD users to five or less. The following example illustrates the changes to the first batch procedure. In this example, the path does not contain the T:. specification:

```
@echo off
rem WORD.BAT
USE T:\KENS\WORD /R
```

```
IF NOT ERRORLEVEL == 0 goto error
SET OLDPATH=%PATH%
PATH=T:.;%PATH%
WORD %1 %2 %3 %4 %5
PATH=%OLDPATH%
USE T:/d
GOTO OK
:ERROR
Echo Application Not Available at this Time
Pause
:OK
SET OLDPATH=
```

This example first establishes a connection to the WORD service and connects it to drive T:. The /R parameter causes the USE command to replace the T: connection if it is in use. If the connection cannot be made, the IF statement executes the GOTO command and transfers control to the :ERROR label, causing the error message to display.

The ERRORLEVEL variable referenced in the IF command is set by the USE statement. If USE is successful, ERRORLEVEL will be 0. Any value other than 0 indicates some type of error. If an error occurs, the procedure skips to the :ERROR label and executes the Echo and Pause statements to display an error message and force the user to acknowledge the message.

The other minor change in this example is the use of the SET and PATH commands. This procedure modifies the PATH command as part of its normal execution by adding the T:. specification to the beginning. Normal programming practices would dictate that you reset the PATH to its original state when you are through.

The first SET statement causes the variable OLDPATH to be set to the contents of the current path. The PATH command follows the SET command and uses the contents of the path itself to add the T:. specification. When PATH executes, it takes the first parameter (T:.) and adds the second parameter (%PATH%) to it to form the new path. Since the PATH is stored in an environment variable (PATH), the %PATH% reference retrieves the current value of the PATH and feeds it to the PATH command. After the application terminates, the last PATH command uses the %OLDPATH% reference to reset the PATH to its original state. The last SET command removes the OLDPATH variable.

By using either of these two methods, you can easily access and maintain most DOS applications on the network. Adding a new application is as simple as copying the desired file and making minor edits.

Simple modifications can also add functions for all network users. The following example shows the same procedure with a minor addition:

```
@echo off
rem WORD.BAT
USE T:\KENS\WORD /R
IF NOT ERRORLEVEL == 0 goto error
SET OLDPATH=%PATH%
PATH=T:.;%PATH%
CD M:\DOC
WORD %1 %2 %3 %4 %5
CD M:\
PATH=%OLDPATH%
USE T:/d
GOTO OK
:ERROR
Echo Application Not Available at this Time
Pause
:OK
SET OLDPATH=
```

The CD command has been added before the command to start Word. In this example, the command changes the M: (personal) drive to the DOC directory. After Word executes, the next CD command returns to the root directory of the user's personal drive. This procedure could be modified further to allow the user to specify as a parameter the directory to change to before executing the program. An example of the additional commands are shown below. They should replace the first CD command in the example:

```
SET _DIR = DOC
IF NOT @%1 == @ SET _DIR = %1
CD %_DIR% > NULL
```

The SET command loads the _DIR variable with the string DOC. This serves as the default document directory if no directory was specified on the command line. If this line is omitted, the procedure will not change directories, unless one is specified. The IF statement resets the _DIR variable to the contents of %1, if %1 is not blank.

In this example, the > NULL parameters are added at the end of the CD command to suppress the output of the command. This prevents the CD command from displaying the current directory if the SET _DIR = DOC line is removed from the procedure or the DIR variable is blank.

The procedures and suggestions in this section will work straight out of the box. They are designed to be functional and have been modified and streamlined over the years on many different networks. Your particular installation may require minor or major changes to one or more of these routines. Feel free to make any changes that you feel are necessary. Just make sure the changes are well thought out and carefully implemented.

THE WINDOWS OPERATING ENVIRONMENT

PATHWORKS comes with support for Windows. A client workstation can run Windows while connected to a server and can access files located on server drives. PATHWORKS will also interact with Windows, providing support for network operations. Windows V3.1 includes support for PATHWORKS as part of the standard installation process. The file manager included with Windows V3.1 supports network drives and is very quick. Other advanced network features are built into Windows for supporting printers, via the control panel, and applications. Future versions of PATHWORKS will be further integrated with the Windows environment.

New applications from Digital such as TeamLinks and PATHWORKS Links show the true potential of linking a GUI with a full-featured network. These applications add a tremendous amount of power to the standard Windows interface and provide users with a truly seamless environment.

Before trying to install Windows, let's review some basics of its configuration.

INI Files

Windows uses several configuration files to store various bits of information. Microsoft has standardized on the .INI file suffix for configuration files of all types, including Windows. PATHWORKS uses the files MSNET.INI and PROTOCOL.INI to store various parameters concerning the network configuration.

Table 8-1 lists the standard .INI files for Windows. Each file stores information about one or more aspects of Windows and its configuration for a particular system. SYSTEM.INI and WIN.INI are the most important and relate directly to every network installation.

SYSTEM.INI is used primarily to store information relating to the hardware configuration of a particular Windows installation. There is some information that does not pertain to hardware, but it is minimal.

WIN.INI is used for storing information about a particular user's preferences and setup. The only troublesome part of this file for network users is normally the ports section, which lists the output ports of the PC.

Table 8-1. Windows Control Files (INI)

File Name	Description
CONTROL.INI	Control Panel
PROGMAN.INI	Program Manager
SYSTEM.INI	System Settings
WINFILE.INI	File Manager
WIN.INI	Windows Desktop Settings

When Windows starts, it looks for SYSTEM.INI and WIN.INI in the current directory, then along the PATH statement, and finally in the directory where Windows is located. It is usually wise to move these files into a separate directory where they are not easily overwritten or deleted. Doing so also simplifies upgrading Windows, although Windows V3.1 upgrades will not overwrite your existing INI files.

The locations for storing INI files can be split into different groups. Everything except SYSTEM.INI should be stored in the user's root directory on the server, which must be in the PATH statement. I suggest placing this directory at the beginning of the PATH statement to override any other directories containing the same files.

The SYSTEM.INI file should be stored in a directory that is linked to a specific PC. If the PC has a hard disk, the file should be in the same directory as Windows if it is on the hard disk or in a directory for hardware-specific files. Make sure the directory containing the file is in the PATH.

Program Group Files

The Windows interface is largely controlled by the various groups that contain the application icons. Figure 8-3 shows a typical Windows screen.

Each window in the Program Manager screen displays the icons for programs in that window or group. The information for each window and its programs is stored in a file with a GRP extension. The PROGMAN.INI file contains references for the current groups, including a reference to the group file.

Like the INI files, the GRP files can be accessed by Windows as long as they are located along the PATH statement. Placing the files in the PATH statement is useful for managing the network, because you can easily store them on a server and provide access to them from each workstation. Standard group files stored on a server also serve as a backup source for files that are corrupted. GRP files can become corrupted with some versions of Windows (including V3.0) when the system is rebooted with

Windows running or when other errors occur. Both the GRP and INI files should be kept in a directory separate from the other Windows files to make upgrading and maintenance easier.

Installing Windows

Before version 3.0 of Windows was introduced, installing Windows on a network server was a frustrating and time-consuming process. Versions 3.0 and 3.1 have simplified the process greatly because of their support for networks.

One of the easiest ways to manage Windows on a network is to install the entire Windows system on the server itself. Once Windows is installed on the server, you can easily configure Windows for different users. This includes client machines with different types of hardware, such as video displays.

Because of the advances in Windows technology, I will not spend a lot of time covering the installation of Windows on the network. There are several publications that are devoted to Windows or cover Windows in almost every issue (e.g., *Windows*

Figure 8-3. Windows V3.1 Program Manager

Magazine, PC Magazine, and *InfoWorld*) and have numerous discussions for installing Windows on a network. Depending on the version of Windows you will be using, you should review these periodicals and your Windows documentation for information on network installation procedures. You should also consult Windows technical support and Digital's customer support centers for information on Windows.

Windows V3.1 is ready for use immediately after it has been installed. Windows V3.0 must be prepared for using PATHWORKS. You do this by running the WIN3SETU program, located on the PCSAV41 system service. If you are running a version of Windows later than version 3.0, you need to run WIN3SETU only if you have an LK250 or LK450 keyboard or are using a DEPCA mouse connected to an older DEPCA interface card.

Installing Windows on a PATHWORKS LAN is a simple process, because network drivers for PATHWORKS are in the Windows V3.1 kit. By your choosing the PATHWORKS driver from the Setup menu, Windows will be ready to run when the setup completes.

The WIN3SETU program copies several files into the Windows directory structure and updates the SYSTEM.INI file for PATHWORKS. This is a simple task, executed by your entering WIN3SETU at the DOS prompt. Be sure to specify the network directory where Windows is stored when it asks you for the location of Windows.

After WIN3SETU finishes, Windows should run with PATHWORKS. Test this by executing WIN and running several applications. If Windows does not start, you must fix the problem before proceeding.

Printing from Windows

After you configure Windows to work with PATHWORKS, any Windows program can access any printer connected to the network. The only concern with printing over a network from Windows is making sure the proper driver is loaded. Table 8-2 lists the correct Windows printer drivers for standard Digital printers. If your network uses other industry-standard printers, such as an HP LaserJet or IBM Proprinter, the normal drivers for these printers should work fine.

There are two ways to use a network printer under Windows V3.x. Both require a connection between the printer and a logical DOS print device such as LPT1, 2, or 3. The first method requires making a printer connection with the USE command. This type of connection is exactly like connecting to a printer for standard DOS programs. Windows can also connect directly to a printer using the Control Panel. Refer to Chapter 6 for examples of using the Control Panel for printer connections and for simple batch procedures for connecting to printers.

Table 8-2. Digital Windows Printer Drivers

Printer	Driver
DEClaser 1100	DEC1100.DRV
DEClaser 2100	DEC1100.DRV
DEClaser 2200	DEC1100.DRV
DEClaser 3200	DEC1100.DRV
LA70	LA70.DRV
LA324	LA324.DRV
LJ250	LJ250.DRV
	PostScript Driver
DEClaser 1150	DEC1150.DRV
DEClaser 2150	DEC2150.DRV
DEClaser 2250	DEC2250.DRV
DEClaser 3250	DEC3250.DRV
PrintServer 20	DECLPS20.WPD
Colormate PS	DECCOLOR.WPD

Program Information Files

Windows runs DOS applications by using a parameter file with a PIF extension. A PIF contains information about where to find the executable program, how much memory it can use, the priority of the process, and several advanced setup features. If a program does not have a PIF, Windows will use the default PIF, which is also used by the DOS session in Windows. PIFs are created and modified with the PIF Editor, which is normally shown in the Windows Accessories group.

PATHWORKS comes with several PIFs tailored specifically for its utilities. The files shipped with PATHWORKS V4.0 are listed in Table 8-3.

Table 8-3. PATHWORKS PIFs

PIF Name	Application
ATTRIB.PIF	Net Attrib Command
DWDOS286.PIF	DECwindows 286
DWDOS386.PIF	DECwindows 386
DWINFO2.PIF	DECwindows Info 286
DWINFO3.PIF	DECwindows Info 386
MAIL.PIF	Mail
NCP.PIF	Network Control Program
NCPDEFO.PIF	NCP Define Object
NCPDEFP.PIF	NCP Define Permanent
NCPEVENT.PIF	NCP Event Logging
NCPLOOP.PIF	NCP Loop Commands
NCPSET.PIF	NCP Set Commands
NCPSHOW.PIF	NCP Show Commands
NCPTELL.PIF	NCP Tell Commands
SEDT.PIF	SEDT (EDT-Style Editor)
SETHOST.PIF	SETHOST
SPAWNER.PIF	Job Spawner

You can enter any of these files in a program group by selecting New from the Windows File menu and clicking on the PIF in the file list. Verify that the program name in the PIF points to the proper location for the program or that the program is located in a directory on the PATH statement.

You can also access PIFs by placing them on the PATH statement. This is handy for networks because the network directory may be connected to a different drive letter on other clients.

CHAPTER 9

Managing Network Applications

Network application management involves both technical aspects, such as managing and tuning applications, and functional aspects, such as determining which applications to use and how users will access the features of those applications. The ease of access and ease of use of the applications you choose for your network will determine the benefits they offer to your organization. Your understanding of the applications' configurations and of configuration files and settings will directly affect both ease of use and ease of access. This chapter takes a cursory look at several popular applications, both PATHWORKS and standard applications, and their configurations.

DOS APPLICATIONS

Many DOS applications can run on various networks. WordPerfect Corp.'s WordPerfect, Borland's Paradox, Borland's dBase, and numerous others will run on most networks and provide some facilities (usually very limited) for managing themselves.

Unfortunately, DOS programs do not standardize on how they maintain their own configuration information, much less on how they operate on a network. Some programs use configuration files stored with the programs, others use files that are located in the user's directory, and some use a combination of the two. Some programs also insist on running only when their directory is the current directory.

Because of the lack of standardization and network support, it is impossible to adequately explain a general approach to managing DOS applications on the network, other than by using the batch procedures mentioned in the previous chapter. If you are running DOS applications on your network, read the information in your manuals and test everything very carefully.

PATHWORKS Mail

One of the greatest and earliest benefits to users of LANs was electronic mail. Long before many people knew what voice mail was, electronic mail was providing communications among people around the world. It not only provided for timely communications, but also served to eliminate telephone tag and to provide documentation of communications among people. Businesses that implemented electronic mail in a test environment soon began to depend on it for day-to-day operations.

Today's electronic mail is viewed as a cornerstone of the LAN, not as an option. PATHWORKS takes the traditional approach to electronic mail to a new level by providing a capable mail system as a standard feature.

The PATHWORKS Mail system serves client users such as DOS, OS/2, and Macintosh users and interfaces to the mail systems located on VMS, OS/2, or ULTRIX nodes. Sites using Digital's powerful ALL-IN-1 system can purchase cost-effective versions of ALL-IN-1 Mail for Windows PATHWORKS for Windows includes an ALL-IN-1 Mail for Windows licence. Also, VMSmail adds power to typical PATHWORKS networks through its ability to interface with applications running on a VMS system.

The PATHWORKS Mail application uses DECnet to communicate with the file server. Mail accesses and stores messages in the user's account on the server. It provides an easy-to-use interface for the user, relying heavily on pull-down menus and simple screens. Mouse support is provided for PCs using a DOS mouse driver (MOUSE.COM or MOUSE.SYS). Mail allows the user to choose the SEDT editor or another editor of choice.

Client Configuration. Before you run PATHWORKS Mail on a client workstation, you must run the MAILSETU program to configure the client. This program prepares the client for running Mail and creates the MAIL.INI file, which maintains the configuration information for a particular client user. The program will ask for the directory for the MAIL.INI file, the username for the server, and the server node name, and it will allow you to change several parameters that affect how mail operates, such as the mouse and keyboard.

The MAIL.INI file may be stored in any directory. Mail locates this file by looking in the directory specified by the DNETMAIL, DECMET, and PCSA environment variables. If the file is not found, Mail will look in the current directory and then in directories located on the DOS PATH. To automatically set the environment variable, include the following statement in the AUTOEXEC.BAT file or in a batch procedure executed at login time:

```
SET DNETMAIL = C:\MAIL.
```

This example specifies that Mail should look in the MAIL directory on the C: drive.

If your users access mail from different workstations, place the MAIL.INI file in their personal directories on the server. The SET statement in the last paragraph should be set in the AUTOUSER.BAT program when they log in. Keeping MAIL.INI on the server and setting the DNETMAIL variable to its location allows users to connect to their mail accounts from any PC on the network.

Mail is executed by typing MAIL at the DOS prompt or including this statement in a batch file or menu statement. If Mail is executed with the -N parameter (i.e., C:\>MAIL -N), Mail will check for new messages.

MAILCHK Utility. The MAILCHK utility allows the user to check the status of his or her mailbox from a client PC, without starting the Mail program. Before MAILCHK is used, it must open a connection to the network Mail account. The simplest way to accomplish this is to include MAILCHK in AUTOUSER.BAT or one of the other standard batch procedures that are executed when a user logs into the personal account. This will ensure that the user is always able to run MAILCHK and can access his or her mail account from any workstation.

The format for executing MAILCHK is:

```
C:\> MAILCHK server username [password] /qualifier
```

MAILCHK uses several qualifiers to control its operation. These qualifiers are listed and described in Table 9-1.

Table 9-1. MAILCHK Qualifiers

Qualifier	Function
/Start	Connects the client to the default node or the node specified with the /Start command. If the node and user information are supplied, they must be in the following order: node, user, password. The password is optional, since MAILCHK will prompt for it if it is not included. Spaces should be used to separate the parameters. If the server and user information are in the DECALIAS.DAT database, you do not need to specify them with the command.
/Status	Displays information about the number of new messages and the status of the mail account.
/Show	Displays the number of new messages.
/Verbose	Displays the number of messages and the date, sender, and subject of each message. This qualifier can be abbreviated to /V.
/Stop	Closes the network connection to the mail account.

In a Windows environment, MAILCHK can be loaded with a special PIF file. PATHWORKS includes a MAIL.PIF file for the Mail program, which provides a good starting point. Figure 9-1 shows the PIF Editor screen with the MAILCHK.PIF file. This file was created by loading the MAIL.PIF file into the editor and choosing the Save As command from the File menu. For a PIF file to be used with an executable file, one or both of the files should be on the DOS search PATH.

In the MAILCHK.PIF file, notice that the display will run in a window and that the Close Window on Exit box is not checked. The dialog box for the entry in the Program Manager is shown in Figure 9-2.

Notice the command line E:\PCAPP\MAILCHK.EXE/V. This command points to the MAILCHK.EXE program in the E:\PCAPP directory on the PCSAV41 service. The /V qualifier causes MAILCHK to run with the Verbose qualifier. Because the PIF is located in a directory on the DOS PATH, when MAILCHK executes, Windows uses the parameters from the PIF for its execution.

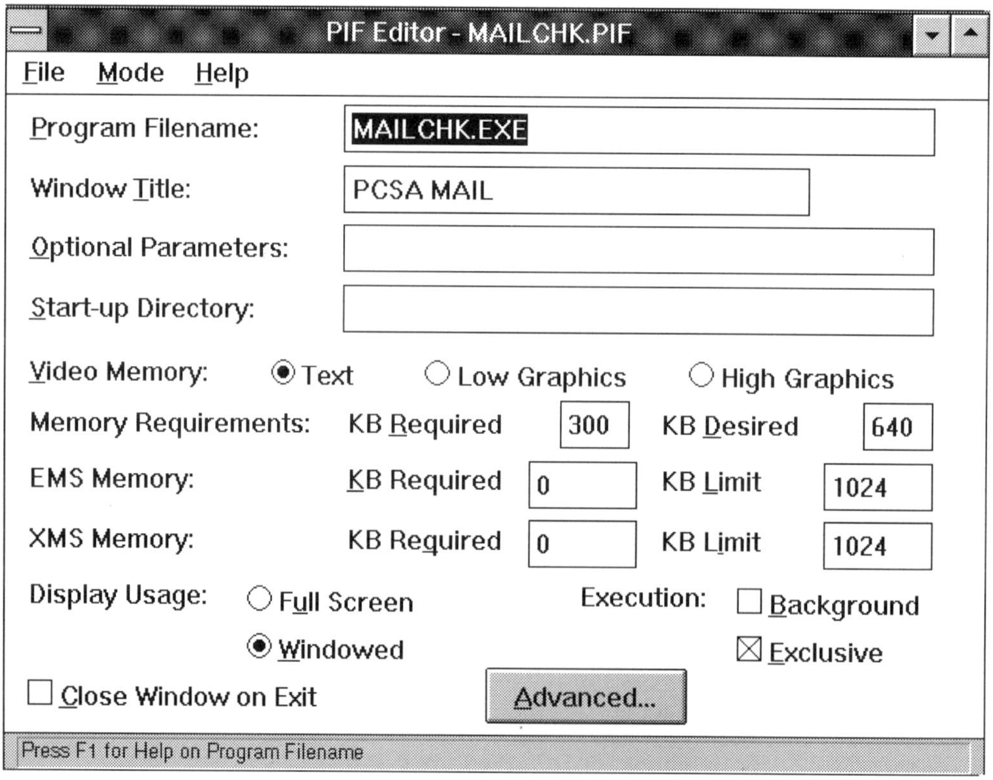

Figure 9-1. PIF Editor with MAILCHK.PIF

The program runs in a window. This example can be expanded for other DOS programs, including other mail and PATHWORKS utilities.

USETSR

SoftTech Solutions' USETSR is a handy utility for both LAN Manager and NetWare networks. It can be used for both at the same time if you are running PATHWORKS for DOS (NetWare Coexistence). USETSR is a TSR program designed to make connecting or disconnecting to network services easier for DOS users. The program loads during the boot process (via AUTOEXEC.BAT) and is available from DOS and other character cell (text) programs by pressing a hot-key combination.

To start the program, enter the command USETSR in your AUTOEXEC.BAT program or the file that starts your network (STARTNET.BAT). USETSR should be loaded after all other TSRs if you will want to unload it later.

The default hot key for USETSR is ALT-U, but you can change it to another ALT key sequence. Pressing the hot key will cause the main screen to pop up over your current application. (See Figure 9-3.) Notice how the main screen displays your current network connections. The example screen shows a PC running NetWare Coexistence, with drives R, Y, and Z connected to a NetWare server and drive H connected to the PCSAV41 service on a PATHWORKS server. This is very handy when you are running an application and can't remember which network connection has the service you are looking for. Pressing ALT-U will give you a quick look at your connections; then pressing ESC will return you to your application.

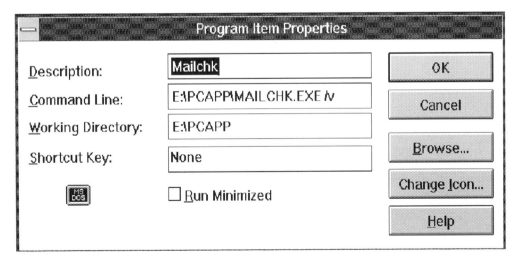

Figure 9-2. Program Item Properties for MAILCHK.PIF

USETSR is really handy when you are running an application and realize that you need to connect to a different file or print service or possibly disconnect from a service and connect to a new one. Pressing the hot key and the Enter key will bring up the connection screen that will allow you to make the connections. (See Figure 9-4.) The connection screen will accept the information required to connect to the network service. If a username and password are required, you can also enter them. Press F10 to complete the connection. Once the connection is complete, press ESC to return you to your application.

To disconnect from a service, you should press the hot key and then press D to access the disconnect screen. You complete the disconnect process by entering the drive letter and pressing Enter.

The Options menu is used to change the hot-key definition and optionally to save the change. If the change is not saved, it will stay in effect until the program is unloaded or the PC is rebooted. You can also use the Options menu to unload the program from memory, if USETSR was the last TSR loaded.

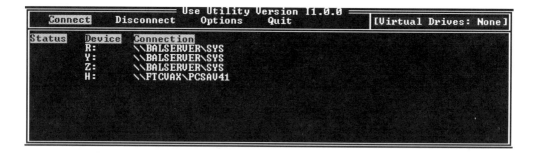

Figure 9-3. USETSR Main Screen

Figure 9-4. USETSR Connection Screen

If USETSR has already been loaded and you try to load it again, it will display a message indicating that it is already active.

WINDOWS APPLICATIONS

Newer Windows application programs and utilities are becoming network aware, and some vendors are beginning to add network capabilities to their programs. The Windows File Manager can access PATHWORKS services just as if they were local drives.

Tools such as File Manager, Digital's File Browser, or Norton Desktop provide a simple interface for users to access network files. The GUI used by all Windows applications is an intuitive interface for users and administrators. The Windows V3.1 File Manager is much easier to use than earlier versions and offers several new features.

The File Browser from Digital is especially well suited for use on a network because of its place in Digital's NAS strategy and the extensions it offers. For example, if a user wants to mail a file from DOS or Windows File Manager, the user must load the mail program, then select the person to whom the file will be sent, and finally select the file. Using the File Browser, the user selects the file, clicks on the mail button, and with a click of the mouse selects the addressee and mails the file.

The major difference between the File Browser and the other Windows file managers is the native network support. File Browser lets you select only certain files with filters and lets you create a named icon for a particular directory, providing one-click access to commonly used files. There is also an icon bar on the left side of the screen that can be customized to load certain functions with one click. File Browser can also display various file types (including graphics), directly print files, and convert from one file type to another, although not all files can be converted.

Word Processing

There are a multitude of word processing packages for PCs. Recent versions of WordPerfect and Word for Windows offer support for network installations. Word for Windows V2.0 is easy to install on a network and provides some support for using files on the network. Figure 9-5 shows a Word for Windows V2.0 dialog box for selecting template files. The template selection dialog box allows the user to select templates located either on the network or on a local disk.

Word for Windows stores the configuration information in the WIN.INI file used by Windows and many other programs. The following example shows a section of

WIN.INI for Word V2.0. The information shown is approximately one-third of the information stored in WIN.INI for Word V2.0 and its related applications:

```
[Microsoft Word 2.0]
AUTOSAVE-path=M:\DATA
INI-path=M:\INI
programdir=S:\WW
Spelling 1033,0=S:\DICT\SPELL.DLL,C:\DICT\SP_AM.LEX
Hyphenate
1033,0=S:\WW\HYPH.DLL,S:\WW\HY_AM.LEX,S:\WW\SP_A
M.LEX
Thesaurus 1033,0=S:\DICT\THES.DLL,S:\DICT\TH_AM.LEX
Grammar
1033,0=S:\DICT\GRAMMAR.DLL,S:\DICT\GR_AM.LEX
ButtonFieldClicks=2
DOT-PATH2=S:\WWDOT
DOT-PATH1=c:\data
DOT-PATH=c:\ww
doc-path=M:\data
```

Notice how the files are spread across the S:, M:, and C: drives. The program files for Word for Windows V2.0 are stored in the WW directory on the S: drive, while the INI file for Word for Windows V2.0 is located in the INI directory on the M: drive, which happens to be the home directory location. Other files such as the various dictionary and grammar files are stored in the DICT directory, also located on the S: drive.

The directory for documents is the DATA directory, located on the M: drive. Remember that the M: drive is mapped to the user's personal directory at login time. This means that every user will find his or her personal files on the M: drive when he or she logs in, even though the users are using the same WIN.INI file.

Moving the different types of files into each user's own directory structures allows the network manager to manage the different pieces of the system separately. When it is time to upgrade to a new version of Word for Windows, the manager can safely move the files into the S:\WW directory without overwriting each user's INI, dictionary, and other files. Other sections of WIN.INI that are not shown provide a mechanism for controlling the other Microsoft applications in a similar manner.

Word for Windows is an important application for PATHWORKS because it fits into the NAS strategy by offering support for electronic mail and Digital's Compound Document Architecture (CDA).

TERMINAL EMULATORS

Two basic types of terminal programs are available today for communicating in a host environment: traditional asynchronous communications programs and programs that use Digital's LAT and CTERM protocols. Standard communications programs, which are the most prevalent, include programs that provide access to the system only through a modem or asynchronous communications line. This requires a direct connection or phone line connection to the host, and these programs will typically not function over a network connection. Examples of these programs are DCA Inc.'s Crosstalk and Datastorm Technologies Inc.'s Procomm.

Other programs provide access over the Ethernet network using Digital's LAT and CTERM protocols. These protocols run over the network and typically are used to communicate between a terminal server and host. By using LAT or CTERM, the programs provide virtually transparent access to the host over the LAN or WAN and allow the users to run host and PC applications, with only the Ethernet cable connecting the client to the network. In a PATHWORKS installation, LAT is used

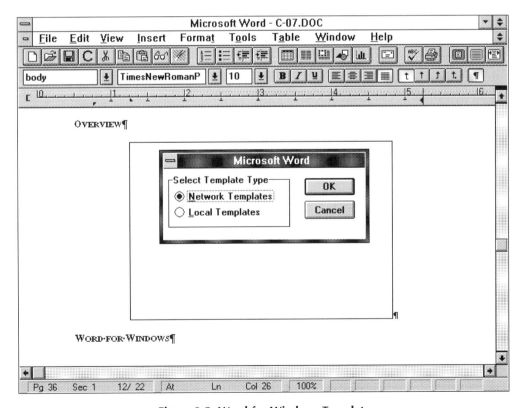

Figure 9-5. Word for Windows Templates

for connecting to hosts over a LAN, while CTERM can provide access to hosts anywhere in the world over a WAN. I highly recommend programs that use these protocols over more traditional programs that provide only asynchronous communications.

PATHWORKS also provides tools for third-party applications via the TRMNLAXS.DLL file. This file is included with PATHWORKS in the kit and includes routines for developing terminal emulation software for PATHWORKS.

SmarTerm

Persoft Inc.'s SmarTerm software, available in both DOS and Windows versions, provides many useful features to PATHWORKS users and MIS staff. It functions over a dial-up line or direct connection and over the PATHWORKS network using LAT. The ability to define different configurations and store them by name is very handy and will simplify life for the MIS staff and users. Other useful features include the ability to define macros and assign them to function keys, remap the PC keyboard to match any other keyboard, and capture screen dialog to a PC file.

VT320

VT320 (for Windows) and SETHOST (for DOS) have one major advantage over other terminal emulation packages: They are included free with PATHWORKS! Both VT320 and SETHOST are patterned after the VT300 series of Digital terminals. Pressing the F3 function key with VT320 and SETHOST installed or on a VT-series terminal will access the SETUP mode. You can also map the function keys to other keys by using the "generic" keymap.

VT320 provides the normal advantages of most Windows applications. (See Figure 9-6.) It runs under Windows V3.x, and provides the cut-and-paste functions found in most Windows applications. You can run more than one copy of VT320 at a time, connecting to the same or different host systems. VT320 also allows you to record sequences of keystrokes and store them in a log file.

VT320 provides access to the server or other system by using serial protocols or by communicating over the network using LAT, CTERM, or TELNET. PATHWORKS comes with both LAT and CTERM. TELNET can be added with the TCP/IP option. If your PC is connected using more than one protocol, you can also run multiple copies of VT320 with different protocols. By using both network communications and a serial connection, you may use the same PC both as a network node and as the system console. The support for serial communications is somewhat limited, providing access only through serial port COM1 or COM2.

Before running VT320, install it in a Windows program group. This is accomplished by selecting File/New and entering the path to VT320.EXE. VT320 is typically stored in the PCSAV41 service directory MSWINV30 (for Windows Version V3.0). Figure 9-9 shows the Program Manager Properties dialog box with the configuration for VT320. In this example, VT320 has been copied to the local C:\ directory. Windows V3.1 has an expanded Properties box that allows the specification of a working directory and shortcut key. This overcomes some, but not all,of the limitations of the Windows V3.0 Properties box.

If you will be using LAT, you must also run LATCP on the client and define enough session control blocks (SCB) for your applications. It is usually sufficient to start off with four and increase this if you encounter problems. You define SCBs by using the WIN3SETU program with PATHWORKS V4.1. If you do not run WIN3SETU, use the following command:

```
LATCP> DEFINE SCB 4
```

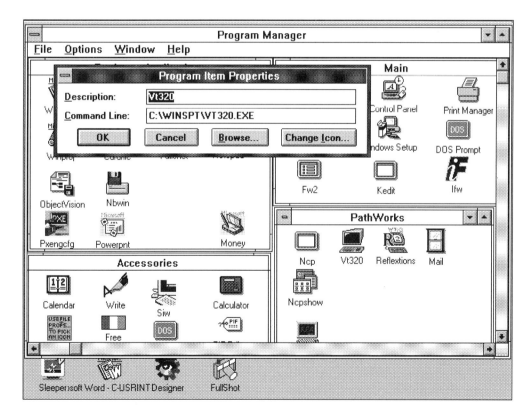

Figure 9-6. VT320 Configuration Screen

If you are running Windows, you must define enough SCBs to handle the number of concurrent sessions of VT320 or SETHOST or a third-party program. The value may range from 0 to 16. Each instance of VT320 or SETHOST will require a single SCB. If you are running no more than four simultaneous sessions, then the default will suffice.

SETHOST

SETHOST is a terminal emulator that runs under DOS. SETHOST provides most traditional features such as the ability to configure the screen, send and capture files, save configurations, and record sequences of keystrokes for storage in a script file.

Like VT320, SETHOST provides access to the server or other system either by using serial protocols or by communicating over the network using LAT, CTERM, or TELNET. SETHOST provides up to four simultaneous sessions over different protocols. By using network communications and a serial connection, you can use the same PC as a network node and as the system console. The support for serial communications provides access through serial port COM1 or COM2. SETHOST will use whichever transport is available for communicating over the network.

SETHOST is designed for the traditional DOS environment but can also run under Windows by using a PIF. You access Configuration mode by pressing the F3 function key. You select options by using the arrow keys to highlight the desired function and then pressing Enter to select the option. Some options have submenus that function in the same manner. To switch from one major option to another (for example, Actions to Communications), press the Page Up or Page Down key.

You may save configurations by selecting the Save Set-Up Parameters option on the Actions menu. Make sure the configurations are stored in a directory that is always accessible and is included in the DOS path or referenced by the SETHOST environment variable. SETHOST looks for its files in the current directory and then checks the directory the SETHOST variable points to (if set). If the SETHOST variable is not set, SETHOST locates the files by checking directories in the DOS path.

CD-ROM AND DISK/TAPE DEVICES

InfoServer

Digital's InfoServer 150 provides storage services to the network, including VMS and PATHWORKS clients. The InfoServer also supports NetWare LANs and can coexist on a network with PATHWORKS and NetWare clients.

The InfoServer 150 is designed to provide a variety of services to the LAN. Services on the InfoServer will be accessible to all users on the network. There is no additional load placed on any of the servers, because the InfoServer sits directly on the network and manages its own devices.

InfoServer supports up to 14 SCSI devices, including tape drives, hard disks, magneto-optical disks, and CD-ROMs. It supports both the ISO 9660 and High Sierra CD-ROM formats. InfoServer automatically mounts DOS-format CD-ROMs and automatically creates PATHWORKS services for them.

The InfoServer 150 attaches directly to an Ethernet network via either ThinWire or ThickWire connections and uses LAST and LAT as the LAN transports. PATHWORKS clients must use LAD to connect to services on the InfoServer. You must also load the MSCDEX driver on the PATHWORKS client. You can use NETSETUP to reconfigure the client and automatically load MSCDEX. Figure 9-7 shows an InfoServer 150 attached to a simple LAN.

A PATHWORKS client can access services on the InfoServer 150 in the same manner as a disk service on a VMS server. To specify an InfoServer CD-ROM device, add the /CDROM qualifier to the USE command. The following command connects the next available drive to an InfoServer service:

```
C:\> USE ?: \\server\service  /CDROM
```

To connect to an InfoServer disk service, type:

```
C:\> USE ?: \\server\service
```

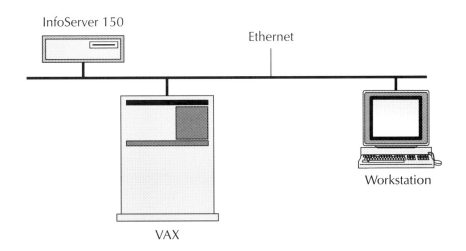

Figure 9-7. InfoServer 150 Attached to a Simple LAN

PATHWORKS users can also query the network to find out what InfoServers and InfoServer services are available. This command displays a list of all InfoServers on the network:

```
C:\> USE  /CDROM /SHOW
```

A slight variation of this command displays the services available on a particular InfoServer:

```
C:\> USE  \\server /SHOW
```

Other CD-ROM Devices

A large part of the CD-ROM revolution is taking place with CD-ROM readers attached to PCs. One example of these popular devices is Sony Corp. of America's CD-ROM device. This device can attach to a PC as a local drive and can be added to an OS/2 LAN Manager server for use across the network. The Sony CD-ROM is cost-effective and efficient.

The Sony CD-ROM (and most other CD-ROMs for PCs) use the Microsoft CD extensions for DOS. When you use a PC with this type of CD-ROM driver on a network, make sure the driver is loaded after STARTNET. If not, the PATHWORKS Redirector will not load.

DISTRIBUTED PROCESSING APPLICATIONS

A discussion of networks would not be complete without a mention of distributed processing. This topic has been cursed and discussed for many years, and it is viewed as either a savior or a killer for business applications.

Distributed processing has been in use for many years. VMS distributed systems in particular have been in use in many different scenarios. The VMS operating system has numerous features that provide an ideal platform for distributed systems.

Digital is a key player in this environment because of its commitment to standards. The Open Software Foundation (OSF) and other standards bodies have specifications for distributed operating environments. Digital has always played a major role in almost every standards organization, and it has built systems that support wide-ranging standards.

PATHWORKS inherits many of the features of VMS, including the ability to build client applications that work in conjunction with applications running on a server. Sample C routines provided with PATHWORKS allow a client to talk to other clients or servers running over the network. A number of applications that are part of PATHWORKS are actually client/server applications. The client Mail utility runs on the client and uses DECnet to access the mail services on the server. Other examples of distributed processing programs are LATCP and NCP on the client, plus most of the other PATHWORKS utilities.

Integrated Systems

The business computer system prevalent in many successful companies provides a perfect environment for using PATHWORKS. Extracting information from corporate databases into word processors or spreadsheets is one of the most often performed tasks in today's typical business. The information may be targeted at an interoffice report, cost analysis, or status report to a customer. The possibilities are almost endless.

One of the easiest ways to pull information from a server-based system is to use the screen-copy facility of most terminal emulators. In a program such as SETHOST or Reflection for DOS from Walker, Richer & Quinn, the user captures the screen to a file. The file may be stored on the user's local drive or on a server directory. After the information is captured, the user must exit the emulator or switch to another DOS session and execute the target program. The information captured may be used directly or may require massaging. Spreadsheets typically are picky about the format of files imported into them.

Windows users are in a better position to use data from other systems because of the multitasking and cut-and-paste facilities of Windows. It is easy to move text from one program to another using the cut-and-paste facility and the Windows clipboard. Applications that have no knowledge of each other can transfer information using the clipboard. Most Windows applications also support Dynamic Data Exchange (DDE), which can be used to automatically pick up the information from the server application.

Screen-copy features are available in almost every emulator on the market, including programs that do not support LAT or networks. PATHWORKS provides a more efficient method of extracting a large amount of data by extracting the information directly onto a server drive. A report could be saved in a typical server directory with a DOS file name of eight characters or less. This file would be available immediately for a client application to access and manipulate.

Many programs can transfer a report file to disk and format it for a typical spreadsheet at the same time. The most often used file types are Lotus 1-2-3 format and comma-delimited. All of the top spreadsheets can read Lotus 1-2-3 and comma-delimited files with no problem. A comma-delimited file is very easy to produce if you are writing your own report programs. The following is a section of a simple comma-delimited file:

```
"No","Description","Qty","Category"

12355, "Hammer ",10,"A"
44421, "Screw - 1/4-20 2In",B
44422, "Screwdriver",13,"A"
55522, "Nail - 10p",200,"B"
```

Each column, or field, in the file is separated by a comma. If the field contains alphanumeric information, it is enclosed by quotes. When this file is imported into a spreadsheet or database, each row in the file becomes a row in the spreadsheet or database, and the columns become columns or fields. Figure 9-8 shows the setup parameters for the import operators, while Figure 9-9 shows the imported data.

Figures 9-8 and 9-9 illustrate how easy it is to move data from a server-based application to a spreadsheet or database. A perfect application for this ability is producing

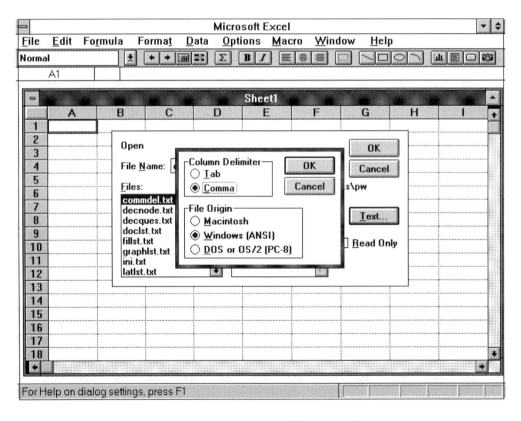

Figure 9-8. Importing a File into Excel

the many graphic reports that most managers are looking for to manage their business. Today's managers understand and expect color graphics instead of traditional reports showing multiple columns and pages of confusing numbers.

Excel, Quatro Pro, and a number of other PC-based programs provide excellent graphics that are easy to generate. Extracting data from a server-based application and generating the graphics with Excel is much easier and more flexible than trying to develop the graphics on the server. Figure 9-10 shows the same spreadsheet from Figures 9-8 and 9-9 with a graphic incorporated into the document.

The simple graph in the figure was made with five clicks of the mouse, using the data from the ASCII file example. This entire process could be accomplished in 5 to 10 seconds, after the data is extracted from the other system. The bottom line results from these examples: We accomplished the task very quickly and reduced the processing load on the server by moving the graphics process to the client workstation.

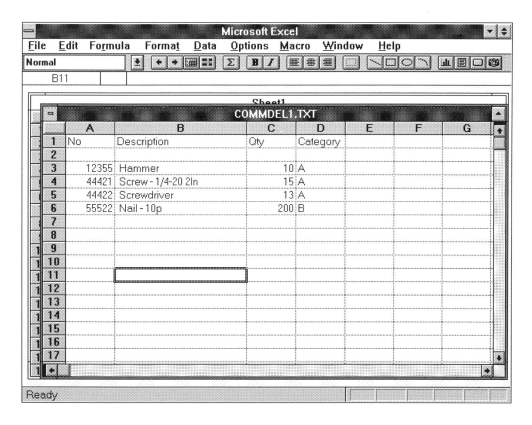

Figure 9-9. Excel with Imported Data

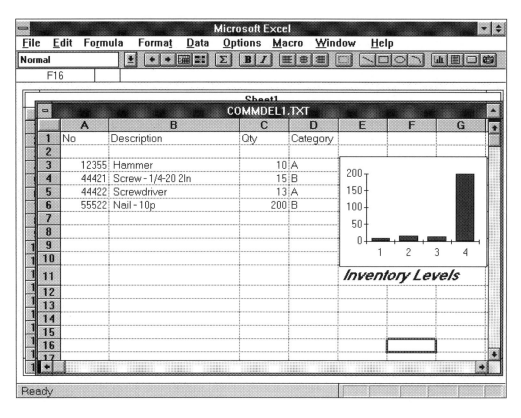

Figure 9-10. Excel Graphic Figure

Computer-Aided Design

Many organizations are using client machines for tasks that were traditionally performed on large workstations or computers. PC-based computer-aided design (CAD) systems such as Intergraph Corp.'s MicroStation and Autodesk Inc.'s AutoCAD have brought powerful design capabilities to the PC and Macintosh. Intergraph and Autodesk offer both PC- and minicomputer-based packages. Intergraph also provides a Macintosh version.

PATHWORKS provides an ideal environment for integrating these systems together. UNIX-based Intergraph workstations running the powerful Engineering Modeling System can use a VAXserver to store their graphics files. Client PC and Macintosh systems running MicroStation can share files with the UNIX machines, using the VAX as the interface. Files created on either system can be accessed by the other systems, with no conversions.

One bothersome task faced by most manufacturing organizations is the process of entering a bill of material into the manufacturing system. This process can be simplified by having the manufacturing system automatically pick up the bill of material from the CAD system.

This example is the reverse of the data extraction example, because information will be moved from the client PC, Macintosh, or UNIX workstation to the server application. The CAD system simply generates the bill of material and exports it to a flat ASCII file. This file is either moved to a file server directory or stored directly in a file-server directory. The only complicated piece is the program that loads the bill of material. This program normally runs on the server as a background task at a standard interval. The incoming file should have an identifying name or extension that signifies that it is an incoming bill of material. Once the file is loaded, the ASCII version is deleted or marked as loaded.

This process may sound complex, but it involves generating only one program and possibly a macro for the CAD package and creating some simple standards for file names and storage. Once this system is in place, it eliminates a labor-intensive task and reduces the chance for errors when new or modified bills of material are loaded.

Desktop Publishing

Desktop publishing functions can also benefit greatly from the proper implementation of PATHWORKS. Programs such as Aldus Corp.'s PageMaker and Ventura Software Inc.'s Publisher bring tremendous power to PC and Macintosh clients. PageMaker runs on both the Macintosh and PC.

Desktop publishing has the same problem as the CAD and data extraction examples: the sharing of information with other client and server applications. Many organizations use PC CAD packages and Macintosh desktop publishing packages. Conversion programs and "sneaker net" are the most often used methods of moving CAD graphics into the Macintosh publishing system. This is very time-consuming and generates lots of duplicate files, further adding to user's management problems.

The solution is to use PATHWORKS as the common storage medium. The Macintosh can directly read the files created by the CAD system. PATHWORKS also lets you easily extract data from a server-based system and integrate it into the document.

With the addition of Word for Windows to Digital's CDA family, the task of moving documents and graphics from one application to another is becoming easy for the CDA family and for packages that support exchanging information with Word for Windows.

Client/Server Applications

Client/Server applications have been the talk of the industry for several years. While many vendors and users have been struggling to understand and implement this technology, Digital has been quietly evolving and using it. As discussed earlier, many PATHWORKS commands use client/server technology to perform their functions. Digital and other vendors now offer several ways for users to implement a client/server strategy over a PATHWORKS network. The high-level discussion in the next several sections is designed to introduce you to different aspects of the client/server architectures available on a PATHWORKS network.

Visual Basic. Microsoft's Visual Basic is a tremendously powerful tool for application development. Visual Basic provides tools for quickly developing the Windows user interface and for allowing programs to focus on the system logic. Visual Basic has been extended in the Digital environment by Digital as well as by third-party vendors.

Digital and Microsoft are both developing Visual Basic APIs for key products. Digital has developed an API for SQL Services that allows Visual Basic applications to read and write to an Rdb database. Digital is also building a Visual Basic API for TeamLinks that will call a Visual Basic application to call TeamLinks functions.

Using Visual Basic and CONNX, you can enhance the Visual Basic Cardfile sample program to read and write records to the vendor file of an integrated system. The free-form comment section of the file could store comments either on the VAX or on the network and link the index to the RMS records. If you take this example a step further, Visual Basic could be used to build a system that displays images stored on the network whenever the user looks up an item number on the VAX.

Another tool for building applications with Visual Basic is the Desktop ACMS product from Digital. Desktop ACMS allows Visual Basic programs on client PCs to read and write to a relational database located on a VAX somewhere on the network. Because ACMS is used to manage the database interface, true client/server applications can support large numbers of users.

Fourth-Generation Languages

Paradox, dBase, and many other packages for client workstations provide users with the technology to quickly generate custom applications and reports. Many of these databases can run over a network and allow access to the database by concurrent users.

Powerful minicomputer software packages, such as Oracle Corp.'s Oracle, Digital's Rdb, Cognos' PowerHouse, and Ingres' Ingres, are available for VMS servers and provide a foundation for building enterprisewide systems that can stand the strain of large numbers of simultaneous users. There are many software packages available for

VMS that are based on one of these databases. The current VMS software directory (which is 2 inches thick) gives an indication of the wide variety of applications available for these database systems.

Systems such as Paradox and Microrim's Microrim's Vanguard have optional features that provide integration with systems running on other computers. The SQL Link option for Paradox allows Paradox applications to read and write to an SQL database running on a server. Borland's Rdb Link provides similar features for systems using Rdb.

A combination of server and client fourth-generation language (4GL) packages provides an ideal environment to build client/server systems. A typical client/server application will share data between the server and client with no intervention by the user.

The X Window System

Any discussion of client/server systems should at least mention the X Window System and DECwindows. The X Window System standard took the UNIX world by storm in the 1980s. Digital has implemented the Motif version of the X Window System in its DECwindows/Motif product. In the world of X, the client and server roles are reversed. This means that a PC running some type of X emulator is actually the server, and the VAX is the client. Confusing? At least we don't have to understand this terminology to use the X environment.

A full discussion on X is outside the scope of this book, but I would like to mention how PATHWORKS and the X Window System are linked. PATHWORKS is shipped with a DECwindows/Motif emulator for PCs that allows a PC to access X applications running on a VMS, ULTRIX, or UNIX system. PC DECwindows/Motif can access multiple X sessions running anywhere on the network. DECwindows/Motif is fully documented in the *PC DECwindows/Motif Guide* included with the PATHWORKS documentation.

Digital also offers another X product called eXcursion, which provides similar features to PC DECwindows/Motif. The eXcursion product is also a full-featured Microsoft Windows application. If you plan to use X of any flavor on your system, you should explore both DECwindows/Motif and eXcursion to compare the costs and benefits.

NETWORK APPLICATION SUPPORT

NAS is an architecture that encompasses a set of standards-compliant products that support the running of applications on many different types of hardware. NAS-compliant software provides the assurance that your investment in software will be compatible with current and future versions of hardware and software and will be able to grow with your organization.

The NAS product sets are offered from Digital in packages designed to support a particular need. They are grouped according to needs such as Application Portability (NAS 100), Distributed Applications (NAS 200), and so on. PATHWORKS is a member of the NAS 200 package, which also includes SQL support, DECnet with Open Systems Interconnect (OSI) extensions, and other options. Numerous third-party products also support NAS, including Windows, Word for Windows, Excel, and Visual Basic. In 1992, Digital estimated that more than 2,400 third-party packages used one or more NAS services.

CHAPTER 10

Practical Approach to Network Management

Managing any computer system is an adventure that places conflicting requirements on system managers. Organizational management, systems personnel, and users often have very different expectations for the system. News reports, computer publications, business magazines, and many other media sources compound the problem by constantly bombarding everyone with new ideas and promises. This adds to the confusion prevalent in most organizations. Technology changes so fast that it is impossible for managers to keep abreast of the current trends and implement useful portions of the new technology throughout an organization. LANs, open systems, UNIX, and other trends are all touted as the way of the future.

Other perspectives add to the problems of managing an enterprisewide system such as a LAN. Software maintenance, managing the cable plant and other network components, planning for the future, and implementing new applications can totally consume a systems department, leading to frustration within all segments of the organization. Let's begin our discussion of LAN management with a review of the different perspectives within an organization.

NETWORK MANAGEMENT PERSPECTIVES

Network management must be viewed in several contexts to properly understand the expectations of everyone involved with the network. Users have a much different view of proper network management than personnel in the systems administration department. High-level managers of an organization will have an even different view from all others. Proper LAN management requires understanding all perspectives.

Upper Management

In most organizations, upper management personnel view the computer system (including the support groups) as a relatively necessary overhead. Their focus is the mission of the organization, involving customer service, marketing, manufacturing, and so on. Available funds are normally targeted toward manufacturing equipment, vehicles, buildings, and other traditional business equipment. Funding for computer systems is usually seen as a drain on capital and expense dollars that could be used for another purpose.

Managers are aware of all the hoopla over downsizing and using LANs to reduce overall systems costs. Many companies are also investigating outsourcing systems management to obtain more efficient systems or reduce systems management costs.

The performance expectations of company managers for the internal systems are very different from some other groups. Timely reporting for every business segment is one of company managers' most requested aspects for a system. Today's managers also expect critical information to be available in clear graphic formats, depicting current trends, results, and other information useful in making important decisions.

Systems managers are also expected to provide reliable, functional systems for all areas of the business. Upper management expects systems to be available most of the time and to be repaired quickly when they fail. Functional systems that link all facets of the business and meet the various needs of all departments are taken for granted.

Systems Management

Most medium-size organizations have information systems (IS) departments for managing their computer systems. These groups view the systems from a management perspective, with concerns over uptime, technology, program modifications, and so on.

If the systems are minicomputer- or mainframe-based, this perspective will probably be from the viewpoint of the big system, where one or more large computers serve many different users in a timesharing fashion. Most systems personnel will view the computer systems as their concern and not the users'. It is normally very difficult for users to obtain data from these systems, as the systems department backlog is very long. Support for obtaining new applications may be delayed because of the long analysis phase that most IS departments go through.

To implement new technology in this type of organization can be very difficult, as everything may be forced through the systems department. IS personnel may feel that LANs are a threat to their department or position. Many people in these groups are also driven by systems, not by the business objectives for the organization. This can cause problems when changes or new technologies are needed immediately.

Client Environment

A user's perspective is very different from the IS and the company management point of view. Most organizations operating today are very lean and place very high demands on all employees. Computer systems offer users a tool that promises to reduce or simplify their workload. Professional departments such as engineering, administration, and maintenance push for advanced systems to use the latest technology available. These users typically are computer literate and demand systems that support their job requirements. Others such as production schedulers, clerks, and others in areas directly involved in running the business may be frustrated with their current systems but may not understand what needs to change to correct the problem, or they may resist changes because of the disruption it would cause.

Many people today have experience with LANs and PCs. These people will be tremendously frustrated when placed in an environment that provides access to out-of-date systems that are awkward to use and go down frequently. People who move from Windows or Macintosh environments to character-based timesharing applications become frustrated very quickly. In a LAN environment, these people expect applications that match their job requirements and take advantage of current technology.

Technology

Viewing system management from the technology perspective is a very big concern today. Arguments over LANs versus minicomputers, UNIX versus everything else, Windows versus DOS, and so on, are examples of technological arguments that are confusing many people and driving purchase decisions for many new systems. Companies are purchasing UNIX systems because they are scared by the open-systems argument. Others are moving to PC LANs because they believe that is the only way to downsize.

The proper way to view technology is to use what is appropriate for your application. If an application requires UNIX, put it on a UNIX box. If another application requires a PC, use a PC. Just buy the appropriate hardware for the application at hand. To protect yourself in the technology war, always buy the most cost-effective hardware. If the difference in the price for a 386 versus a 486 PC is $400, buy the 486. This box should run any software that comes out for many years to come. If you always purchase the lowest cost alternative, you will be forced into replacing systems frequently, as the demands of your software exceed the capabilities for your systems.

Network management tools are an important technology to consider for your network. Management software and smart network components such as bridges and routers are improving every day. These tools provide the capability to tune and remotely manage your network. They can help reduce the cost and improve the reliability of the overall system.

Technology is a key ingredient of every network and provides a lot of excitement for the future. Always keep technology in perspective, but do not let it drive your purchase decisions. New technology should be used to improve your systems and provide usable applications for your users.

The LAN

The LAN should be viewed as both a strategic and a tactical tool for the organization. It can be used to link all the functions of the organization and provide tools for users in many diverse departments. A properly managed LAN also increases uptime, ease of use, and data sharing, which are critical to the organization. Tools such as word processing or spreadsheets that were once nice to have are now mission-critical tools. As the organization slims down and new functions are undertaken by many personnel, the organization can no longer afford systems that fail frequently and take a long time to repair.

LANs should also be viewed as tools to place information into the hands of the users. Users should take ownership of the data for their areas and learn to manipulate that data into useful information to support their job goals. When LANs are well designed and well maintained, this happens very quickly. Most companies find that users are demanding access to the data necessary to accomplish their jobs. The LAN serves as the facilitator to make this happen.

NETWORK MANAGEMENT COMPONENTS

One of PATHWORKS' hidden features is its use of standard facilities found in the various file server operating systems. VMS has been around for a long time and has many robust management tools. Network control and monitoring programs, wide-area networking, and other facilities are well developed.

Server Tools

Network tools such as NCP and LATCP are standard VMS features shipped with every system. SYSGEN, AUTHORIZE, MONITOR, and other numerous tools are also part of the basic VMS system.

When you access a tool such as NCP, your first impression may be that the tool is not as flashy as programs such as NetWare's various utilities. By further researching NCP (or any other VMS utility), you will realize that most PC network operating systems do not support the level of functionality provided by VMS. The NetWare Fconsole utility provides some server monitoring facilities, but it is not as comprehensive a tool as NCP is.

After using NCP or LATCP for a while, you begin to understand why they do not have fancy menus. Menus can get in the way of an experienced user if the menus are not carefully thought out. Even the best menus are cumbersome when a simple command will suffice. The interactive mode of PCSA Manager commands offers the flexibility to execute many different types of commands in sequence. In addition to the interactive mode, *every* VMS management command can be driven from a command file. Most VMS systems will contain references to NCP or LATCP in the system start-up files. This unique feature provides the system manager with the tools to easily customize the management of a system. Command files can be created for system start-up, adding users, and building print queues.

Some VMS system management programs are beginning to add an option for a front-end menu. PCSA Manager uses its Menu command to bring up a point-and-shoot-style menu for accessing most program functions. All commands within PCSA Manager can still be executed from the PCSA> command line or from DCL.

Note that systems such as NetWare have begun adding batch routines in limited areas of the system. Their developers became aware of the requirements for these tools after the systems were used in a production environment for several years. VMS utilities benefit from having many years of solid production experience. Their management tools have grown to support many wide-ranging environments and to resolve the problems encountered over the years in different business situations. Most other PC networks have been in production environments for a very limited number of years and are only now beginning to move into complex environments.

Network Tools

NCP and LATCP are examples of the powerful network features within VMS. Both of these programs control various aspects of your network architecture. NCP and LATCP each maintains its own database of network objects and provides tools for adding, deleting, and displaying various parts of the database and the current status of the system. NCP is typically used to show the current status of DECnet and to monitor or change certain network parameters. Most network tools can also perform certain levels of testing between the server and another area of the system, such as a client PC.

User Accounts

The VMS AUTHORIZE utility is used to manage user accounts. User accounts control access to one or more servers and to specific services within those servers. Providing the ability to manage services effectively and provide proper security for the network is a very important feature of a PATHWORKS LAN. VMS account features are robust and include items such as group codes and proxy access to remote systems.

User Groups

User groups are a powerful feature provided by PATHWORKS (and most other LANs). Groups are used to provide and restrict access to different services. You define groups by giving the group a descriptive name (e.g., ENG_DB_R) and assigning members to the group. Groups are also linked to a service with a particular access method such as read or read/write.

Groups are especially useful since different departments require access to the same application or database. For example, engineering, production, and research and development all require access to the manufacturing and CAD database, but each needs different levels of access. Engineering needs access to manufacturing but needs to maintain the CAD database. Production needs to maintain manufacturing and access the CAD database. Research and development needs access to both manufacturing and the CAD database, but it does not need to maintain either of them. Creating access for each user in each group would be an arduous and time-consuming task. Using groups to define the access and placing users in groups accomplishes the task quickly and efficiently.

PATHWORKS MANAGEMENT COMPONENTS

PCSA Manager

PCSA Manager provides facilities for managing the various services offered by PATHWORKS. Additional options are provided for tuning the server, managing user accounts, managing workstations, and performing other miscellaneous functions. PCSA Manager offers a menu interface and command line interface, which provide the system manager with a powerful tool for managing the server, including automating almost any function performed by PCSA Manager.

PCSA Manager works with the operating system to perform many functions. Setting up a print queue via the menu creates a command procedure for creating and starting the queue. You may modify this file and include it in the system start-up procedures. Security and user accounts also interface with the standard operating-system features. The tight integration of PCSA Manager and the server operating system is very important to organizations that have large networks or run networks and server applications. Because PCSA Manager uses the standard features of the operating system, any maintenance performed in either VMS or PCSA Manager will affect the other automatically.

PCSA Manager can be executed from DCL by entering the following command:

```
$ PCSA
```

It can also be executed from DOS by entering:

```
C:\> USE \SERVER %username *  /PCSA
```

PCDISK

The PCDISK utility provides access to virtual disks residing on the server. It allows a VMS user to have simultaneous access to multiple virtual disks and to access virtual disks on remote servers. VMS command line editing is supported for all commands.

PCDISK emulates certain DOS commands, enabling a VMS user to manipulate files on a virtual disk. PCDISK is necessary only for LAD drives, because PATHWORKS file services store files in RMS format to allow VMS users to manipulate the files with standard VMS commands.

NETCONFIG

NETCONFIG is used to configure a new system for DECnet. When a new VAX is installed, this program must be run before the node will have access to the network. Running this program is a fairly simple fill-in-the-blank process, provided you understand node names, DECnet addresses, and other parameters.

This program should be run only before PATHWORKS is installed, because it blows away all DECnet objects in the DECnet database. Do not run this program after installing PATHWORKS, or some features such as USE/SHOW will not work.

USER ACCOUNT MAINTENANCE

Most PATHWORKS users will access a server with a user account. This account will consist of a username, UIC, and password combination. The account may be maintained by either the account management facility of the server (AUTHORIZE) or the PCSA Manager account management functions. Some account modifications may use the facilities of one method or the other. For instance, to change the VMS quotas, you would use the VMS AUTHORIZE utility. To modify the user's AUTOUSER.BAT file, you would use either the PCSA MANAGER MODIFY command or a DCL or DOS editor.

When you add a PATHWORKS user with the PCSA_MANAGER ADD USER command, the account information is stored in the server's user file (UAF for VMS). You should add PATHWORKS users by using the ADD USER command. If the user account is a VMS interactive user, the system will ask if you wish to use this account.

You may specify parameters that allow the user to log in to the server interactively, set the user's password, specify a different directory for the user's login directory, and set the file version limit. The following command adds a user, sets the password (the default is WELCOME), and specifies a root directory:

```
PCSA_MANAGER> ADD USER/PASSWORD=JOHN -
_PCSA_MANAGER> /ROOT=DKA300:[USERS]: SMITH
```

239

This command creates the account SMITH, creates the directory DKA300:[USERS.SMITH], and allows the administrator to edit the AUTOUSER.BAT file. The user information is stored in the standard user file for the server and can be accessed with the standard server user maintenance programs.

To modify the AUTOUSER.BAT file for an existing user, use the MODIFY USER command or edit the file with a DOS editor or other ASCII editor. The MODIFY USER command invokes EDT (or the editor you have specified) and allows you to make changes to the user's AUTOUSER.BAT FILE. The format is:

```
PCSA_MANAGER> MODIFY USER KEN
```

To remove a user record, use the REMOVE USER command. This command deletes the user record in the UAF and the PCSA database. If the /NOKEEP qualifier is used, it will also delete files and directories in the user's home directory. If the /KEEP or /NOKEEP qualifier is not specified, the user will be prompted for instructions. Although you may delete a user with the standard user maintenance program for the server, this does not remove the user directories and files as the REMOVE USER /NOKEEP command does. The command format is:

```
PCSA_MANAGER> REMOVE USER KEN /KEEP
```

SHOW USERS displays all the currently registered PATHWORKS users. The display may be restricted by the USERNAME qualifier. The following commands display information for all users and then user KEN. These commands could also be executed from DCL by entering PCSA SHOW USER as shown in the screen on page 241.

User Access to Services

DENY and GRANT are PCSA MANAGER commands that allow or restrict access to services for specific users. These commands override group access to a service. If the user is a member of a group that allows access to a specific service and the DENY command is used to restrict access to the same service, the user-specific restrictions created with DENY take precedence.

The DENY command is used to restrict access to a service for a particular user account. It can be used to selectively override access that has been granted to a group. The command format is:

```
PCSA_MANAGER> DENY KEN WORD20
```

The GRANT command allows access to a file or print service for a specific user. Information concerning access granted to users is stored in the service database. The

```
PCSA_MANAGER> SHOW USER

REGISTERED USERS:

USER NAME   UIC           LOGINS            DIRECTORY
---------   -----------   --------------    --------------

KEN         [360,100]     ENABLED           DKB300:[KEN]
TRISH       [360,101]     DISABLED          DKB300:[TRISH]
JOE         [360,102]     DISABLED          DKB300:[JOE]

TOTAL OF 3 REGISTERED USERS


PCSA_MANAGER> SHOW USERS /USER=KEN

REGISTERED USERS:

USER NAME   UIC           LOGINS            DIRECTORY
---------   -----------   --------------    --------------

KEN         [360,100]     ENABLED           DKB300:[KEN]

TOTAL OF 1 REGISTERED USER
```

default access is read for file and disk services, and the default access is read, create, and write for printer services. The command format is:

```
PCSA_MANAGER> GRANT KEN WORD20 /ACCESS=(READ,WRITE)
```

This example grants read and write access to user KEN for the WORD20 service.

PATHWORKS GROUPS

PATHWORKS supports different levels of access for users belonging to various groups. A PATHWORKS group is typically used to define access characteristics for different users. In a typical manufacturing organization, one group could be created for the engineering department defining read/write access to the engineering database and read access to the manufacturing and research and development systems. A group for manufacturing may include read/write access to the manufacturing system and read access to the production engineering database.

Groups can also control access to print services and applications. This is a nice mechanism for providing access to public services such as high-volume laser printers and limiting access to slow-speed devices such as plotters or PostScript printers. Applications that require limited access may also be linked to groups.

A user link to a PATHWORKS group is not mutually exclusive, as is a UIC group. Users may be in one group, no groups, or any number of groups. By carefully planning for the use of this facility, you can easily modularize groups according to functional requirements. In our manufacturing example, different groups with varying levels of access to the engineering database could be controlled by PATHWORKS groups. A group such as ENG_PROD could be used to define access to the engineering production database, while ENG_R&D could define access to the research and development database. These groups could be further defined by ENG_PROD_R and ENG_PROD_RW, signifying read only and read/write access. One group that is always defined for PATHWORKS users is PUBLIC, which all users belong to.

By planning and exploring user groups, you will find that a network can be easy to manage. You should determine which types of programs and devices require access by which groups of users. Carefully plan on the limits required for your network, taking care to limit access where necessary and not to place undue restrictions on users. Too many restrictions will be as cumbersome as not enough.

Groups are created by using the PCSA Manager command line or menu. Once you create a group, you should establish the access rights to group services. Then add users to the group.

Figure 10-1 illustrates adding a group code with PCSA Manager from the command line. This could also be accomplished from the PCSA Manager menu by selecting the Users/Group menu and following the prompts. Figure 10-2 shows the PCSA Manager Group menu. Although using the menu is quick and easy to use for the most part, not all group command functions are available from it.

Group Maintenance

The ADD GROUP command/Create a Group menu item creates a new group and adds it to the server database. The format is:

```
PCSA_MANAGER> ADD GROUP EXCEL
```

Once the group is added, you must add members to the group with ADD MEMBER. The next command adds users KEN and JOE to the group EXCEL:

```
PCSA_MANAGER> ADD MEMBER KEN,JOE EXCEL
```

DENY/GROUP is used to restrict access to a service for an entire group of users. The operation of the command is the same as the DENY command.

The GRANT/GROUP command operates similar to the GRANT command, except it authorizes access to a service for an entire group. The format is exactly the same as GRANT, except that a group name is specified in place of the username. If both GRANT and GRANT/GROUP are used for particular user, the user-level access information will override the group access.

The REMOVE GROUP command deletes a group and removes the member connections to the group:

```
PCSA_MANAGER> REMOVE GROUP EXCEL
```

The REMOVE MEMBER command removes one or more members from a group. Members cannot be removed from the group PUBLIC. The following command removes the members KEN, JOE, and JANE from the service WORD:

```
PCSA_MANAGER> REMOVE MEMBER KEN,JOE,JANE WORD
```

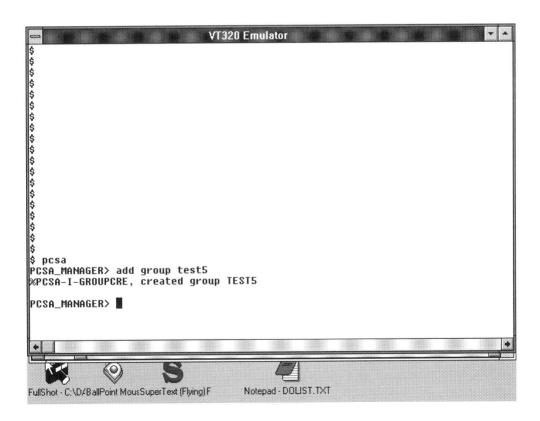

Figure 10-1. PCSA Manager Add Group Command

The SHOW GROUP command displays information for a user or group. Information for the group PUBLIC cannot be displayed by SHOW GROUP. Qualifiers for the group are GROUP, MEMBER, and USERNAME. GROUP and USERNAME limit the display to a particular group or user. The MEMBER qualifier cannot be used with USERNAME.

The following commands display information for the group WORD20, all groups, and the user KEN, respectively. The last command displays the members of the WORD20 group:

```
PCSA_MANAGER> SHOW GROUP /GROUP=WORD20

PCSA_MANAGER> SHOW GROUP

PCSA_MANAGER> SHOW GROUP /USERNAME=KEN

PCSA_MANAGER> SHOW GROUP /GROUP=WORD20 /MEMBER
```

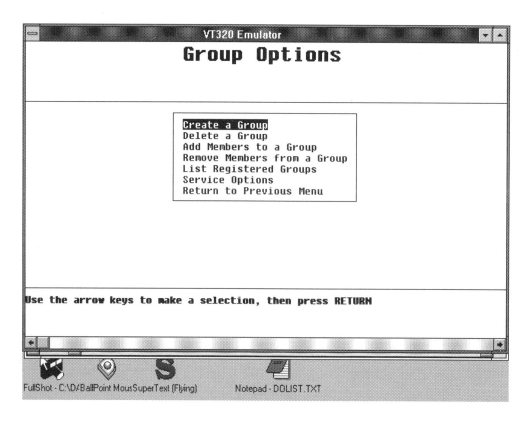

Figure 10-2. PCSA Manager Group Menu

Figure 10-3 illustrates examples of the commands to add a group and assign members. It also shows two uses of the SHOW GROUP command.

Figure 10-3. Group Examples

```
PCSA_MANAGER> ADD GROUP WORD20
%PCSA-I-GROUPCRE, CREATED GROUP WORD20

PCSA_MANAGER> ADD MEMBER JOE,KEN WORD20
%PCSA-I-ADDGROUPMEM, MEMBER JOE ADDED TO GROUP WORD20
%PCSA-I-ADDGROUPMEM, MEMBER KEN ADDED TO GROUP
WORD20
%PCSA-I-ADDGROUPMEMSUMM, 2 MEMBERS SUCCESSFULLY
ADDED, 0 MEMBERS NOT ADDED

PCSA_MANAGER> SHOW GROUP /GROUP=WORD20

REGISTERED GROUPS:

GROUP NAME

-------

WORD20

TOTAL OF 1 REGISTERED GROUP

PCSA_MANAGER> SHOW GROUP /GROUP=WORD20 /MEMBER

REGISTERED GROUPS:

GROUP NAME USER NAME

----- ------

WORD20     JOE
WORD20     KEN

TOTAL OF 1 REGISTERED GROUP
```

Automating the Addition of New Users

All PATHWORKS management components can be driven from an application program or command file. If you are managing a large or complicated network, this ability can greatly simplify your management chores. You can create a command procedure to simplify adding users and assigning them to a group. The following example illustrates a command file for creating a user, assigning the user to different groups, and creating an AUTOUSER.BAT file:

```
$ !                                                              ADD_ENG.COM
$ !
$ PCSA ADD USER 'P1'
$ PCSA ADD GROUP ENG_PROD_R    'P1'
$ PCSA ADD GROUP ENG_R&D_RW 'P1'
$ PCSA ADD GROUP MFG_R 'P1'
$ !
$ !
$ OPEN USER$DIR:['P1']AUTOUSER.BAT
$ WRITE CALL STD_DPT ENG
$ WRITE CALL STD_PRT ENG_LJ
$ CLOSE FILE
```

This program is executed from DCL by the following command:

```
$ @ADD_ENG NEWUSER
```

NEWUSER is the PATHWORKS username for the user being added. This simple program adds the user, assigns the user to the groups ENG_PROD_R, ENG_R&D_RW, and MFG_R. It also creates the AUTOUSER.BAT file and establishes access for common file and print services via the two WRITE statements. These two lines write the CALL STD_DPT and CALL STD_PRT statements into the AUTOUSER.BAT file, to force these procedures to execute each time the user logs in. The ADD_ENG.COM example file automates with one command a process that would take eight to 15 individual steps using PCSA Manager's menu or command mode. If you are using ACLs in addition to or in place of PATHWORKS groups, you could easily add the commands to update the ACLs or place the user in an ACL group.

Every network is unique and has its own set of requirements for configurations, users, and so on. You should take this example for adding a user and modify it to suit your own needs.

PATHWORKS SERVICES

PCSA_MANAGER is used to manage the PATHWORKS service database, which maintains information for all PATHWORKS services. Some of the service commands also affect server directories and/or printers. Remember that it is not necessary to create a service for a particular directory or printer to use it as a PATHWORKS service. Since PATHWORKS users can access VMS directories and print queues, you need not explicitly define a directory or print queue to PATHWORKS. When you define a service with PCSA Manager, the information is stored in the PATHWORKS database. Each time you access services via PCSA Manager, this database is accessed.

The larger the database, the longer operations will take. Unless your environment requires the group features or other management features of PCSA Manager, you may want to define the directory or queue from VMS. This is particularly true of print queues if your environment does not require restricting access to them.

File and Print Service Maintenance

File services are managed primarily from within the PCSA Manager utility. They may also be manipulated from the operating system, with some limitations. Although some actions, such as creating a new service, at first glance appear to duplicate the create directory function from the operating system, they perform several other jobs at the same time. Pay close attention to the notes on each command and review the appropriate command syntax in Appendix E of this book and the appropriate PATHWORKS manuals.

Creating a New Service. The ADD SERVICE/DIRECTORY command creates a service and directory (if the directory does not exist). It also creates an ACL for the service. You may specify the service name (1 to 25 characters), attributes, connections limit, default RMS protection mask, root directory, and service type. The following command creates a common service named ADMIN on the disk DKA300::

```
PCSA_MANAGER> ADD SERVICE/DIRECTORY ADMIN
_PCSA_MANAGER> /TYPE=COMMON /ROOT=DKA300:
```

The menu version of this command does not allow the specification of another device for user directories. This becomes critical as your system grows and you wish to manage the location of directories across multiple disks to optimize the performance of your server.

The ADD SERVICE/PRINTER command creates a print service and optionally a spool directory. You may specify the service name (1 to 25 characters), queue name, connections limit, form name, default RMS protection mask, root directory, and service type. The following command creates a common service named LASER and links it to the HP_LASER queue:

```
PCSA_MANAGER> ADD SERVICE/PRINTER LASER HP_LASERJET
```

Viewing Service Information. Often you need to view information about a service. The SHOW FILE_SERVER SERVICES command displays information about file or print services. The display includes the service name, type, attribute, maximum connections, number of active users, user or group name, alias, access, and RMS protection. If the service is a print service, the spool directory, queue name, and form name will also be displayed. The exact information displayed will depend on which qualifiers are used.

The major qualifiers for this command are ACTIVE, AUTHORIZED, and REGISTERED. These qualifiers determine what information is displayed. The ACTIVE qualifier displays information only about active file or print services. AUTHORIZED will display information about authorized (granted) file or print services. The REGISTERED qualifier displays information about all file and print services, whether or not the service is active or has any authorized users. These qualifiers are considered major because they specify the global information the command retrieves.

Other parameters such as the service type, name, alias, group=public, username, and whether to display full or brief information may be used. You may use some of these qualifiers with only one of the major qualifiers. Check your *Server Administrators Guide* for the exact parameter list.

This example displays all authorized services:

```
PCSA_MANAGER> SHOW FILE_SERVER SERVICES/AUTHORIZED
```

The next example uses the same command as above, but it also uses the ACTIVE qualifier to display all active service connections:

```
PCSA_MANAGER> SHOW FILE_SERVER SERVICES/ACTIVE
```

The following example displays the same information but restricts the display to those services authorized for the client KEN:

```
PCSA_MANAGER> SHOW FILE_SERVER SERVICES/AUTHORIZED
_PCSA_MANAGER> /USERNAME=KEN
```

To display all services that allow access by the PUBLIC group, use the /GROUP=PUBLIC qualifier. The GROUP qualifier may be used only with the group PUBLIC.

The first command that follows displays information for all registered services on this server. The second command restricts the display to print services with the PRINTER qualifier. The SERVICE qualifier may be used with either command to restrict the display to a specific service:

```
PCSA_MANAGER> SHOW FILE_SERVER SERVICES/REGISTERED
```

```
PCSA_MANAGER> SHOW FILE_SERVER SERVICES/REGISTERED -
_PCSA_MANAGER> /PRINTER
```

The SHOW FILE_SERVER CONNECTIONS command displays information for the active connections to the file server. It can be limited to a particular client or service. Information on the connection ID, client, username, alias name, service name, and access is displayed.

SHOW FILE_SERVER CONNECTIONS is very useful when you wish to modify a file or print service. Let's say you wish to work on the printer connected to the LASER service but wish to notify any people using the printer first. The following command displays all connections to the service LASER, providing you with a quick list of users to notify either by phone or with a broadcast message:

```
PCSA_MANAGER> SHOW FILE_SERVER CONNECTIONS -
_PCSA_MANAGER> /SERVICE=LASER
```

This command can be used for file services by specifying the file service name in place of the print service. The FULL qualifier may be used to display the root directory for the listed services.

Changing Service Parameters. The SET FILE_SERVER SERVICE command changes characteristics, maximum connections, attributes, file length, and RMS protection for a file or print service. The parameters may be changed permanently or for the current session only. This example shows the format:

```
PCSA_MANAGER> SET FILE_SERVER SERVICE DOC -
_PCSA_MANAGER> /CONNECTIONS=20 /PERMANENT
```

This example changes the maximum connections for the WORD20 disk to 20 and specifies that the change is permanent.

Stopping Connections to a Service. Occasionally you will need to terminate a connection or stop the file server totally. The STOP FILE_SERVER CONNECTIONS command is used to stop file server connections, terminate the file server process, disconnect a specific connection, disconnect all connections to a particular service, or stop the file server from accepting connections from unregistered nodes. This process may take several minutes to complete, depending on the activity of the server. The following command stops the file server and all connections:

```
PCSA_MANAGER> STOP FILE_SERVER CONNECTIONS -
_PCSA_MANAGER> /ALL_SERVICES
```

The next command terminates only connections to the WORD20 service:

```
PCSA_MANAGER> STOP FILE_SERVER CONNECTIONS -
_PCSA_MANAGER> /SERVICE=WORD20
```

Showing File Server Status. The SHOW FILE_SERVER STATUS command displays the status of the file server. The status information displayed includes whether the server is accepting connections, whether the server is accepting connections from unregistered workstations, the status of server logging, and the information being logged. There are no qualifiers. This command is useful for quickly checking the status of the server. If users cannot connect to their server, the STATUS command will give a quick indication of whether the server is accepting connections or not.

Displaying Version Information. The SHOW VERSION command displays version information for the currently executing components of the server. The command is shown below. When a problem occurs with the server, this command is also useful for checking whether the server is running. If one of the servers is not running, it will display "Not Available" in place of the version:

```
PCSA_MANAGER> SHOW VERSION

LAD$KERNEL   VERSION   : LAD$KERNEL V1.2
LADDRIVER    VERSION   : LADDRIVER V1.2
PCFS_SERVER VERSION : PATHWORKS FOR VMS S4.ØE
PCSA_MANAGER VERSION : PCSA_MANAGER S4.ØE
```

Displaying File Server Sessions. The SHOW FILE_SERVER SESSIONS command displays the active sessions for the file server. The display can be for all sessions or can be restricted to a particular client. Information displayed includes the session ID (a unique ID assigned by the file server for each connection), workstation name, number of current workstation connections, and number of files the workstation has open.

The format for the command is shown below. To restrict the display to one client, add the CLIENT qualifier as shown in the second command:

```
PCSA_MANAGER> SHOW FILE_SERVER SESSIONS

PCSA_MANAGER> SHOW FILE_SERVER SESSIONS /CLIENT=KEN
```

Disk Service Maintenance

Adding a New Service. The CREATE DISK command creates a DOS virtual disk on the server, including formatting the disk for DOS. You may specify the server file specification and location, number of blocks allocated, whether the virtual disk should use all contiguous disk space, virtual disk size, and type. The type may be SYSTEM, BOOT, APPLICATION, or USER. The following command creates a 15-MB disk for Word for Windows:

```
PCSA_MANAGER> CREATE DISK WORD20 /SIZE=10MB
_PCSA_MANAGER> /TYPE=APPLICATION
```

If the disk is a boot disk for a workstation, the disk size should be 360 KB, 760 KB, 1.2 MB, or 1.44 MB and should correspond to the size of the floppy defined on the workstation.

The NET CREATE command functions like CREATE DISK and creates and formats a virtual disk on a file server from a DOS client. You may specify the disk name, size, and location on the server.

Viewing Service Information. SHOW DISK_SERVER SERVICES displays information for disk services, including services on other nodes in a cluster. You can display information for all disk services by entering the command with no qualifiers. This command is useful for obtaining a quick look at the current state of the disk server, including which users are connected to particular services. The following command displays information for all services on the current server:

```
PCSA_MANAGER> SHOW DISK_SERVER SERVICES
```

Adding the /CLUSTER qualifier will display additional information for client connections to other nodes in a cluster environment. A server node name may be added to the /CLUSTER qualifier to restrict the display to a cluster node other than the current node. Other useful parameters are FULL (display the disk file specification), SERVICE (limit the display to a particular service), and TYPE (limit the display to a particular service type).

SHOW DISK_SERVER CONNECTIONS displays connection information for active disk server users. Information displayed includes the client name, service name, access method, and container file name. The information can be restricted to certain services or clients. The command format is:

```
PCSA_MANAGER> SHOW DISK_SERVER CONNECTIONS
```

This example displays information about all connections to the disk server. The CLIENT and SERVICE qualifiers can be used to select specific clients or services. The command shown below displays information only for the client KEN:

```
PCSA_MANAGER> SHOW DISK_SERVER CONNECTIONS /CLIENT=KEN
```

The REMOVE SERVICE command removes a file service or print service entry from the service database. All users are denied access to the service, any current connections are dropped, and any files located in the service may be deleted. The command format is:

```
PCSA_MANAGER> REMOVE SERVICE OLDAPPS /KEEP
```

This example removes the service OLDAPPS but does not delete the files located in the service. If KEEP or NOKEEP are not specified, the system will prompt for instructions.

To delete a disk service from a client, use the NET DELETE DISK command. Before executing the DELETE command, you must dismount the disk. You should use this command to delete a virtual disk, instead of using the SERVER DELETE command. DELETE DISK checks to make sure the disk is dismounted and deletes information for the disk in the PCSA database.

NET DELETE will also delete a virtual disk from a client PC. To delete the 12322.DSK virtual disk on KENS, type:

```
C:\>NET DELETE \\KENS%SYSTEM * /FILE=DKB0:[12322]12322.DSK
```

Changing Service Parameters. To change service characteristics, maximum connections, the password, and the rating for a mounted virtual disk, use the SET DISK_SERVER SERVICE command. For this command to execute correctly, the disk must be mounted and at least one parameter must be specified. The format is:

```
PCSA_MANAGER> SET DISK_SERVER SERVICE WORD20 -
_PCSA_MANAGER> /CONNECTIONS=20 /NOPASSWORD
```

This example changes the maximum connections for the WORD20 disk to 20 and specifies that no password is required.

You can also change parameters for a service from a client. NET MODIFY changes characteristics for a virtual disk service, such as the password, number of connections, number of blocks allocated, and priority rating. To modify the number of connections, type:

```
C:\>NET MODIFY \\KENS\APPDISK[%SYSTEM * /CONNECTIONS=20
```

Preparing a Disk Service for Use. Before a user can access a disk service, the disk must be mounted. The MOUNT DISK command opens the disk container file and allows connections to the service.

Qualifiers specify the access method, whether the disk is available to all nodes in a cluster, the maximum number of concurrent connections to the disk, the password, whether the disk is permanent or nonpermanent (the default is nonpermanent), the disk rating, and the disk type. The following command mounts the disk WORD20 as a permanent service:

```
PCSA_MANAGER> MOUNT DISK WORD20 /TYPE=APPLICATION
_PCSA_MANAGER> /PERMANENT
```

From a client, use NET MOUNT to make a virtual disk available for network connections. NET MOUNT optionally allows you to establish usage parameters for the disk. The disk may be mounted either permanently or temporarily. (It does not remount when the server is booted.)

Dismounting a Disk. Some maintenance actions on a disk service may require that the service be dismounted. DISMOUNT DISK removes all connections to a virtual disk and closes the disk file on the server. This command must be used before a disk is deleted or modified. The command format is:

```
PCSA_MANAGER> DISMOUNT DISK WORD20
```

From a client, you may dismount a disk with the NET DISMOUNT command. To dismount the disk connected to drive E:, type:

```
C:\>NET DISMOUNT E: \\KENS1:%SYSTEM * /TYPE=USER
```

Stopping a Server Session. STOP FILE_SERVER SESSION terminates a session between a particular workstation and the file server. There are no qualifiers. The following command terminates the session between node KEN and the file server:

```
PCSA_MANAGER> STOP FILE_SERVER SESSION KEN
```

The STOP DISK_SERVER CONNECTIONS command stops the disk server, disconnects all connections, dismounts all mounted disks, and stops the LAD$KERNEL process. This process may take several minutes to complete, depending on the activity of the server.

MISCELLANEOUS MANAGEMENT FUNCTIONS

File Server Event Logging

Regardless of the size of the network you are managing, you should track events as they occur over time. This is useful for detecting errors, file problems, security problems, and any number of other events. PATHWORKS provides the ability to log a number of different events over time. When the logging process is started, you can specify the time interval for collecting statistics and the type of statistics collected. You should also investigate the features of the AUDIT and ANALYZE VMS commands (and other VMS utilities) for additional logging capabilities.

The START FILE_SERVER LOGGING command starts logging file server events and may also open a new log file. You can specify the events to be logged, including all events, connections only, default events, errors (nonfatal), errors (fatal), locks, opens, operation actions, protocol errors, read requests, security violations, and session information. The events logged by default are errors, errors (fatal), operator, protocol, and security.

The LOG_FILE qualifier is used to specify the name of the log file. The default server log is PCFS_SERVER.LOG. If no qualifiers are entered, the current log file will be closed (if logging is enabled) and a new log file created. The following command starts logging for the default events:

```
PCSA_MANAGER> START FILE_SERVER LOGGING
```

The STOP FILE_SERVER LOGGING command stops logging events on the server. The /EVENT qualifier may be used to stop logging only specific events.

Open File Maintenance

The CLOSE FILE_SERVER FILE command closes a file that is open on the file server. It is useful if a remote user has left his or her workstation with a file opened. To use this command, you must know the numerical file ID, which can be found with the SHOW FILE_SERVER OPEN_FILES command. The format of the CLOSE command is:

```
PCSA_MANAGER> CLOSE FILE_SERVER FILE 5
```

This command closes the file with file ID 5.

Managing the Network Databases

Maintaining the Node Database. Some network functions require that definitions for remote systems be listed in the DECnet database. This can be done with NCP, using the DEFINE NODE and SET NODE commands, or with PCSA Manager. The PCSA Manager ADD NODE command updates the DECnet database (both volatile and permanent) with the node name and address. The function is the same as the NCP DEFINE and SET NODE commands.

REMOVE NODE deletes an entry for a workstation or other node from the DECnet database. You may specify the node to delete either by node name or address. The following commands add and delete the node MYVAX from the local database:

```
PCSA_MANAGER> ADD NODE MYVAX
```

```
PCSA_MANAGER> REMOVE NODE MYVAX
```

There are several client tools that can be used for managing parts of the network. These include the some of the various NET commands, NCP, and LATCP. NCP and LATCP are client counterparts of the same programs on the VMS server. They are used to update the NCP and LAT databases for the client. The NET command offers options for listing the NCP database, performing loop tests, and defining new objects.

A node must be registered to connect to another node over DECnet, send broadcast messages outside your LAN, and use file services outside your LAN. You must also define the node of the primary server in the client DECnet database. You may want to define other nodes in the client and server NCP databases if you wish to communicate with them using file access listener (FAL) and network file transfer (NFT).

It is also a good idea to define local nodes on your network in the server NCP database. The NCP SHOW KNOWN NODES command will display all active nodes and their node names, if the nodes are defined. Nodes that are not defined in the server NCP database will have only their DECnet addresses displayed.

NET DEFINE will register a node name and address in the client DECnet database (DECNODE.DAT). This file should be in the DECNET directory on the client boot device. To define the node KENS, type:

```
C:\> NET DEFINE   KENS 1.200
```

KENS represents the node name of the node being registered. It must be from one to six alphabetic characters. The address is a standard DECnet address in the form aa.nnn (a = area 1 to 61; n = node 0 to 999). KENS and the 1.200 address in this example define the main server for this client.

NET LIST lists all nodes currently in the client DECnet database:

```
C:\>NET LIST
```

Broadcast. The BROADCAST command is used to send messages to one or more workstations or users:

```
PCSA_MANAGER> BROADCAST KEN "Lets do lunch!"
PCSA_MANAGER> BROADCAST * "System is going down at 4:00PM!"
```

Maintaining the Remote-Boot Database. Client workstations that remote boot from the server must be defined with PCSA Manager. The remote-boot database is used to define the workstation's name, address, and other specific information required for the remote-boot procedure. When the workstation is booted, the server responds by using the address to send the required boot information.

The ADD TEMPLATE command creates a template to be used to create other workstation boot profiles. After the creation of a template, new remote-boot workstations can be added very quickly. This command can save tremendous amounts of time when you are adding new workstation definitions.

ADD TEMPLATE requires the template name (1 to 39 characters), node name (1 to 6 characters), and an optional comment (1 to 35 characters). The node name is the name of the node profile that will be used for the template. The following command creates a template called DOS5_DEPCA:

```
PCSA_MANAGER> ADD TEMPLATE DOS5_DEPCA KEN "DOS 5.x with DEPCA"
```

The REMOVE TEMPLATE command deletes a template record from the server database:

```
PCSA_MANAGER> REMOVE TEMPLATE DOS5_DEPCA
```

The SHOW TEMPLATES command displays all templates defined for remote-boot workstations:

```
PCSA_MANAGER> SHOW TEMPLATES
```

The ADD WORKSTATION command adds a definition for a new workstation to the PCSA database. This definition is used by PATHWORKS for remote-boot nodes. If the ADD TEMPLATE command has been used to define a standard template for a workstation with a similar setup, the /TEMPLATE qualifier may be used. This reduces the information that must be entered, because it uses values from the template definition.

You may specify the node name, node address, a comment for the definition, workstation network adapter type, operating system version, server controller device name, DOS name, network key disk size, and/or template name. You should not use the Type, Client, DOS, and Size qualifiers with the /TEMPLATE qualifier. The following command adds a boot configuration for the workstation KEN, using the DOS5_CQ template:

```
PCSA_MANAGER> ADD WORKSTATION KEN 6.124 "KENS WKSTN" -
_PCSA_MANAGER> /ADAPTER=(ADDRESS=08-00-2A-00-25-66) -
_PCSA_MANAGER> /TEMPLATE=DOS5_CQ
```

The MODIFY WORKSTATION command changes information in the remote-boot database for a specific workstation definition concerning the Ethernet address, network adapter, server Ethernet adapter, client software version, and workstation comment. This command is used only for remote-boot clients. The format is:

```
PCSA_MANAGER> MODIFY WORKSTATION KEN /qualifier
```

The qualifier is either /ADAPTER=(TYPE=adapter, ADDRESS=address), /CLIENT_VERSION=version, /COMMMENT=comment string, and /DEVICE=device name.

REMOVE WORKSTATION is similar to REMOVE TEMPLATE but causes a number of things to happen. When this command executes, the remote-boot disk is dismounted and deleted, and the workstation record is removed from the server, NCP, and remote-boot databases. The only parameter needed is the workstation node name.

The SHOW WORKSTATION command displays all remote-boot workstations. The format is:

```
PCSA_MANAGER> SHOW WORKSTATION
```

Log Files

Several log files are maintained by PATHWORKS to monitor various aspects of the server. The log files maintain information on such actions as starting the disk or file server and information on events affecting NetBIOS, security, and performance. Log files are stored in directories pointed to by the PCFS$LOG_FILES and LAD$LOG_FILES logicals. Table 10-1 lists log files relative to the server.

The file of particular interest to security is the PCFS_SERVER.LOG. Security violations are tracked by the SECURITY event flag. Table 10-2 shows the types of events that may be stored in the PCFS_SERVER. LOG.

Table 10-1. Log Files

Log File	Description
File Server Log File:	
PCFS_OUTPUT.LOG	Contains errors written by VMS when the server starts.
PCFS_ERROR.LOG	Contains errors written by the file server before it terminates.
NETBIOS_OUTPUT.LOG	Contains errors written by VMS when the server starts.
NETBIOS_ERROR.LOG	Contains errors written by NetBIOS before it terminates.
PCFS_SERVER.LOG	Contains information related to file server security events such as invalid usernames, changes to files, and unsuccessful attempts to connect to file services.
Disk Server Log File:	
LAD$KERNEL_OUTPUT.LOG	Contains errors written by VMS when the server starts.

Table 10-2. PCFS_SERVER.LOG Structure

Event	Function
ALL	All event types
CONNECTIONS	Connections to services
DEFAULT	Default events
ERRORS	Nonfatal errors
FATAL	Fatal errors
LOCKS	DOS file lock and unlock requests
OPENS	File open and close requests
OPERATOR	Operator actions
PROTOCOL	Protocol errors
READS	File read and write requests
SECURITY	Violations
SESSION	DECnet connections

Whenever a security-type event occurs, the client workstation and the event description are recorded. This includes the target of the security problem (i.e., Invalid Directory = DKA300:[000000.USR]), the date and time, and other pertinent information.

CHAPTER 11

Functional Approach to Network Management

COMMAND PROCEDURES

VMS DCL is a powerful tool for managing a network and automating many day-to-day tasks. It is a full-featured programming language, not a simple batch facility like the DOS batch language. DCL features tools and functions to perform IF/THEN logic, launch application programs, query and set system parameters, perform numerous functions such as string manipulation, and accomplish many other tasks.

The various VMS and PATHWORKS utilities add to the functionality of DCL because of their ability to be integrated simply and cleanly within a DCL program. This capability was illustrated earlier in our discussions concerning the command line interface to all standard VMS and PATHWORKS utilities.

The examples shown in this chapter barely scratch the surface of DCL, using only the minimal functions necessary for each task. The procedures shown here could be easily enhanced with error checking and an interactive interface.

When a VMS system boots, the SYSTARTUP_V5.COM command procedure is executed. This file contains specific commands required for that particular VAX, including commands to start PATHWORKS, application programs, and other network tools, to configure and start printers, and to perform any other specific commands for that system.

Instead of loading a lot of commands into SYSTARTUP_V5, you should organize commands by function and place them in separate command files. Doing so will make it easier to troubleshoot problems and work with the functions independently. Calls to these procedures should be placed in the start-up file, where they will be executed as the system boots.

Placing these commands into separate procedures allows them to be tested independently and gives the system manager the ability to restart different system components easily. This also makes it easy to upgrade to new versions of VMS, since the number of things to add to the new start-up file is greatly reduced.

The start-up file is also a good place to start command procedures that must run on a certain schedule. Procedures to purge files, clean up temporary files, back up procedures, and start batch processes can all be started automatically.

VMS also provides useful tools for creating shortcuts to commands and files. VMS utilities and VMS applications use logical names and symbols extensively to standardize location names for files and directories and to access programs quickly. These are often created in a user's LOGIN.COM file to customize the operation of the system for that user.

Use a symbol for frequently used commands such as PCSA_MANAGER. To define this command with a symbol, type:

```
$ PCSA == RUN PCSA_MANAGER MENU
```

After you enter the command above, typing PCSA will execute RUN PCSA_MANAGER. Symbols can also be defined for NCP, AUTHORIZE, and any other frequently used commands. Default actions for certain commands can also be created using symbols. For example, to cause the TYPE command to always display one page at a time, use:

```
$TYP*E == TYPE /P
```

The * indicates that the command can be shortened to TYP. Symbols also are handy for shortcutting entire commands. To define a command for displaying all file service connections, use:

```
$FILEU*SERS == PCSA SHOW FILE_SERVER SERVICES/ACTIVE
```

Now if you enter FILEU at the $ prompt, you will get a list of active users, just as if the entire command were entered. I normally have a number of symbols created in my LOGIN.COM to simplify managing the network. The following list is included in my LOGIN.COM:

```
$CD == SET DIRECTORY
$MD == CREATE/DIRECTORY
$FILEU*SERS == PCSA SHOW FILE_SERVER SERVICES/ACTIVE
$AUTHU*SERS == PCSA SHOW FILE_SERVER SERVICES/AUTHORIZED
$TYP*E == TYPE /P
$ PCSA == RUN PCSA_MANAGER
$ NCP == RUN SYS$SYSTEM:NCP
```

If you spend a lot of time using the VMS server, you should explore DCL, including symbols and logical names, in more detail.

Server and Client Tricks

During the daily management of a network, impromptu tasks will pop up from time to time. Chores such as moving one or more files to numerous directories, deleting a group of files that do not fall neatly into wildcard categories, deleting one file in numerous directories, and many other similar tasks must be performed quickly and flawlessly.

Performing these tasks one by one is very time-consuming and error-prone. (Did you ever delete a file by accident?) The tasks become more distasteful when they must be done after people are off the system, that is, at night or weekends. Wouldn't it be nice if this could be automated?

Well, it can, if the proper tools are used. In the following examples, we will look at several typical problems that occur from time to time and explore how to automate them. In these examples, we will use an editor called Kedit from Mansfield Software Group. Any other ASCII editor could be used but may lack some of the functionality of Kedit, such as sorting, moving/copying of columns, macros, and numerous other useful features, including speed and compactness.

The command files shown in the two examples that follow, moving a file and deleting a file, are DOS batch programs. They could just as easily have been VMS DCL programs. Directories may be captured with the VMS DIR command, edited with a DOS editor, and executed with VMS. This is important because VMS may provide more functionality with a particular command than the DOS version, as in the VMS DELETE command with the /EXCLUDE parameter.

Moving a File to Numerous Directories. Once in a while, you will need to copy or move a file into several directories. If the file should be moved into all subdirectories within a given directory, the file may be manipulated with the VMS copy command by using the ... qualifier with the command.

If the target directories are only a few of the subdirectories in a particular parent or if the target is several directories under different parents, the problem is a little more complicated. Neither VMS nor DOS provides a good tool to perform this task.

An easy way around this problem involves using standard features of VMS and/or DOS and an ASCII editor. Here are the steps required to move the files:

1. Redirect the target directories to the file (i.e., MOVEDIR.BAT).

2. Strip directory headers/footers and columns.

3. Add the file name to the beginning of each line.

4. Add the MOVE/COPY command to the front of all directories.

5. Rename the file.

6. Execute the command.

Step 1 involves capturing the target directories to a file, usually with a simple system command. If the target directories are under different parents, this may require capturing several directory listings to different files and then combining the files. The target directories can also be entered into the file manually. The following shows a sample of the directory commands and the resulting file:

DOS:

```
C:\> DIR *. > MOVE.BAT
```

VMS:

```
$ DIR *.DIR /OUTPUT=MOVE.BAT/COL=1
```

Below is the contents of MOVE.BAT, created from the first command:

```
MOVE.BAT
Volume in drive E is PCSA
Directory of E:\
JOE            <DIR>                11-19-92 10:20a
JAN            <DIR>                10-07-92 10:24a
NAN            <DIR>                10-07-92 10:25a
JACK           <DIR>                10-07-92 10:27a
DANNY          <DIR>                10-07-92 10:29a
DEF            <DIR>                10-07-92 10:30a
KEN            <DIR>                10-07-92 10:30a
RAT            <DIR>                10-07-92 10:31a
JEZ            <DIR>                10-07-92 10:32a
RAC            <DIR>                10-07-92 10:33a
TTT            <DIR>                12-03-92  8:39p
RAC            <DIR>                10-07-92 10:35a
12 file(s)      0 bytes
33460224 bytes free
```

This particular file was captured by redirecting the output to a file, as illustrated in the sample commands. Notice the headers, footers, and detailed information about each file. The VMS command shown above would produce the same output but with fewer header and footer lines and without the detailed information for each file. This is a key distinction if you are using an editor that does not do column operations.

Once you have captured the target directory listings in a file, you must reformat the file into a batch program. The first step is to edit the file and remove any directories that will not be used in this step. Typically some directories already have the required file or for some other reason do not need the update.

The next step involves stripping any directory information from the file with an editor. The simplest way to accomplish this is to sort the file and delete the lines with header and footer information.

If the directory is captured with the DOS directory command, it will include several additional columns on the right-hand side of the file. These can be removed easily with Kedit by blocking the columns (CTRL-B) and deleting the block (CTRL-G). The entire file should then be shifted over one column, creating a column with one space. In Kedit, you accomplish this with the SHIFT RIGHT command (SHIFT RIGHT 1 *).

Now that you have a single space in column 1, you can easily create the actual command structure. The Kedit CHANGE command will allow you to change the space in column 1 and turn it into a copy command. This is done by issuing the command CHANGE\ \COPY D:\UTIL\AUTOUSER.BAT \. The CHANGE command in this example changes the first space in each line into the copy command, including the full file specification. Additional spaces are not modified because COPY only affects the first space in the line.

At this point, we are almost finished. If the directory was captured with the DOS directory command, it will contain spaces in the target directory names between the name and the period (.) delimiter for the extension. You can remove these spaces easily by using the Kedit ZONE command to bracket the columns containing the spaces. If the names are in columns 8 through 16, the command ZONE 8 16 will restrict the CHANGE command (and others) to only these columns. The command CHANGE\ * * will delete all spaces in the file names, without affecting any other spaces. The following shows a completed file, ready to execute:

```
COPY D:\UTIL\AUTOUSER.BAT JOE
COPY D:\UTIL\AUTOUSER.BAT JAN
COPY D:\UTIL\AUTOUSER.BAT NAN
COPY D:\UTIL\AUTOUSER.BAT JACK
COPY D:\UTIL\AUTOUSER.BAT DANNY
COPY D:\UTIL\AUTOUSER.BAT DEF
COPY D:\UTIL\AUTOUSER.BAT KEN
COPY D:\UTIL\AUTOUSER.BAT RAT
COPY D:\UTIL\AUTOUSER.BAT JEZ
COPY D:\UTIL\AUTOUSER.BAT EAC
COPY D:\UTIL\AUTOUSER.BAT TTT
COPY D:\UTIL\AUTOUSER.BAT RAC
```

Notice that we used DOS to move the files into the user directories. The next procedure uses the VMS SET FILE/PROTECTION command to set the file protections to the owner of the directory, which is the same as the owner's username. It would be very simple to combine both of these procedures by appending this next file to the one above and using the VMS COPY command:

```
$ SET FILE/OWNER=JOE    [.JOE]AUTOUSER.BAT
$ SET FILE/OWNER=JAN    [.JAN]AUTOUSER.BAT
$ SET FILE/OWNER=NAN    [.NAN]AUTOUSER.BAT
$ SET FILE/OWNER=JACK   [.JACK]AUTOUSER.BAT
$ SET FILE/OWNER=DANNY  [.DANNY]AUTOUSER.BAT
$ SET FILE/OWNER=DEF    [.DEF]AUTOUSER.BAT
$ SET FILE/OWNER=KEN    [.KEN]AUTOUSER.BAT
$ SET FILE/OWNER=RAT    [.RAT]AUTOUSER.BAT
$ SET FILE/OWNER=JEZ    [.JEZ]AUTOUSER.BAT
$ SET FILE/OWNER=EAC    [.EAC]AUTOUSER.BAT
$ SET FILE/OWNER=TTT    [.TTT]AUTOUSER.BAT
$ SET FILE/OWNER=RAC    [.RAC]AUTOUSER.BAT
```

Both of these files were built with the DOS Kedit editor, illustrating that PATHWORKS allows you to use all the tools at your disposal to accomplish a task. VMS provides a tremendously powerful command language, which is light-years ahead of DOS. The editors and other tools provided running under the DOS environment offer ease of use and other features. By combining tools from both environments, you can accomplish tasks quickly and painlessly.

This example illustrates an important point concerning whether to execute the procedure from VMS or DOS. If the copy procedure was done from VMS, the second procedure to set the permission on the file would be unnecessary. This is because VMS sets the permission on the file correctly when it is copied into the user's directory, and DOS does not.

This trick can save you many hours of frustration when resolving problems, configuring a system, or just performing incidental chores. You can usually build command files of this nature in 2 to 10 minutes. The file may be executed immediately or submitted to a batch job to execute later. It is a good idea to use a dummy command (one that performs no function, such as LOGIN.COM) in place of the actual command for test purposes. By testing the command with a dummy action, the test can take place immediately, allowing the command to be executed later with confidence.

Deleting a File in Numerous Directories. The following example involves deleting several unique files that do not lend themselves to using wildcards. A good example of this situation is when several files with different extensions and unique names must be deleted, such as several .EXE, .COM, .BAT, or other files beginning with A and ending with J. If you have several hundred files to delete, this may take awhile. This could be further complicated if the files are located in numerous subdirectories.

The first step to automating this process is capturing a list of the files, in the same manner as the last example. The only difference is this time you want file names, not directories. Once the file names are captured, edit the file to remove directory information and to remove any files that should not be deleted, as in the previous example. The major difference in these two examples is replacing the COPY command with the DELETE command. The following code illustrates a completed file:

```
$ DELETE      [.JOE]AUTOUSER.BAT
$ DELETE      [.JAN]AUTOUSER.BAT
$ DELETE      [.NAN]AUTOUSER.BAT
$ DELETE      [.JACK]AUTOUSER.BAT
$ DELETE      [.DANNY]AUTOUSER.BAT
$ DELETE      [.DEF]AUTOUSER.BAT
$ DELETE      [.KEN]AUTOUSER.BAT
$ DELETE      [.RAT]AUTOUSER.BAT
$ DELETE      [.JEZ]AUTOUSER.BAT
$ DELETE      [.EAC]AUTOUSER.BAT
$ DELETE      [.TTT]AUTOUSER.BAT
$ DELETE      [.RAC]AUTOUSER.BAT
```

This file uses the VMS DELETE command syntax, indicated by the $ command prefix, the brackets around the directory entries, and the period (.) prefix before the directory name. If the syntax is changed to the DOS format, this procedure can be executed from DOS.

This example must be used with great caution because it can create havoc with your system and delete files with great abandon. I usually test-delete files by replacing the DEL command with the DIR command and verifying that the appropriate results are obtained.

Managing Client Configurations

One of the most difficult tasks for managing client workstations with hard disks or floppy disks is automating the task of updating files on those disks. When the network has only four or five clients, you can easily to go to each PC and load the files on the disk or carry a new floppy to the machine.

If your network has only a few PCs, this can be managed by loading the new software on a network disk and going to each PC and copying the files to the local drive using the XCOPY command with the /S parameter.

An easier way to accomplish the update involves using the PERMIT command. Create a network batch procedure called BYE, STOP, SHUTDOWN, or some other easily remembered name. Then have each user execute this procedure from DOS as he or she leaves the office. Next, you can make a connection to the PC with USE and copy the files directly to the local PC drive from your own desk. This method can be further streamlined by creating a batch procedure that contains the commands to connect to each PC in turn and then execute a procedure called UPDATE.BAT. This procedure would contain the XCOPY command or whatever other commands are required to perform the update. Samples of these three procedures are shown below.

Here is the BYE.BAT command:

```
@ECHO OFF
REM BYE.BAT
PERMIT COPYKLS=C:\  /RCW    SUPER
```

This is the MOVEAPP.BAT command:

```
@ECHO OFF
REM  MOVEAPP.BAT
USE L: \\KLS\COPYKLS
CALL UPDATE
USE L: \\JOE\COPYJOE /REPLACE
CALL UPDATE
```

This is the UPDATE.BAT procedure:

```
@ECHO OFF
REM UPDATE.BAT
SET _DIR=C:
IF NOT "%1" == "" SET _DIR=%1
XCOPY E:\WINNEW %_DIR%\WIN3 /S
```

Note the third and fourth lines in the UPDATE procedure, which set or reset the _DIR variable. This defaults the target drive for the update to C: and allows the user to override it by supplying the drive on the command line. Additional intelligence could be added to this file to check for certain files and modify the update procedure accordingly. UPDATE.BAT can be changed to update virtually any program (including PATHWORKS) except for DOS. Since DOS requires updating the boot sector before the new files are copied or using a special update procedure as in MS-DOS V5.x, the update procedure won't work.

Another method of updating applications involves using the UPDATE.BAT procedure covered in our last example. Instead of running the procedure directly from the server, create an entry in the news file for your network. The news file should be displayed whenever a user logs in. This message should display information on what software updates are available and the commands to update them. In this scenario, UPDATE would be renamed to something like UPTWIN, enabling the user to upgrade Windows, by entering:

```
C:\> UPTWIN D:\
```

or

```
C:\> UPTWIN
```

SYSTEM BACKUPS

Backup procedures are one of the most important elements of any system, especially a LAN. A network quickly becomes a vital part of an organization, one on which users rely to perform their day-to-day functions. When the system or a component breaks, it is absolutely critical that no data is lost. Critical data may range from corporate systems to databases and spreadsheets. Each piece of data is critical to someone and may be very expensive to the enterprise if lost.

If you are using disk services, understanding mounted and dismounted services is important. When a service is mounted, a backup that includes the service cannot guarantee the integrity of the data. You should make sure that all disk services are dismounted when they are included in a backup. Dismounting services before backup should be included in an automated procedure to place the server in a known state before the backup runs, unless they are read-only application services that are not updated frequently. Commands to dismount the services and remount them after the backup completes should be inserted into your normal backup procedure or called as subroutines.

If your system runs 24 hours a day, dismounting and remounting disk services may be a problem, unless the disks are read only, in which case they may be loaded when they are created and will not require a daily backup. If backups are required, you may be able to create a new service each day, using the date as a suffix for the service. If the service name is DATA, the new name would be DATA121291 for a disk created on December 12, 1991. Creating a new service each day requires a command procedure to create and mount the new disk, dismount the old disk, and copy files to the new disk. The normal backup can then pick up the old disk. Make sure the timing of the disk creation procedure is sequenced before the backup procedure.

Backup Equipment

What is equipment doing in a discussion on backup? The hardware available today has made some of the old issues regarding backup a moot point. Backup devices are available with capacities of 1.2 to 5 GB on one tape. These devices allow a single backup to cover a tremendous amount of data. Powerful systems from numerous vendors combine multiple tape drives and/or stackers that allow a single backup to cover vast amounts of data, without changing tapes.

With the batch and backup features of VMS, unattended daily backups can be performed in the middle of the night, every night. If a system has more disk space than can be covered in a single data backup, the system should have more tape capacity.

If your system uptime or access to backup data is critical, consider using mirrored disk drives or adding a spare drive and backing up to that drive. Backups to a spare drive are quick and can allow users to do their own restores.

Backup Issues. Now that we have discussed user files, shared data files, and application files, let's review issues concerning system backup. A backup is one of those things that seems to be too much trouble until the moment the system crashes and the disk turns out to be dead. Then there is a lot of crying and gnashing of teeth.

Directory structures have a direct bearing on your backup procedures if you have a tape drive that has less capacity than your total disk space. This is frequently a problem on many systems, especially on very small and very large systems.

By establishing parent directories for user and shared data files, the backup process can be simplified. Since all data directories originate from two root directories, your daily backups can pick up only data files easily. If your VAX applications use a similar data structure, backups can be simple to construct. The backup command below shows an example of the command syntax for a system that has both PATHWORKS users and VMS applications. Note that the backup also covers files that reside on the system disk (such as SYSUAF.DAT):

```
BACK.COM

$ FROM_FILES   == 'DKB300:[000000.DATA...]*.*"
$ FROM_FILES1  == 'DKB300:[000000.USERS...]*.*"
$ SYS_FILES    == 'SYS$SYSDEVICE:[000000...]*.DAT"
$ BACKUP/LOG/REW' -
     ASSIST/IGNORE=(INTERLOCK,LABEL) -
     'FROM_FILES' , 'FROM_FILES1','SYS_FILES'-
     MKA500:BACKUPNAME
```

This command will back up the data directories, user directories, VMS data directories (from DKB300:[000000.DATA]), and certain files from the system disk

(SYS$SYSDEVICE). You should determine exactly which file types and structures should be backed up from each disk before implementing any backup procedures.

Backups are a concern for PATHWORKS because DOS will allow users to create directories deeper than the maximum VMS depth of eight subdirectories. This is not a problem unless you try to back up with a standard VMS utility such as BACKUP. VMS commands and programs in general cannot go deeper than the maximum depth of eight. If you have a directory structure deeper than eight and use the BACK.COM command file in the previous example, directories beyond eight will not be backed up. If the /IMAGE or /PHYSICAL qualifiers are used, BACKUP will back up the entire disk, including the problem directories. The problem with this approach is you have to perform a full backup of the disk.

Your procedures should include printing a backup log each day and reviewing the log for errors. This log may be a summary log showing only errors, or the entire backup log. Make sure the log is a manageable size but contains enough details to catch any errors. If the printout is too large, it may become unmanageable. With an ULTRIX or VMS server, consider modifying the backup procedure to mail the backup log to your mail account.

Scheduling Backups

Daily. Some type of backup should occur every day on your system. If the capacity of the available tape drives exceeds the disk capacity of your system, this should be a full backup. If this is not the case, then a daily data backup should be performed. This should occur when the system is least busy and users are logged out. This may cause the backup to be split into several pieces, each occurring at a different time, if your system is heavily used 24 hours a day.

Weekly. A full backup should be performed every week, usually on a weekend. This backup should be rotated offsite to a secure location. Some weekly backups may not cover applications and other executable programs because of time, capacity, or other constraints.

Monthly. Each month, there should be a scheduled full backup that covers everything on the system. This should include everything the weekly backup does and anything it skips. This backup should also be rotated offsite.

General Management Issues

As discussed at the start of this section, successful backup strategy is critical. Your strategy should include a schedule for backups, stating when backups will be performed, what type they will be, and who will perform them. You must also make provisions to perform the backups at a time when users are off the system.

The number and type of tapes needed are also key factors in a successful backup strategy. Tapes should be high quality and from a well-known and well-respected vendor. Don't trust your priceless data to questionable tapes just to save a few dollars. In order to determine the number of tapes you need, you have to determine the tape rotation schedule. The number of tapes in a rotation depends on how far back you wish to safeguard your data. If you wish to go back 4 weeks, you will need 20 tapes (5 x 4 weeks) for the daily backup. Weekly and monthly backups may consume one additional tape per week. Offsite copies for weekly and monthly backups may require another tape per week. If your system is used in a plant subject to a government body or other certification organization, you may need to keep periodic tapes for archive purposes.

So far, we have taken a cursory look at the backup procedures for your system. You should get the idea that backups are very serious business and require a fair amount of planning.

Procedures

VMS provides a number of options for automating backup procedures. The DCL language is useful for performing a number of other functions, such as mounting and dismounting LAD disks and building automated backup logs. The following procedures are a simple introduction to the VMS backup command and some of its options. If you will be writing or updating backup procedures for your system, you should consult other documentation, including your system manuals, for backup procedures.

Data Backups. Data backups do exactly what the name implies; they back up only the data, consisting of a user's personal data, corporate databases, departmental databases, and system databases, on your system. Data backups should be performed daily. Executable programs and applications are normally skipped during a data backup.

Certain system files must be included in your data backup. VMS systems use the .DAT file suffix for files that contain system parameters. Examples of these files are the UAF, DECnet and LAT database files, and all of the PATHWORKS database files. These files may usually be picked up by the backup procedure by including the specification SYS$DEVICE:[000000...]*.DAT in your backup file specifications. These files are normally not large and do not have a large impact on the capacity of the backup. Any other system files that change frequently are also good candidates for the data backup. This may include COM files or other program files.

Data backups can be split into multiple streams if required. If the system is running 24 hours a day, the daily backup may have to back up data application-by-application. The individual backups can be scheduled over breaks or lunch hours or some other downtime.

Full Backups. A full backup backs up everything on the system, including all data disks and system disks, programs, and applications. If a system failure occurs, you normally restore all or part of a full backup before restoring the latest data backup.

VMS Backup Commands

BACK.COM is a simple backup procedure that backs up data files, critical system files, and start-up files. The following procedure is a very simple, but functional, example. It can be executed from DCL by entering @BACK at the $ prompt, or it may be executed via one of the batch queues by using the SUBMIT command:

```
$!                              BACK.COM
$ BACKUP/LOG/REWIND -
    /ASSIST/IGNORE=(INTERLOCK,LABEL) -
    DKB300:[000000.USERS...]*.*, -
    DKB300:[000000.DATA...]*.*, -
    DKA300:[000000...]*.DAT, -
    SYS$STARTUP:*.COM -
    MKA500:SAVE/SAVE_SET/
```

BACKLIST is a simple command for listing the files on a tape. The procedure mounts, rewinds, and lists the files. As with the BACKUP command, it requires no parameters and is executed from DCL by entering @BACKLIST:

```
$!                                      BACKLIST.COM
$ MOUNT/FOREIGN/ASSIST     MKA500:
$ BACKUP/REW/LIST          MKA500:
```

A key element to any backup process is a tool for restoring files. Below is a simple RESTORE procedure that accepts two parameters, designating the files to restore and where to place them. The command is executed by entering @RESTORE FILES LOCATION:

```
$!                              RESTORE.COM
$!
$ BACKUP/LOG/REW -
      /ASSIST -
      MKA500:SAVE./SELECT.'PI'-
      'p2
```

The BACKUP command also operates interactively, which is more appropriate for restore operations for one or more files. To restore the file TEXT, use:

```
$BACKUP
From: MKA500:BACK/SELECT=TEXT
To: USR$DISK:[KEN]*.*
```

If you plan to use BACKUP, explore the documentation in your VMS users manuals and third-party references.

Third-Party Packages

Third-party offerings bring powerful and user-friendly tools to the backup process. Because backups are such a critical part of operating any system, investigating third-party tools is a very important part of planning any system. The best of these tools offer many more options than VMS BACKUP and are much easier to use when you are restoring files.

Some of the more popular third-party programs are offered by Raxco Inc., a provider of many different tools for VMS. TapeControl is an example of a program that adds to the functionality of the standard VMS commands. TapeControl stores the identifier for the tapes used in the backup process, the volume label, creation date of the tape, tape expiration date, owner, usage, error indicators, and numerous other information in the TapeControl database. You can use the normal DCL backup commands and command procedures, because the VMS backup commands are actually enhanced, not replaced, by TapeControl. Searching for and retrieving information from a tape is accomplished quickly by using the menu features of TapeControl.

Raxco also offers a package called ArchiveCommand that can automate the process of moving dated files from disk to tape. This product is useful in maintaining the integrity of your data and keeping infrequently used files off your disk but still accessible. Other vendors also offer products that perform similar functions to ArchiveCommand.

SERVER TUNING

All computer systems must be tuned in order to deliver optimum performance. Even PC and Macintosh users must tune their systems as they demand more and more from the systems. Memory usage is a particularly important area to tune, because memory is available in limited quantities and offers high performance. The PC laptop used to write this book has 8 MB of RAM. While this seems like a lot, it can use another 8 MB to really improve performance. New and improved application programs continue to place heavier demands on memory and other components of systems.

Servers suffer even more from this balancing act because of the tremendous demands from the network. Instead of one user, they may have 10 or 200 clients hanging on the LAN. VMS servers may also be running timesharing applications that place additional requirements on system resources.

When you are tuning a computer system, compromise is the name of the game. System changes to improve file server response time may cause a decrease in performance for timesharing or client/server applications. Even tuning the server by maximizing the cache may limit the number of clients that can connect to the server.

Tuning a system is a continual process. All changes should be made in small increments and monitored. This cycle should continue on a routine basis as the demands on the network change.

VMS Servers

Tuning a VMS server involves tuning PATHWORKS and many other system components, including VMS, DECnet, and LAT. VMS utilities such as SYSGEN, AUTOGEN, NCP, and LATCP can have an impact on server performance. Other utilities, layered products, and third-party products such as Monitor (VMS utility), Analyze (Digital), and Monitor/Plus (Data Center Software) provide tools for analyzing the performance of the server and network. Most of our discussion will concentrate on tuning the PATHWORKS server. To learn more about tuning VMS, review your system manuals and other publications such as VMS *Performance Management* and *The Hitchhiker's Guide to VMS*.

Seventy-five percent of VMS tuning involves memory. Changes to VMS system parameters typically will cause performance increases of 10 percent if correct and performance decreases of 90 percent if wrong. Cache size, number of workstations, open-file cache parameters, and cache buffer size are a few of the parameters that are used to tune PATHWORKS and affect memory. The cost of memory has dropped drastically in recent years, making it foolish to run a system with too little memory. However, it is still important to maximize memory usage.

You can also change the priority of the file server, giving the server more access to the CPU. The file server runs at Priority 8 by default.

Any changes to the server configuration will not take effect until the server is stopped and restarted. Some changes may also require reconfiguring VMS with AUTOGEN and rebooting. Changes made with PCSA Manager will display a screen explaining the steps to reconfigure and boot the server when required.

File Server Tuning

You should distribute resources among different disks (and systems, if you have multiple servers). Use a system disk and separate disks to distribute applications, users, and any heavily used programs. No PATHWORKS components should be located on the system disk, including system files, services, and user files. PATHWORKS is very I/O-intensive and benefits greatly from spreading the load over multiple disks.

Use available resources, such as memory and disk, effectively. When resources are reaching their maximum potential, add memory if necessary and feasible. Increased memory can cause tremendous performance benefits.

If your server is dedicated to PATHWORKS, allocate as many resources as possible for the server. In this type of scenario, timesharing resources are not an issue, so dedicating all of the server resources to PATHWORKS does not cause a drop in performance for other users.

The server processes such as LAD and NetBIOS should never swap. The NO SWAP qualifier should be used when starting these processes to prevent swapping.

You can gain another performance improvement by using end-node servers instead of routers. Routing tasks add another layer of overhead that pulls resources from PATHWORKS. With the price of VMS systems falling to the level of PCs, routing tasks should be moved to a dedicated router, possibly running on a workstation or other low-cost VMS platform.

Caching

Caching is an important tool for improving file operations. VMS uses caching internally to improve performance. A cache operates by temporarily storing information in memory that the system will need before it requests it. Since memory is very much faster than disks, reading the information from the cache instead of disk is much quicker. PATHWORKS augments the VMS caching by adding data caching and open-file caching. By carefully tuning these two features, you can significantly improve the performance of a PATHWORKS server. The PCSA Manager configuration screen is used to modify these parameters. (See Figure 11-1.) Both forms of PATHWORKS caching affect only stream files.

Data Caching. Data caching works by caching requests for data from the server. When a program requests part of a file, PATHWORKS will read past the point requested and store this information in the data cache. When the application requests another read, the cache will contain the data.

All I/O requests on the server are cached. The tuning goal for data caching is to keep the cache hit rate above 70 percent and cache availability near at least 80 percent.

The hit rate is the percentage of time that data requested (reads only) is located in the cache. This is a direct indication of how effective data caching is on your system. The availability is the percentage of time cache memory is available when requested. When cache memory is not available, the system must reorganize the memory used for cache operations. This causes an extra load on the server that adversely affects performance.

Open-File Caching. Open-file caching retains files in memory when they are closed for a certain period of time after a file close request is received. (The default is 15 seconds.) Open-file caching is very useful for programs that open and close the same file frequently, such as DOS batch files. Applications that open numerous unique files do not benefit from this type of cache.

The open-file hit rate shows the percentage of time that a closed file was reopened while still in the open-file cache. For open-file caching to be effective, the hit rate should be more than 70 percent. The PATHWORKS manuals recommend disabling open-file caching if it is less than 70 percent.

Microsoft Excel is an excellent tool for creating performance graphics. The data for these graphs can be stripped and pulled into the spreadsheet automatically with a simple command procedure on the VAX and a macro in Excel.

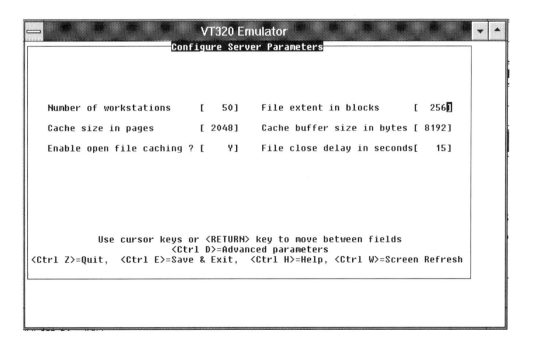

Figure 11-1. PCSA Manager Configuration Screen

Using graphics to display server performance data is a powerful way to view the data. The graphs should be built with standard markings to quickly identify when something needs to be changed.

Creating a program on the VAX or the PC to review the data on a regular basis and suggest changes is also fairly simple. Automating the process of collecting and reviewing server performance data is a critical part of keeping your system running on an even keel. This is an area in which VMS really brings a lot to the table because of its robust tools and the ability to drive programs from within another program. For example, a DCL program can call PCSA Manager and then read the output.

Changing Cache Parameters. The configuration screen in PCSA Manager is used to modify the cache parameters. Changing the cache requires stopping the file server, updating the values in the configuration screen, and restarting the file server. The steps for this process are outlined in the chapter "Improving Server Performance" in the *Server Administrator's Guide*.

Other Memory Issues

The page fault rate is an indication of how often the server generates a page fault and swaps a program from disk to memory or vice versa. When a page fault occurs, it is disastrous to the performance of the server, because a disk is incredibly slow compared with memory. To display the page fault rate, type:

```
$ SHOW SYSTEM
```

If the page fault rate is high, consider increasing the VMS parameters that affect paging, or obtain more physical memory. The file of particular interest to security is the PCFS_SERVER.LOG. Security violations are tracked by the SECURITY event flag. Table 10-2 shows the types of events that may be stored in the PCFS_SERVER. LOG.

Another area of memory to monitor is the virtual page count. If the system is out of virtual memory, you should increase the size of the VMS parameters affecting the page count. The SHOW MEM/FULL command will show the size of the page file, the free virtual memory, and the total. This information is usually located at the end of the SHOW MEM/FULL display.

VMS uses a priority scheme to manage the processes concurrently executing on a server. The range is from 0 to 31, with 31 having the highest priority. The PCFS_FILE_SERVER process has a default priority of 8. When a server is exclusively used for PATHWORKS or has a high number of PATHWORKS users relative to interactive VMS users, increase the priority of the server. The procedure for this is also in the "Improving Server Performance" chapter of the administrator's manual.

Disk Server Tuning

LAST Group Codes. Group codes can be used for the LAST transport to segment LAST users on large networks. However, servers and clients will not recognize each other if group codes are used but do not match. If server KENS is in LAST group 0 and workstation JOE is in LAST group 3, they will not communicate with each other. Restricting nodes to certain servers via group codes may also improve the servers' performance if there are several servers on the network and they are heavily used.

These are the steps necessary to set up group codes:

1. Set LAST group codes on the client. Edit AUTOEXEC.BAT on the client and add:

   ```
   C:\> LAST /G:5  (Where 5=GROUP CODE)
   ```

2. Set LAST group codes on the server:

   ```
   $ MCR ESS$LASTCP  STOP TRANSPORT
   ```

3. Edit the LAST start-up file and add the group code:

   ```
   $ EDT SYS$STARTUP:ESS$LAST_STARTUP.DAT
   ```

   Change the GROUP= line to:

   ```
   GROUP=5  (Where 5=GROUP CODE)
   ```

4. Restart LAST:

   ```
   @SYS$STARTUP:LAD_STARTUP
   ```

The LAST group code only affects operations that use LAST, including virtual disks and possibly file services if LAST is used in place of DECnet.

Clients will not be able to connect to servers that are not in the same group as the client. Servers that offer remote boot services must be in group 0. Remote boot clients must also use group 0 to connect to the boot server. After booting, they may change to another group.

Disk Server Caching. Performance of the disk server can be improved by changing the cache size. This should increase the cache hit rate. The hit rate for the disk server is an indication of the effectiveness of caching. The rate should be at least 80 percent. The rate is checked with the following command:

```
PCSA_MANAGER> SHOW DISK_SERVER COUNTERS/CACHE
```

Changes in the size of the cache should be made in increments of 256 pages. Review the average read size to determine the cache size. If you have plenty of memory, try setting the size to 3,096. The default size is maintained in the ESS$LAD_STARTUP.DAT file, located in the SYS$STARTUP directory. The cache size is entered with the CACHE = statement, with a default size of 512.

After the cache parameter is changed, the disk server must be stopped and restarted. The steps for this procedure are:

1. Check the current values of the cache:

```
$PCSA_MANAGER SHOW DISK_SERVER COUNTERS/CACHE
```

2. Stop connections to the server:

```
$PCSA_MANAGER STOP DISK_SERVER CONNECTIONS
```

3. Change the CACHE= parameter in ESS$LAD_STARTUP.COM. Also change the NPAGEDYN parameter, if required.

4. Restart the disk server:

```
$@SYS$STARTUP:LAD_STARTUP
```

NPAGEDYN Parameter. The NPAGEDYN parameter is used by LAST and LAD and may require changing when the cache size is modified. The following list shows the values that make up NPAGEDYN. Lines 1 through 5 must be calculated and the totals added together with lines 6 and 7 to get the new NPAGEDYN value:

1. Cache size + 256 bytes

2. (Number of servers) + (Number of clients) + 250 bytes

3. Number of mounted disk services + 100 bytes

4. Number of node connections + 100 bytes

5. Number of service connections + 350 bytes

6. 30,000 (bytes for driver images)

7. 300,000 (contingency)

The NPAGEDYN parameter should be changed in MODPARAMS.DAT. After changing the parameter, run the AUTOGEN procedure and reboot the VAX.

Tuning the Lookaside Lists. The performance of the disk server can be further improved by managing the lookaside lists that VMS uses to manage memory for network applications such as LAST. The sizes of the IRP, LRP, and SRP lookaside lists are controlled by the MIN_IRPCOUNT, MIN_LRPCOUNT, and MIN_SRPCOUNT SYSGEN parameters.

To check the current values, use the DCL SHOW MEMORY/FULL/ALL command. If the current size of either IRP, LRP, or SRP is equal to or close to the maximum for that list, the minimum value should be increased.

The new value for IRP, LRP, and SRP should be increased in increments of 30 percent per change. These values should be entered into MODPARAMS.DAT.

Additional Programs (Third-Party and Digital)

Another source of help for managing and tuning your system can be one of the numerous third-party programs available for VMS. Raxco markets a program called SystemCommand that can automate many of the tasks we have discussed throughout this book. This program can monitor VMS performance (swapping, paging, CPU utilization, processes, and other parameters) and disk performance (file size, I/O rate, and so on). When certain conditions are met (e.g., free space drops below 20 percent), SystemCommand can trigger certain actions to begin correcting the problem. Status reports and log files can be automatically created and archived to collect historical data.

Other programs are available for assisting in tuning your VAX. VAX Performance Analyzer (Digital) and PerfectTune (Raxco) can directly assist in the tuning process. Numerous other vendors also offer competing products.

Print Queues

The Queue Manager Buffer Count parameter may require increasing if your system has a lot of queues. The value may range from 1 to 1,500. The formula for this parameter is:

Q = Number of Queues + Number of Files Per Queue + 100

The maximum value is 1,500, but the value cannot be larger than the size of JBCSYSQ.DAT.

DECnet

Several DECnet parameters can affect the performance of your network. The following list shows several parameters that you may want to change. Before making a change, be sure to record the existing values for each parameter and document the current performance of your system:

- ◆ Pipeline Quota
- ◆ Maximum Broadcast Nonrouters = Number of Nodes + 1
- ◆ Maximum Links

The Maximum Links value may require changing because DOS frees up links only when the PC receives an ACK from the server. This can cause a delay in releasing links from clients, which will appear confusing because the server will not show the links as available.

If your system has PATHWORKS running on a cluster, do not use the cluster alias for PATHWORKS services, because the maximum number of alias links is 200.

Physical Disk Drives

One of the biggest bottlenecks for PATHWORKS is the server disk I/O. If the number of I/Os to a disk is extremely high or if the disk is heavily fragmented, PATHWORKS users will suffer. Tuning VMS management of the disks on a server can improve performance for everyone using the network.

You should also take advantage of Digital and third-party products that affect performance. Adding a RAM disk for the server, such as DECram from Digital, can trigger major performance gains for applications that perform many read operations. Placing these files on the RAM disk will drastically improve performance of the server for all applications.

Other products such as Digital's Movefile, Executive Software Inc.'s Diskkeeper, and Executive Software's I/O Express can improve the performance of your disks. Diskkeeper and Movefile are defragmenters that will reorganize a disk, placing all files into contiguous disk space. On a heavily used system, this can offer a major benefit. The same thing can be accomplished by doing a backup and restore, but that is much more time-consuming. I/O Express is a caching utility for VMS that improves the caching performance of the system if there is adequate memory available.

Another procedure that will improve performance of the disk systems is spreading files over numerous disks. If the files on a system are spread over multiple disks, a system will always perform better than a system with fewer disks of the same total capacity or with files grouped together on one disk. Use some logic in this process, taking into account which files are used most frequently and the time during the day when the access occurs. System files, PATHWORKS system files, heavily used applications, and large data files should have their own disk or be grouped according to use. The goal is to minimize the number of files being accessed on one disk at a time.

STANDARDS

To complete setting the stage of a proper network, we need to touch on the issue of potential problems. It is never pleasant to discuss problems or failures, but it is much more enjoyable to have this discussion now, instead of when trouble occurs. Every network will have a failure or problem somewhere during its lifetime. This may be a simple case of a user's not being able to access a file, which would be a software or configuration problem, or a workstation's not being able to access the network. Both of these examples are local failures that cause problems for just a few users. A traumatic failure occurs when the file server dies or when a network problem drops access for a number of users.

The best problem-resolution method is always prevention. As we move through detailed discussions in each segment of the system, we will cover relevant issues relating to preventing problems and what to do when and if they occur. A variation of Murphy's law states: "A piece of equipment designed and built by humans will fail." As your network grows, the likelihood of this happening increases dramatically.

One of the best methods of problem prevention and resolution in computer networks is to establish standards for your network and carefully document procedures, methods, techniques, and useful ideas as they occur. Standard configurations for network-access batch files are an efficient method of maintaining the user interface and a valuable control mechanism for problem prevention. AUTOEXEC.BAT, CONFIG.SYS, STARTNET.BAT, and LOGON.BAT files are also areas where you can prevent problems before they happen.

Workstation Types and Configurations

You may ask, "What if we only have to replace a PC every once in a while?" When managing a LAN, you almost never have a small problem. A PC may get flaky when a chip on the motherboard begins to fail. If this PC is a network workstation, you may experience timing, boot, network, and other failures from this slightly malfunctioning unit. The worst problem is the length of time it takes to resolve the problem and the havoc created before it is found.

A second problem occurs when there are PCs of many different types and brands on the network. You may have problems with replacement parts, setup configurations, and installation of specific types of hardware or software in the PCs. One of the companies I work with has an 80386 machine that locks up occasionally, especially when running Windows. This particular machine has 4 MB of memory and a 40 MB disk drive. It had similar problems before being installed on the network, causing some complaints from the user. Now that the machine is a network workstation, every time it locks up it kills the network connection to the server and kills the user login to the VAX. This can be very aggravating and can cause the loss of data, depending on what the user was doing. The hardware vendor is not very responsive and cannot supply quality advice. Of the 15 to 20 PCs on this network, this is the only machine that exhibits these problems.

With the many different PCs on the market today, what is the solution to this dilemma? Standards, standards, standards! The first thing you should do is to standardize on configurations for different workstations (e.g., 80286, 80386) that will be used on your network. Standards should include the amount of memory, types of memory (i.e., conventional, extended, expanded), option cards, vendors, machine type (VAX, PC, Macintosh), and so on. Anything that will be used on more than one PC should be spelled out in some type of standard for your organization. This does not have to be a formal or lengthy document, but simply a reference guide to standardize configurations for your system. Whenever a new configuration will be added to your network, it should be thoroughly tested by the system support staff or the end user. Once the testing is complete, add the configuration to your standards.

Other equipment should not escape your scrutiny when developing standards. These items include printers, mice, monitors, video adapters, hard disks, and so on. Network cards are especially important, as a bad or nonstandard choice will haunt you for years. Cheap network cards are often made to lower standards than cards purchased from other sources. It is easy to find what appears to be a bargain in low-cost network cards; you can save $50 to $100 or more per card. The actual cost of the cards may not surface until later when they have been in service for several months and begin to suffer sporadic or permanent failures, often bringing down an entire segment of your network. The real cost in dollars and lost efficiency of your organization's work force will quickly cancel any savings on the initial purchase of the cards.

One important point to consider concerns the PATHWORKS software. Since PATHWORKS is a Digital product, you can always be certain that your Digital network card will work with the latest version of PATHWORKS. Third-party cards often lag behind a new release by several months before all the required drivers are available. You may also find yourself with a heavy investment in low-cost cards that will not work at all with the latest release of PATHWORKS.

I have also seen networks brought down repeatedly by cheap cards such as video and serial/parallel adapters. Unless you want to make a career of fixing rampant problems, standardize your equipment configurations and always purchase quality components.

Figure 11-2 shows a section of a typical configuration document. Feel free to copy this format and add to it as necessary. This will save you many hours of frustration over the years to come.

Figure 11-2. Sample Standards Document

Computers

Type:	VAX Workstation
Vendor:	Digital
Model:	VAXstation 4000 Model 60
Memory:	8-32 MB
Disk:	0-2 GB
OS:	VMS

Type:	PC
Vendor:	Digital
Model:	DECPC-433
Processor:	486-33 MHZ
Memory:	4 MB
Disk:	80 MB
OS:	DOS
Options:	Mouse, Super VGA,
Ports:	Serial (2), Parallel (1), Ethernet ThinWire (1)

Type:	PC
Vendor:	Digital
Model:	DECPC
Processor:	386-25 MHZ
Memory:	4 MB
Disk:	60 MB
OS:	DOS
Options:	Mouse, VGA
Ports:	Serial (2), Parallel (1)

Network Cards

Type:	Ethernet—8-bit ThinWire or ThickWire
Vendor:	Digital
Model:	DE100-AA
For:	PC-AT bus

Type:	Ethernet—8-bit Twisted-Pair or ThickWire
Vendor:	Digital
Model:	DE100-AA
For:	PC-AT bus

Network Equipment

Network Interface Cards and Drivers. Client workstation network interface cards are almost a commodity item in today's market. Digital and other top vendors sell these cards for premium prices, while others sell similar cards at discount prices. Prices for the same type of card may range from $150 to $450, creating a great deal of confusion for consumers.

Before buying a large quantity of cards from Digital or another reputable vendor (with no-question return policies), you should test these cards thoroughly in your environment. These tests should include every type of workstation planned for the network plus a full suite of software.

Technology is advancing at a tremendous rate for both software and hardware. In a typical network, the network interface card is where these two meet. Buying a network card from a reputable vendor is low-cost insurance for protecting your network against technology hassles involving network cards. Quality cards are also less likely to fail and can be supported under your network service agreement with Digital and some other vendors.

After deciding which cards will be used on your network, document the cards in the same manner as workstations and other components. Standardizing on a minimum of different types reduces the number of different software configurations for each client. Cards from different vendors often require drivers and start-up files of different configurations, including executable files, CONFIG.SYS files, .INI files, and others.

As you test different cards, determine the software requirements for the drivers and start-up files. Some interface cards, such as most Digital cards and the ThickWire and ThinWire Xircom Inc. adapters, may use the same files and configurations. Documenting these requirements saves a tremendous amount of time when configuring new workstations and troubleshooting problems.

Cabling. A typical business will have a vast quantity of various types of cable running to numerous places within the facilities. Cable usually runs in the ceiling, under the floor, and in the walls. Common types of cable are telephone, electrical, and computer-related. Most of this cable will be undocumented and probably unnumbered. The hunt for the opposite end of a particular cable can be a nightmarish experience. It is vital to establish standards for the type of cable, connections, numbering schemes, and methods of running the cable.

In previous chapters, we discussed different types of cable that are suitable for your LAN. Once you have standardized on cable types, you should establish standards for cable vendors. The specification should include the cable type, authorized vendors, connector type and number, and any other information critical to that particular type of cable. This could include RG specifications for ThinWire, for example.

Connectors should also be documented carefully. Quality varies from vendor to vendor with cable connectors just as with any other product. Some connectors may also come in many flavors. A good example of these cables are fiber-optic and ThinWire coaxial connectors. The reliability and ease of installation may vary greatly from one type of connector to another.

Numbering Schemes and Network Maps. Numbering schemes are another often debated topic. The purpose of this discussion is not to try to convince you to use any one method, but to demonstrate different methods that may be applied to your situation. Unless you are using professional technicians to install your network, the installer will usually resist using a thorough scheme because the installation may take a little longer. I have seen people grudgingly follow a certain scheme until they run out of prenumbered labels, and then switch to any old number without saying a word until it is all over. Make sure you account for the proper amount of labels in the correct formats before starting on the installation.

The major emphasis in developing a numbering scheme is on designing a format that will document your network and provide a growth path for the future. This includes planning for an adequate number of devices within each scheme and developing numerous schemes that will accommodate your network in the future.

The cable number should be imprinted in the cable cover or placed on the cable via a standard cable-identifying label. Standard labels are available that actually wrap around the cable and adhere to the cover with some type of contact cement. All labels should be sturdy, legible, and reliable. Cable numbers should appear at each end of the cable and on each side of any splice in the cable. When faceplates are used, they should be labeled with the numbers of the cables attaching to the faceplates.

Numbers on components should meet the same criteria as labels for cables. Standard labels are sufficient, if they are resistant to fading and peeling off. Cheap, imprinted labels usually will not adhere to a component for a long period of time and are not recommended. Bridges, repeaters, and other components should be labeled according to their own numbering scheme. This applies to every component on the network, including clients, servers, printers, and so on. Remember that nodes such as servers and clients are already assigned network numbers (i.e., Area.Node), which should be marked on the outside of the unit. Table 11-1 shows some possible cable numbers for various types of network components.

Using the format in this figure, ThinWire cables would be numbered TH-0001 to TH-9999. Twisted-pair would be TW-0001 to TW-9999. If you are using twisted-pair for printers, terminals, and network devices, you may want to add a designation for network or terminal device. This can be accomplished by adding either an N or a T to the format shown above. TWN-0002 would indicate a network cable, while TWT-0002 indicates

285

Table 11-1. Numbering Schemes

Component	Format	Description
Cable	XX-NNNN	XX= TH =ThinWire TW=Twisted-Pair TT=ThickWire N=Number
Bridge	BR-NNNN	
Repeater	RP-NNNN	
Router	RT-NNNN	
Server/Client	Area.Node	

this cable is for a terminal or printer. This is particularly important when you are using standard modular jacks that either a terminal device or network device can plug into.

Your documentation should also include legible maps of all components on your network, complete with clear markings for each cable or component number. Every item listed in your network database should appear on the network diagram. The diagram does not have to be fancy or pretty, but it must be functional and must be updated as your network changes.

An accurate diagram is essential to efficient network management. This tool will be used when problems occur, when your system needs expanding, and when your organization reorganizes. With an up-to-date diagram, you will be able to quickly see where components are located and find the path for each cable on your system.

To create this diagram, you should invest in a good software package that will produce legible diagrams and provide for their maintenance in a timely manner. This is critically important, because a hard-to-use or slow software package makes it cumbersome to maintain your diagram and will probably mean the diagram gets out of date. Selecting a package for this task usually means choosing some type of CAD software.

One of the best tools I have found for the job is Micrografx Designer. This program is a CAD and graphics package rolled into one piece of software. Designer makes it easy to build standard components (PCs, servers, etc.), label them, and store them in a clip-art file. Once this is done, you can place them into a network diagram in seconds. Designer also provides a Parts List feature that will build a table of all components in your drawing. This table can be placed in the drawing or saved as a file. It also supports color and multiple layers, a standard CAD technique for placing different items on separate layers. By turning layers on or off, you can control which components are displayed at one time and speed up the response of the system.

Network Database

The network database is one critical component of successful network management that is often overlooked until it becomes a real problem, at which time it is very difficult and expensive to implement. This database should not be confused with the PCSA Manager, NCP, or other databases used by the server or client. It should be a traditional application created with one of the popular PC database packages or a VMS package. Key items to store in your network database are shown in Figure 11-3. Items with an asterisk (*) indicate key fields.

Figure 11-3. LAN Configuration Database

```
    *   Node name
    *   Node address
    *   Username
        User department
        Network cable number
        Primary server
        Client configuration
                Machine type (PC, Macintosh)
                Serial number
                Memory
                Mouse type
                Monitor type
                Memory
                Network adapter
                        Type
                        Ethernet address
        Problem history
                Last problem date
                Description
    *           Problem key (physical, machine, etc.)
```

This database should support numerous reports for managing the network. Lists of all active components (i.e., devices with a network address), lists of clients with network numbers, cable listings showing devices on each end of a cable and all splices, and comprehensive reports on selected components (e.g., a detailed report on a particular client) should be available. You should also have a report that will select one device and list all cables and other devices attached to it. For example, you would enter a repeater number and list all cables attached to it.

The information we have dealt with so far in the database example concerns the equipment on the network. A second major part of the database should be a problem-solving database that consists of information relating to past problems and their resolution. This should include key words, node and component identifiers, problem and resolution descriptions, and other relevant information. A sample format is shown in Figure 11-4.

Figure 11-4. Problem Database

```
*    Node or component name
*    Key link to system database
*    Key words
     Problem description
     Searchable fields for symptoms
     Resolution description (360 characters)
     Link to external file(s) for additional information
```

The problem database should provide the data for reports relating problems by type, symptom, node or component, and resolution. This should include look-ups by key word, symptom, and node to provide quick retrieval when a problem occurs.

A comprehensive database can be a real asset in maintaining this type of information. Just make sure it is accessible, via hard copy or preferably on a PC (with backups for another PC of course), if the system goes down. Along with the database, a network log book and solutions book are essential for tracking past problems and documenting items that are not easily stored in a database. You should, however, store references in your database, via the Link to external file(s) field, to items in any book or file to provide a readily accessible path to the information. There is nothing more frustrating than knowing you have the information close by and remembering seeing it last week, but knowing you can't put your finger on it.

It is also advisable to store this system on more than one node or be able to restore a backup to more than one node. The database is a valuable tool when the system goes down. If you store the files only on the server, and the tape drive can connect only to the server, then you may not have access to the information if the server or the network goes down. I like to use a PC database for storing this database, with the main database stored on the server. Each night it is backed up to a client hard disk. This provides some security, because it is unusual for two machines to fail at the same time.

User Accounts and Access

You should also create standards for user accounts, directories, and access methods. These should serve as models for creating a new user and setting up access to the system.

I suggest a simple format for this standard, using the UAF and login files as a guide. Each particular type of user will probably have the same type of access requirements, resulting in the same format within the PCSA database, UAF files, and login files. This format should include the required directory structure, system privileges and quotas (if the user is also a VMS user), sample AUTOUSER.BAT file, and required applications. Security concerns and procedures should also be documented.

Site Guide

A critical document for any system is the operations procedure manual, or site guide. This document should describe all of the key procedures for operating and maintaining your network. It should not be a document that takes 5 years to create and is out of date before it is completed. This document will provide you with a tool to solve problems quickly, assure that problems are averted during normal and abnormal system operations, and be a handy reference for your system. It can also be a handy training tool when new employees are hired.

I suggest using a good word processor such as Word for Windows or a document management tool to create your procedures. They must be in an easy-to-access format that can be retrieved by the appropriate personnel and updated when necessary.

If you have a complex and/or large network, using a tool such as Digital's Bookreader, VAX Notes, or PATHWORKS Conferencing will ease the task of maintaining and accessing your documentation. These types of products can be used to build online documentation that is widely available to your users and can be maintained in a timely manner.

The information contained in the site guide includes backup and restore procedures, daily operations, monthly and year-end operations, operations of application software, network diagrams, numbering schemes, and so on. The manual may be broken into several parts by category.

Figure 11-5 lists some of the various components for a typical site guide. This example is not meant to be an all-inclusive list, but to illustrate the types of information to be included in your manual. This type of document cannot be designed and created in a day, so make sure the format is one that can grow over time.

Valuable tools for documenting parts of the database are clear, short, and concise flow charts. A good flow chart can replace an entire page or more of text. (See Figure 11-6.)

If you try to block out a period of time and generate a site guide in a day, week, or month, you will be severely disappointed. This undertaking must be planned and managed over the lifetime of your organization. It should grow and change as your systems evolve. A good way to start this project is to begin with a simple outline like the one in Figure 11-5 and use it as a working tool. Working 15 minutes a day or 1 hour per week on this project can yield a tremendous result over time. Plan to use the proper tools to build and manage this project. Trying to do it on a simple word processor may seem fine at first but can become unmanageable as your documents grow.

Figure 11-5. Site Guide Components

```
Administrative
Production jobs
Troubleshooting
Backup
      Daily
      Weekly
      Monthly
Restore
      User-requested
      Disk failure
Disaster recovery
Server configuration
Client configuration
Hardware inventory
Startup and shutdown procedures
      Server
                  Automated
                  Manual
      Network
                  Automated
                  Manual
Installed applications
      Server
      Clients
Account management
Security
```

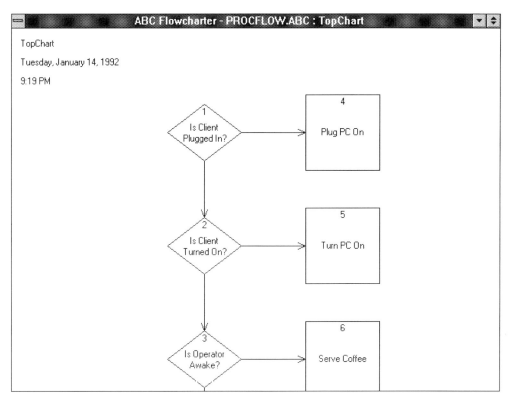

Figure 11-6. Troubleshooting Flow Chart for Dead PC

CHAPTER 12

Problem Solving

As your network grows in complexity and size, it will become an integral and vital part of your business. Features that were once nice to have will become necessities, and people who were resistant to the network will not be able to function when it is down. When network problems occur, they must be isolated, diagnosed, and solved quickly to avoid causing havoc in the organization.

This chapter focuses on another piece of the network puzzle, the art of problem solving. This involves the relationship of the network transport software and the physical network components. Try to imagine the vast amount of cable, connectors, and components scattered throughout a building or organization. The cable in a typical building usually consists of electrical wiring, telephone cables, computer cables, and any number of other types of wiring that might extend for several miles if they were laid end-to-end. The cable plant for any network is often a real puzzle in itself, because the many different parts may not be labeled clearly or may have been improperly installed.

With this great tangle of cable in your mind, now try to picture the network software communicating over this fragile mess at a very high speed. A good comparison would be a very fast race car running around and around over an old road, with numerous potholes that are covered loosely by straw, just waiting to grab a wheel at any moment. When a problem occurs in the cable plant of a network, it can cause problems for one or possibly many users. Problems in the cable layer usually show up in other areas, such as a program intermittently reporting errors or possibly reports from DECnet that a particular task cannot be completed.

The best solution for solving network-related problems is prevention and planning. The old adage, "An ounce of prevention is worth a pound of cure," is very appropriate for maintaining a functional and problem-free network. Careful planning should cover cable plants, network components, system standards, client standards, configuration management (clients, servers, and other nodes such as routers and bridges), and management tools. Carefully document all aspects of your system during installation.

You should also read the *PATHWORKS Network Troubleshooting Guide*. This manual includes descriptive chapters on DECnet, LAST, LAT, and TCP/IP. Each chapter details how the product functions and describes numerous tools used for management and troubleshooting. The guide also includes detailed discussions on specific problems and troubleshooting methods. A good understanding of how the different pieces of network software work together is helpful for quickly solving network problems and effectively planning your network.

PROBLEM NOTIFICATION

Network problems come in many shapes and sizes, ranging from problems with certain applications to nodes that cannot communicate with the network. Notification of these problems may come from a multitude of sources. Problem reports may come from users, errors on the system console, system error logs, and network analysis systems. The key to solving a problem is quickly identifying the problem, isolating the problem section of the network, and implementing a quick resolution.

Probably the most frequent method of problem notification is from the user community. A user may call and report that his or her workstation or terminal is not working. This may be simply that the user's password has expired or the user's PC or some other device is not plugged into the network or electrical outlet. It could also indicate a problem with a network interface card, cable, or connector.

Network managers may also find problems by using reports from VMS utilities, PATHWORKS server programs, or specific network management programs from Digital or third-party vendors. Many of the standard VMS network programs such as DECnet, LAT, and LAST will report errors to the system console or any other device that is set up to receive errors. These error messages will point to a problem completing a task to or from a particular node.

WHERE TO START

Troubleshooting a network can be a very time-consuming and often fruitless process. One key to quickly finding and solving problems is a good set of tools. Tools can consist of software, hardware, and a healthy set of checklists.

The OSI network model shown in Figure 12-1 is a handy tool for understanding network problems. When a problem that does not have an obvious cause occurs (such as when a cable breaks or PATHWORKS fails to load on a client), start at the lowest level of the OSI model and work your way up. For instance, if a workstation cannot connect to the server, check the cable connections, the cable itself, the network adapter, and network drivers. The cabling and connectors are at the bottom layer of the chart, and the network adapter and drivers belong to the data link layer.

To effectively troubleshoot a network, you don't have to memorize this model, but it helps to understand the relative order of the various components and the likelihood of a problem at each level.

Always consider whether something new has been added or if something has changed on the network. If you add a new client and it cannot access the server, start at the client. If you add a new client on Saturday and it works fine, and then on Monday someone else cannot access the server, check both client addresses and node names.

The environment surrounding your network is another good place to search for problems. Always be conscious of what has changed around the network (new lights, electrical lines or outlets, radio transmitters, and so on), and think about the impact on the network. When a problem occurs, consider whether an outside source could have had an impact on the network.

PROBLEM ANALYSIS TOOLS

Troubleshooting a network problem has one thing in common with fixing a faulty engine on a car: To be successful, you must use the correct tools. In addition to the standard tools that come with PATHWORKS, Digital and other companies offer many tools that are useful for finding a problem. The tools are in the form of service, software, and hardware.

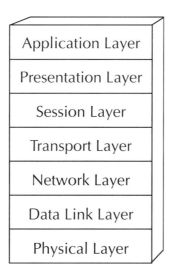

Figure 12-1. OSI Network Model

Digital Customer Support

The first line of defense in supporting your network should be Digital's Customer Support Plan. This program provides different levels of onsite or depot support to fit your requirements. This is a typical pay-for-what-you-get program, with options for 9 hours per day, 5 days a week (9 x 5) support, to 24 hours per day, 7 days a week (24 x 7) support. This program includes hot-line support and onsite hardware support via a local field service office. Digital support is usually better than most support programs, with occasional glitches.

If support stopped at this point, it would still be classified as very good. Current advances in the support area are evidence of how Digital is moving far ahead of its competition in supporting its customers. Digital has developed several products that are used internally to track and solve problems. These tools include a comprehensive problem logging and tracking database (including a history of problems for different products) called CHAMP. CHAMP also interfaces automatically with the local field service office to automatically dispatch technicians to customer sites, with the correct problem diagnosis if possible.

DSN Link is a recent addition that electronically links the customer to the support database. DSN Link allows the customer to search the database and then print or extract problem descriptions, patches, and news about critical problems. News about critical problems or issues relating to the customer's problems will be automatically mailed to the customer's mail account of his or her machine. The customer can also enter an electronic service request that will be sent to the server center, which will respond electronically, including downloading patches or suggestions. This is an exciting product and is free if you have a Digital support contract. DSIN is a subset of DSN Link and includes access to the problem database and allows entering of electronic service requests. DSIN users can access this network by using a PC or terminal with a modem.

A second powerful program for supporting your VAX is a product called VAXsimPLUS. This product is also free to all support customers. VAXsimPLUS is an acronym for VAX System Integrity Monitor Plus. After installation on your machine, VAXsimPLUS monitors your machine, looking at the CPU, memory, and disk systems. VAXsimPLUS is an artificial-intelligence tool that analyzes system component problems and attempts to predict when a failure is likely. If you have multiple disks of the same type and at least one of them is shadowed, VAXsimPLUS can also automatically copy a suspect disk to a spare disk before the problem disk fails. When a failure threshold is reached, VAXsimPLUS sends a message to your mail accounts. The message includes the suspect device name, suspected problem, a problem diagnosis code, and a note to call the support center (including the phone number). The DSN Link interface may be restricted to certain processors in initial releases.

Support technicians also have access to a full suite of tools, including Standard Package for Error Analysis and Reporting (SPEAR), Crash Analyzer and Troubleshooting Assistor (CANASTA), and Modular Analysis Expert (MAX). These tools enable technicians to analyze system dumps, diagnose a down or hung system, and analyze VAXsimPLUS logs. The sooner you involve Digital support for typical problems, the quicker you will be on the road to finding a fix and possibly hearing suggestions for avoiding future problems.

CompuServe

Another good source of information for preventing and solving problems is the CompuServe Information Service. There are numerous Digital forums, including a PATHWORKS forum, available to CompuServe subscribers. PC Magnet (from *PC Magazine*) is also available on CompuServe, although you must subscribe to it separately. PC Magnet offers information on PCs and provides a library for obtaining free utilities.

Time-Domain Reflectometry

Several companies make tools for detecting network problems at the physical level. One of the most valuable types is the cable scanner that uses time-domain reflectometry to detect network problems. This technique can pinpoint problems such as an open or short in a segment of cable, and it will show the exact distance to the problem. This will be invaluable when a cable problem occurs in your network. The scanner can also perform other testing of network wiring such as impedance checking. It will work with most coaxial and twisted-pair cable.

In addition to using the scanner when a problem occurs, you should use the scanner to test every cable run that has connectors or is over 100 feet long. Testing the cable before using it to connect a network node will save a lot of time, especially if the node is new or has had its network software modified. When a new node is added to a new cable, it is very difficult to pinpoint a problem, because there is no way to tell whether the node or the cable is causing the problem.

The scanner can also be used to determine the noise level of the cable. This can be important for determining when a cable will cause problems in the future because it is run too close to a fluorescent light or other source of interference. By checking the cable at installation and checking the noise level against other cables on your system, you can spot a problem cable very quickly. It is a good idea to document the average noise level of particular types of cables in your network and note any cables with high levels. A noisy cable can affect any node on that segment.

Multimeters

An old-fashioned multimeter is often an indispensable tool for network management. It is simple to use and can test for short or open conditions of twisted-pair cable, RS-232/MMJ cables, and connectors. A multimeter should never be used to test coaxial cables. If you wire your own RS-232 cables, a multimeter is indispensable.

A multimeter does not provide the capabilities of a cable scanner (except for checking for an open or short). To use a multimeter, you must short the two wires that will be tested before beginning the test. With the multimeter selector set to the position to test resistance, it will test the cable by sending a very low voltage over the wires and measuring the resistance of the return signal.

Standard Utilities

VMS provides a number of standard utilities for troubleshooting and managing the network. Several of the programs in the following list have been mentioned in previous chapters on using and managing the network. They can also be used for troubleshooting or displaying information about the network. If your network uses DECservers, they also provide some test capabilities for each port connected to the server:

◆ NCP (client and server)

◆ LATCP (client and server)

◆ LASTCP

◆ NET.EXE

◆ USE.EXE

◆ DECserver Software

VMS Layered Products

Digital has several layered products that will help you analyze your network. These products can monitor network traffic, pinpoint which nodes are the cause of problems, analyze the performance of the network, and perform many other tasks. Some of the products, such as Extended LAN Management System (ELMS) and DECmcc, can be used to manage nodes on the network, in addition to troubleshooting. The following list shows several products that were available when this book was written:

◆ Lan Traffic Monitor (LTM)

◆ DECmcc

◆ Terminal Server Manager (TSM)

◆ ELMS

Common Sense

A successful network will not run without a good dose of common sense. Common sense in network management means following the rules. Checking for loose cabling and cable that runs on the floor (where it can be stepped on or run over by a chair) and making sure that your network standards are in place and adhered to are important in making sure your system runs reliably. One of my professors in college had a saying: The fastest way to do anything with a computer is not to do it at all. Using a common sense approach to your network is like getting in out of the rain. Make sure things make sense, and follow the rules.

GENERIC TROUBLESHOOTING

The following list specifies a general set of steps for finding a particular problem. The steps should normally be performed in order, unless you have an indication of where to start (for example, if one particular client can't communicate with the server):

1. Read system release notes.

2. Review PATHWORKS and system log files.

3. Check lower network layers first, and then work up.

4. Isolate problem segments of the network.

5. Check if multiple workstations are affected or only one workstation is affected.

6. Check if affected workstations are on one segment only.

7. Check for hardware or software configuration errors.

8. Verify that no two nodes have the same address.

9. If multiple workstations are affected, check the server.

This list also hints at several things that can minimize future problems. Notice that the third step mentions starting at the lower network layers. Remember from Chapter 11 that most problems occur in the cable plant. That is the physical layer. The fourth item mentions isolating problem segments from the rest of the network. This will prevent the problem from affecting other nodes, and it usually points toward the problem. The eighth point mentions checking for duplicate network addresses. The network database should be referenced and updated every time a node is added to the network. This prevents duplicate node addresses.

As you gain experience with the procedures mentioned in this chapter, you should update them in your site manual. The procedure updates should include techniques for using any new products or upgrades to existing products, and any improvements you note from your own network. Be sure to include any steps or techniques introduced by third-party or Digital products that may be installed on your system.

Loop Tests

Loop tests are a powerful tool for detecting network problems. A loop test functions exactly as its name implies: Messages generated on one node are sent to another destination, and they loop back to the originating node. The test can detect hardware and cabling problems, either on a single node or between a node and the server. General users should not be given access to this test.

The loop test is very flexible and can test server-to-server, workstation-to-workstation, and workstation-to-server connections. The workstation components for using the loop test are shown in Figure 12-2.

Figure 12-2. Workstation Loop Test Components

PATHWORKS client programs on the boot disk:
SCH.EXE
DLL.EXE (data link driver)
Program files on the PCSA troubleshooting disk:
DNP
NCP
NCPSET
NCPDEF
NCPLOOP

The scheduler (SCH), data link driver (DLL), and DECnet (DNP) should be running on every client connected to the network. DECnet may not be loaded if you are only using LAST. The items mentioned above are required for the loop test, but other components such as LAT may also be loaded. I usually start with the workstation in its normal configuration as it is loaded via STARTNET.BAT.

Before running any of the loop tests from a client, you must install the NCP files from the troubleshooting disk in the client. You can copy these files to the hard disk or run them from a floppy. I suggest preparing a standard troubleshooting floppy that includes the required files to perform any of these tests plus any standard editors or utilities you normally use on a PC.

Before running a loop test, zero the NCP counters on the node that will run the test:

```
C:\>NCP
NCP> ZERO CIRCUIT
NCP> ZERO LINE
NCP> ZERO EXECUTOR
NCP> EXIT
```

It is often useful to reset all of the counters at once by using a batch procedure similar to this:

```
@ECHO OFF
REM RESETERR.BAT
NCP ZERO CIRCUIT
NCP ZERO LINE
NCP ZERO EXECUTOR
```

When the loop test runs, it will update the NCP counters with the results of the test. To fully understand what the counters are showing and to detect if they indicate an error, you must know what a "normal" reading is. You should review the error counters and log the results from time to time when there are no problems with your network. These values will be an invaluable tool when you begin to look for problems, because you can compare the test results with the values in your log. At the conclusion of your testing, you can display the counters by using:

```
C:\>NCP
NCP> SHOW CIRCUIT COUNTERS
NCP> SHOW LINE COUNTERS
NCP> SHOW EXECUTOR COUNTERS
NCP> EXIT
```

Do you remember the trick for capturing values to a file with the redirection facilities of DOS? This is useful for recording the results of your testing in a file for later review or printing. The double redirection symbols (>>) on the second and third commands append the results of those commands to the file created by the first NCP command. The following batch procedure runs all of the commands to show the NCP counters, and it captures the output:

```
@ECHO OFF
REM TRCKERR.BAT
NCP SHOW CIRCUIT COUNTERS                    >> NCPERR.LOG
NCP SHOW LINE COUNTERS                       >> NCPERR.LOG
NCP SHOW EXECUTOR COUNTERS                   >> NCPERR.LOG
```

The procedure can be modified to store this information over multiple runs if you add a second redirection symbol to the first command. The following procedure also adds a separator bar between each run:

```
@ECHO OFF
REM TRCKERRA.BAT
ECHO -------------------------------NEW RUN-------------------------
NCP SHOW CIRCUIT COUNTERS                    >> NCPERR.LOG
NCP SHOW LINE COUNTERS                       >> NCPERR.LOG
NCP SHOW EXECUTOR COUNTERS                   >> NCPERR.LOG
```

The loop test performs three different types of tests: client loop-back test, loop node test, and loop circuit test.

Client Loop-Back Test. This test checks the data link level of the client and will determine if the network interface card has a problem. This test can run only on a client with a ThinWire network connection, because it requires that a T connector with a terminator on each side be installed on the client. The T connector echos the test commands back to the test program on the client. Run the test by entering:

```
C:\> NCP LOOP LINE CONTROLLER
```

The test will report success or failure by displaying a message at the end of the test. If the test fails, a hardware problem exists with the controller card or the PC.

Loop Node Test. This test verifies communications with a specific remote node by checking the complete DECnet connection. The remote node must be running MIRROR from the troubleshooting disk. NCP will display the following types of failures:

◆ Invalid access control information

◆ Node executor information not set

◆ Undefined node name and address

This procedure will test connections from server to server, client to server, and client to client.

In Figure 12-3, the node is used for the server-to-server test to indicate the remote server, and the node KLS is the remote client node for the client-to-client test. For the client-to-client test, the NCP MIRROR command is used on the remote node to echo the test commands back to the node running the test.

The client-to-server test shows the results of the loop node test. Notice how the test reports the status of the test as it progresses and displays the success of the test.

Figure 12-3. Loop Node Tests

Client-to-Server Loop Test
On the client:

```
C:\>NCP LOOP NODE KENS
        LOOP NODE test started at 18-Jan-1992 11:11:38
        Connect complete to node KENS
        Remote node maximum buffer size for loopback: 4096
        Sending loop message 1, 46 bytes.
        Successful send and receive, message 1.
        LOOP NODE test finished successfully at 18-Jan-1992 11:11:38
```

Client-to-Client Loop Test
On the remote client (KLS):

```
C:\>NCP MIRROR
```

On the local client:

```
C:\>NCP LOOP NODE KLS
```

Server-to-Server Loop Test
On the server:

```
$ NCP LOOP NODE KENS
```

The best way to approach using any of the loop node tests is by running the test between two nodes that are exhibiting no problems. Once you have the test running on these nodes, stop the test on one node and start it on the node exhibiting the problem. If this command does not complete successfully, it indicates a problem with the connection to the node or a problem with the remote node itself.

Loop Circuit Test. This can test a specific node anywhere on the network. A failure may indicate a physical connection problem. You can perform this test from anywhere on the network. It is performed almost exactly like the client-to-client loop node test:

On the remote client (KLS):

```
C:\>NCP MIRROR
```

On the local client:

```
C:\>NCP LOOP CIRCUIT
            LOOP CIRCUIT test started at 18-Jan-1992 11:13:22
            Sending loop message 1, 46.
            Message echoed by remote circuit loopback 1, 46 bytes.
            LOOP CIRCUIT test finished successfully at 18-Jan-1992
            11:13:22
```

If this test is not successful, it indicates a problem along the link to the remote node.

NET ERROR

NET ERROR displays error statistics for network and virtual disk services. Statistics shown are based on information gathered since the last time the counters were zeroed. The errors displayed by NET ERROR include file service errors (line and circuit) and virtual disk errors (LAD). The LAD counters can be reset with NET ZERO LAD, while the NCP ZERO commands must be used to reset the line and circuit counters. NET ERROR is equivalent to executing the NCP commands for showing the line and circuit errors and also includes the LAD errors. To execute the command, type:

```
C:\>NET ERROR
```

NET TEST

The NET TEST command conducts a loop node test between a client and a server. NET TEST will report the results of the test as it runs and will indicate whether the command was successful when it completes. It is equivalent to the loop node test between a client and server. The only parameter is the name of the server, as shown in Figure 12-4, which checks the connection to the server KENS.

Figure 12-4. NET TEST

```
C:\>NET TEST KENS

    LOOP NODE test started at 18-Jan-1992 11:10:57
    Connect complete to node KENS
    Remote node maximum buffer size for loopback: 4096
    Sending loop message 1, 512 bytes.
    Successful send and receive, message 1.
    Sending loop message 2, 512 bytes.
    Successful send and receive, message 2.
```

Figure 12-4. NET TEST (continued)

```
         Sending loop message 3, 512 bytes.
         Successful send and receive, message 3.
         Sending loop message 4, 512 bytes.
         Successful send and receive, message 4.
         Sending loop message 5, 512 bytes.
         Successful send and receive, message 5.
         Sending loop message 6, 512 bytes.
         Successful send and receive, message 6.
         Sending loop message 7, 512 bytes.
         Successful send and receive, message 7.
         Sending loop message 8, 512 bytes.
         Successful send and receive, message 8.
         Sending loop message 9, 512 bytes.
         Successful send and receive, message 9.
         Sending loop message 10, 512 bytes.
         Successful send and receive, message 10.
       LOOP NODE test finished successfully at 18-Jan-1992 11:10:59
         Command completed successfully.
```

You should notice from the output of the LOOP NODE command that it sends 10 messages and reports on the status of each. It also reports on the complete success of the command.

NET ZERO LAD

The NET ZERO LAD command resets to zero all error counters for LAD services. This is a useful command to run after LAD problems have been resolved. Running NET ZERO LAD and then tracking the LAD error statistics will provide information about the reliability of LAD services since the last problem was resolved. If the command is not executed after fixing a problem, the counters will continue to accumulate errors and will not provide an accurate picture.

Noise Levels

In addition to testing for noise with devices that use time-domain reflectometry, you can also use NCP to display errors that indicate high noise levels. The SHOW KNOWN LINES COUNT command will display error counts and information on different types of errors. Each line (Ethernet, asynchronous, and so on) will be listed, followed by numerous statistics for that particular line. The statistics on collisions will indicate whether or not a lot of noise is present on the line by the magnitude of the error number. You should check the number of collisions frequently for new trends. Increasing numbers of collisions usually indicate problems at the physical level, such as a loop in a cable, a cable running too close to a light, a missing terminator, or another physical problem.

You should investigate other capabilities of NCP and look further into the capabilities of other DECnet tools. The system manuals for VMS will provide an in-depth review for NCP and other standard commands. Digital also provides other suggestions for DECnet in the *DECconnect Planning and Configuration Guide* (order number EK-DECSY-CG-002).

SERVER PROCEDURES

One area where problems affect a large number of users is the server. If a server problem occurs, it may bring down only certain services or the entire network. There are a number of facilities provided by VMS to test components of the network that reside on the server. You can use NCP, LATCP, PCSA Manager, and LASTCP to perform tests of various parts of the network. You can also use the DCL SHOW command for reviewing memory or the status of a process.

The following list shows the general order for testing the server. You can change the order in which the tests are performed if you know which service the problem affects (for example, if everything works but file services):

1. Test DECnet.

2. Review the file server checklist .(See Figure 12-5.)

3. Review the disk server checklist. (See Figure 12-6.)

4. Review the remote-boot checklist. (See Figure 12-7.)

5. Review the remote-printing checklist. (See Figure 12-8.)

6. Test LAT.

Explaining the management and testing of DECnet is outside the scope of this book. To fully cover this product would require another book the size of this one. To begin the process of understanding DECnet, review the PATHWORKS DECnet manual chapters on troubleshooting.

The following checklists show the steps for testing the file server, disk server, remote boot clients, and printing functions. As new versions of PATHWORKS, DECnet, VMS, and other products are introduced, new features and capabilities will be introduced. Becoming familiar with these products and their capabilities will make your life much easier.

Figure 12-5. File Server Troubleshooting Checklist

❏ Verify that VMS file server objects are defined properly:

```
$ NCP>SHOW KNOWN OBJECTS
```

❏ Verify that the file server is running and accepting connections:

```
$PCSA> SHOW VERSION

$SHOW SYSTEM (Look for PCFS_SERVER.EXE.)
```

❏ Verify that the desired service exists by using PCSA Manager.

❏ Verify that the user attempting to connect to the service is authorized to use the service.

❏ Verify that the file server or service has not reached any limits on the number of sessions or number of connections.

❏ Verify that the file server's serverwide sessions total is two less than the NCP MAXIMUM LINKS parameter.

Figure 12-6. Disk Server Troubleshooting Checklist

❏ Verify that the disk server is running:

```
$PCSA> SHOW VERSION

$SHOW SYSTEM (Look for LAD and LAST drivers.)
```

❏ Verify that the server node and workstation are communicating:

❏ Test with the USE /V to connect to a disk service:

Figure 12-7. Remote-Boot Troubleshooting Checklist

❏ Determine the hardware address of the workstation.

❏ Verify that the circuit service state is enabled at the server:

```
$ NCP SHOW KNOWN CIRCUITS
```

❏ Verify that the workstation node is registered as a boot node:

Is the node address correct?

Is the node name correct?

Is the hardware address correct?

Figure 12-7. Remote-Boot Troubleshooting Checklist (continued)

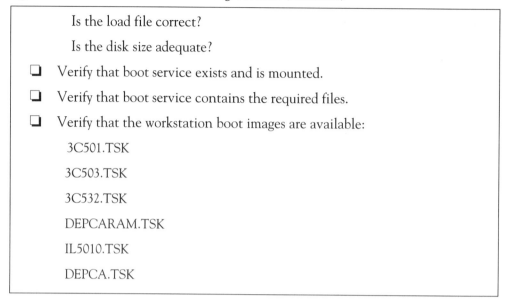

Is the load file correct?

Is the disk size adequate?

❑   Verify that boot service exists and is mounted.

❑   Verify that boot service contains the required files.

❑   Verify that the workstation boot images are available:

3C501.TSK

3C503.TSK

3C532.TSK

DEPCARAM.TSK

IL5010.TSK

DEPCA.TSK

Figure 12-8. Remote-Printing Troubleshooting Checklist

❑   Verify that the printer is ready (online) to print.

❑   Verify that the print queue is defined and running.

❑   Test printing from VMS. (Use the DCL PRINT command.)

❑   Specify the queue name used by the server:

`$ SHOW QUEUE`

❑   Verify that the print service exists.

❑   Verify that the service alias is correct.

❑   Review the file server checklist. (See figure 12-5.)

CLIENT PROCEDURES

Troubleshooting on the client involves the same concepts as troubleshooting for the server. The problem must be isolated as quickly as possible, and then the problem must be fixed. The following list is an overall guide for testing the client:

1. Review the general considerations. (See Figure 12-9.)

2. Test DECnet.

3. Review the file services checklist. (See Figure 12-10.)

4. Review the disk services checklist. (See Figure 12-11.)

5. Review the remote-boot checklist. (See Figure 12-12.)

6. Review the remote-printing checklist. (See Figure 12-13.)

7. Test LAT.

Figure 12-9. General Client Troubleshooting Considerations

❏ Verify that required network components are loaded in CONFIG.SYS, AUTOEXEC.BAT, and STARTNET.BAT.

❏ Try loading components in conventional memory.

❏ Unload all TSRs.

❏ Try removing other installed options:

   Test DECnet by removing LAT, LAST, etc.
   Test LAD by removing DECnet, LAT, etc.

When a client cannot reach a file server or other node, use the loop node test. You can also test from one client to another with PERMIT or FAL and NFT.

Figure 12-10. File Services Troubleshooting Checklist

❏ Check that file services are running:

```
C:\>USE /STATUS
```

❏ Verify that the file service exists.

❏ Verify that the user is authorized for the file service.

❏ Check CONFIG.SYS for minimum parameters:

   BUFFERS=8
   FILE=20
   LASTDRIVE=Z

Figure 12-11. Disk Services Troubleshooting Checklist

❏   Verify that the LAD driver and LAD.EXE are running:

    `C:\>USE /STATUS`

❏   Verify that the desired service exists and is mounted.

Figure 12-12. Remote-Boot Troubleshooting Checklist

❏   If you are not using a floppy to boot, verify that Jumper W16 is removed (DEPCA).

❏   Verify that no hardware errors occur on power-up. (DEPCA Error 72 is OK, if a mouse is not present.)

❏   Verify that the workstation is registered as a boot node.

❏   Reboot the workstation (CTRL-ALT-DEL).
    Error Codes:

Remote boot code/data is in place =	1
Scheduler has been initialized =	2
Datalink has been initialized =	3
LAST has been initialized =	4
LAD has been initialized =	5
All responses for services have been received =	6
Manual boot checking (CTRL-C) completed =	7
First connection to boot service completed =	8
DECPARM.DAT found and parsed correctly =	9
First connection broken. DLL, LAST have been reinitialized =	10
Reconnected to first service. Transferring control to the boot block =	11

Figure 12-13.-Remote-Printing Troubleshooting Checklist

❏   Verify that remote printer is ready (online) to print.

❏   Verify that the print service (or queue) exists.

❏   Verify that the print device is correct:

    `C:\>USE`

CHAPTER 13

Network Security

A cornerstone of any network security plan involves analyzing the requirements of the organization, environment, customers, government, and so on. Your security procedures must be tailored to all these requirements and must be flexible enough to change over time as the requirements change. Remember the old adage: "The only thing for certain is death and taxes." A wise security manager will add "change" to the front of that list.

The user and network administrator have somewhat paradoxical requirements for using the network. The administrator must determine a particular user's requirements and establish the proper access to resources for this user, but at the same time the administrator must maintain a level of protection for other users. Users always strive for more access, while administrators try to control and limit access.

In a properly designed network, many security issues are managed by the default structure of the network. Network standards, login procedures, menus, directory structures, and user accounts will simplify the lives of both administrators and users. Network security is a good example of how the KISS concept works. Establishing and maintaining the standards mentioned above is a simple process, but it is absolutely essential to having a well-run and secure network.

This chapter will focus on some of the available security operations for a PATHWORKS network. I will not try to cover security in an exhaustive manner or provide the final word in security features, but I will provide an overview of security that will suffice for many networks. If your requirements are based on government standards or otherwise exceed the topics discussed here, you should refer to other texts relating to your security needs. You should also seek the guidance of Digital and other vendors of security products and services to ascertain the proper products for your requirements. Remember that the techniques used by hackers evolve over time just as the security tools improve. A few years ago, typical hackers would spend hours trying different passwords to access a system account. Today, they use sophisticated programs that try thousands of passwords in minutes. They also have access to programs that can scan thousands of phone numbers looking for a modem connection.

The Digital Equipment Computer Users Society (DECUS) is a very useful tool for staying on top of security issues. There are several special interest groups (SIG) that deal with security, some of which are security specific (Security SIG) or frequently deal with security (Personal Computing SIG). These SIGs provide an ideal environment to meet with others with similar concerns and to share solutions. The Security SIG Session Notes from the DECUS meetings held twice a year provide a wealth of information on various aspects of security.

DOCUMENTING SECURITY REQUIREMENTS AND POLICIES

The first phase in developing a security plan for any system is to begin documenting the security requirements and policies for your organization. This document will include the security needs and procedures and the reasons they were developed. The security manual should become a key part of your site manual.

The security requirements of your enterprise should be organized into a detailed outline, with references to supporting documents such as government or industry regulations. The documentation should be in a format that can change as your requirements change. You should consider all aspects of your organization in pulling the requirements together. The following list suggests several possibilities:

◆ Corporate guidelines.

◆ Customer policies (requirements, audits, etc.).

◆ Government regulations.

◆ Industry standards.

◆ The likelihood of security problems.

◆ Protection of data from competitors.

◆ Employee environment (e.g., hostile employees).

Once you have documented your requirements, you can begin to design your security policies. The policies should outline what will be done to secure your network and should refer to which requirements they fulfill.

VMS provides a number of features for maintaining the security of your network. If you turn on all of the security features, you will spend your life responding to, researching, and maintaining the alarms and reports they generate. You should carefully decide which tools should be used. Always focus and report on key issues, and use enough security, but not too much.

NETWORK ARCHITECTURE AND PHYSICAL SECURITY

The network itself is a security problem because of its openness. Anyone accessing the cable directly or through a modem can capture the information traveling over the wire or through the air. Instead of having to log into a central computer, someone could tap onto the LAN and monitor the traffic. This is not a very fruitful enterprise, however, because the data the person is looking for must be actually traveling over the LAN when he or she taps in and would be difficult to find.

If you are concerned with the physical aspects of securing your network, there are several steps you can take. You should restrict access to network devices such as bridges, routers, and the system console by locating them in areas that are not readily accessible. Using locked offices for the console, and ceilings and secure rooms for the other components, will put these devices out of sight and out of reach. You may also want to secure access to network connections, such as structured cable faceplates, splices, and T connectors on ThinWire. If necessary, structured cable faceplates can be installed in boxes recessed in the wall and locked.

You should also secure modems and other external access ports to your network or any component on the network. If you do not secure them, they provide a place for someone to change the phone line to an unsecured line, remove modem security, or replace the device with another device. Remember that connecting to any device on the network usually means connecting to the network.

Backup tapes, software, blank tapes, and any other item that provides an input to your system should also be locked up. If someone has access to your backup tapes, they have access to your data. They also may use backup tapes to place security breach software on your system by adding the program to the backup set and waiting until you restore the system. Bang, you're dead.

The PC provides another point where problems can enter your network. One of the most obvious types of problems are computer viruses. Viruses have been in the news frequently over the last few years, especially after a virus infected the Internet. To protect your network against PC viruses, you should restrict access to directories other than the user's personal and shared directories. All other directories should be write protected, and you should require explicit permission to gain access to them. This should prevent users from loading programs into the system, other than in their personal or shared directory. You can also create a command procedure on the server that will search the entire disk looking for certain types of files. Suspicious files can then be killed or reported. DECUS and third-party vendors have programs that look for different types of viruses and remove them.

SECURING YOUR NETWORK: VMS FEATURES

A nice feature of VMS is that the different utilities that affect security work well together. Many utilities can be used alone or in conjunction with others. When used together, they build on each other, providing a layered security similar to the way you layer clothing in the winter to keep out the cold. This allows each site to install only the security features required by that site and still retain the ability to add more features as changes occur.

Authorize Utility

User account information is maintained for VMS users and possible PATHWORKS users by the Authorize utility. This utility is executed by setting your default directory to SYS$SYSTEM: and entering the command RUN AUTHORIZE. Access to Authorize should be restricted to certain users by a group code or ACL identifier. The ACL identifier is the best choice, since it can be granted and removed easily.

The information stored and maintained by Authorize includes the username, account name, default login directory, password, password parameters (e.g., length and expiration period), system privileges, proxy information, allowable system managers (e.g., MAXJOBS and BYTLM), and ACL identifiers.

The SYSUAF.DAT database is the main VMS security file. This database is maintained by both Authorize and the PCSA Manager ADD USER command. Authorize also maintains the NETUAF.DAT, NETPROXY.DAT, and RIGHTSLIST.DAT databases.

VMS V5.4 introduced two new security qualifiers (PWDHIS and PWDDIC). PWDHIS enables password history tracking for a user. PWDDIC enables checking the password dictionary for a user. These flags are turned on by default for all new users.

When PWDHIS and PWDDIC are on, a user cannot use a password twice in the same year, nor can he or she use passwords found in the password dictionary. The PWDDIC stores words that are considered to be invalid and currently has over 40,000 words in its file. The default limit on storing password history is 1 year, up to a maximum of 60 passwords. The limit can be adjusted to the last 2,000 passwords and up to 28,000 days.

User Identification Codes

The UIC is the key for records in the UAF. Whenever a user logs in, the UAF is read and updated, using the username to access the UIC record for that user.

The UIC is the primary mechanism for users to connect to services on the system. The UIC is linked with the username when a user is added to the system by PCSA Manager. The group code is automatically set to 360, and the user code is set to the next available code.

UICs always have the format [Group,User], using brackets as delimiters and a comma as the separator.

The group code in the UIC is used to establish mutually exclusive user groups. UIC groups are normally used to separate users for a particular VMS application. Because they are mutually exclusive, a user may be in only one UIC group.

Identifiers

VMS uses identifiers to provide access to the system and to identify certain characteristics about a user or a process. Any process or user may have more than one identifier at any given point in time. An identifier may indicate who the user is (i.e., UIC), what type of access the user has (i.e., system identifier), and what groups the user belongs to. You can view or access identifiers by lexical functions within a DCL file.

System-defined identifiers are used for certain processes or tasks running under VMS. They normally are used to identify processes or users. Examples include the LOCAL identifier, which is associated with users logged in through local terminals, and the BATCH identifier, which flags batch processes.

General identifiers are created with the Authorize command to establish groups of users. These identifiers are not mutually exclusive, as users may belong to one or more groups. They are also very flexible, providing a mechanism for creating any number of groups or classes of users or resources.

The power of general identifiers becomes evident as you explore the various options for their use. Along with enabling you to create nonexclusive groups, general identifiers can also control resources for overlapping groups (where a user is a member of two groups that access common resources) and mutually exclusive groups (where a user can be in only one group or the other at the same time). They can also be used in very complex schemes where a user could be in two of three groups, but not in all three.

Network Control Program

NCP can be used to provide several elements of security to the PATHWORKS VMS environment. It can be used to define objects and link them to both a user ID and a file (executable or otherwise). It can be used to restrict systems to certain communications with a particular node, such as in from a node, out to a node, both, or no communications with a node.

Access Control Lists

ACLs are used by VMS to provide tighter security than that provided by the UIC alone. Defining an ACL for an object such as a file or directory will provide a control mechanism that is linked to a user via the Rightslist database and an identifier specified on the user's UAF record. You normally use identifiers to group users by assigning the same identifier to multiple users, on the basis of function or some other criteria. The user is linked to the ACL by placing the identifier in the ACL with certain access privileges. Each entry in the ACL is an ACE.

Each time a user logs into the system, VMS builds a rights list for the user, indicating the active rights for this particular login. Each time the user tries to access that which is protected with an ACL, VMS checks the user's rights list against the identifiers listed in the ACL. As soon as it finds a match, it grants access to the object on the basis of the ACE. If the user has two ACEs in an ACL for one object, the access is granted on the basis of the first ACE in the list.

Using ACLs in addition to the standard UAF and PATHWORKS features adds another layer of security to your network. It also provides a great mechanism to improve on the access capabilities of the standard PATHWORKS services.

The first step in creating an ACL is to decide what objects will be controlled and what groups and users will have access to them. Groups may be mutually exclusive or totally independent. Access may also be denied explicitly to a user or group. Examples of identifiers are:

MFG, SALES, ACCTG	Based on department.
WORDPROCESSING, SPREADSHEET	Based on function.
ADMINISTRATOR, USER, PROGRAMMER	Based on access requirements.

A particular user may be in the MFG, WORDPROCESSING, SPREADSHEET, and USER groups at the same time.

Once the identifier and object criteria have been established, you are ready to begin setting up the ACL. The first step is to create the general identifier using the Authorize utility. The following commands create the identifier SALES and assign it to the user KEN. The first command sets the default directory to the SYS$SYSTEM: directory, which contains the SYSUAF.DAT database:

```
$ SET DEFAULT SYS$SYSTEM:
$ RUN AUTHORIZE
UAF> ADD/IDENTIFIER SALES
UAF> GRANT/IDENTIFIER SALES KEN
```

The next step is to define the ACL and enter the ACEs. You add the first ACE entry in an ACL when the ACL is created, using the SET ACL command. This command is executed from DCL:

```
$ SET ACL /ACL=(IDENTIFIER=SALES,-
   OPTIONS=DEFAULT ACCESS=READ+WRITE+DELETE) -
   SHARE.DIR
```

This example creates an ACL for the object (directory) SHARE. The OPTIONS=DEFAULT qualifier causes the ACL to be added to any new files and directories created using the service. This resolves one problem with PATHWORKS COMMON file services. If users are added to a PATHWORKS group that has read/write access to a COMMON service, they can add new files to the service and access files they create on the service. They cannot access files created by others. By placing an ACL on the service directory using the format illustrated in the previous example, users who have the SALES identifier may read and write to any files on the service. You can override access to a particular object within the service by adding an ACL to the object and restricting access by using stricter ACEs in the individual ACL.

The order in which ACEs appear in an ACL controls who has access to the object. Remember that the first ACE that gives a user access is the one that will be used. You should always review all the entries in an ACL when adding a new ACE.

Digital recommends several techniques for managing ACLs. The following list contains a short description of each recommendation:

◆ Review all ACEs using ACCESS=NONE.

◆ Carefully review the order of all ACLs.

◆ Do not use ACLs on all objects.

◆ Use general identifiers relating to groups.

◆ Update ACLs when you delete accounts.

If you are planning to use ACLs on your system, you should consult your VMS documentation and test the ACLs on your system.

Network Auditing

Alarms. The standard features of VMS provide the ability to monitor a number of security concerns, delivering real-time notification to consoles and tracking certain information to log files. You may set alarms to monitor Authorize functions, break-in attempts, login failures, ACL events, all possible events, file access, installation of images, successful logins, logouts, and volume mounts and dismounts. Monitoring of Authorize functions and break-ins is turned on by default when the SET AUDIT/ALARM command is executed.

The SET AUDIT command provides options for controlling which alarms to report and how to report them. You can report alarms to a device, such as the console, and write them to the security log. The /ARCHIVE parameter controls which types of alarms are written to the security file.

To ensure that alarms are properly set, make sure your start-up procedures properly start the operator communications (OPCOM) process. The start-up procedure should also include the commands to enable security alarms on your systems. I suggest placing the commands related to security procedures in their own startup file and calling this file from your system-specific start-up procedure.

In most implementations, LOGFAIL, BREAKIN, FILE=FAILURE, and LOGIN should be monitored. Logins should be limited for resources such as REMOTE and DIALUP. This will aid in checking likely sources of problems. You should also monitor ACL access and privileges for secure files and system services, to detect attempts to access these resources.

Alarms are sent to operator consoles that have been enabled for security alarms. Any number of terminals can be enabled at the same time. You can enable alarms on a terminal or hard-copy device by using the following command:

```
$ REPLY/ENABLE=SECURITY
```

Use a hard-copy terminal for security alarms to provide a permanent log. If the alarms are sent to a normal CRT, they will scroll off the screen and be lost. You may use a CRT for alarms if you have a system operator who continually monitors the system. If you are using a hard-copy device, keep it in a secure environment.

The following commands can be added to your start-up procedures to activate security alarms on a particular device:

```
$ DEFINE/USER SYS$COMMAND TTA2:
$ REPLY/ENABLE=SECURITY
```

This triggers alarms to the device on TTA2: for any security events.

Analyze Utility. The Analyze utility provides the ability to selectively report on the alarms logged in the security log file. Using the ANALYZE/AUDIT command and its qualifiers, you can quickly create lists (/BRIEF), detailed reports (/FULL), summary reports (/SUMMARY), and a secure output file for future reports (/BINARY).

This utility provides a quick way to look at your security log a number of different ways. You can bracket certain dates (/BEFORE and /SINCE), event types (/EVENT_TYPE), and users (/USERNAME). This flexibility provides a handy tool to hone in on suspected problems and review your system security on a daily basis. The standard /OUTPUT parameter allows you to dump any reports to a file.

You should frequently review and track summary reports to develop a picture of your system. Recording key information from a summary each week will give you a good picture of your system's activity. You should also understand which security events are normal for your system. Security can be controlled only if you understand what is normal.

A feature of ANALYZE/AUDIT is the ability to jump from a full or brief report display to an interactive mode. This allows you to enter commands to select a new report to look at suspicious activity. Enter the interactive mode by pressing CTRL-C when viewing a full or brief report. You can return to the report by entering CONTINUE or exit to DCL by entering EXIT.

The *VMS System Managers Manual* provides a detailed overview of the ANALYZE/AUDIT command, along with a number of suggestions for its use. I advise you to read this section of the manual and try the many different suggestions shown.

Automating the Audit Process. Monitoring security is no different than monitoring any other aspect of system performance, in that it must be a routine part of your system operations. One way to facilitate this is to automate everything possible. Automating security reporting should focus on automating the standard reports and collection of data, and alerting the system manager when a suspicious event occurs. The actual probing and detection of problems should be a manual process that is assisted by automated tools.

DCL command procedures can be used to automate many of the reports you will need in the normal security operations of your system. The following example illustrates running the ANALYZE/AUDIT utility from a command procedure and mailing the output to a mailing list of security reviewers:

```
$! DAILY_SUMMARY.COM
$!
$ANALYZE/AUDIT/BRIEF/SUMMARY/SINCE=TODAY/-
         OUTPUT=DAILY.LIS
$!
$ SUBMIT DAILY_SUMMARY.COM -
    /AFTER= TOMORROW +4 -
    /PRINTER=SECURITY$LASER -
    /QUEUE=SECURITY$BATCH -
    /RESTART
$!
$MAIL DAILY.LIS "@SYS$SYSTEM:SECURITY_.LIST"
```

Notice the SUBMIT command in the middle of the procedure. This command is used to automatically trigger the DAILY_SUMMARY.COM command file to run again the next day at 4:00 a.m. The print and batch queues used for this command are special security queues that should have restricted access. The actual printer should be located in a secure area. The /RESTART parameter is used to cause the procedure to restart after the system is rebooted or the STOP/QUEUE/REQUEUE command is executed. The command procedure serves as a quick daily security procedure.

The reason for using the mailing list file is to protect the mailing list and make it easy to update when changes occur. By maintaining a few central mailing lists, you can easily make updates when things change on your system. All of your security procedures should reference the common mailing lists and should not have hard-coded mail addresses.

This very simple example of automating your security reporting should be viewed as a starting point. After you have decided what is important to your organization, you should tailor the reports and command procedures to your environment.

SECURING YOUR NETWORK: PATHWORKS FEATURES

The security features of PATHWORKS center around the File, Print, and Disk services and the UAF. Changes made to users via PCSA Manager are entered in the same UAF file maintained by Authorize. The groups created by PATHWORKS are not the same as UIC groups or identifier groups and are not stored in these databases.

File Services

When a new file service is created from within PATHWORKS, an ACL is attached to the root directory of the service. ACEs are added to the ACL to allow access to the service.

PATHWORKS also uses a default account that allows all users to access file services that are granted PUBLIC access. Any user may attach to a PUBLIC service, regardless of whether he or she has a VMS account. The default account can be disabled by the following command:

```
PCSA_MANAGER> SET FILE_SERVER CHARACTERISTICS -
_PCSA_MANAGER> /NODE=DEFAULT_ACCOUNT
```

Application services are controlled by the PCFS$READ and PCFS$UPDATE identifiers, which provide read and update identifiers that are entered in the ACL. These identifiers are not part of the VMS UAF but are added by the file server when the user connects to the service. The GRANT command is used to establish whether access is read only or read/write for a user or group. Service access can be granted to all users or to an individual.

ACL and RMS protection is propagated to all files handled by the file server. When a file is added to a common service, the file inherits the RMS protection assigned to the service.

Common and Personal Services. Security for common file services can be controlled at the individual file level. Application file services can be controlled at the service level only. The level of security for a common service is controlled by the VMS username, RMS protection on individual files, and ACLs placed on individual files.

When you add common services from the menu, a default RMS protection is set for the service. Adding a service with the command line allows you to specify a different mask. The default RMS protection mask is SYSTEM:RWED, OWNER:RWED, GROUP:None, and WORLD:None. When a user connects to a service, the UIC is checked for account access to the service and ACLs are checked for specific files within the service. ACL access to a file is overridden by UIC access only when permission is explicitly denied.

ACEs are not used to determine access for common services. The user account must be listed in the UAF. Access is by a specific user's UIC or the UIC of PCFS$ACCOUNT (the default account).

The default RMS protection for file services is the same as for application services. The ACL and RMS protections are not propagated to all files created on the service. Any common service or file within the service can be accessed if a user knows the password to an account that is listed in the UAF with the appropriate permission. Group and world access is not checked if an ACL denies access.

There are problems to accessing files on a common service. If a user accesses a common service by username, the user cannot access a file created by another user accessing the service in the same manner, unless the file has world access or the user is in the same UIC group and the file has group access. The problem occurs because the PATHWORKS group permits access to the service but not to the files within the service that are created by others. Users can access the service via the default account, but this opens up all the files to all users. If you place all users in the same UIC group, this may create problems with VMS programs or limit the groups to mutually exclusive groups. The quickest solution to this problem is to set up identifiers for various groups of users and create ACLs on the common service directory. See the section "Access Control Lists" in this chapter for more information.

Default access is public and is used when no username/password is specified. To stop default access to a specific service, use this command:

```
PCSA_MANAGER> Deny Public Access SERVICENAME
```

The PCSA Manager GRANT command is not used for common and personal services.

PCFS$SERVICE_DATABASE.DAT. The PCFS$SERVICE_DATABASE.DAT file maintains the service name, root directory, and ACL for the service. There is also an access list of users of specific file services. A list of file services to which all users can connect is also maintained here. When a client connects to a service, PCFS$SERVICE_DATABASE.DAT is checked by the server process PCFS_SERVER, and the appropriate access is granted. ACLs override the PATHWORKS security and RMS file security.

Disk Services

Use passwords for disk services on a per-service basis, since VMS security is not used for disk services. The number of connections can be limited and/or a disk can be mounted read-only or read/write.

When a disk is mounted, it is available to anyone on the LAN. There is no way to audit the disk server.

Disk services should be used for remote-boot clients and applications. Using password protection at the service level and controlling the number of connections should suffice for these services.

LAD$SERVICE_DATABASE.DAT. LAD$SERVICE_DATABASE.DAT serves a different purpose than PCFS$SERVICE_DATABASE.DAT. It is used to resolve conflicts in a cluster environment for disks that are offered on multiple nodes. It also provides a list of disks to mount when VMS boots, and it keeps track of access information.

PASSWORDS

Password-based security is one of the most widely used security procedures today. It can be found on computer systems, bank teller machines, garage door openers, home security systems, and so on. Passwords may have a trick name to hide their identity, such as a personal identification number, or may be called your special code or security code. Lengths typically range from four characters on up.

VMS passwords must be from six to 31 characters and contain at least one alphabetic character, and they may use the character set A-Z, 0-9, _, -, and $, in any combination. VMS V5.4 and higher augments this with the PWDHIS and PWDDIC flags mentioned with the Authorize utility earlier in this chapter.

Reliable passwords have certain common characteristics. A basic rule for passwords and usernames is this: The longer the better. Adding a single character to the length of a password dramatically increases the difficulty of trying to guess the password. This is especially important in this age of computerized password-guessing programs.

A good password is one that is hard to guess and is not obvious. Using your birth date or hire date opens the door to a lot of people who know you or have access to this critical information. Your Social Security number, phone number, and other similar numbers introduce the same problem, as do family names, streets, common terms for your business, and so on. Computer-generated passwords have the opposite problem: They are so unique that they are written down, usually close to the computer.

I believe that good passwords are made up of phrases that are common to the user but meaningless to others. Good phrases can be interspersed with special characters (_, -, $) and can be turned around to further confuse the meaning.

Setting password expiration dates is often useful, but it is subject to some debate. When passwords must be changed frequently, people tend to write them down. (Most people have at least three or four passwords to remember — bank, garage, computer at work.) If they don't write the passwords down, they may fall into a pattern (changing the first or last letter or number), which makes the password easier to guess. If you automatically expire passwords, the time period should be geared to your organizational requirements.

System Passwords

A system password can be created with Authorize to restrict access to certain system components. System passwords are normally used when you wish to control access to the system console or modems. It forces users to enter this password before they gain access to the device and enter their username/password.

The Authorize utility is used to establish a system password, while the DCL SET command designates which devices it applies to.

Two areas of concern arise from using system passwords:

◆ Since the password will normally be required on certain devices, it adds a layer of confusion to the user interface, because users must enter the password on some devices and not on others.

◆ There is only one system password per VAX. If you protect five different devices with the system password, all five use the same password. This means that if you protect the console and two modems, the modem users have access to the console.

POTENTIAL ACCOUNT PROBLEMS

Default Accounts

There are potential problems with some of the standard accounts used by VMS and PATHWORKS. PATHWORKS uses a default account that provides access to public services without users' supplying a username and password. Access to services by this account should be reviewed. This account can be disabled by using PCSA Manager.

Several other accounts are installed by VMS for use by the system manager and field test personnel. The SYSTEM account is used by the system manager and should not be disabled. This account should have a secure password that is fairly long (10 characters or more) and is frequently changed.

The FIELD and SYSTEST accounts should be disabled with Authorize after your system is up and running. They can always be turned on when field service or someone else requires them.

DECnet may also have one or more default accounts that permit users to access services like MAIL, MIRROR, and so on. These accounts may create problems by providing a method of accessing several resources on your system without using a username and password. If you want to enable access to resources by a default account, you can create a default account for each object that requires access. This requires users to use an individual account for accessing each object, which provides a more secure form of access and gives a more detailed method of tracking access to the objects.

If a default DECnet account is used (either one or multiple accounts), users should not have access to type 0 objects (TASK objects). Allowing access to TASK objects will provide a method for a user to execute command procedures on that node. NETCONFIG.COM will set the default account to no access for TASK objects.

Installation Procedures and Other Programs

What do installation procedures and other programs have to do with potential account problems? The inherent flexibility of VMS provides a possible hole into your network security. This occurs because programs may directly modify the protection schemes (including ACLs and RMS protection) on directories, files, and the various UAF files.

Many programs are executed by users with system or other privileges. If these programs modify either the system files or protections, they may open holes in your security scheme. For example, users may change protections, which would give them direct access to the files at a later time. Or, they could add new accounts to the UAF, RIGHTSLIST, or NETPROXY databases. This would also allow someone access either to the entire system or to certain files at some later time.

To protect yourself against this type of access, you should be familiar with the programs on your system and monitor the installation of new software. Tracking changes to UAF, RIGHTSLIST, and NETPROXY can also notify you of changes made by other programs. You can create simple command procedures to review these databases periodically to detect new accounts or accounts that have changed.

Disabling Accounts. Every organization needs some type of procedure for restricting access for people who leave. Notice of departing users will normally come from the personnel department.

Once you have determined that a user has left, deactivate the account with AUTHORIZE and the DISUSER flag. This leaves the account intact until you know for sure the user is gone and the user's files have been disposed of.

You should also contact the user's former supervisor to determine what happens to the user's files and any system functions he or she may have been responsible for. Remember that the user's data is the most valuable asset on your system.

Access to Programs. If your organization has a concern about people running certain programs such as PERMIT or FAL, you can move these programs from the system service with PUBLIC access to a restricted service. If they are not used at all, delete the programs. This also applies to programs on the server, especially management programs or other programs that could affect security or provide unauthorized access, including NCP, AUTHORIZE, and PCSA MANAGER.

Education. Education is an important part of any set of security procedures. Everyone using the system must know what to do, when to do it, and why they should do it. Without adequate training, users will not properly adhere to the security procedures and will probably do exactly what you are trying to stop. This may not be intentional, but it will happen as a matter of habit.

Most illegal access to systems happen by people who have obtained a valid account and password from a valid user.

Security education must include all elements of your security procedures, including discussions on passwords and how to create them, what to do with them (don't write them down or discuss them), and why they are required. Users should also understand why accounts cannot be shared.

Site Guide Procedures and Audit. The security procedures documented in your site guide must be followed and audited. Operations personnel, development groups, system managers, and users must all follow the routine procedures.

Everyone in the organization will be affected by the procedures, making accurate and timely audits a necessity. Even if your security requirements are not strict, the procedures should be audited occasionally for adherence and to make sure they are still adequate for your requirements.

The security requirements of any computer system depend on the local environment. PATHWORKS for VMS provides one of the most robust environments for maintaining a secure and flexible network. In addition to the many security features of both VMS and PATHWORKS, there are many products available for VMS, DOS, and the PC itself. Some companies (Dell and others) are providing security features in the BIOS that enable you to password-protect the PC.

To properly protect your system from intruders, you should follow the guidelines in this chapter. Seek outside guidance if you require a more secure system. There is an entire industry supporting the security requirements of computer systems. Just remember that locks usually keep out only honest people and that the best defense is a common-sense approach to security.

APPENDIX A

Ethernet Guidelines

ETHERNET CABLE TYPES

Baseband ThickWire 50-ohm Coaxial Cable — 10Base-5
Baseband ThinWire Coaxial Cable — 10Base-2
Broadband 75-ohm Coaxial Cable
Twisted-Pair Cable — 10Base-T
Fiber-Optic Cable

ETHERNET CONFIGURATION RULES

Rule 1: Coaxial ThickWire Segment

Maximum Length:	500 meters
Maximum Connections:	100
Cable Attenuation:	50 meters
Minimum Spacing:	2.5 meters
Grounded Once Per Segment	
Terminated	

Rule 2: ThickWire LAN

Maximum Distance Between Nodes:	2,800 meters
Maximum Nodes:	1,023
Fiber-Optic Cable (Aggregate):	10,000 meters
Maximum Number of Repeaters Between Nodes:	2

Rule 3: ThickWire XLAN

Maximum Distance Between Nodes:	44,000 meters
Maximum Nodes:	8,000
Fiber-Optic Cable (Aggregate)	10,000 meters
Maximum Number of Bridges Between Nodes:	7

Rule 4: ThinWire Coaxial Segment

Maximum Length:	185 meters
Maximum Connections:	30
Minimum Spacing:	1.5 meters

Rule 5: Twisted Pair

Maximum Length:	100 meters
Maximum Connections:	64

Rules 1, 4, and 5 apply to 80 percent of all small companies.

PCSA Manager Commands

This appendix lists the commands for PCSA Manager, most of which are covered in Chapters 10 and 11 of this book. For details on the operation of these commands, consult the *PATHWORKS for VMS Server Administrator's Command Reference*.

Command	Function
ADD	Creates a new entry for an object or objects in the PCSA Manager or DECnet database.
GROUP	Adds a group definition.
MEMBER	Adds members to a group.
NODE	Adds a workstation or server to the DECnet database.
SERVICE/DIRECTORY	Adds a file service.
SERVICE/PRINTER	Adds a print service.
TEMPLATE	Adds a template for remote-boot workstation definitions.
USER	Adds a PATHWORKS user to the PCSA Manager database and possibly the SYSUAF database.
WORKSTATION	Adds a version 2.2 workstation to a version 4.0 server.
BROADCAST	Sends messages to clients.
CLOSE FILE_SERVER FILE	Closes a file on the file server.
CONFIG	Confirms the current configuration of the file server.
CREATE DISK	Creates a virtual disk.

Command	Function
DELETE DISK	Deletes a virtual disk.
DENY	Denies a user access to a file or print service.
DENY/GROUP	Denies a group of users access to a file or print service.
DISMOUNT DISK	Dismounts a virtual disk.
EXIT	Exits the PCSA Manager and returns to DCL.
GRANT	Grants a user access to a service.
GRANT/GROUP	Grants a group of users access to a service.
HELP	Displays help for PCSA Manager commands.
MENU	Starts the menu interface.
MODIFY	
DISK	Modifies the virtual disk characteristics.
USER	Modifies a user's AUTOUSER.BAT file.
WORKSTATION	Changes the hardware address or Ethernet adapter of a workstation or the comment in the remote-boot database. Can also be used to change the VAX adapter that services remote-boot requests.
MOUNT DISK	Mounts a virtual disk.
REMOVE	
CLIENT_OS	Removes a client operating system.
GROUP	Deletes a group definition.
MEMBER	Deletes a member from a group.

Command	Function
NODE	Removes a workstation or server from the DECnet database.
SERVICE	Deletes a file server directory or printer service entry from the service database.
TEMPLATE	Removes a remote-boot template.
USER	Removes a user definition.
WORKSTATION	Removes the network key disk and disables remote boot for a workstation.
SET	
DISK_SERVER CHARACTERISTICS	Changes disk server characteristics.
DISK_SERVER SERVICE	Changes disk service characteristics.
FILE_SERVER CHARACTERISTICS	Changes file server characteristics.
FILE_SERVER SERVICE	Changes file service characteristics.
SHOW	
DISK_SERVER CHARACTERISTICS	Displays disk server characteristics.
CLIENTS_OS	Lists client operating systems located on the server.
DISK_SERVER CONNECTIONS	Lists active disk service connections.
DISK_SERVER COUNTERS	Displays disk server cache counters.
DISK_SERVER SERVICES	Displays disk services information.
FILE_SERVER CHARACTERISTICS	Displays file server characteristics.
FILE_SERVER CONNECTIONS	Displays active file service connections.
FILE_SERVER COUNTERS	Displays caching statistics for the file server.
FILE_SERVER OPEN_FILES	Displays open files for file and printer services.

Command	Function
FILE_SERVER SERVICES	Displays active file and print services.
FILE_SERVER SERVICES-/AUTHORIZED	Displays file and print services, including authorized users.
FILE_SERVER SERVICES-/REGISTERED	Displays registered file and print services.
FILE_SERVER SESSION	Displays active file service sessions on the server.
FILE_SERVER STATUS	Displays file server status information.
GROUP	Lists the members in a group.
TEMPLATES	Displays templates for remote-boot workstations.
USERS	Lists registered PCSA users.
VERSION	Displays the current versions for the VMS server components and their status.
WORKSTATIONS	Lists remote-boot workstations.
START	
DISK_SERVER CONNECTIONS	Starts the disk server.
FILE_SERVER CONNECTIONS	Allows the file server to accept service connections.
FILE_SERVER LOGGING	Begins logging file server events.
STOP	
DISK_SERVER CONNECTIONS	Stops the disk server and all connections.
FILE_SERVER CONNECTIONS	Stops all file server connections.
FILE_SERVER LOGGING	Stops logging server events, and closes the log file.
FILE_SERVER SESSION	Stops a particular file service session.
ZERO DISK_SERVER COUNTERS	Resets the counters for the disk server.

APPENDIX C

PCDISK Commands

This appendix lists the commands for the PCDISK program. Most PCDISK commands perform functions similar to client commands, such as USE or DIR. PCDISK is designed for a PATHWORKS manager to manipulate files on a virtual disk from VMS. For details on the operation of these commands, consult the *PATHWORKS for VMS Server Administrators Command Reference*.

Command	Function
ATTRIBUTE	Sets, clears, or displays DOS file attributes.
CHDIR or CD	Changes to a new directory or displays the current directory.
COPY	Copies DOS files between and within DOS devices (virtual disks), similar to the DOS copy command.
CREATE	Creates and formats a DOS virtual disk file.
DELETE	Deletes a file from a DOS device.
DIRECTORY	Displays files and information about files.
EXIT	Disconnects from any assigned DOS devices, and then exits the PCDISK utility.
EXPORT	Copies (exports) a DOS file from a DOS device to a file in the VMS file system.
FORMAT	Formats a DOS device.
HELP	Displays help about PCDISK commands.

Command	Function
IMPORT	Copies (imports) a file from the VMS file system to a DOS file on the virtual disk.
LABEL	Creates, changes, or deletes a disk volume label on a drive.
MKDIR or MD	Makes a new directory on a DOS device.
RENAME	Renames a file.
RMDIR or RD	Removes a directory entry from a DOS device.
SET	Sets disk and file information within a connected DOS device.
SHOW	Displays information about active connections, services, and the version of PCDISK.
SPAWN	Creates a subprocess, suspending the current PCDISK session.
TYPE	Displays the contents of a file on the CRT.
USE	Connects or disconnects a DOS device.
VOLUME	Displays the disk volume name of a drive.
XCOPY	Simulates the DOS XCOPY command for copying files.

Client LATCP and NCP Commands

LATCP and NCP share the standard prompt format used for almost all PATHWORKS management programs. All commands can be executed from the LATCP> or NCP> prompt, as well as from the DOS command line. The HELP command is used to display command and syntax information in both programs. The following example illustrates the LATCP SHOW command, as it is executed from the LATCP prompt:

```
LATCP> SHOW CHAR
    LAT characteristics as of 7-April-1992 11:23:01

    Server Name              = LAT_AA0003004455
    Protocol Version = 5
        .               .
        .
        .
```

Both LATCP and NCP can be used from the DOS command line, either to execute a single command from DOS or to execute LATCP or NCP commands from a DOS batchfile. The following example shows the same SHOW command as it is executed from DOS:

```
C:\>LATCP SHOW CHAR
    LAT characteristics as of 7-April-1992 11:23:01

    Server Name                  = LAT_AA0003004455
    Protocol Version = 5
        .               .
        .
        .
```

Executing LATCP and NCP commands from DOS or within a batch file adds a tremendous amount of flexibility to network management on the client. If you examine the STARTNET.BAT program, you will notice that both LATCP and NCP are called to establish paramaters at client boot time. The ability to control network transport parameters via batch programs makes setting and resetting parameters for various programs very easy.

LATCP

LATCP manages LAT services for a client node. It creates and modifies the LAT database that stores the configuration parameters for a client machine (i.e., C:\DECNET\declat.dat). You can also use LATCP to create preferred network services and configure network printer services for parallel printers attached to a client workstation.

LATCP is executed from the DOS command line, as illustrated below:

```
C:\>\DECNET\LATCP
    LATCP>
```

The most common LATCP commands for PATHWORKS V4.x are listed in Table D-1.

Table D-1. LATCP Commands and Functions

LATCP Command	Description
ADD	Displays current LAT services from the network and allows you to select services to add to the local LAT database. Entering ADD without parameters will cause LATCP to listen for available services. Pressing the space bar will stop LATCP from listening and display the services. Once the services are displayed, you can add a service by using the cursor keys.
Parameters:	
node address	DECnet address of the node offering the service.
Ethernet address	Ethernet address of the host offering the LAT services.
node name	Name of the node offering the service.
service name	Name of the preferred service.

Table D-1. LATCP Commands and Functions (continued)

LATCP Command	Description
ADD LPT*n*	Logical name of the printer you are offering as a service (LPT1, LPT2, LPT3). ADD LPTn adds a definition for a local printer to the LAT database, allowing the printer to be used as a LAT printer.
Qualifiers:	
/RATING=*n*	Priority for the service (0 to 255). Defaults to 255.
/PASSWORD=*string*	Password for the service.
/NOPASSWORD	A password is not required. This is the default.
DEFINE	Stores information in the local LAT database.
DEFINE FALLBACK	Enables LAT to try every available LAT service for making a connection. If FALLBACK is not enabled, LAT will try only the highest rated service.
Qualifiers:	
ON	Tries all known LAT addresses.
OFF	Accepts only the entry with the highest rating for a particular service. This is the (default).
DEFINE GROUP CODES	Establishes group codes in the LAT database for all LAT connections.
Parameter:	
code	The group code defined (0 to 255). Multiple codes can be defined, separated by a comma (,).
Qualifier:	
/ALL	Enables all group codes (0 to 255) /ALL is the default.

Table D-1. LATCP Commands and Functions (continued)

LATCP Command	Description
DEFINE LPT THROTTLE	Controls the rate at which LAT sends information to a local printer being used as a LAT service. This setting is dependent on the speed of the PC. The faster the clock, the higher the throttle setting.
Parameter:	
n	Throttle value.
DEFINE MAX CIRCUITS	Establishes the maximum number of concurrent LAT circuits allowed.
Parameter:	
n	Maximum number of virtual circuits (1 to 32). The default is 4.
DEFINE MULTICAST	Enables or disables whether LAT listens for available services. The default is enabled.
Parameters:	
ON	Causes LAT to listen to service announcements. This is the default.
OFF	Turns off listening for service announcements. ADD LPTn overrides the OFF parameter.
DEFINE RETRANSMIT LIMIT	Establishes limits on how many times LAT will retransmit a message before declaring the circuit down.
Parameter:	
n	The number of times a message will be retransmitted (1 to 255). The default is 24.

Table D-1. LATCP Commands and Functions (continued)

LATCP Command	Description
DEFINE SCB	Updates the current number of session control blocks.
Parameter:	
n	The number of SCBs to allocate (0 to 10). The default is 0.
DEFINE SCB BUFFER	Allocates a selected numner of buffers for each SCB allocated with DEFINE SCB.
Parameter:	
n	The number of SCB buffers (1 to 8). The default is 6.
DEFINE SEARCH	Allows LAT to request information from other nodes about their available services. It also enables FALLBACK.
Parameters:	
ON	Turns on a search of other nodes that results in a connection. The default is OFF.
OFF	Turns off search mode.
DEFINE SERVICE TABLE	Establishes how many services may be stored in the local service table.
Parameters:	
n	Maximum number of services allowed in the service table (1 to 255). The default is 10.
DEFINE SESSION THROTTLE	Limits the maximum number of bytes sent in a slot.

Table D-1. LATCP Commands and Functions (continued)

LATCP Command	Description
Parameter:	
n	Maximum number of characters sent in a slot (1 to 225). The default is 127.
DELETE	Removes a preferred service from the local LAT database.
Parameters:	
service name	Name of the preferred service to delete.
/ALL	All services in DECLAT.DAT.
DELETE /LPT*n*	The logical name of the local printer offered as a LAT service. DELETE LPTn removes a LAT printer definition from the LAT database.
EXIT	Exits from LATCP.
HELP	Provides information on LATCP commands.
LIST SERVICES	Displays preferred services from the LAT database.
SHOW	Displays information about the current LAT configuration and existing services.
SHOW CHARACTERISTICS	Displays information about the current configuration of LAT.
SHOW CIRCUITS	Displays information about the current LAT virtual circuits.
SHOW COUNTERS	Displays LAT error counters and their current values.
SHOW PORTS	Displays information about the current LAT printer ports.
SHOW SERVICES	Displays information from the LAT service table, including preferred and any known services.

Table D-1. LATCP Commands and Functions (continued)

LATCP Command	Description
SHOW SESSIONS	Displays information about the current sessions.
ZERO COUNTERS	Resets all LAT counters to zero.

NCP

NCP is used to manage DECnet on the client. The format for the command is the same as for LATCP. The NCP.EXE program should be in the DECnet directory for each client. Programs for some NCP commands (such as NCP SHOW) are located on the PATHWORKS troubleshooting disk.

NCP is executed from the DOS command line, as illustrated below:

```
C:\>\DECNET\NCP
  NCP>
```

All NCP commands for PATHWORKS V4.1 are listed in Table D-2. You should refer to the *DECnet Network Management Guide* in the PATHWORKS documentation for the NCP qualifiers.

Table D-2. NCP Commands and Functions

NCP Command	Function
CLEAR	Removes a specific option from the volatile DECnet database of the client. CLEAR commands do not affect the permanent database.
CLEAR EXECUTOR	Removes executor node parameters stored in memory for the current client.
CLEAR LOCAL-ADAPTER NAME	Removes a local adapter name from the volatile database.
CLEAR REMOTE-ADAPTER NAME	Clears a remote adapter name from the volatile database.
COPY KNOWN NODES	Copies the node database to a specific file. Access information is not copied.

Table D-2. NCP Commands and Functions (continued)

NCP Command	Function
COPY NODE	Copies information about a single node name from a remote node into the node database.
DEFINE	Changes parameters in the permanent DECnet database or an auxiliary DECnet database such as the JOB SPAWNER database. Permanent characteristics take effect when you restart DECnet.
DEFINE ACCESS	Defines incoming access information for a designated user in the incoming access database (DECACC.DAT). Access information consists of a user ID, password, and type of access.
DEFINE CIRCUIT	Defines the circuit characteristics in the permanent database.
DEFINE EXECUTOR	Defines and stores executor node characteristics in the permanent database.
DEFINE LINE	Establishes line parameters.
DEFINE NODE	Assigns a node name and optional access control information to a unique node address.
DEFINE OBJECT	Stores information in the JOB SPAWNER database (DECOBJ.DAT).
DEFINE REMOTE-ADAPTER-NAME	Defines a remote adapter name for NetBIOS. The remote adapter name includes a node name and an object associated with that node.
EXIT	Exits from NCP.
HELP	Displays a summary of NCP commands on your screen.

Table D-2. NCP Commands and Functions (continued)

NCP Command	Function
LIST	Displays information from the permanent DECnet database.
LIST ACCESS	Displays entries in the incoming access database (DECACC.DAT).
LIST CIRCUIT	Displays permanent information about the circuit from the DECnet database (DECPARM.DAT).
LIST EXECUTOR	Displays permanent information for the executor node from the DECnet database (DECPARM.DAT).
LIST KNOWN	Displays permanent information about all occurrences of an entity from the DECnet database. Information may come from DECPARM.DAT, DECNODE.DAT, DECOBJ.DAT, DECREM.DAT, and DECACC.DAT.
LIST LINE	Displays information about the line from the DECnet database (DECPARM.DAT).
LIST NODE	Displays information about a remote node that is contained in the node database (DECNODE.DAT).
LIST OBJECT	Displays information about an object in the JOB SPAWNER database (DECOBJ.DAT).
LIST REMOTE-ADAPTER NAME	Displays information about a remote adapter name from the remote adapter name database (DECREM.DAT).
LOOP	Executes a loop test.
LOOP CIRCUIT	Runs a loop test to a specific Ethernet address, a multicast Ethernet address, or an adjacent node on a DDCMP line.

Table D-2. NCP Commands and Functions (continued)

NCP Command	Function
LOOP EXECUTOR	Runs a loop test within the local node to a local loop-back mirror.
LOOP LINE CONTROLLER	Runs a loop test within the local node to the Ethernet controller. This test requires the use of a loop-back connector and is frequently used to determine local hardware problems.
LOOP NODE	Runs a loop test to a remote node that has a loop-back mirror.
MIRROR	Used on a local node to allow loop node tests from remote nodes to the local node.
MONITOR LOGGING	Displays event logging information on the screen.
PURGE	Removes information from the permanent database.
PURGE ACCESS	Deletes incoming access information for a specified user from the incoming access database (DECACC.DAT).
PURGE EXECUTOR	Removes specified executor parameters from the DECnet database (DECPARM.DAT).

APPENDIX E

PATHWORKS Client Commands

Table E-1 lists the various client commands for PATHWORKS.

Table E-1. PATHWORKS Client Commands

Command	Description
BCAST	Broadcasts a message over the network.
LATCP	Adds and Modifies LAT parameters.
LOGON	Connects the client to a personal directory on a VMS or ULTRIX server.
MEMMAN	Displays memory statistics and may be used to unload network components.
NET ATTRIB	Sets or displays file-protection information. May also be used to change ACL information on a VMS server.
NET CONTINUE	Restarts suspended file or print services.
NET CLEAR	Deletes a node from the network database.
NET CREATE	Creates and formats a virtual disk.
NET DEFINE	Defines a DECnet node name and address to the network.
NET DELETE	Deletes a virtual disk.
NET DISK SERVICES	Displays information about available network disk services.
NET DISMOUNT	Removes a virtual disk connection from the network.
NET ERROR	Displays statistics on network errors.

Table E-1. PATHWORKS Client Commands (continued)

Command	Description
NET FILE SERVICES	Displays information about available network file and print services.
NET HELP	Provides help information about commands and syntax.
NET LIST	Lists nodes in the DECnet node database.
NET LOAD	Restores saved network connections.
NET MODIFY	Changes characteristics of a virtual disk service.
NET PAUSE	Temporarily suspends connections to file or print services.
NET PASSWORD	Allows a client user to change the server password.
NET PRINT	Prints a file on a network printer and displays print service information.
NET SAVE	Saves current network connection information for possible restoration a later time.
NETSYS	Creates a bootable floppy from the system service.
NET TEST	Establishes a loop test between the server and the client.
NETTIME	Sets the date and time on the client from the server.
NETVER	Displays the PATHWORKS for DOS version and versions of DOS on the PATHWORKS service.
NET ZERO LAD	Clears error counters for virtual disk drives.

Table E-1. PATHWORKS Client Commands (continued)

Command	Description
PERMIT	Permits another client to establish a connection to your client machine.
SETLOGON	Used with an OS/2 server to register a client username and password with the server.
SETNAME	Sets a client node name on the server.
RCV/TRCV	Used with TCP/IP and DECnet to display messages on a client.
USE	Establishes and modifies file, print, and disk service connections for a client. Also displays information about connections and available services.

NET COMMANDS

Many of the PATHWORKS commands begin with the NET parameter. In most cases, you enter the NET command from DOS followed by an action. When a NET command is executed, DOS loads NET.EXE and reads the MSNET.INI file found in the DECnet directory on the PC. Some NET commands are performed locally on the PC, whereas others execute on the PC and trigger actions on the server.

NET commands are stored in the MSNET.INI file, a text file that contains actions for NET.EXE and the definitions for each action. An action is indicated by a label in MSNET.INI that matches the command entered with the NET command. Following the action label are the functions the action will perform. Below is a sample of an MSNET.INI file:

```
create $*
    ldu create $* /*

Start LAD
    sch
    dll /irq:5 /t:2
    \netrun last /n:-1 /m:e /c:d /g:-1
    \netrun lad /r:-1 //w:-1 /a:-1
```

The create command executes a single function called ldu. This is an example of a command that is executed on the server. When NET CREATE is executed, it sends the command line to the server for execution. NET.EXE communicates with the server via the PCSA$RMI object, which is running on the server.

The Start LAD action executes several commands to start the scheduler, the data link layer, LAST, and LAD on the client. Some of the parameters for the commands may be entered on the NET command line, as in the following example:

```
c:\> NET Start LAD /n:JOEPC          ,
```

COMMAND REFERENCE

Table E-2 lists the most important client commands and their parameters.

Table E-2. Client Commands and Parameters

Command and Parameters	Description
BCAST	Broadcasts a message to a node or nodes. *Note*: You can create a file called BCAST.ID in your PATH statement and place your name or other information in this file. When you send a message, the receiver will see your node name and the information in this file.
Format:	`C:\>BCAST [/C] NODE [,NODE,NODE,...]` `filename message`
Parameters:	
/C	Returns an error if the message is not sent.
NODE	The node to receive the message. If the node name is a group, all members of the group will receive the message.
filename	The file name of a distribution file with a listing of addresses and a file type of DIS. The file type is not specified.
message	The message to send.

Table E-2. Client Commands and Parameters (continued)

Command and Parameters	Description
LOGON	Logs onto your personal network account.
Format:	`C:\>LOGON server username` `[password	*] [/virtual]`
Parameters:	
server	Server name.
username	Username for the account on the server.
password	Account password.
*	Flag to prompt for your password.
/virtual	Virtual disk account. Specifies that your account is on a virtual disk.
MEMMAN	The MEMMAN program is a memory manager that displays information about a workstation's memory and optionally unloads programs from memory.
Format:	`C:\>MEMMAN /qualifier`
Parameters:	
/B	Provides a brief display of information when you are using the /E, /M, and /S screens.
/E	Displays detailed information on expanded memory usage. You must have an expanded memory driver loaded via the CONFIG.SYS file for this command to work.
/F	Provides detailed information when used on /E, /M, and /S screens.
/H	Displays help information on MEMMAN.

349

Table E-2. Client Commands and Parameters (continued)

Command and Parameters	Description
/M	Default parameter. Displays the memory map for DOS.
/S	Displays summary information for all types of memory in the client machine.
/U	Unloads all network components from conventional memory. Components to unload are all components up to and including the PATHWORKS memory mark.
/X	Displays detailed information on extended memory usage. You must have loaded the HIMEM.SYS memory driver via the CONFIG.SYS file for this command to work.
/Y	Does not prompt before performing the unload procedure and is used only with the /U parameter. Use the /Y parameter very carefully.
NET ATTRIB	Sets the attributes on a file or files located on a server directory.
Format:	`C:\>NET ATTRIB [drive:path	filename]` `[identifiers]`
Parameters:	
drive:path	Specifies the drive and/or path where the file is located.
filename	Specifies the file to be changed. Wildcards (e.g., *.*) may be used, if you have sufficient access.
identifiers	Used with the /ACCESS option to establish ACL information.

Table E-2. Client Commands and Parameters (continued)

Command and Parameters	Description
/ACCESS=	Specifies the access to be established on the VMS server. May be read, write, or none.
/Bottom	Adds an ACE to the bottom of the ACL.
/Default	Establishes the default protection for any new files created or modified on a particular drive.
/Query	Prompts for information necessary to change the ACL on a VMS server.
/Protection=	Specifies the file protection code. Valid codes are R (Read), W (Write), E (Execute), and D (Delete). You specify the protection by type of ownership (System, Owner, Group, and World).
/Remove	Removes an ACE from the specified ACL. Cannot be used with wildcards.
NET CLEAR	Removes a node from the DECnet database.
Format:	`C:\>NET CLEAR node`
Parameter:	
node	Specifies the node to remove.
NET CONTINUE	Continues a printer or file service that has been paused with Net Pause.
Format:	`C:\>NET CONTINUE DRDR	PRDR`
Parameters:	
DRDR	Reconnects file services.
PRDR	Reconnects print services.

Table E-2. Client Commands and Parameters (continued)

Command and Parameters	Description
NET CREATE	Creates a virtual disk on the server.
Format:	`C:\>NET CREATE \\server[%username]` `[password	*]`
Parameters:	
server	Name of the server to contain the disk.
username	Name of a valid account for the user creating the disk. You must have privileges on the server to create the disk. To create a system, boot, or application disk, you must have system privileges.
password	Password for the username specified.
*	Flag to prompt for password.
/alloc=	Number of blocks the virtual disk will occupy on the server. If /size is used, the system will allocate a default number of blocks. You may allocate fewer blocks than the default but not more.
/file=	File specification for the virtual disk. This includes the VMS drive/directory name and the name of the virtual disk.
/query	Prompts for information not specified on the command line.
/size=	Size of the disk in kilobytes or megabytes. Allowable sizes are: 360 KB, 720 KB, 1.2 MB, 1.44 MB, 5 MB, 10 MB, 20 MB, 32 MB, 64 MB, 128 MB, 256 MB, and 512 MB.
/type=	Determines the default device and directory for the virtual disk. Allowable classes are system, boot, application, and user. See your PATHWORKS documentation for the current list of default devices.

Table E-2. Client Commands and Parameters (continued)

Command and Parameters	Description
NET DEFINE	Registers a node name and address in the DECnet database.
Format:	`C:\>NET DEFINE name address`
Parameters:	
name	Name of the new node.
address	DECnet address of the new node.
NET DELETE	Deletes a virtual disk on the server.
Format:	`C:\>NET DELETE \\server[%username]` `[password | *]`
Parameters:	
server	Name of the server that contains the disk.
username	Name of a valid account for the user deleting the disk. You must have privileges on the server to delete the disk.
password	Password for the username specified.
*	Flag to prompt for password.
/file=	The server specification for the file containing the virtual disk.
/query	Prompts for parameters not specified on the command line.
/type=	Specifies the default device and directory for the virtual disk.
NET DISK	Displays information about available network disk services.
Format:	`C:\>NET DISK [SERVICES] [\\server]` `[service[%username] [password | *]`

Table E-2. Client Commands and Parameters (continued)

Command and Parameters	Description
Parameters:	
SERVICES	Optional keyword.
server	Name of the server that contains the disk.
service	Valid disk service name. If this parameter is entered by itself, the command will display all servers that offer this service.
username	Name of a valid account for the requested service.
password	Password for the username specified.
*	Flag to prompt for a password.
NET DISMOUNT	Removes a virtual disk connection.
Format:	`C:\>NET DISMOUNT[drive] \\server` `\service [%username] [password	*]`
Parameters:	
drive	A logical drive letter that maps to the virtual disk. If this parameter is used, the client is disconnected from the virtual disk after it is dismounted.
server	Name of the server that contains the disk.
service	Name of the disk service to be dismounted.
username	Name of a valid account for the user dismounting the disk. You must have privileges on the server to dismount the disk.

Table E-2. Client Commands and Parameters (continued)

Command and Parameters	Description
password	Password for the username specified.
*	Flag to prompt for a password.
/cluster	Causes the virtual disk to be dismounted from each server in the cluster. The default is to dismount the virtual disk on the specified server only.
/query	Prompts for information not specified on the command line.
/temporary	Dismounts the virtual disk for a temporary period of time. Once the server is restarted, the disk will be restored.
/type=	Specifies the default device and directory for the virtual disk.
NET ERROR	Displays statistics on network errors.
Format:	`C:\>NET ERROR`
NET FILE SERVICES	Displays information about file and print services available on all servers on the network or a particular server. It may also be used to find servers that provide a particular service.
Format:	`C:\>NET FILE [SERVICES] [\\server]` `[service[%username] [password	*]`
Parameters:	
SERVICES	Optional keyword.
server	Name of the server that contains the service.
service	Valid file/print service name. If this parameter is entered by itself, the command will display all servers that offer this service.

Table E-2. Client Commands and Parameters (continued)

Command and Parameters	Description
username	Name of a valid account for the specified service. If this parameter is left blank, default access information is used.
password	Password for the username specified.
*	Flag to prompt for a password.
NET HELP	Displays help information about NET commands.
Format:	`C:\>NET HELP command`
Parameter:	
command	NET client command for which to display help.
NET LIST	Displays a list of nodes currently in the DECnet database.
Format:	`c:\>NET LIST`
NET LOAD	Restores saved network connections. It uses a file created with NET SAVE.
Format:	`c:\>NET LOAD [drive:path\]filename`
Parameters:	
drive	DOS drive letter.
path	The DOS path pointing to the location for the configuration file. This must be exactly the same as the specification used with NET SAVE.
filename	The file name for the configuration file.
/log	Displays connections as they are restored.
NET MODIFY	Changes the characteristics of a disk service.

Table E-2. Client Commands and Parameters (continued)

Command and Parameters	Description
Format:	`C:\>NET MODIFY \\server\service` `[%username] password| *]`
Parameters:	
server	Name of the server that contains the disk.
service	Name of the service.
username	Name of a valid account for the specified service.
password	Password for the service.
*	Flag to prompt for a password.
/connections=	Limits the number of connections. The default is 30.
/extensions=	Number of additional blocks to allocate to the virtual disk when the disk size is increased. The size cannot be extended beyond the maximum size of the disk.
/file=	The VMS file specification for the disk.
/nopassword	Deletes the password for a disk.
/password=	Sets the password for a disk.
/query	Prompts for all parameters.
/rating=n	Priority rating for the service.
/type=class	Determines the default device and directory for the virtual disk. Classes are SYSTEM, BOOT, APPLICATION, and USER.
NET MOUNT	Mounts a virtual disk.
Format:	`C:\>NET MOUNT \\server\service` `[%username][password| *]`

Table E-2. Client Commands and Parameters (continued)

Command and Parameters	Description
Parameters:	
server	Name of the server containing the service.
service	Name of the service to mount.
username	Name of a valid account for the user creating the disk.
password	Password for the service.
*	Flag to prompt for a password.
/cluster	Mounts the virtual disk on each available server in the cluster.
/connections=	Limits the number of connections. The default is 30.
/file=	The VMS file specification for the disk.
/password=	Sets the password for a disk.
/query	Prompts for all parameters.
/rating=n	Priority rating for the service.
/ro	Mounts the disk read-only.
/rw	Mounts the disk read/write. Only one user at a time can connect to a disk service in read/write mode.
/temporary	Mounts the disk until the server is stopped or rebooted.
/type=class	Determines the default device and directory for the virtual disk (SYSTEM, BOOT, APPLICATION, and USER).
NET PASSWORD	Used to change a user's password on the server.

Table E-2. Client Commands and Parameters (continued)

Command and Parameters	Description
Format:	`C:\>NET PASSWORD [\\server[%username]`
Parameters:	
server	The server name on which you wish to change your password.
username	The username for which to change the password.
NET PAUSE	Temporarily suspends connections to file or print services.
Format:	`C:\>NET PAUSE [drive:][path]DRDR	PRDR`
Parameters:	
DRDR	Suspends all file service connections.
PRDR	Suspends only connections to network print services.
NET PRINT	Prints files, displays print queue information, and controls a printer.

Format:	`C:\>NET PRINT`
	`[drive:][\path\]filename`
	`device:|server [/parameter]`
	
	Basic NET PRINT functions are listed in Table E-3.

Parameters:	
drive	DOS drive letter. This is a logical drive letter that maps to the drive containing the file to print. This may be a local or network disk.

Table E-2. Client Commands and Parameters (continued)

Command and Parameters	Description
path	DOS path specification. This is The DOS path that points to the location of the file to be printed. The drive and path are necessary only when you wish to print a file that is not in the current directory and/or drive.
filename	Name of the file to print.
device:	DOS print device. This is the specification for the print device. This should be LPT1:, LPT2:, or LPT3:. This device is mapped to a particular print queue with the USE command.
server	Server and/or print queue specified. This indicates the server and optionally the print queue.
/after	Allows you to control the date and/or time at which the file will print. For example: `/after=09-sep-1992:18:30`
/binary	Specifies that the file is a non-ASCII file. Use this parameter for files such as printer control language, CAD drawings, and other files containing special printer codes. This parameter must be specified immediately after the NET PRINT command.
/burst	Causes a burst page to print immediately before your document. The default is noburst.
/noburst	Suppresses printing a burst page.
/characteristics=	Allows you to specify special print characteristics for a particular printer.

Table E-2. Client Commands and Parameters (continued)

Command and Parameters	Description
/copies=	This parameter may range from 1 to 255 and controls the number of copies to print. The default is 1. For example: `/copies=2  /copies=3`
/delete	Deletes a print request. The print queue and request number must be specified. For example: `\\vax1\LJ$office 55 /delete`
/flag	Causes a flag page to print immediately before your document. The flag page contains useful information about your print request, such as username and information about the file. The default is /noflag.
/noflag	Suppresses the flag page.

/form=	Specifies the number of the form to use for this print request. Each type of form (e.g., 8 1/2- x 11-inch, legal, purchase order) is assigned a name and number, usually by the system administrator.
	
	When /form is used, the print request will not print until the proper form is loaded into the printer and a mount form request is issued to let the server know the form is loaded.
	
	The form number may be a numeric number or the form name. For example:
	
	`/form=110`
	`/form=legal`

/header	Prints a standard VMS header on the top of each page.

Table E-2. Client Commands and Parameters (continued)

Command and Parameters	Description
/job_count=	Equivalent to the /copies parameter.
/lowercase	Used for printers that support lowercase printing. The default is /nolowercase.
/nolowercase	Used when you are using a printer that does not support lowercase printing.
/name=	Specifies a name for your print request that will print on the flag page. Name is an alphanumeric field that can be 1 to 39 characters. The name field cannot contain spaces or file extensions. For example: /name=(Engineering_Weekly_Report)
/note=	Specifies a message up to 255 characters that will print on the flag page. For example: /note=(Revision_No_1)
/operator=	Specifies a message up to 55 characters that will be sent to the operator console when the request begins to print. For example: /operator=(Notify_KLS_when_out.txt_complete)
/pages=low,up	Specifies a range of pages to print from an ASCII file. You may select a single page or a range of continuous pages, but not random pages. All pages print by default. For example: /pages=(1,10)
/parameters=	See /form.

Table E-2. Client Commands and Parameters (continued)

Command and Parameters	Description
/passall /nopassall	Passes all print codes to the printer without interpretation by NET PRINT.

/priority	Allows you to specify a new priority for a particular print job. This will cause the request to print sooner or later than originally planned. For example:
	
	`/priority=5`
	`/priority=10`

/restart	Allows a request to begin printing after a queue is restarted either after a crash or after being stopped manually.
/norestart	Stops a print job from automatically restarting at the beginning after a crash.
/set	Causes parameters to remain in effect until you change them or disconnect from the print device. When used by itself, /set will remove all qualifiers that were previously set. You may retain previously set parameters by using the /* as a wildcard and changing only the new parameters. For example: `/set` Clears all parameters. `/set /copies=2` Sets the copies parameter. `/set /* name=JIM` Sets the name parameter and retains all other parameters.

Table E-2. Client Commands and Parameters (continued)

Command and Parameters	Description
/setup	Used primarily for testing new print control modules. It copies the selected module from the print control library to the printer. The module and names are checked for validity only at the time the file is printed, not when the print request is submitted.
/show	Lists the server and service connected to the client's logical print devices. /show will also display information for all qualifiers that are currently set for a printer.
	/show with a device name will display the server and print service to which the device is connected. For example:
	`/show lpt1:`
	/show without a device will display servers and services for all print devices on the network.
/space /nospace	The /space and /nospace flags control the spacing of the printer output. /nospace is the default and specifies that the output matches the incoming print file. /space causes NET PRINT to double the spacing of each line in the print file.
/trailer /notrailer	These commands specify whether a trailer page is printed at the end of your print request. The default for this option may be set by your system administrator.

Table E-2. Client Commands and Parameters (continued)

Command and Parameters	Description
NET SAVE	Saves the current network connections for later restoration.
Format:	`c:\>NET SAVE [drive:path] filename /qualifier`
Parameters:	
drive:path	The drive and directory where the file is located.
filename	The name of the context file.
/log	Displays the connections as they are saved.
/network	Saves only file and print service connections.
/virtual	Saves only disk service connections.
NETSYS V4.1	Creates a bootable floppy disk using the DOS system files from a directory on the server. The directory must be located on the system service.
Format:	`C:\>NETSYS drive:path floppy`
Parameters:	
drive:path	The drive and directory where the DOS system files are located.
floppy	The drive letter for the bootable diskette.
NET TEST	Executes a loop test between the client and server.
Format:	`C:\>NET TEST server`

Table E-2. Client Commands and Parameters (continued)

Command and Parameters	Description
Parameter:	
server	Server that is running the test.
NETTIME	Sets the date and time of the workstation from the server.
Format:	`C:\>NETTIME [server]`
Parameter:	
server	Server from which to retrieve the date and time.
NETVER	Displays information about the PATHWORKS for DOS version and all versions of DOS that are loaded on the system service.
Format:	`C:\>NETVER`
NET ZERO LAD	Zeros the LAD counters.
Format:	`C:\>NET ZERO LAD`
PERMIT	Makes a client disk or directory available as if it were a server file service. Other clients can connect to the disk or directory and access it via the USE command.
Format:	`c:\>PERMIT alias=drive:[path] /flag [node | *]`
Parameters:	
alias	Alias name. This name represents the service the client is making available. The alias is used by another client via the USE command to connect to the service.

Table E-2. Client Commands and Parameters (continued)

Command and Parameters	Description
drive	DOS drive letter. This is a logical drive letter that maps to the drive you wish to make available.
path	DOS path specification that points to the directory you wish to make available. The path is necessary only when you wish to limit access to a particular directory structure.
flag	The default flags are /CRW.
/C	Permits the client to create new files on the server.
/R	Permits read access to files in the service.
/W	Permits write access to the service.
node *	User node. The node parameter indicates the node that is allowed to connect to the service. If the wildcard (*) is used, the service will be available to all users on the network.
RCV/TRCV	The RCV and TRCV commands load the Receiver program on a client. This program receives messages from the BCAST command and other programs such as the PC Mail program. RCV is used for systems running the DECnet protocol, while TCP/IP systems must use TRCV. VMS servers will also send messages to clients when their passwords enter the expiration period.
Format:	`C:\>RCV /qualifier`
Parameters:	
/A:name	Adds a group name to receive messages.

Table E-2. Client Commands and Parameters (continued)

Command and Parameters	Description
/D	Displays stored messages.
/H:n,m	Specifies the colors of the broadcast message header.
/L:0 | 1	Specifies the NetBIOS adapter to use.
/M:n,m	Specifies the colors of the broadcast message.
/N:n	Sets the number of messages (1 to 10) stored by RCV. The default is 10.
/O:n	Determines the number of minutes time-out. The default is no time-out between receipt of a message and the resumption of the client task.
/P:T | B	Determines whether messages are displayed at the top (T) or bottom (B) of the screen. T is the default.
/R:n	Specifies the source from which to receive messages (server only, other clients only, or both). The default is both.
/S:Y | N	Enables (Y) or disables (N) a beep when a message is received in graphics mode The default is Y.
/T:n	Determines the type of messages received.
SETLOGON	Sets account information for DOS clients on an OS/2 server.
Format:	`C:\>SETLOGON username password`
Parameters:	
username	Username of the account.
password	Password for the account or for * (flag to prompt for a password).

Table E-2. Client Commands and Parameters (continued)

Command and Parameters	Description
SETNAME	Sets the client computer name. It is run once after the redirector has been loaded.
Format:	`C:\>SETNAME computername`
Parameter:	
computername	Name of the client computer.
SPAWNER	Allows a DECnet system to trigger the execution of client commands on another DECnet system.
Format:	`C:\>SPAWNER /log /help`
Parameters:	
/log	Logs messages to C:\DECNET\SPAWNER.LOG.
/help	Provides onscreen help.
USE	Establishes and manages connections to file and print services on the server.
Format:	`c:\>USE device \\server\service [%username password	*] [/parameter]`
Parameters:	
device	Logical DOS device (LPTn:, D:, M:). This is the logical device name for DOS.
	For printers, it refers to the standard printer devices LPT1:, LPT2:, or LPT3:.
	Disk drive devices have the format D:, M:, and so on. Network drive letters typically start with D: or E:, depending on the number of client drives, and go through Z:.
	Device names are always followed by a colon (:).

Table E-2. Client Commands and Parameters (continued)

Command and Parameters	Description
?	The ambiguous device specifier. USE will connect to the next available device when ? is specified.
*	When the wildcard (*) is specified, the USE command will affect all device connections.
server	File server where the service is located. If the server name is used, precede it with two backslashes (\ \ ).
service	Service name. The service name is preceded by one backslash (\ ) and specifies the service the client will connect to.
username	Username on the server. The username must be a valid username for the service specified. If no username is specified, USE will use the default connection for the service, if possible.
password	User password.
*	Flag to prompt for password.
/brief	Brief information display (default).
/cdrom	Specifies that the device is a CD-ROM device.
/check	Checks the error status of the device. If a problem is encountered, the error level is set to 1.
/click /noclick	Turns on or off a clicking sound when a virtual disk is accessed.
/connect	Causes USE to prompt for the device, service, and password (V4.1).

Table E-2. Client Commands and Parameters (continued)

Command and Parameters	Description
/disconnect	Disconnects from a service. This option removes a connection. The current connection cannot be removed.
/environ	Sets environment variable. The /environ option is used only from a batch file. It causes the device used in the connection to be loaded into the environment variable specified with the command.
/except	Excludes specified drives from the disconnect option.
/fixup	Makes disconnected virtual drives appear as invalid drives.
/full	Displays maximum information about the specified service.
/help	Displays help information.
/list	Shows services. This is the default option if USE is executed with no options.
/load	Remaps network connections that were saved with USE/SAVE.
/log	Displays process information.
/network	Identifies the device as a file or print service.
/nonw	Used with NetWare Coexistence to exclude NetWare connections from wildcard operations.
/noprompt	Causes USE to not prompt when a component is missing from the command.
/remove	Removes disconnected drive references from the PATH statement. /remove is always used with /disconnect.

Table E-2. Client Commands and Parameters (continued)

Command and Parameters	Description
/replace	Replaces a connection with a new connection.
/restore	Same as USE/load.
/save	Saves current network connections in a file.
/setdir	Connects to any directory. Allows the client to connect to any device or directory on the server even if the device is not offered as a service. /setdir only works with a drive letter (A:, etc.) that is already connected to a service. It cannot be used at the same time the connection is made.
/show	Displays service information.
/status	Displays status information.
/virtual	Specifies that the disk service is a virtual disk.
/X	Ethernet address of the node offering the service.

Table E-3. Basic NET PRINT Functions

Function	Description
NET PRINT \\server	Lists all print requests on the server.
NET PRINT \\server\queue	Lists all print requests on the queue.
NET PRINT \\server\queue /USER=username	Lists all print requests for a specified user.
NET PRINT device: /USER=username	Lists all print requests for a specified user.
NET PRINT device: jobnumber	Shows the status of a specific job number.

PASSWORD Program Source

The PASSWORD program is a public-domain program and is available free of charge from the Digital Customer Support Center. To obtain the program, place a service call and ask the technician to send it to you. The Center will supply both source and executable code. The program can be modified and compiled with Turbo Pascal V6.0.

PASSWORD Program

```
This program is for PATHWORKS users who want to have the server name,
username, and password entered once as environment variables and used until
they are deleted.

The program is invoked as:

PASSWORD  [/N]

  PASSWORD is the name of the executable.
   /N  is an optional parameter. It means "Don't ask for the server name and
the username if they are already defined in the environment."

The parameters entered will be stored in the MASTER environment as:

  SERVER
  USER
  PASS

When PATHWORKS is executed, if SERVER and USER are already defined in the
environment, then these will be shown as defaults, and you can accept them by
just pressing RETURN or you can change them before pressing RETURN.

If the environment is full, errorlevel 1 will be set if the password cannot be
entered, errorlevel 2 will be set if the username cannot be entered, and
errorlevel 3 will be set if the server name cannot be entered.

uses

    opdos,opcrt;
```

```
var

    Menv:EnvRec;
    j:Integer;
    i:char;
    SwitchChar,pass,server,user,Userver,UUser:String;
    OK,askit,endit,ChangeThem:Boolean;
begin

  CheckBreak:=False;  {don't allow CTRL-BREAK}

     {switch is /n - means don't ask for server and username if set}

  askit:=true;
  if paramcount > 0 then begin
      switchchar:=paramstr(1);
  if upcase(switchchar[2]) = 'N' then
    · ASkit:=False;
  end;

{find the master environment}

   MasterEnv(Menv);

{now, look for the variables 'SERVER' and 'USER'}

  Server:=GetEnvStr(Menv,'SERVER');
  User:=GetEnvStr(Menv,'USER');

  ChangeThem:=False;
  if AskIt or (server = '') or (user = '') then begin
      ChangeThem:=True;
      Write('Please Enter Server name [',server,'] ');
      readln(Userver);
      if Userver<>'' then
         Server:=Userver;

      Write('Please Enter user name [',user,'] ');
      readln(UUser);
      if UUser<>'' then
         User:=UUser;

  end;
```

374

```
{now, get password - don't echo, of course}

    endit:=False;
    j:=1;
    Write ('Please enter password ');
    while not endit and (j<80)do begin
      i:=readkey;
      if ord(i)=13 then
          endit:=true
      else begin
          if ord(i)=8 then begin
              if j > 1 then
                  dec(j);
          end
          else if (ord(i)<>3) then begin
            pass[j]:=i;
            inc(j);
          end;
      end;
    end;
    pass[0]:=(chr(j-1));

{got password; now set environment}

    OK:=False;
    OK:=SetEnvStr(Menv,'PASS',Pass);
    if not OK then
        halt(1);

    if ChangeThem then begin {we need to amend user and server}

        OK:=False;
        OK:=SetEnvStr(Menv,'USER',User);
        if not OK then
            halt(2);
        OK:=False;
        OK:=SetEnvStr(Menv,'SERVER',Server);
        if not OK then
            halt(3);
    end;
  end.
```

NETSETUP WIK Command Reference

Command	Function
$BEGIN, $END	Marks the beginning and end of a WIK block.
$DO_CASE variable	Begins a Case statement and indicates the variable to be tested.
$CASE value	Begins a Case Test Block and indicates the value to test for. The commands to execute when the test variable equals the test value follow the CASE statement. CASE is the only Case command that can contain multiple entries.
$END_CASE	Ends a Case statement.
$DESTINATION disk "comment"	Establishes the destination disk to receive the PATHWORKS client files. The disk parameter can be either a drive letter or a WIK variable (i.e., DESTINATION). The comment will be displayed when NETSETUP prompts to insert the key disk.
$CLEAR_SOURCE	Clears indicators for the source disks containing PATHWORKS files. It is normally used only before a series of $ADD_SOURCE statements.
$ADD_SOURCE disk disk_label "comment"	Establishes a possible source disk for PATHWORKS files required by NETSETUP. Parameters are the disk drive letter (A-Z), disk label, and a comment. If the disk label is included, it will be verified before NETSETUP copies files from the disk.

Command	Function
$SET variable value	Enters the specified value in the variable name specified after $SET. Any WIK variable can be loaded with $SET, including up to 20 user-defined variables.
$COPY source_file target_file	Copies files from the PATHWORKS source disk to the key disk. The complete source and target paths (including file name) must be specified.
$DELETE {DESTINATION} file name	Deletes the specified file. You should ensure that the key disk is clean before beginning to copy files.
$IF	Begins a conditional (IF) statement.
$ELSE	Begins a conditional ELSE section within an IF statement.
$END_IF	Ends an IF statement.

Acronyms

4GL	fourth-generation language

A ················

ACE	access control entry
ACL	access control list
ACMS	Application Control and Management System
ANSI	American National Standards Institute
API	application program interface

C ················

CAD	computer-aided design
CANASTA	Crash Analyzer and Troubleshooting Assistor
CDA	Compound Document Architecture
CI	Computer Interconnect

D ················

DDE	Dynamic Data Exchange
DECUS	Digital Equipment Computer Users Society
DSIN	Digital Software Information Network
DSSI	Digital Storage Systems Interconnect

E ················

EMI	electromagnetic interference
EMS	expanded-memory specification

F ················

FAL	file access listener
FDDI	Fiber Distributed Data Interface
FRB	floppy remote boot

H · · · · · · · · · · · · · · ·

HMA	high-memory area

I · · · · · · · · · · · · · · ·

IPX	Internetwork Packet Exchange
IS	information systems
IVP	installation verification procedure

K · · · · · · · · · · · · · · ·

KISS	keep it simple, stupid

L · · · · · · · · · · · · · · ·

LAD	local-area disk
LAN	local-area network
LAST	Local-Area Systems Transport
LAT	Local-Area Transport
LATCP	Local-Area Transport Control Program
LAVc	Local-Area VAXcluster
LTM	LAN Traffic Monitor

M · · · · · · · · · · · · · · ·

MAU	multistation access unit
MAX	Modular Analysis Expert
MIS	management information systems
MMJ	modified modular jack
MOP	Maintenance Operations Protocol

N · · · · · · · · · · · · · · ·

NAS	Network Application Support
NCP	Network Control Program
NFS	Network File System
NFT	network file transfer

O · · · · · · · · · · · · · · ·

OPCOM	operator communications
OSF	Open Software Foundation
OSI	Open Systems Interconnect

P ················

PIF	personal information file
PIM	personal information manager
POSIX	Portable Operating System Interface

R ················

RFI	radio frequency interference
RJE	remote job entry
RISC	reduced instruction set computers
RMS	Record Management Services

S ················

SCB	session control block
SIG	special interest group
SNA	Systems Network Architecture
SPEAR	Standard Package for Error Analysis and Reporting
STP	shielded twisted pair

T ················

TCP/IP	Transmission Control Protocol/Internet Protocol
TSM	Terminal Server Manager
TSR	terminate and stay resident

U ················

UAF	user authorization file
UIC	user identification code
UMB	upper memory block
UTP	unshielded twisted pair

W ················

WAN	wide-area network

X ················

XMS	extended-memory specification

Suggested Readings and Online Services

BOOKS

Mastering VMS, David W. Bynon, CBM Books, 101 Witmer Rd., Horsham, PA 19044.

Structured Cabling Guide, Digital Equipment, P.O. Box CS 2008, Nashua, NH 03061.

VMS Performance Management, James W. Coburn, CBM Books, 101 Witmer Rd., Horsham, PA 19044.

Writing Real Programs in DCL, Paul C. Anagnostopoulos, Digital Press, 12 Crosby Dr., Bedford, MA 01730.

MAGAZINES

DEC Professional, 101 Witmer Rd., Horsham, PA 19044.

LAN Computing, 101 Witmer Rd., Horsham, PA 19044.

LAN Times, P.O. Box 652, Hightstown, NJ 08520.

PATHWORKS Complete, Digital Equipment, PC/PCI Applications Group, 305 Forrester St., Littleton, MA 01460.

VAX Professional, 101 Witmer Rd., Horsham, PA 19044.

Windows Journal, Windows User Group, P.O. Box 1967, Media, PA 19063.

ONLINE SERVICES

DEC PC Integration Forum, CompuServe, 5000 Arlington Centre Blvd., Columbus, OH 20212.

The VAX Forum, CompuServe, 5000 Arlington Centre Blvd., Columbus, OH 20212.

.

Index

Also Available from CBM Books

B O O K S

VIDEOTAPES AND KITS

Desktop Systems Integrator Kit (disk included) by Al Cini	$49	1-878956-28-0
The Hitchhiker's Guide to VMS Performance Part I: VMS Memory Management and Paging Performance (1 tape/1 study guide) with Bruce Ellis	$499	1-878956-09-4
The Hitchhiker's Guide to VMS Performance Part II: I/O Performance (1 tape, 1 study guide) with Bruce Ellis	$499	1-878956-12-4
The Hitchhiker's Guide to VMS Performance Part III: CPU Performance (1 tape, 1 study guide) with Bruce Ellis	$499	1-878956-15-9
How They'll Hack Your VAX, and How to Prevent It (2 tapes, 1 study guide) with Bruce Ellis	$599	1-878956-18-3

Available at your bookstore or, in the U.S., order by phone: (215) 957-4265. Prices subject to change.

CBM Books

VAX I/0 Subsystems: Optimizing Performance by Ken Bates

Learn how to analyze and improve I/O performance from leading expert Ken Bates, a member of the original development teams for both the HSC and KDM70 controllers, and the developer of the first striping product offered by Digital.

"(This book) explores the right strategies to help system managers obtain the greatest total performance from their systems."
— Grant Saviers, Vice President, PC & Systems Peripherals Group, Digital Equipment Corporation

"A landmark book."
— DEC Professional

1-878956-02-7/$49

Mastering VMS by David W. Bynon

This handbook uses step-by-step examples and explanations on how to apply VMS system operation and management techniques. Hands-on instruction for system managers, programmers, operators and analysts.

"Provides the reader with information on everything from the rise of the VAX machine and study of the VMS operating system to information on VMS operation management, utilities and commands."
— The Office

"A valuable book for those using the VMS operating system."
— CHOICE

0-9614729-7-9/$40

The Open Desktop Companion: A Guide for PC and Workstation Users
by David W. Bynon

A must-have, easy-to-use guide to the Open Desktop graphical user interface, Open Desktop DOS, the underlying SCO UNIX operating system and Open Desktop's networking capabilities.

"This handsomely presented technical volume will have most value to system administrators as well as sophisticated and committed end users."
— Small Press

1-878956-23-X/$28

VMS Performance Management by James W. Coburn

With in-depth discussions of VMS tuning, this book includes a wealth of information that goes beyond the Digital manuals. It describes techniques for analyzing VMS systems and correcting performance-related problems.

"VMS tuning methods are thought by many to border on the mystical. Mr. Coburn dispels that myth. His concise, easy-to-follow examination of VMS performance management reduces system tuning to a level approachable by mere mortals — or system managers."

— DEC Professional

1-878956-21-3/$30

The Hitchhiker's Guide to VMS by Bruce Ellis

This unusual programmer's guide from VMS internals guru Bruce Ellis transforms hands-on system programming tips into a fast, fun read. From VMS internals and process concepts to system data structures and security, *The Hitchhiker's Guide to VMS* covers all the bases.

"Bruce Ellis is the only author I've found who can write entertainingly about the low-level details of VMS. The book is amazingly fun to read…you'll learn a lot."

— DECUSCOPE

"… put your thumb up, this hitchhike could be the most enjoyable learning experience you've had."

— ON$DECK Magazine

1-878956-00-0/$35

The Hitchhiker's Guide to VMS Performance: Part I—VMS Memory Management and Paging Performance with Bruce Ellis

In this videotape, VMS internals guru Bruce Ellis describes techniques for enhancing VMS memory management and paging performance. Comes with a follow-along study guide.

"Ellis knows VMS so intimately that he can talk about a subject as heady as VMS performance tuning almost in a stream-of-consciousness style… As your guide in the Vastek Hitchhiker video, Ellis gives an enlightening and enjoyable tour of VMS memory management and paging performance."

— DP Labs

1-878956-09-4/$499

A Manager's Guide to Multivendor Networks by John Enck

This book defines fundamental network architectures and explores the standards, topologies and technologies that affect multivendor networking and data communications strategies.

"Without reading like alphabet soup, (A Manager's Guide to Multivendor Networks) rounds up the key functions, services and equipment that managers must grasp conceptually to spearhead successful networking projects."

— *Computerworld*

"A Manager's Guide to Multivendor Networks takes a simple approach to a complex subject. It is recommended reading for anyone desiring a block-diagram look at network implementation."

— *Workstation*

1-878956-03-5/$35

UNIX, Quick! by Andrew Feibus

It doesn't get much easier than these shortcuts and simple techniques for learning the UNIX operating system fast. Step-by-step instructions show you how to use basic functions and features and more advanced techniques.

"Andrew Feibus' book aims to give DOS users a trouble-free transition to UNIX by cutting out unnecessary commands, procedures and utilities."

— *IBM Computer Today*

1-878956-01-9/$30

Introduction to Data Communications: A Practical Approach by Stan Gelber

For systems analysts, programmers, engineers, customer service reps, sales support personnel, mid-level managers... anyone whose job requires knowing and understanding data communications concepts and applications.

"(Author Stan Gelber) skillfully uses his extensive experience to provide very detailed, useful, hands-on information for the MIS professional and systems analyst building corporate networks... His understanding of the public telephone network and equipment that interfaces to it to provide corporations with a variety of capabilities is unmatched in the literature."

— *LAN Computing*

1-878956-04-3/$39

The Dictionary of Standard C by Rex Jaeschke

C guru Rex Jaeschke has written the only comprehensive resource defining the terminology of the C language.

"Rex Jaeschke's books have always focused on making the C language more accessible and understandable to all C programmers. The Dictionary of Standard C continues this tradition by providing clear, concise definitions for the many concepts and technical terms with which both novice and experienced programmers should be familiar."

— Jim Brodie, Chair of ANSI C Standards Committee X3J11

"I would recommend this indispensable book to students and C programmers...it is equally valuable as a complete C language reference."

— Wilson Mbakweni, *Computing*

1-878956-07-8/$24

Mastering Standard C: A Self-Paced Training Course in Modern C by Rex Jaeschke

A self-teaching workbook on the statements and constructs of the C language written by Rex Jaeschke, internationally acclaimed C expert and voting member of the ANSI C Standards Committee X3J11.

"If you want to learn the C language and are willing to spend some time learning it end to end, Mastering Standard C is a good way to go."

— *Dr. Dobb's Journal*

0-9614729-8-7/$40

Data Communications & Networking Dictionary by T.D. Pardoe and R.P. Wenig

This book provides definitions for communications and networking terms ranging from the most basic to the most complex — a useful learning aid for beginners and a valuable reference for experts. Over 2,000 listings define networking standards, acronyms, and common abbreviations of communications and networking terms.

"If you need help understanding the difference between a bridge, a hub and a router, this dictionary deserves a place on your bookshelf."

— *Engineering Automation Report*

1-878956-06-X/$24

Available at your bookstore. Or, in the U.S., call to order: (215) 957-4265

Networking Titles from CBM Books
Written by and for Computing Professionals

▼ ▼

The Complete Guide to PATHWORKS: PATHWORKS for VMS and DOS

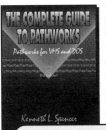

"... a current and lucid presentation ..."
— *Chris Lord, Senior Software Engineer, Digital Equipment Corp.*

Order more copies and save as much as $15.00 per book. Put a copy on every network manager's desk. Helpful for all MIS staff — even for end users.

Kenneth L. Spencer
$39
Softcover, 390 pages

3 1/2" disk included

Ethernet Pocket Guide: A Practical Guide to Designing, Installing and Troubleshooting Ethernet Networks

Your handy guide to installing an Ethernet network. From the basic design to the final installation, you'll learn everything from what Ethernet is to troubleshooting after you're up and running. A complete, easy-to-use reference.

Byron Spinney
$15
Softcover, 96 pages

Introduction to Data Communications: A Practical Approach

"... very detailed, useful, hands-on information for the MIS professional and systems analyst building corporate networks."
— *LAN Computing*

This user-friendly handbook covers the design, configuration, security and management of data communications networks. A technical as well as practical approach to computer networks.

Stan Gelber
$39
Softcover, 314 pages

A Manager's Guide to Multivendor Networks

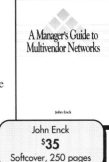

"... a simple approach to a complex subject."
— *Workstation*

For executive managers, technical managers, engineers and analysts designing and building multivendor networks. Without the technical jargon, a clear guide to the connectivity strategies and networking architectures of the major players.

John Enck
$35
Softcover, 250 pages

Data Communications & Networking Dictionary

"... for help understanding the difference between a bridge, a hub and a router, this dictionary deserves a place on your bookshelf."
— *Engineering Automation Report*

The defining resource for networking and data communications terms — from the most basic to the most complex. Over 2,000 listings. Plus explanations of networking standards and all the acronyms you need to get around.

T.D. Pardoe and R.P Wenig
$24
Softcover, 155 pages

To order, complete the reverse side and mail or . . .

Phone (215) 957-4265

FAX (215) 957-1050

Through CompuServe User ID 76702,1565

CBM
B O O K S

Satisfaction Guaranteed!

CBM Books Order Form

For fast, easy ordering . . .

- **By Phone (215) 957-4265** ■ **FAX (215) 957-1050**
- **Through CompuServe Mail — User ID 76702,1565**

. Title		Quantity	Subtotal
The Complete Guide to PATHWORKS: PATHWORKS forVMS and DOS (includes 3 1/2" disk)			
1-5 books	**$39.00 each**		
6-15 books	**$33.15 each**		
16-49 books	**$27.30 each**		
50 + books	**$23.40 each**		
Ethernet Pocket Guide: A Practical Guide to Designing, Installing, and Troubleshooting Ethernet Networks	**$15**		
Data Communications & Networking Dictionary	**$24**		
A Manager's Guide to Multivendor Networks	**$35**		
Introduction to Data Communications: A Practical Approach	**$39**		
PA residents add 6% sales tax.			
UPS shipping: In the U.S., $4 for the first book, $1 for each additional book. Outside the U.S., please call (215) 957-4265 for shipping information.			
TOTAL ORDER			

Name _____

Title _____

Company _____

Address _____

City _____ State _____ Zip _____

Country _____

Telephone (_____) _____ FAX (_____) _____
Street address required.

☐ Payment enclosed $_____ payable to CBM Books.

Charge to: ☐ [MasterCard] MasterCard ☐ [VISA] VISA ☐ [AMERICAN EXPRESS] American Express

Account #: _____ Exp. Date _____

Signature _____ Date _____

☐ **Please send me a FREE catalog.**

PMBI 12/92

Mail to:

CBM Books
101 Witmer Road
P.O. Box 446
Horsham, PA 19044

Phone (215) 957-4265 FAX (215) 957-1050
Through CompuServe User ID 76702,1565

Satisfaction Guaranteed